MIRACLES ON THE WATER

MIRACLES
ON THE
WATER

THE HEROIC SURVIVORS OF A
WORLD WAR II U-BOAT ATTACK

Tom Nagorski

NEW YORK

LIBRARY OF CONGRESS CATALOGING-IN-PUBLICATION DATA

Nagorski, Tom
    Miracles on the water : the heroic survivors of a World War II U-boat attack / Tom Nagorski.—1st ed.
      p. cm.
    Includes index.
    ISBN 1-4013-0150-9
    1. City of Benares (Steamship).   2. World War, 1939–1945—Naval operation, German.   3. World War, 1939–1945—Naval operations—Submarine.   4. Shipwrecks—North Atlantic Ocean.   5. Survival after airplane accidents, shipwrecks, etc.—Anecdotes.   6. Passenger ships—Great Britain—History—20th century.   I. Title.

D782.C6N35   2006
940.54'293—dc22   2005052540

Hyperion books are available for special promotions and premiums. For details contact Michael Rentas, Assistant Director, Inventory Operations, Hyperion, 77 West 66th Street, 11th floor, New York, New York 10023, or call 212-456-0133.

Book design by Richard Oriolo
Maps by James Sinclair

FIRST EDITION

10 9 8 7 6 5 4 3

For Anne

CONTENTS

BOOK ONE

THE YOUNG AMBASSADORS

BOOK TWO

LIFEBOAT 12

ACKNOWLEDGMENTS

This book is based primarily on the accounts of survivors—given in writings, recordings, and interviews—of a terrible ordeal at sea. As such I owe a debt, first, to the children who survived the attack on the *City of Benares*, a remarkable and resilient group of men and women who have inspired me greatly. I also feel a profound gratitude and empathy toward those who did not survive; the record shows that many of these unfortunate souls exhibited uncommon courage during a terrifying time.

Two people were responsible for convincing me that this story merited more than just an essay for the family records: the literary agent Cynthia Cannell, and my longtime friend and colleague Peter Jennings. From the beginning I was mindful of the fact that the story of the *Benares* could hardly be classed among the great epics of the Second World War, the larger-tapestry stories whose datelines—Normandy and Dresden, Stalingrad and Iwo Jima, to name but a few—are so familiar. Cynthia and Peter, each in a different way, convinced me that the saga of the *Benares* had an epic quality of its own. "It's a great story," Cynthia stressed. "Plain and simple—a great story." I gave Peter an outline on a Friday during the summer of 2002; he called that Sunday, less than forty-eight hours later, urging me on, and in the years that followed he inquired often about my progress. I had not yet finished when Peter received his diagnosis of lung cancer; that same week he asked that I bring him whatever chapters were complete. I will forever remember his support—particularly given all he had on his mind, even before he became ill. Those who knew Peter Jennings will recognize these qualities: an unbridled curiosity and profound loyalty. They are greatly missed.

Several people volunteered to read the manuscript and offer constructive criticism. I would like to thank my ABC colleague Martha Raddatz; my friends Blair Effron, Phil Gordon, and Christopher Voss; my father-in-law, Rod Heller; and in particular my uncle Zygmunt Nagorski, Jr., for their encouragement and excellent suggestions. Barbara and Christine Nagorski told me their father's story and then unearthed letters and newspaper clippings that were the first documents I saw describing the torpedoing of the *Benares* and the rescues that followed. Bill Strachan has been a superb editor and reassuring voice; and when I hired Sabine Goodwin to help with research I had no idea how much valuable advice she would offer vis-à-vis the manuscript itself.

I have benefited from the help of three historians. The Harvard professor John Stilgoe provided essential background on the subject of lifeboat journeys; I recommend his book *Lifeboat* to anyone with even a passing interest in stories of the sea. Thomas Parrish's volume *Submarine: A History* was another source of background and another terrific read. And Ralph Barker's *Children of the Benares* was an excellent treatment of this particular story.

I would have accomplished nothing without the support and love of family. First and foremost, thank you, Anne, with all my heart. To say that my wife has been "supportive" does her no justice at all. Anne has been my editor and unparalleled booster, encouraging me in countless ways, even when it meant more sacrifice for her. This book is dedicated to her, together with a promise, to Anne and to our children, Natalie and Billy: I owe you one. More than one.

Finally, I would like to thank my parents, Ingrid and George Nagorski, who instilled in me a curiosity about family history and about World War II in particular, through the prism of their own very different but intense experiences. I was captivated by their stories about the war years; my greatest regret is that my father died before we were able to finish the conversation.

AUTHOR'S NOTE

All quotes in this book are taken from personal accounts—written journals, statements made to survivors or rescuers, interviews given to reporters, recordings made for museums or documentaries, or interviews with
the author. Where possible I have checked quotes with others who were present for a conversation. Not surprisingly, I have found that writings, recordings,
and statements made in 1940 hold up better to scrutiny than recollections
shared six decades on. Where I attribute thoughts to any individual, the source
is an interview with the author or statements made by that individual in writing or to other survivors.

A full list of all interviews and other source material appears at the end
of the book.

Bohdan's Story

I first heard the story on a Christmas Eve sometime during the late 1970s, at the New York apartment where *Wigilia*, the Polish Christmas Eve dinner, had been celebrated in my family for as long as I could remember. My father was Polish, born in Warsaw in 1920, and my mother Norwegian—Oslo, 1925—and when I was a child my Christmas holidays were divided roughly between Norway and the apartment in lower Manhattan where my father's cousins lived.

The patriarch of the New York family was my father's uncle Bohdan, and he could make several claims to his place at the head of the *Wigilia* table. He was the oldest living Nagorski, for one thing; his birthday happened to fall on December 24, for another; and he was a warm and charming man, funny and above all a superb raconteur. By the time I came to know Bohdan, he was a hunched figure, slow-moving and almost completely deaf—the gesture I came to associate with him was a hand cupped over an ear as he leaned close, watching the lips of whoever was speaking. He was a frail man by then, but his wit and warmth shone through.

"It isn't fair," he would say to me. "You are growing like a tree—and I am only getting smaller and smaller!"

The annual Christmas Eve highlight was Bohdan's poem, verse that he composed and which he would recite without notes sometime between the main dish and dessert. It was his survey of the year, essentially, a collection of musings, and it was invariably interrupted by laughter—real laughter, not the polite or sympathetic kind. Bohdan delivered his poem in Polish, the language of the *Wigilia*, and my mother and I would struggle to grasp the essence, helped by my father, or a cousin, with the translation. But we never missed the twinkle in Bohdan's eye, or the delight etched on faces around the table. These were unmistakable.

It was on one such evening, in the din of cross-table conversation, that I picked up what seemed a remarkable phrase, the punch line to a story.

"The obituary was written . . . ," Bohdan's wife, Zosia, was saying, waving a hand in the air. "Imagine—I was reading about the death of my husband, in a newspaper. And look—he is sitting here now, all these years later!"

Fragments of the story followed: Bohdan had been a passenger on a ship sunk by a German submarine during the Second World War, and then a passenger in one of the ship's lifeboats. Logic and reports from the scene had made it clear: He was lost in the North Atlantic, starved or drowned, hundreds of miles from land. London press dispatches described a harrowing night and the following day's rescue of only a few dozen frostbitten souls. Bohdan Nagorski had not been among them. At the time he was forty-nine years old.

"She had no faith!" Bohdan cried, smiling at his wife. More laughter echoed around the *Wigilia* table.

"Bohdan, Bohdan," Zosia said, sounding exasperated. "Of *course* I had faith. You *know* I had faith."

She shook her head, laughing softly. She had heard Bohdan's story many, many times.

But for those of us who hadn't, it was easy to understand why Zosia, or anyone waiting for the ship's lost passengers, might have abandoned faith that September, all those years ago. The story came to me in patchy fashion, snippets tossed across the dinner table. It was fascinating to imagine my great-uncle drifting in a lifeboat, or sitting later in some London apartment, reading his own death notice. But I was young, a teenager, and I suppose my curiosity fizzled.

One evening in the summer of 2001, my wife and I enjoyed a dinner with Bohdan's daughters—they had been young girls in 1940, waiting in Montreal for their father's ship to arrive. We sat on the terrace of their home in Hampton Bays, New York, and talked about Bohdan and Zosia, about the older generation generally, and the talk drifted to stories about the war. It was during dinner that the story of the SS *City of Benares* resurfaced, this time absent the frenetic atmosphere of Christmas Eve, and this time I was a journalist with a fairly intense curiosity about the war and about this astonishing story that unfolded, Barbara and Christine Nagorski telling it in greater scope and with much richer detail.

It was enough to keep me awake for a while that night, enough to send me on something of a mission to learn more: to find the people who had shared in Bohdan's miracle—the children in particular—to uncover the accounts not only of his fellow passengers but of his rescuers, as well as the men on board the submarine that had fired the deadly torpedo. Enough, in short, to produce this book.

Because it was, by any measure, an almost unbelievable story.

The story we are about to hear is one of great horror.
But it is also one of remarkable courage and endurance.
Of fortitude in the face of danger. Of hope in the face of
despair. And it is that which we celebrate today.

    —Reverend John Foulds
       Memorial service commemorating the fiftieth
       anniversary of the attack on the SS *City of Benares*
       September 17, 1990

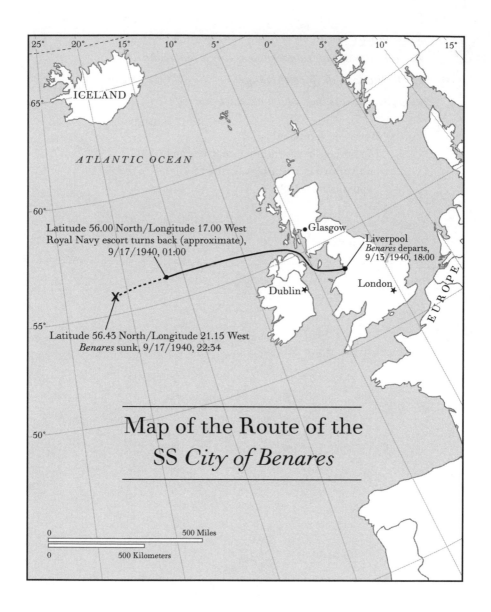

25°　　20°　　15°　　10°　　5°　　0°　　5°　　10°　　15°

ICELAND

65°

ATLANTIC OCEAN

60°

Latitude 56.00 North/Longitude 17.00 West
Royal Navy escort turns back (approximate),
9/17/1940, 01:00

•Glasgow

Liverpool
Benares departs,
9/13/1940, 18:00

Dublin★

London
★

EUROPE

55°

Latitude 56.43 North/Longitude 21.15 West
Benares sunk, 9/17/1940, 22:34

50°

Map of the Route of the
SS *City of Benares*

0　　　　　　　　500 Miles

0　　　　500 Kilometers

MIRACLES ON THE WATER

BOOK ONE

THE YOUNG AMBASSADORS

CHAPTER 1

"We've Been Hit!"

Beth Cummings sat upright, lifted suddenly from sleep, and not sure why. It was dark, black-night dark, nothing stirring in her small cabin, and she was wide awake.

A bad dream, perhaps. But then she felt the ship shudder. *Rough seas,* Beth thought. *Very* rough seas.

She felt for the light switch. The light wouldn't come on.

An alarm sounded nearby. She heard groans and rustling, someone in the adjoining cabin. That might be her friend Bess, up and about. Maybe *she* knew what was happening.

Beth Cummings stepped gingerly from her bed into a gathering pool of water.

BESS WALDER HAD NEVER BEEN a sound sleeper. She was in the top bunk next door. The jolt woke her instantly.

That's a torpedo! she thought.

She heard another bang, felt the floor shake, then a sound like a closet full of glass, things rattling and breaking inside. Bess came down the ladder and called to the girl in the lower bunk.

"C'mon! Get out!"

The girl shivered under her blanket. She didn't want to go.

Bess Walder was fifteen years old. Beth Cummings was fourteen.

. . .

FRED STEELS WAS ELEVEN, AND in his cabin there was chaos. The room shook, glass shattered, an armoire crashed, and when Steels tried to leave his bed he found himself trapped. Heavy planks of wood had fallen, making a misshapen X just inches above his body.

Parts of the bunk had collapsed, right on top of him.

Steels, a strong and stocky child, pushed up at the wood. *Good thing there's nobody in my top bunk*, he thought. One of Steels' cabinmates was crying for his glasses. Alarm bells rang. He heard nothing from the third boy in the cabin, an eleven-year-old named Paul Shearing. *He sleeps through anything.*

Steels worked at the wood, nudged a fat piece up, away from his face. *I can do it*, he thought. *I can get out.* He shoved another plank aside.

Then Fred Steels realized he was soaking wet.

It's blood, he thought, but then he felt a soft spray coming from the washbasin. Water, not blood. The pipes had burst.

Suddenly Steels understood what had happened. "We've been hit!" he cried, trying to rouse his cabinmates. The two other boys shifted in their bunks, still fuzzy-headed.

"Come on, then!"

Finally Steels was free, squirming through a narrow space he had made between the wood planks and the side of his bed. He pulled on his bulky life jacket and felt for his shoes in the dark. *There they are.*

He tried to find his suitcase, then realized there was no point in carrying anything to the ship's deck. Water shot from the basin. Steels' life jacket was getting wet.

Paul Shearing was up now. He had found his life jacket, and a coat his mother had bought for her son's journey. Then, searching for his shoes, Shearing felt a jab in his foot.

"Oww!"

Steels spun around. "What's happened?"

Shearing winced. He had cut his heel on a piece of glass. "It's all right."

He stepped gingerly in the water, feeling a sharp sting in his foot. After a while he found a pair of sandals. The third boy in the cabin had found his glasses.

They fumbled about in this way, and then, perhaps two minutes after the initial jolt, the three boys shuffled out the cabin door and along an already-crowded hallway.

Bess Walder and Beth Cummings were making their way somewhere behind them. Together they were among the youngest, and arguably the most important, passengers on board the British liner SS *City of Benares*.

THE *BENARES* CARRIED 215 CREW and 191 passengers, including 90 boys and girls who were pioneers in a program designed to spirit British children to safer shores. These young evacuees had been chosen from the country's most vulnerable communities, from households particularly battered by the German bombardment. It was a bold and controversial experiment, involving thousands of children. They were sailing for Canada, away from war, and they had no idea how long they would be gone.

It was mid-September, 1940. World War II was one year old.

For several days the mood on board the *Benares* had been cheerful, almost festive. They had left home and family, to be sure, but they had also bid farewell to air raids and rations, put behind them what one of the boys called the "everyday horror" of the German *Blitzkrieg*. Adolf Hitler's air force had pummeled Liverpool in the days before the *Benares* set sail from that same port; the children and their escorts had watched the bombs as they fell. Now their home was an eleven-thousand-ton luxury liner, clean and elegant, comfortable and richly stocked. Onboard meals were feasts—heaping buffets of meat and chicken, fresh fruit in large baskets, limitless ice cream for dessert—served by Indian waiters in bright blue and white uniforms. The ship's decks were a virtual playing field, the playroom a huge and colorful space where imaginations might run, and memories of war recede.

Jack Keeley, an eight-year-old from Brixton, told his little sister, Joyce, "We've gone from one world to another." Indeed they had. The ship's older passengers relished the calm and opulence, unheard-of commodities in wartime England. All manner of terror and deprivation had disappeared.

MARY CORNISH WAS A PIANIST and music teacher from London, one of ten children's escorts traveling on the *City of Benares*. She was forty-one years old. On the night of September 17, Cornish had tucked in her charges—fifteen girls aged six to thirteen—at about eight o'clock. After dinner, she and two of the other escorts had chatted over coffee in the lounge. At perhaps half past nine, they had decided to take a stroll on deck.

It had been a rough day on the water. Now a steady rain blew across the deck, but every so often the women could make out the moon, nearly full, fat clouds drifting past. The women sang songs, gazed out at the water, and compared notes.

They had been at sea for four days. Seasickness had come and passed for many of the girls in their care. Homesickness, too. Now the mood and camaraderie were first-rate, they agreed, children and escorts smitten by the thrill of the journey. In five days they would land at Montreal.

Mary Cornish was relaxed and happy when she left her fellow escorts and descended the stairs to the main deck. She was a few steps from her cabin when she felt a sharp thud and heard the sounds of smashing glass.

The passageway went dark. She stumbled, feeling for a hallway railing. Some faint light showed itself in the distance, illuminating the bulkheads. The path ahead was cluttered with debris. It was also filling rapidly with water.

The torpedo had struck port side, one deck below. It had detonated directly beneath the children's bathrooms.

My girls are down there, Mary Cornish said to herself, peering into the blackness. *I must get to the girls.*

BOHDAN NAGORSKI HAD BEEN WALKING on deck, too, and he was still there when the *Benares* shook, at three minutes past ten. To Nagorski the sound was like the report of a revolver, fired close to the ear. But that was a fleeting impression; in fact he knew almost immediately what had happened.

Three Royal Navy vessels had flanked the *City of Benares* as she moved into the Atlantic, precisely because British commanders understood the risks associated with the journey. Hitler's submarines had torpedoed more than three hundred vessels in the previous four months. Two weeks earlier the SS *Volendam* had been hit, carrying 320 children from the evacuation program. But the *Volendam* had been struck close to shore; all her children had survived.

The *Benares* had sailed for four days and nights without incident. By the time her naval escort turned about, on the morning of September 17, the ship was nearly five hundred miles northwest of Liverpool. Royal Navy officers supervising the escort—as well as the *Benares*' crew and passengers—had believed their liner was safe, far from the prowling U-boats, and beyond the theater of war.

It was just before ten o'clock at night on the seventeenth when Nagorski took his after-dinner stroll with his friend and compatriot Zygmunt Gralinski, a Polish diplomat. Two other passengers joined them—the British parliamentarian James Baldwin-Webb and an Indian medical student who was traveling to the United States for postgraduate research. The men were examples of an eclectic passenger list, reflecting what the historian Ralph Barker called "a colorful mixture of the cosmopolitan, intellectual and the persecuted." Bohdan Nagorski was a bit of each—a port engineer and shipping executive who had been made a refugee by the war. For a half hour or so they talked about Canada, and they discussed the situation in Poland. At about a minute after ten, Gralinski said he was tired. Nagorski suggested it might be wise to spend the night on deck; if a torpedo struck, he said with a smile, better to be here— closer to the lifeboats, fully dressed, and wide awake.

His remark had been meant as a joke. Gralinski chuckled, Baldwin-Webb bade them good night, and then came the crash. The force of it shook the deck. In a matter of seconds the four men were separated.

Nagorski righted himself and searched for his friend. In these first moments, as the *Benares* listed slightly and the rain turned hard and icy, he felt strangely calm. *I need to get to a lifeboat,* he said to himself. *And I should get some of my things.*

But as he made his way below deck, he also imagined that this would be the last night of his life. In the last year alone Bohdan Nagorski had fled the German bombardment of Poland, traveling "in a railway carriage or motorcar or a peasant's cart." He had escaped Nazi-occupied France and survived the opening salvos of the London blitz. Now Nagorski stood in his cabin, studying the little room in an almost disinterested way, wondering what belongings were worth carrying to the lifeboat station. He had made similar calculations before—gathering possessions in his home in Gdynia, on the Baltic Sea, stuffing a small suitcase in Bordeaux.

After a quick survey, Nagorski took his coat and homburg hat and a diplomatic pouch, leaving a trunk and that same small suitcase behind.

All the while the thought beat in his mind like a drum: *I am going to die. I will lose my life, somewhere in these waters.*

NOT FAR FROM THE *City of Benares*, the submarine *Unterseeboot* 48— U-48, for short—cut through the water, just below the surface. Several of her crewmen had gathered to celebrate their latest achievement.

U-48 had already distinguished herself as a fearsome piece in Hitler's maritime arsenal, and in time this submarine would achieve unparalleled successes for Nazi Germany. Her commander was Heinrich Bleichrodt, a hard-drinking thirty-year-old who had taken the reins only a few days earlier. U-48 had left L'Orient, in Nazi-occupied France, on September 8. For Bleichrodt the mission would mark the beginning of a storied career. Eventually U-48's commander would win Germany's prized Knight's Cross with Oak Leaves, for leading a crew that sank more enemy vessels than any other submarine during World War II.

Bleichrodt had spotted the slow-moving shapes of Convoy OB213 in the early afternoon of September 17. Under his orders, U-48 had tailed the *City of Benares* in a zigzag pattern for nearly ten hours.

In Heinrich Bleichrodt's mind there was no question that the *Benares* was fair game. She was sailing in a large convoy, she had gunners positioned at either end, and she was a large liner, an inviting target at a time when U-boat achievements were measured by the tonnage of ships destroyed.

These were arguments the Germans would make years later, when they stood in the dock at Nuremberg, charged with crimes against humanity for attacks including the one on the SS *City of Benares*. For now U-48's men were jubilant. "A success," Bleichrodt said simply. Through U-48's conning tower they could see that the liner was sinking by the stern and listing badly. Some of her lifeboats had already begun their descent. Bleichrodt knew they had struck a particularly stinging blow that night in the North Atlantic.

THE EXPLOSION HAD TORN INTO the *Benares*' side, throwing children from their bunks and crushing furniture and equipment over a wide swath of the ship. Lights flickered, dimmed, and went dark; water cascaded into the ship's interior from burst pipes and from the Atlantic itself. Within minutes several people on board the *Benares* were dead.

Mary Cornish kept looking for "her girls." After a frantic quarter hour she found some of them, only to miss her own lifeboat's launch. At an officer's order, she went instead to a boat jammed with men, and six of the evacuee boys. *All right, then*, she thought, *I shall care for these children instead.* It comforted her somewhat; if she was here, perhaps the boys' escort was in another lifeboat, tending to her girls. The boat went down on the command of an officer, teetering for a moment and then landing with a splash.

Two of the boys in her boat were Fred Steels and Paul Shearing. They had lost contact with their cabinmate, the boy with the glasses. Now, teeth chattering, Steels took hold of the boat's Fleming gear mounted between the seats, small iron levers that propelled the boat forward. Steels tugged hard, helping the men pull clear of the hulking liner. *An adventure*, he thought. *If Mum and Dad could see me . . .*

Mary Cornish huddled close to another boy, rubbing his shoulders.

"I'm freezing, ma'am," he said.

She could hardly hear the boy over the roar of the sea.

Bodies passed, bobbing on the water. Cornish looked away and massaged the boy's feet.

"Don't worry," she told him. "It's only a torpedo."

OTHER LIFEBOATS DANGLED VIOLENTLY FROM their davits. Fred Steels had watched as one of them—crowded with people—cracked against the ship's side, hurling its occupants into the water.

The Polish diplomat Zygmunt Gralinski stepped down a rope ladder into a lifeboat that was swamped at precisely the moment it touched the water. He fell into the cold sea.

Baldwin-Webb, the British MP, stayed on deck longer than most other passengers, helping women and children board the lifeboats. Suddenly he found himself alone at the ship's railing, gazing down at the water. He had missed his chance; the lifeboats had all been lowered. People beckoned from below, some forty feet down.

Baldwin-Webb hesitated. Then he stepped to the edge and jumped. He landed on his stomach, hitting the water with a sickening slap.

The teenagers Bess Walder and Beth Cummings reached their lifeboat—Lifeboat number 5—but the boat took on water almost immediately. After a wild struggle on the waves, it was upended. Bess and Beth were thrown into the sea. The girls spent a harrowing few minutes slashing and crawling to stay above water, and somehow they both found their lifeboat. It was upside down.

Bess Walder swam to the boat, and there she saw Beth, barely, through the sea spray and the rain. Beyond that Bess could see only hands—a row of wrists and knuckles curled over the opposite side. Perhaps a dozen people were clinging desperately to the keel of Lifeboat 5.

"*Beth!*" Bess cried out. "*Hang on!*"

In the tumult of the storm and waves, the two girls languished there, ice-cold, holding on, crying out and no one able to hear them. They tried desperately to elevate themselves, to keep their bodies above the water. Every few minutes a flare shot up in the distance. Beth Cummings watched as a pair of hands on the keel lost their grip and slipped away.

A fresh, fiercer storm broke over the scene, and the winds reached gale force. At about half past ten the waters were illuminated suddenly, splashed by a powerful searchlight.

"Rescue!" came the cry from one of the lifeboats. A smattering of cheers went up on the waves. But almost as suddenly the light was gone, having swung an arc around the site and then dipped below the water level. Darkness returned.

The shivering, dying refugees of the *Benares* never knew it, but the searchlight belonged to *Unterseeboot* 48. Captain Heinrich Bleichrodt had passed close by on a reconnaissance mission, a visit to the scene of his crime. He could see, from that fleeting look, that no more torpedoes were needed.

THE *CITY OF BENARES* SLIPPED into the sea.

U-48 sped away, to the east.

Three hundred miles away, the warship HMS *Hurricane* made a horseshoe turn.

Hurricane's senior officer, Lieutenant Commander Hugh Crofton Simms, had read a decoded message from the Office of Western Approaches, the Royal Navy's station near Liverpool that monitored maritime activity in the North Atlantic. A civilian liner had been hit.

"Proceed with utmost dispatch to position 56.43 N, 21.15 W, where survivors are reported in boats."

Immediately Simms set a fast course for the search area, racing the *Hurricane* through increasingly rough and dangerous seas. His crew was excited, but the seas raged, and the ride became as turbulent as any they had known. Hugh Crofton Simms doubted he would reach the scene in time to be of help.

IN LIFEBOAT NUMBER 12, BOHDAN Nagorski thought of war, of all the times he had considered life and family, and loss. For the moment at least he believed he had cheated death once more. He had a seat in a lifeboat, a warm coat draped across his knees and over the frame of a cold boy at his side. They had pulled those Fleming handles hard, away from the doomed liner. There were forty-six people crammed in this boat, six more than it was meant to hold. The group was quiet and showing no signs of panic. Presumably a rescue vessel would find them.

But as the storm rose, and the awful cries of the dying filled the night, Nagorski said to himself, *We will not make it. We will not last until morning.*

Lifeboat 12 was drifting in a particularly unforgiving patch of the Atlantic, six hundred miles from land and three hundred miles from the nearest warship. Nothing in this hellish scene at position 56.43 N, 21.15 W suggested that any of these people would live.

IT WAS THE WORST MARITIME disaster of the war to date. Entire families were wiped out. Businessmen, diplomats, and professors were lost. So were scores of crewmembers and evacuee children.

But the fact was that the *City of Benares*—while an immediate and powerful symbol of tragedy and the horror of war—would also prove herself a mother of miracles in the waters where she went down. Mind-bending examples of courage, endurance, and good fortune took shape in the hours and days that followed the attack—the children in particular exhibiting what one naval officer later called "courage beyond praise."

Sudden, almost imperceptible shifts in fortune were to determine who survived and who perished: the choice of the port-side lifeboat; a delay in reaching the embarkation deck; a foot massage offered by an adult escort to one of the children; or a cheerful talk administered by a child to a failing elderly passenger. Mother Nature played her role. So did bravery. So did patience and discipline, stoicism and keen minds.

But it was chance, more than anything, that dictated who would live.

CHAPTER 2

The Young Ambassadors

On the night of September 9, 1940, in the London neighborhood of Brixton, Eddie Grimmond heard the rumble of planes before his wife did, before the children had stirred. By the time the air raid sirens screamed, he had roused the entire family, which was no small achievement. He and Hannah Grimmond had eleven children, six boys and five girls. Soon Hannah and all the children were bustling about the cramped two-story home, pulling on coats and shoes and walking down Lilford Road to the neighborhood bomb shelter. They made a ragged picture, mother and father and a group of sleepy, scarcely clad boys and girls.

When they arrived at the shelter, roughly thirty-five neighbors were already there.

"Getting tired of this, Hannah," Eddie Grimmond told his wife.

The German *Blitzkrieg*—literally, "lightning war"—was in its third night, and already it was an uncompromising, ferocious aerial assault on targets across England. The *Luftwaffe* had opened its barrage as darkness fell on September 7, sending more than three hundred bombers and six hundred fighter planes to carry out the most savage attacks of the war to date. The Germans dropped hundreds of bombs on London that first night, torching docks along the Thames, killing 448 civilians and rescue workers and wounding some 1300 others. Thousands more were left homeless.

London power stations and factories were hit, and many of the bombs had been strapped to oil drums, so that their damage would be multiplied by firestorms on impact. Flames lit the night sky, and all along the docks the "smells of empire" rose in the air, as barges and storage houses filled with rum, pepper, and rubber burned through the night.

It would come to be known as "Black Saturday." From that night on, Londoners by the hundreds of thousands took to basements, bomb shelters, and metro stations, girding for the next strike from the air.

Eddie Grimmond believed the blitz would be short-lived, that British Spitfires and Hawker Hurricanes would soon repulse the *Luftwaffe*. He was also convinced that the family's frequent visits to the fortified shelter were a waste of time. Worse, they were a concession to Nazi terror, emboldening the enemy while each rush down the road filled his children with fear. His youngest was three, the eldest eighteen. Eddie Grimmond would have preferred they sleep in their own beds, forgo the shelter, and take their chances.

That night the *whoosh* of an approaching bomb seemed particularly close. The shudder and reverberations of impact followed, tremors felt below ground. Some of the children screamed.

When the all-clear came, the sun was lifting over Brixton. The Grimmond family walked quietly back to Lilford Road. They were startled by what they found. A bomb had crushed their home, leaving a small mountain of rubble atop their modest possessions. Nearly everything the Grimmonds owned had been broken, buried, or burned, including five suitcases that had been packed with clothes and lined near the door, one each for Augusta, Constance, Edward, Leonard, and Violet Grimmond. These five were to travel to Canada in less than a week as part of a large-scale evacuation of British children.

"They can't possibly go now," Hannah Grimmond said to her husband. "Not without their things."

Eddie Grimmond was stone-faced and silent. They could all have been killed, he knew. Had they taken their chances, as he had suggested, and slept in their own beds, they would probably have been buried under all that rubble.

He moved about his ruined home, a rage building slowly. Grimmond had been bitterly opposed to the idea of sending his children away. It was a form of surrender, he thought, precisely what the Germans were hoping for. But within hours, after a long morning spent surveying the destruction, he had changed his mind. The children must leave London. As much as he hated the idea, he did not want them to hear one more siren or one more bomb whistling from the sky, everyone guessing where and when the crash would come.

Eddie Grimmond had already lived one odyssey of war, a life's worth of violence and romance. He had been a machine-gunner in World War I, a teenager in the trenches in northern France and prisoner of the Germans in the months before the armistice. He had seen his best friend killed, and upon his return from the front he had befriended and later married the friend's widow, Hannah, taking on her child and ultimately fathering ten more. On the morning of September 10, 1940, Eddie Grimmond told his wife that the bombing would only get worse. "I know the Germans," he said. The children would have to go, suitcases or no.

Hannah Grimmond was still reluctant. That night they withdrew once more to the shelter, this time because it was the only place to sleep. They talked well into the night about the choice they faced. All eleven children lay nearby on a long, neat row of mattresses. However horrible the war became, Hannah Grimmond wondered, was it not better for a family to endure together? Was it not unfair to dispatch only five of the eleven children to safety— simply because they were the right age for the evacuation program—and leave the rest in London? Could any family survive such a rupture?

That night it was quieter—heavy cloud cover slowed the *Luftwaffe*— although Buckingham Palace was damaged slightly by a German bomb. By the following afternoon Eddie and Hannah Grimmond had made their decision. The children would go to Canada.

They told Augusta, the thirteen-year-old, that she would have to act as a "little mother" to the others.

ACROSS ENGLAND THAT SUMMER, IN household after household, parents had faced the same wrenching choice. In London, government billboards showed pitiful images of children, forlorn faces staring up at fretful-looking mothers. "The children deserve a better life," one of the notices said. "Mothers, send them out of London."

To some parents the decision came easily; a battlefield was no place for a child, and by that first fortnight in September, no one doubted that England would be a battlefield—or at least a bombing target—for some time. The blitz had made a ferocious debut; a land invasion was considered imminent. Hitler's *Reich* appeared unstoppable. The evacuation program offered a ticket to freedom, and safety. It was reasonable to think that evacuation might also mean the difference between life and death.

But the idea was attacked on two fronts. Some saw it as unpatriotic. Certainly Winston Churchill did. The new prime minister detested the idea. He believed the mass departure of children would soften the national backbone and damage public morale. Worse, he thought, the enemy would see it as a sign of weakness.

This was precisely the moment, Churchill argued, "when all must brace themselves for the supreme struggle." Churchill was already immensely popular, and powerful. His opinion on such matters held obvious weight.

For mothers and fathers, there were more personal considerations. Was it not paramount to preserve a family, as Hannah Grimmond had suggested? How could parents in good conscience deliver their children to strangers, half a world away? What if the war were to last several years? An eight-year-old girl, say, might be a teenager before she and her parents were together again. A fifteen-year-old boy might return as a young man. So much would be missed. And of course such calculations assumed that parents and children would survive the war; it was also possible that they would never see one another again.

For countless parents—indeed for many people who had no children, but joined the debate nonetheless—the choice was as the author Elspeth Huxley described it: "Security for the young and helpless was measured against the scars which flight from danger might have upon their minds, and against the bereavement which parents would suffer with their children gone." These sons and daughters of England would either be safe in some faraway land, or home with family under bombardment and a possible German occupation.

Bernard and Rosina Walder had considered the choice for months. They lived in Kentish Town, in North London, with their son, Louis, ten, and a fifteen-year-old daughter named Bess. No bombs had fallen on their street, but war had already touched the family in many ways.

Bernard Walder was a caretaker for the Rhyl Street School, a modest position with a notable perk: a three-story home across the street from the school. From the stone wall of that home, Bess Walder had watched firemen run drills in the school playground. London taxis were parked there, serving as makeshift fire trucks, carrying part-time workers who had been pressed into service as volunteer firefighters. On the first mornings of the blitz, the all-clear would sound, Bess and her family would return from the school's bomb shelter, and soon after Bess would see the fire crews returning home, the men's faces blackened from a night spent fighting blazes on the docks.

The family spent an afternoon filling sandbags and hauling them up against the sides of the house. Town workmen came one day and stripped the railings from a fence in front of the Walders' home; these were to be melted down for scrap metal. Bess helped tape windows so they would not shatter during an air raid, and her parents kept rugs near the front door, ready to seal the vents against a gas attack.

Bess was an intelligent and curious girl, and throughout the summer of

1940 she had heard loud and occasionally rough language in her home, whenever neighbors and friends came to talk politics. Her father had been a com-
mitted pacifist since World War I. The "Great War" had instilled in him a
revulsion for all armed conflict and a profound fear of the consequences war
might impose on his family.

But Bernard Walder had also read *Mein Kampf,* and he had followed the
news from Berlin about Hitler's *Reich.* He was convinced that the Führer intended to destroy Britain. He explained these things to Bess—even read her
passages from *Mein Kampf.* Bess Walder noticed that when her parents and
their friends spoke the word "Nazi," it was spat derisively, with a venom she
had rarely heard.

One morning Bernard Walder watched as his daughter chatted with the
young firemen across the way. It was a sweet scene, in some ways, his daughter
and these brave young Englishmen, but it stirred other feelings. *Why should
they stay here and watch a hell unfold around them?* In truth he hated the idea
of sending Bess and Louis away, but if the Germans were coming and a safe
haven were offered, how could he say no? What sense was there in keeping
children in London if the city risked becoming an inferno?

"Look what's happening now," he told his wife. "What kind of life have we
brought our children?"

Together Bernard and Rosina Walder decided they should apply to send
Bess and Louis away.

IT HAD BEEN A SEASON of almost unrelenting pessimism. In May
alone, Holland had fallen to the Nazis, Belgium had capitulated, and on Britain's
Empire Day, May 24, King George VI had broadcast a chilling message to the nation. "Let no one be mistaken," the king warned. "It is no mere territorial conquest that our enemies are seeking. It is the overthrow, complete and final, of this
empire and everything for which it stands, and after that the conquest of the
world." The British Ministry of Information began circulating leaflets under the
heading "If the Invader Comes: What to Do and How to Do It." The small print
drew on examples from the Polish, Dutch, and Belgian experiences.

It was in this atmosphere that the British government fashioned a program
to send children to the so-called British dominions—Australia, Canada, New
Zealand, and South Africa. A parliamentary committee established earlier
that year had outlined two basic aims for any evacuation program: greater
safety for the children and a better future for the country. The latter would be

achieved, first, by reducing the national burden of feeding so many children, and then by safeguarding these boys and girls who would presumably be the men and women of postwar Great Britain.

The man nominated to lead the program, a member of Parliament named Geoffrey Shakespeare, was initially opposed to the idea. Shakespeare was forty-seven, a career politician and part-time journalist. As a young man he had been private secretary to Prime Minister Lloyd George. He worked diligently to plan an evacuation scheme, but essentially he agreed with Churchill and with those parents who saw evacuation as a kind of betrayal. If the nation was in peril, this thinking went, the better response would be to stand up to the enemy. Several members of Parliament argued that mass evacuation would sow panic and be taken outside Britain as proof that the nation was preparing for defeat. The point was articulated clearly in a letter to the *Times* of London written by the headmaster of Winchester College:

> How can we with any consistency continue to speak of training in
> citizenship and in leadership while at the same time we arrange for
> them . . . to leave the post of danger? Families should face the danger
> together; the nation should face the danger together.

But support grew quickly for the evacuation program, in part because it was cast in the public discussion as a question of fairness. Thousands of children were already being spirited privately to English country estates, and hundreds more to other countries by families who could afford to arrange such passage on their own. London dailies ran pictures of upper-tier children posing happily on elegant manors in Quebec and New York's Long Island. In a memorandum prepared for the war cabinet, Geoffrey Shakespeare warned that "if children are stopped from going under government auspices, while other children can freely proceed overseas at the expense of their parents, there is bound to be a strong feeling that there is a discrimination in favour of the privileged classes." Why, as one writer put it, should "the son of the rich sleep in security in New York's gay lighted towers . . . while the son of a poor man dozes in crowded shelters below our dangerous cities, menaced by the bomber's drone?"

It was a reasonable question. Something had to be done.

On June 17, Winston Churchill acquiesced. Or—more likely—he missed the chance to voice his opposition. That day Shakespeare presented his report to the cabinet, meeting in the War Rooms at Westminster. It included his plan for a Children's Overseas Reception Board, or CORB, to safeguard the young boys and girls of Great Britain.

Churchill recorded several dissenting views. First he argued that ships carrying the evacuees would be vulnerable, and that it would be difficult to draft warships as escorts, given how thinly stretched the Royal Navy already found itself. These points were incontrovertible. Then he repeated the argument about evacuation and Britain's global image. He wished no ill to the children of England, Churchill assured his cabinet, but he asked them to consider the question: What signal would a large-scale evacuation send to the nation, to the enemy, and to the rest of the world?

It was during this discussion that a messenger arrived with a note for the prime minister. According to the minutes of the meeting, "At this point . . . a message was brought in reporting that the French troops had ceased fire at 12:40." France was capitulating. The German Army had marched into Paris three days earlier. Now Britain's ally just across the English Channel was under Hitler's thumb.

The historian Martin Gilbert has said that after the news about Paris, Churchill left the cabinet meeting and was never "fully apprised of what it was he had agreed to." Indeed, while minutes from the June 17 meetings show that Shakespeare's report was endorsed that day, they also suggest that in the end the discussion had been overwhelmed, understandably, by the news from Paris.

It is almost certain that had Churchill devoted more time and attention to the CORB proposals, he would have formally rejected them. Later he would inveigh against the whole idea with characteristic bluntness, arguing in opposition to "any stampede from this country at the present time."

But by then a stampede of sorts was already under way.

On June 18, the cabinet established the CORB, "for the care, supervision, and education of the children . . . until the war is over." The CORB would select the evacuees, match them with families in the "dominions" who had volunteered to act as hosts, book passage on commercial liners, and then monitor the children—albeit from a great distance. It would prove a huge logistical endeavor. Candidates were to be at least five years old and not yet sixteen. They would be "young ambassadors" for Britain, Geoffrey Shakespeare said, representing their country with honor abroad. No parents or other relatives would be permitted to go along; in some cases parents were not even aware until embarkation where precisely their child was going. Adult escorts would be hired, one for every fifteen children. The ships—and their precious cargo—would enjoy the protection of the Royal Navy. "The transport of the children in safety," Shakespeare said, "was the crux of the whole matter."

Asked how he would counsel parents who faced the difficult question of whether to send their children on the CORB ships, Shakespeare said, "This is advice I cannot give." But Shakespeare did feel it necessary to issue a public warning to parents, via the British Broadcasting Corporation:

> You have to weigh the danger to which your child is exposed in this country, whether by invasion or air raids, against the risks to which every ship that leaves these shores is subjected in wartime by enemy action . . . The risks of the voyage are obvious and the choice is one for which you alone are responsible.

The warnings made no mention of submarines. They did not need to. There were probably no parents—and only a few children—who remained unaware of the risks.

HITLER'S U-BOATS HAD BEEN VERY active that summer, patrolling the English Channel and the northeast Atlantic, "always suspected, always unseen." Between June and early September, the fleet of these fast and deadly submarines had sunk 351 ships—an average of more than three per day—and crippled dozens more. More than one million tons of allied shipping had already been destroyed. The fall of France had given Nazi Germany the Bay of Biscay, and with it a submarine base far closer to British shores.

The role of the U-boat in the German war plan had grown steadily since the onset of war. In late 1939 Hitler had decreed that merchant ships communicating by wireless could be intercepted; the order was soon amended to include all vessels. Standing Order 154 directed U-boat commanders to "rescue no one and take no one aboard . . . Care only for your own boat and strive to achieve the next success as soon as possible! We must be hard in this war."

Hard they would be. In August 1940, Hitler authorized a total naval blockade of the British Isles; the U-boat would be his principal tool of enforcement. Now all U-boat commanders had unequivocal instructions: They were to attack any vessel deemed to be violating the blockade, and to do so without warning.

For all the dangers, and all the debate within individual households, the response to the evacuation program was swift and staggering. On June 20, the

CORB opened its doors in an annex of the Thomas Cook and Sons Travel Agency in London's Berkeley Street. The halls were soon jammed with parents; nearly three thousand more people waited outside. By the first week in July, there were 210,000 applications for some 20,000 places. The first evacuee ships were scheduled to sail in late July, but for the moment they would come nowhere near to meeting the demand. On July 4, the CORB temporarily shut its applications office.

Watching these developments, Winston Churchill returned to the debate. On July 18, he said that it was

> most undesirable that anything in the nature of a large-scale exodus from this country should take place, and I do not believe the military situation requires or justifies such a proceeding, having regard to the relative dangers of staying and going.

The dangers inherent in "staying" were magnified by Hitler's latest pronouncement, given in an address to the *Reichstag*, which was really an ultimatum to Great Britain. Hitler called the speech his "Final Appeal to Reason":

> A great empire will be destroyed, an empire which it was never my intention to destroy or even to harm . . . I consider myself in a position to make this appeal since I am not the vanquished begging favors, but the victor speaking in the name of reason.

The threat to Great Britain could not have been more stark or plainly stated. As for the potential dangers of "going," a fresh reminder came in the final days of summer.

On August 29, the Dutch liner SS *Volendam* left Liverpool carrying 606 passengers, 321 of them children traveling under the CORB program, the largest single contingent of evacuee children to date. On her second day out, the *Volendam* was struck by a U-boat's torpedo at a little before midnight, seventy miles off Ireland's Donegal Coast. The ship and her passengers were fortunate; all eighteen lifeboats were deployed successfully, the seas were calm, and there was, according to the ship's captain, "no panic whatsoever." Later that same night the *Volendam* survivors were picked up by the tanker *Valdemosa*. The sole casualty resulted when the ship's purser was crushed in a fall between his lifeboat and the *Volendam* herself. The SS *Volendam* and every one of her child passengers survived.

The episode might have served as a cautionary tale, frightening some would-be evacuees or their families, but before the attack on the *Volendam* could leave any real impression, something else did: the opening night of the blitz, one week later. Britons were confronted with newspaper accounts of "rows of lifeless children in the hospital morgue." Photographs amplified the impact.

The press reports and images pushed many families to the same decision: They would send their sons and daughters away, if provided the chance.

On Monday, September 9, the families of nearly one hundred more children received the news they had been waiting for:

I am directed by the Children's Overseas Reception Board to inform you that your preliminary application in connection with this scheme has been considered and they have decided that (child/children) (is/are) suitable for being sent . . .

Wartime regulations meant that precise details—the ship's name, embarkation port, or even day of departure—could not be given. But parents were told to expect a CORB representative at their home within the next twenty-four hours, and they were informed that their children would leave England before week's end.

THE ENVELOPE WAS MARKED "on His Majesty's Service" and addressed to Bernard and Rosina Walder. It fell to Rosina Walder to tell the children. She thought it would be the most difficult thing she had ever done. A dread came over her as she poured morning tea in the kitchen.

Bess saw her mother's hand trembling. Then came the question.

"How would the two of you like to go to Canada?"

Louis and Bess looked at each other. Smiles spread slowly across their faces.

"Wonderful," Bess said after a few moments. "When can we go?"

Bess had some vague ideas about Canada—the Rockies and rolling wheat fields, a place where food was plentiful and the skies blissfully free of bombers. As far as Bess knew, Canada was not in the enemy's sights. Louis Walder was a weaker, less outgoing child; he had suffered frequent colds and showed little interest in leaving England. When the news came, Louis had a simpler perspective: He believed he would see cowboys and Indians in Canada.

Their mother was relieved. The children had taken the news so well! Then she felt a pang of sorrow. *Almost too well*, she thought.

That Wednesday, September 11, Bess and Louis were taken to London's Euston Station. There the children would meet an appointed adult escort and the train to Liverpool.

It was a gray, rain-flecked morning. Hundreds of people milled at the station, waiting for the same train. Bess and Louis saw other boys and girls with their parents, soldiers with wives or girlfriends, vendors hawking snacks and sweets. Conductors bellowed. Whistles blew. All along the platform there were cries and hugs and long farewells.

Rosina Walder fought back tears, barely. "You grow up and be a good girl," she told her daughter. "And don't forget: You must look after that young man."

Bess promised she would. She embraced her mother, then her father. Then she and Louis turned away and boarded the train.

The two children settled in one of the rear cars with a woman from the evacuation program. As the train pulled away, Bess Walder avoided looking out the window, holding her brother's hand tightly. *We've left all the crying parents behind*, she thought.

Neither child cried—but for much of the ride Bess thought of what her mother had said. *Grow up and be a good girl* ...

What exactly did that mean? "Grow up"? What had her mother had in mind?

Bess Walder believed that leaving England was for the best, and she was thrilled to be going to another country. She and Louis were very lucky—she knew that much. But what had her mother meant? Was she really to "grow up" in Canada? And care for her brother for all that time?

How long would she and Louis be gone?

CHAPTER 3

The *City of Benares*

K en Sparks could not believe this was the ship.

She's enormous, he said to himself. The liner stretched more than a soccer field's length down the dock, her decks rising higher than the boy could see. *She's rich-looking,* Sparks thought. *And she's here for us.*

Sparks was thirteen, an eager, effervescent child from Wembley who had made war reporting a kind of hobby. He had collected shrapnel shards after air raids, and read everything he could about warplanes and warships and about the Royal Navy's engagements with Hitler's submarines. He had peppered family and teachers with questions about the war, about Hitler himself, and about the British defenses. But until this bright afternoon Ken Sparks had never actually *seen* a warship, or a liner, or for that matter any craft larger than the paddle steamers that ferried Londoners along the Thames.

Now Ken Sparks was staring up at the SS *City of Benares.*

"Magnificent," Sparks said to Derek Capel, a boy waiting in line behind him. "And she's waiting for *us.*"

Derek Capel was twelve, and he had never seen anything like it either. In magazines, maybe. He moved slowly in the queue, holding his little brother Alan's hand.

"That'll be our home now, Alan," Derek said. "We'll be living on this thing for a while."

"Gosh!" Alan Capel said. He was five years old.

The children formed orderly lines along the dock, though they were almost bursting with energy and excitement. Some of them jumped in place. When the time came, they bounded up the gangway, forty-six boys and forty-four girls, many craning their necks for a better look. Onlookers cheered and waved from the port and from the *Duchess of Atholl*, a liner moored in the adjacent berth. Hardly any of the children had ever been on board a ship; few had ever laid eyes on Liverpool Bay, much less the Atlantic Ocean.

The children's escort, Mary Cornish, thought she had never seen such a fine and happy procession, and it made her proud. The afternoon was crisp and cool, a breeze lifting smoke from the ship's stacks and carrying salt air over the port. Cornish noticed the smells—not just the sea salt but the rough port odors of tar and rope, and freshly scrubbed decks. Tensions she had felt—worries over the children's mood, their health, and her own jitters about the journey—eased as she drank in the dockside scene. She felt the rush of adventure, a keener sense that what they were doing was good, and right.

Just look, she thought. *Look at the smiles* . . .

CLUTCHING SMALL SUITCASES AND WEARING identification tags around their necks, ninety children bade farewell to their families that week at bus depots and train stations across Great Britain. They came from Wales in the west, Sunderland in the north, from cities along the southern coast, and from the grittier neighborhoods in and around London. They were sons and daughters of miners and policemen and factory workers, children of blue-collar, bomb-ravaged communities. Their circumstances and back-grounds were in no small measure their tickets out of the country.

None had known rougher times than the five sons and daughters of Eddie and Hannah Grimmond. Much of the CORB procedural work had been rushed or waived entirely for the Grimmond children once word came that their home had been leveled. On September 11, Eddie Grimmond brought Augusta, Constance, Edward, Leonard, and Violet—none of whom had been able to bathe since the bombing two nights before—to Euston Station. A train took them west from there to Sherwood's Lane School, in the Fazackerlay district of Liverpool. Sherwood's Lane would be a place for orientation and last-minute checks, a chance for the children to get to know one another and their adult escorts.

Rosemary Spencer-Davies took that same train to Liverpool. She would be the oldest in the CORB group, a highly independent fifteen-year-old traveling from Brixton with her younger brother, John. Rosemary made a fast impression at Fazackerlay as one of the more mature and sophisticated of the young evacuees. She was tall and slender, with brown eyes and long brown pigtails, and she was already an accomplished writer and painter. She read to the other children and helped bathe the youngest girls, many of whom mistook Rosemary for one of the adult escorts. A Sherwood's Lane schoolmistress thought Rosemary Spencer-Davies had the gift "of winning almost instantly the respect of those who met her." She was planning to pursue studies as an artist in Canada.

Like the Grimmond children, Rosemary and John Spencer-Davies had come to Liverpool after considerable debate at home. Throughout the summer their mother had insisted the children stay in England; their father had countered that Rosemary, at least, should leave before she turned sixteen, the cutoff age for the CORB program. Soon, he reminded his wife, their daughter's chance would expire.

As was the case in many of these family disputes, the father was in favor of evacuation, the mother against—and the father often won the argument. The letter inviting the Spencer-Davies children was delayed in the mail; only a frantic, last-minute effort brought John and Rosemary to Liverpool.

Eleven-year-old Paul Shearing had actually encouraged his parents to let him go. Shearing was a slight, self-conscious boy from Bournemouth, along England's south coast, and he felt ambivalent at best about his childhood. He had been teased at school, and occasionally at home as well. His shy nature and fair curly hair had provoked occasional cruelty from older boys. "Well, *Pauline*, when's your mommy coming . . ." Walking in his neighborhood of Moordown, Paul Shearing had kept quiet, too shy to speak to schoolmates or shopkeepers he saw along the way. Even before the blitz, Shearing had wanted to be somewhere else, and he had told his parents so. Canada, he thought, sounded delightful.

Terrence Holmes had begged to go, too, not because he wanted to leave home and certainly not because he wished to see Canada. He didn't know a thing about Canada. What Terrence Holmes wanted was to sail the Atlantic. He loved ships, and the sea, though he had scarcely seen either as a child growing up in Wembley. Terrence was ten years old. In the days before he left home, he spent hours at a desk in his room, sketching all manner of liners and warships for his parents.

There were twenty-three sets of siblings in the group that met at Fazackerlay. Jack and Joyce Keeley, at eight and six respectively, were among the youngest. Their father, a veteran of both World War I and the Boer War, had wanted desperately to send his children away from this war. Jack Keeley romped happily over the Sherwood's Lane grounds in a brand-new pair of boots his parents had bought for the journey. Rex Thorne, a thirteen-year-old from Wembley, was traveling with his ten-year-old sister, Marion. Rex carried an idyllic picture in his mind of a farm in Saskatoon, Saskatchewan, where he and Marion were to wait out the war. The names—"Saskatoon," "Saskatchewan"—conjured images of Indians and wilderness. It never occurred to Rex Thorne that his sojourn would amount to anything more than a few weeks or months. Surely the war would be over by then.

Robert and John Baker, twelve and seven, were headed all the way to Vancouver, British Columbia. John Baker was a restless child, and to him the voyage loomed like a dream, almost too wondrous to imagine. They were going on a kind of holiday, he and Robert and all these other boys and girls, to places none of them knew, in a land utterly unaffected by the war. Robert, or Bobby as his brother called him, was a more sober boy. It would fall to him to watch over his little brother, to be sure that little Johnny didn't run off when no one was looking.

Eleven of the ninety children had come from Sunderland, near the Scottish border. Nine-year-old Billy Short spoke a Scottish brogue so strong that some of the other boys had difficulty understanding him. Billy and his brother, Peter, five, had never been to London, or Liverpool, or for that matter to any place more than a short drive from their home. Their family had always vacationed within a small radius of Sunderland; the borderlands there were really the only places Billy and Peter Short knew. Eleanor Wright was thirteen, eldest of the Sunderland children. She had corresponded for months with a pen pal on Prince Edward Island, her ultimate destination.

Wright's schoolteacher, a Miss Gills, had given a last-minute talk to the Sunderland evacuees.

"We want no tears or fuss," Gills admonished. When the time came for farewells, the evacuees were to remember that they were "British to the backbone." Parents were asked by teachers and CORB representatives to stand at a distance as their children boarded the train for Liverpool. This way, presumably, any "tears or fuss" might be minimized. Peg Steels had anguished over the decision, and when the time came to bid farewell to her son, Fred, she cried and held the boy tight. Leaving his mother, Fred Steels thought, was "like trying to get away from an octopus." For the most part, the children took the farewells better than their parents.

Elizabeth Capel had brought sons Derek and Alan by train to London, and then by taxi across the city to Euston Station. Once there, in the noisy crowd, she felt the need to remind herself that what she was doing was right. In the Capel family, there had been little doubt about the decision to send Derek and Alan away; they believed the boys would benefit not only from an absence of danger but also from a stable education and a "start in life" that now appeared unattainable in England. For the Capels there was another consideration: There was Jewish blood on Mr. Capel's mother's side of the family. Still, Elizabeth Capel found it wrenching to see her boys in the train car windows. She winced at the conductor's last call for Liverpool.

In a strange way, parents were helped by the knowledge that the blitz was getting worse, the bombings more frequent and ferocious. More and more children were listed among the casualties. A German invasion seemed a certainty now. Bernard and Rosina Walder, sad as they were to watch their son and daughter board the Liverpool train, were grateful for the escorts and the CORB program, and for the chance to spirit Bess and Louis to safety. "We've done the best for them," Rosina Walder told her husband. "Even if it breaks our heart." Still, many mothers and fathers remained wracked with guilt after the trains pulled away, and they returned to homes that felt changed and empty. The parents fretted over a single, basic question: Had they done the right thing?

THE CHILDREN SPENT TWO DAYS and nights at the Sherwood's Lane School. They slept in a pair of cottages, on blankets arrayed in neat rows. In each cottage forty-five children and their escorts shared spaces meant for twenty-eight. "We are like seeds in a pod," one boy wrote home.

Here the children met and came to know their escorts: three men, three women, a supervisor, a reserve escort, a doctor, and a nurse. Together they were charged with caring for the evacuee boys and girls until they reached Canada. The escorts were educators and artists, health-care professionals and ministers. Though all were volunteers, the group had faced fierce competition; several thousand people had applied for the chance to chaperone the evacuees to Canada.

The lead or supervising escort was Marjorie Day, fifty-three-year-old headmistress of the Wycombe Abbey School in Buckinghamshire, one of England's finest schools for girls. The women in charge of the three groups of girls were Maud Hillman, forty-four, a preschool teacher; Sybil Gilliat-Smith, twenty-five, a painter and art teacher who was sailing to Canada to rejoin her husband; and Mary Cornish, forty-one, a classical pianist who had been teaching music for twenty years. The reserve was a teacher and part-time London ambulance driver named Lillian Towns, a mother of two originally from New Zealand and a last-minute addition to the group.

The doctor and nurse were both women. Dr. Betty Margaret Zeal, thirty, was on leave from Hammersmith Hospital, where she had specialized in child psychiatry. The nurse was a twenty-eight-year-old named Dorothy Smith.

As for the men, two were ordained ministers, and the third a minister-in-waiting. Reverend William King was a twenty-eight-year-old Canadian Protestant who had run religious education programs for boys in his native Ontario. Father Roderick O'Sullivan, thirty-two, a Roman Catholic from Herne Bay, England, had lived and taught for a decade in France before fleeing the Nazi occupation in July, via boat from St. Jean de Luz to England. Rory O'Sullivan, as he was called, belonged to the Order of St. Francis deSales, and he had applied for a chaplaincy in the Royal Navy. While O'Sullivan waited, he would escort fifteen English boys to Canada.

The youngest and most eccentric of the escorts was a strapping young scholar and athlete from Hampstead named Michael Rennie. Rennie was charismatic and strikingly handsome, the son of a vicar and descendant of the celebrated Scottish engineer John Rennie, whose design credits had included the blueprints for London Bridge. Michael Rennie was only twenty-three, but he was already something of a Renaissance figure. He had gone to Oxford to study engineering, in the footsteps of his famous ancestor, only to grow disillusioned and prepare instead for the priesthood. In 1940 Rennie had completed his degree studies at Oxford's Keble College with distinction, managing along the way to train as a sea scout, build and race cars, and star at rugby.

Michael Rennie was due to begin his divinity studies at Westcott House, Cambridge, in October. The escort job would be a kind of sabbatical—another adventure for an adventurous young man.

Beyond adventure, these men and women were united in the belief that what they were doing was right, and that it was important. They considered the work a form of national service.

THE GERMANS POUNDED LIVERPOOL DURING the two nights the children spent at Sherwood's Lane. The school was roughly two miles from the nearest strikes, but air raid sirens rang in the cottages. Many children had been too excited about the journey to sleep; now nearly all of them were awakened by the alarms and rushed to shelters. An antiaircraft battery near the school fired round after round, a *pop-pop-pop* heard through the night. Whatever anxieties the children had felt about leaving home were now displaced by fresh fears: Why had they left—if only to sleep in one more dangerous bed? Would they ever make it to Liverpool port? When, if ever, would they actually set sail?

On their first morning together, Paul Shearing and Derek Capel used "free time" to gather bits of shrapnel in the school courtyard. Metal fragments dotted the grounds, the detritus of a night's worth of firing from the antiaircraft guns.

Shearing found himself enthusiastic and unafraid. Neither the sudden separation from family nor the trip itself had fazed him. Already he had made new friends. Soon he would be in Canada.

Derek and Alan Capel had spent most of their childhood in Hanworth, near the old London Air Park, and for as long as Derek could remember he had loved airplanes, loved to read about them and to build model planes, and of course to see the real things, parked in rows at the airfield. Once the war began, Derek Capel had spent long afternoons watching the skies for German Stukas, imagining himself a kind of early warning lookout for his country. He had seen oil bombs land near Hanworth. Once, his father had found an unexploded bomb in their front garden.

Like many English boys, Derek Capel had a shrapnel collection at home, a small pile of metal kept near his bed. His parents had struggled to convince him not to stuff all that metal in his suitcase when he left for Liverpool.

On his first morning at Fazackerlay, Derek Capel found a large chunk of shrapnel and carried it back to the dining hall. He made a present of the gray metal to his little brother, who pocketed the gift and ran happily to the other younger boys.

"Souvenir!" Alan Capel cried.

Derek Capel believed it would bring them good luck.

Michael Brooker of Kent and Liverpool's Patricia Allen spent a good part of those days trying to comfort anxious children. Young though they were—ten and twelve respectively—theirs were voices of experience. Brooker and Allen were the only children in the group who could call themselves veterans of the evacuation program. "Second-chancers," someone said. They had been passengers aboard the SS *Volendam*, the ship torpedoed less than two weeks earlier. The other *Volendam* children had been returned to their homes, but Brooker and Allen came back to learn that their homes had been badly damaged in a *Luftwaffe* raid and their families were living in shelters. So Michael Brooker and Patricia Allen were sent instead to Sherwood's Lane, listed as "priority candidates" for the next available passage.

Many children needed comforting. Jack Keeley's little sister, Joyce, a six-year-old from Brixton, was homesick and wanted to leave. The Sherwood's Lane headmistress, Margaret Abraham, tried to soothe the girl.

"Look at your brother!" Abraham cried. Eight-year-old Jack was busy running with other boys in the school courtyard. "You look at him. You'll be happy as that soon enough."

Seven-year-old John Snoad detested Sherwood's Lane, ached for his parents from the moment he arrived, and dreaded the prospect of the Atlantic crossing. The heavy *Luftwaffe* strafing only made him more depressed and frightened. Snoad screamed at the wail of the air raid sirens, and again as bombs landed in the distance. It did not help that he and his cottage mates could also hear—or feel—the occasional rat skittering across the schoolhouse floors.

"You'll have luxury at sea," Headmistress Abraham told Snoad, but he did not believe her. Snoad passed two fitful, largely sleepless nights at the school, contracted a deep asthmatic cold, and in the last minute was deemed unfit for travel. He returned, sick but relieved, to his family in London.

Other children had last-minute reasons to stay behind. Sunderland sisters Violet and Marion Gustard, eleven and nine, were preparing to leave when Violet saw her mother sewing name tags into their clothes and was overcome with dread. She cried and clutched her mother's dress, pleading to be kept home. After a half hour her mother relented, holding them both back. Violet's sister, Marion, was furious; she had been keen to go. At the same station, Dorothy Wood's little brother, Lenny, fell ill—"broke out in spots" just as they were to board the bus for Liverpool. Wood's parents suggested that both children wait for the next departure, when they might be "shipshape," as their father put it. But Dorothy Wood was wildly excited about the trip, and she "made a scene" at the bus station. Within the hour she was kissing her brother good-bye, waving brightly to her parents, and marching toward the bus.

SOME OF THE CHILDREN MADE fast, close friends during those forty-eight hours at Fazackerlay. Derek Capel and Billy Short were three years apart, from opposite ends of the country, but they both had younger brothers to watch and both loved carousing on the school grounds. Bess Walder found a friend in Beth Cummings, the fourteen-year-old from Liverpool. Beth had lost her father when she was four; he had been killed in a train derailment. She had two older brothers, one in the British Army and the other in training to be a naval gunner. Beth's mother, Anne Cummings, had wanted to keep at least one child at home—but more than that she was desperate to keep at least one child *alive*. It was a terrible choice, but once she learned that the CORB children would have Royal Navy warships guarding them in the Atlantic, Anne Cummings became convinced her daughter would be safer as an evacuee than she would be at home.

A woman from the CORB came for Beth Cummings at eleven in the morning of September 10. Beth gave her mother a quick hug and kiss and walked with the woman down the street. She turned to wave; Anne Cummings waved back. That was that.

At Sherwood's Lane Bess and Beth "larked about," singing loudly and trading stories about the war and about their families. Mostly they imagined the trip ahead. How big would the ship be? What would they be fed? What might they do for fun? And what on earth would Canada *look* like? Both girls were destined ultimately for Toronto; neither knew much about what that city might hold in store.

For all the worrying their families had done that summer, neither Bess nor Beth was at all anxious about the journey, and after a day spent together they were almost inseparable. They were both heavyset, physically strong, and independent-minded girls, but in some ways they were quite different. Beth Cummings was an extrovert, playful, eager to introduce herself to the other children. Bess Walder was quieter, more restrained, a serious child who had listened intently to her parents talk about the war. Beth was traveling alone; Bess was with her younger brother, Louis.

Beth Cummings had always loved geography, always yearned to travel. *Now I'll have an adventure, just like my brothers.* To her new friend she said, "I can't wait, Bess! We shall have a grand time at sea."

EACH CHILD HAD COME TO Liverpool with a single suitcase and small duffel bag, a spare collection of clothing, toiletries, and other items recommended by the CORB. The board had sent families the following list, together with letters of acceptance:

1 overcoat and mackintosh

1 suit

1 pullover

1 hat or school cap

2 shirts

2 pairs stockings

2 undervests

2 pairs pants

2 pairs pajamas

1 pair boots or shoes

1 pair plimsolls (for the girls)

6 handkerchiefs

1 comb

1 tooth brush and paste

1 face flannel

1 towel

1 suitcase—about 26" × 18"

stationery and pencil

ration card

i.d. card

birth certificate (if possible)

bible or new testament

✱✱✱

no trunk permitted

no passport required

On the morning of Thursday, September 12, the children were given medical examinations and their bags were inspected for necessities. When the time came to leave, they were given gas masks and name tags, which were looped through shoelaces, to be worn around their necks. Then it was time to board a bus for the short ride to the port. They sang all the way, until the Liverpool docks came into view and the sea-salt air drifted through the open windows. The teachers and escorts agreed that virtually all their charges were in good spirits, sorry perhaps to have left their homes but excited—giddy, even—as they prepared to embark.

The Sherwood's Lane headmistress, Margaret Abraham, would always remember those two days and nights. She remembered the youngest boys and girls, remembered that they had seemed particularly fearless—Peter Short, five years old and seemingly fascinated by the sirens and the bombs; Ann Watson, six, a tiny, doll-like girl with a mass of blond, corkscrew curls, who pestered the escorts with questions about Canada.

But mostly Margaret Abraham would keep a mental snapshot of Augusta Grimmond, eldest of the five Grimmond children. Gussie, as they called her, was tall and thin, an almost scrawny girl who had arrived looking exhausted, her hair "hung in scraggy rats' tails." But Gussie Grimmond was obviously clever and quick-witted, and determined to show that she could care for her brothers and sisters and for herself. She had taken her parents' parting orders seriously: She was "a mother now," with "children"—her siblings—aged five, eight, nine, and ten. She took charge of her brothers and sisters, and took pains to see that they were as well bathed and groomed as possible. Gussie Grimmond left a profound impression as a child whose spirit and demeanor (her "Cockney tyranny," Abraham called it) suggested not a thirteen-year-old but an adult much traveled and well versed in the gravity of war.

Margaret Abraham saw to it that the Grimmond children were given new clothes before they left Sherwood's Lane, and she insisted to Gussie that she be in touch once the children reached Canada. Gussie never wrote to Abraham, but before the *City of Benares* left port, she penned a letter to the London shelter where her parents and remaining siblings were staying.

Dear Mum and Dad,
It is very lovely here on the ship. I wish you were here with us ... We had our photo taken as we were coming on the boat, and we are going to have it taken again now. We are drinking milk in the lounge. Our boat is in the middle of the river. We are all eager to start off ...

Eddie and Lenny are sharing a cabin. Connie, Violet and me are sharing a cabin. The cabins are all furnished. Connie and Violet are sharing a wardrobe ...

Please, Mum, do not worry as we have been fitted up with clothes ... There are men to guard us at night in case our boat got sunk. Please do not answer this letter as I will be in Mid-Atlantic. Excuse writing and spelling.

Good-bye must close now from your loving Gussie and from the others. Your loving daughter Gussie
XXX

Gussie Grimmond's description—"very lovely here on the ship"—was an understatement.

Arriving at the top of the gangway, Bess Walder was met by the most exotic-looking man she had ever seen. She saw the shoes first, shiny and black, and turned up at the toes. Lifting her gaze, she found a brown-skinned man in a turban, wearing a loose-fitting white uniform rimmed by a turquoise sash.

"Little madam?"

Startled, Bess took the man's outstretched hand.

"Please madam, welcome!"

"Thank you!"

The man turned next to her brother, Louis.

"Welcome, little sir! Welcome! Welcome to you!"

It's like the Arabian Nights, Bess thought.

The man was in fact from India, one of 166 Indian crew and servants on board the *City of Benares*. Nearly everywhere the children wandered they were met by Indians who bowed and clasped their hands. For more than a half century British shipping companies had recruited in India for seamen, and by 1939 laborers from India and Southeast Asia accounted for roughly one-third of the shipping industry's workers. The *City of Benares* had run a Liverpool-to-India service (hence the name, "City of Benares"—Benares being the northern Indian city known today as Varanasi). The ship's officers and petty officers were British, but nearly three in four of the *Benares* crew and staff were from India. Some were Hindu and others Muslim, but otherwise little is known of their backgrounds. The *Benares'* manifest listed home addresses or at least home cities and towns for all the other crew and passengers; for the Indians there were often no such details, and scant information of any sort. In many cases there were not even full names on the register. Hence one finds records of "Aziz, General Servant" or "Bhakua, Scullion." Their professional titles are given as "seaman," "wenchman," "baker," "butler," and the pejorative "boy."*

The turbaned man's greeting and colorful dress were only the first of many rich images the children drank in that afternoon. To children and adults alike, nearly all of whom had left some war-wracked place, the *Benares* was a wonderland. If not quite "Arabia," it was certainly a world apart from what they had left behind.

The children were shown to their cabins. The CORB had reserved an aft

---

*Many official records pertaining to the *City of Benares*—as well as several unofficial accounts of the journey—suggest second-class treatment of the Indians if not outright racism. The absence of full names was a small example.

section of the lowest deck, forty-three cabins that could hold more than one hundred people. The children and escort staff would be virtually cordoned off from the paying passengers, all of whom were accommodated at the forward end of the ship. The CORB had wanted it this way, to ensure easier supervision of the evacuees. There would be forty-six boys on the ship's starboard side, forty-four girls port side. Each set of cabins opened to a hallway, with bathrooms in between. The CORB group would share the dining area, one deck above, with paying passengers. Mealtimes would be staggered.

Bess Walder worried initially that the cabin assignments would leave her unable to care for her brother. Her mother's admonition—"you must look after that young man"—still rang in her ears. It had never occurred to her that she and Louis would not share a room on board. But then Bess found her own cabin—clean and comfortable, a wardrobe near the door that could have held all the clothes her family owned. She met and took a liking to her roommates—ten-year-old Ailsa Murphy and the *Volendam* veteran Patricia Allen—but mostly Bess was happy to find her new friend Beth Cummings just one cabin away. Beth had two Liverpool girls for cabinmates—Joan Irving, fifteen, and twelve-year-old Betty Unwin.

By the time one of the Indians appeared at Bess Walder's door—"Young ladies, is everything all right?"—Bess' anxieties had dissolved. She no longer fretted about Louis. The girls chatted happily, wondering when the ship would leave its moorings. They had almost forgotten about the war.

That afternoon the Indian sailors gave a brief tour. Nothing disappointed. The playroom was enormous, the size of a gymnasium, its walls a colorful fresco of nursery rhyme characters. A large, ornate rocking horse sat against one of the walls, a basket at either side of the saddle. It could hold three children. *I'm too old for that,* Bess Walder thought, but she took a turn on the top seat anyway, rocked awhile, and loved every moment.

There were boutiques along one hallway, selling everything from sundries to clothing to fine jewelry. Nine-year-old Billy Short gawked at the displays, wondering what his small stash of pocket money might fetch from one of the shops. The dining room was sleek and elegant, like a fancy London restaurant, and the kitchen was at that hour sending up blissful aromas of roast meat, curries, and freshly baked bread.

Everywhere they explored, the children feasted their senses. *It's a floating palace, is what it is,* Ken Sparks thought. *We are going to enjoy this.*

. . .

BENEATH HER ELEGANT TRIMMING, THE *City of Benares* was a strong and well-built ship. She was the largest and most modern vessel in Britain's Ellerman Lines, built at Glasgow in 1936 to Lloyd's first-class specifications and known as the "pride of the peacetime run to India." The *Benares*' typical "run" had taken her from Liverpool to Bombay, but in the summer of 1940 Ellerman had offered the *Benares* and two other liners to the CORB program. Since then the ship had been made over, painted deep brown, and fitted with guns. This would be her first Atlantic crossing.

The *City of Benares* held four decks, ran 485 feet bow to stern, and weighed more than eleven thousand tons. Earlier that Thursday she had been vigorously tested—boilers and emergency generators checked, lifeboats launched and lowered. All twelve boats had descended cleanly; none leaked. The ship also carried twenty-two rafts, cork life jackets for every passenger, and small kapok life vests for the children.

At Liverpool that afternoon, a surveyor for the Ministry of Shipping was on hand to monitor a full lifeboat drill, alarm bells ringing, emergency lights switched on, children and adults marched to gathering points and then to the boat stations themselves. Two boats were lowered to the embarkation deck, and several children were helped aboard to show how this was done. The children's escorts were told that if the alarms rang, they were to "see that the children get their lifebelts and suitable clothes, and proceed to the assembly station allotted for your group." The surveyor, a Captain White, reported that the *City of Benares*' lifeboats and the falls and ropes used to lower them "were all that could be desired."

Bohdan Nagorski—a shipping executive and paying passenger—was impressed by other qualities. He walked the decks and corridors that first day, noting approvingly the *Benares*' ventilation system, her large cabins, the general sturdiness of the vessel, and the knowledge and professionalism of her crew.

To a fellow passenger Nagorski remarked, "It is a delightful ship."

THEY WERE ALL ON BOARD by mid-afternoon, Thursday, September 12, 90 children from the CORB program, 10 escorts and other CORB staff, 91 paying passengers, a crew of 209, and 6 representatives from the convoy. All told, 406 passengers and crew.

The paying passengers were nearly as giddy as the children. Whatever their circumstance and particular reason for sailing, they had all experienced the terror of the blitz. Many had lost property or family; nearly all had known deprivation in the home. Stiff upper lips notwithstanding, it had been a hellish time, and to walk from Liverpool port—itself bombed during every one of the past three nights—into the elegant cabins and carpeted common rooms of the *City of Benares* was a remarkable thing.

The passengers were an eclectic group of businessmen and refugees, journalists and entertainers, diplomats and agents, a collection of people as exotic as the *Benares* herself. They represented at least fourteen countries, and they had all been touched in some way by the war.

Florence Croasdaile, a thirty-eight-year-old American, had married a British Merchant Navy officer in 1928. Her husband's ship had been torpedoed off the coast of Norway; now he was a prisoner of the Nazis. Croasdaile's mother had invited her and their two children—Patricia, nine, and Lawrence, two—to join her in America, while they awaited word of her husband's fate.

Arthur Wimperis, a sixty-five-year-old London playwright and screenwriter, was traveling to Hollywood, hoping for another hit. Wimperis' film credits had included the 1934 adaptation of *The Scarlet Pimpernel* and the critically acclaimed *The Private Life of Henry VIII*, made with the producer Alexander Korda in 1933. Now Wimperis was to collaborate with Korda on a new picture.

Monika Lanyi, daughter of the great German writer and Nobel laureate Thomas Mann, was traveling with her husband, Jeno Lanyi, an art historian from Hungary. Ruby Grierson, a Scottish filmmaker, was under contract to the National Film Board of Canada for a documentary about the child evacuees. And the British Broadcasting Corporation's Eric Davis was on board for the first leg of a long journey to the Far East. Davis was going to run the BBC office in Singapore.

The *Benares* also carried refugees from Nazi Germany—among them a doctor named Martin Bum; the writer Baroness Amelie von Inglesleben; and Rudolf Olden, a German Jew who had waged an intellectual battle against Hitler and National Socialism for the better part of a decade. Olden was a left-wing lawyer, human rights advocate, and journalist whose stinging criticisms of Hitler were published in the *Berliner Tageblatt* in 1934. Olden had been harassed and ultimately deported from Germany, only to be imprisoned as a "hostile foreigner" in England once the war began. Evidently the English authorities had not known Olden's politics. In any event, Rudolf Olden's case had been resolved in the summer of 1940 when the New School for Social Research in New York offered him a teaching position. Together with his wife, Ika, Olden was now sailing for New York.

Among business travelers on board the *City of Benares* were Maurice Maher, an oilman from Dublin who was headed for oil fields off Venezuela; Ernest Szekulesz, a prominent Hungarian publisher; and John Percival Day, not a businessman per se but an authority on banking in Canada and a well-respected professor of economics at McGill University in Montreal. Prior to his academic career, Day had been cited for gallantry as a light infantry captain during World War I. Henry and Phyllis Digby-Morton—thirty-eight and thirty-four years old, respectively—were up-and-comers in the fashion industry; their ultimate destination was a New York trade show called "Britain Delivers the Goods."

One prominent businessman was shipping his entire family to Canada on the *Benares*. Emil Bech was a London-based managing director for the Royal Danish Porcelain Company, manufacturers of some of the world's finest china. Bech lived with his wife and three children in Aldwick, along England's south coast, where German aircraft were now visible nearly every day. Like so many families in the south, the Bechs had come to believe they were living on a potential front line. Surely the Germans were coming—and no doubt the first salvos of a full-fledged German invasion would be fired along their coastline.

So Emil Bech had chosen to send his wife, Marguerite; daughters Barbara, fourteen, and Sonia, eleven; and his nine-year-old son, Derek, to Canada. Marguerite Bech had tangled with her husband over the decision to leave, much as the evacuee families had done. The great difference in their case was that they had the means to arrange a trip of their own; the children would travel with their mother, and they had family waiting for them—Marguerite Bech's distant relatives in Montreal. So Emil Bech would stay on in England, watching over their home and his company. Marguerite and the three children would go to Canada to wait out the war.

Barbara Bech, eldest of the children, boarded the *City of Benares* with some trepidation, and a strong tinge of remorse. Was it right to leave England, she asked herself, when the country was fighting so bravely for its survival? Barbara Bech had friends who would have no such opportunities, and she knew it. She wondered when and whether she would see them again.

The Bechs were three of ten children on board the *Benares* who were traveling outside the CORB program. The one in this group who made an immediate impression was a fair-haired eleven-year-old from St. John's Wood named Colin Ryder Richardson.

In part this was because Richardson was traveling alone, and in part it was because he sported a knitted balaclava cap and fancy scarlet life vest, both of which had been last-minute gifts from his mother. "Interesting-looking boy," the Canadian professor J. P. Day remarked to another passenger. Colin's vest was sewn in deep red waterproof silk and lined with kapok; almost immediately the boy felt the stares and odd looks from *Benares* crewmen. Colin imagined their thoughts—*What's the boy doing with that shiny life vest? Ours ain't good enough?* Richardson explained to all who asked—and many who did not—that his mother had been very firm. "You must never take it off," she had said. "Go to bed in it. If you are torpedoed, the British Navy will rescue you, even if they take two or three days to come. So don't worry. Just keep that vest on." She was a South African; Colin's father was a London barrister, and they had arranged privately to send their son to a family on New York's Long Island. The benefactor was Henry Stickney, a Wall Street banker and one of many well-to-do New Yorkers who had offered to take in English children.

"We are all looking forward to welcoming your son Colin," Stickney's wife, Helen, had written to Colin Richardson's parents. Helen Stickney had asked questions: Did the boy have any particular character traits? Any contagious disease? What was his usual bedtime? She assured the Richardsons that two maids and a caretaker awaited their son, and that there were other British children coming to New York. Colin, she wrote, "should not feel too expatriated."

One night in early September, Richardson's parents had sat him down after supper. "What would you think if we send you to America?"

Colin responded as many of the evacuees had—without hesitation. *Great,* he thought. *Cowboys. Hollywood. Lots more food.* It would not be Hollywood, his mother and father explained, and he might never see a cowboy. But the boy was thrilled nonetheless.

Once on board the *Benares*, Colin Richardson stood out as an uncommonly intelligent and self-assured child. He had no sibling with him, no nanny, no official escort, only the promise that someone from the mysterious Stickney family had arranged his passage from Montreal to New York. His cabinmate, a young Hungarian journalist named Laszlo Raskai, had offered to keep an eye on the child, but after an hour spent talking with Colin Richardson, watching him unpack and then select a book from the ship's library, Raskai was convinced the boy would require no special attention.

The *Benares* also carried her share of politicians, military men, and diplomats. Lieutenant-Colonel James Baldwin-Webb, a member of Parliament, was on a fund-raising mission for the British Red Cross. He had meetings planned with New York financiers to help fund the purchase of new ambulances. Retired Royal Navy Lieutenant-Commander Richard Deane had been sent to train Canadian forces; Herve de Kerillis, a French Air Force lieutenant, was on a secret mission to Quebec; and Zygmunt Gralinski, undersecretary of state for foreign affairs for Poland's government-in-exile, was traveling to Washington, D.C., for consultations with Poland's ambassador.

Bohdan Nagorski's reasons for sailing blended diplomacy, business, and family. He carried a diplomatic pouch for the Polish government-in-exile; he had business in both Canada and the United States on behalf of the Gdynia-America Shipping Line; and his wife, Zosia, and two young daughters awaited him in Canada. The family's wartime odyssey had taken them—in just one year—from Warsaw to Naleczow, in the Polish countryside, to Romania, to France, and finally by boat from southern France to England. Nagorski had dodged danger several times along the way, and now he believed—as did so many people on board the *City of Benares*—that he was sailing into calmer seas, as it were. For now at least, he was leaving the war behind.

THE *BENARES*' DEPARTURE WAS DELAYED, held over because the *Luftwaffe* had dropped mines in the channel the previous night. A maritime traffic jam built in the channel, and on the afternoon of Thursday, September 12, passengers were told it would be Friday afternoon before the *Benares* actually left Liverpool.

The wait exasperated the children. It also made the thrill of departure that much greater, when the time finally came. At about six o'clock Friday evening, the crew pulled fast the *Benares'* watertight doors, the lifeboats were swung out, and the rafts shifted to ready position. A cheer went up from the deck.

It was a theatrical farewell. Nearly all the children had gathered on the promenade deck in neat rows, some of them carrying small Union Jacks. They waved back at the port and at the crew of the *Duchess of Atholl*, the steamer docked in the adjacent berth. The *Duchess* was an Atlantic liner that had been requisitioned by the admiralty; her crew was sailing for Halifax, on a mission to man reconfigured American destroyers.

The *Duchess of Atholl*'s sailors waved back at the *Benares'* boys and girls. J. R. Creswell was a young sailor on board the *Duchess*, excited about his mission and greatly warmed by what he saw and heard across the harbor. When the children sang "Wish Me Luck (As You Wave Me Goodbye)," Creswell and his fellow sailors joined in, hollering the verses across the water. Creswell felt a rush of pride as the song echoed across Liverpool Bay. When it was over, the

Duchess of Atholl and other ships in the harbor sounded a series of foghorn salutes.

The tide was right. The euphoria was palpable and it was contagious. Bohdan Nagorski had boarded the *City of Benares* in a businesslike frame of mind, but now he felt a profound respect and admiration for the child evacuees and gratitude for his own circumstance. *How strange*, he thought, *that we are leaving Europe.* The screenwriter Arthur Wimperis watched the children. *Fine ambassadors*, he thought. Little Jack Keeley held his sister's hand. "We're going to have an *adventure!*" he told her.

The sun was dropping out over the water. The children shouted "hurrah" from the deck. The *City of Benares* edged from her berth.

ORDINARILY THE CREW WOULD HAVE waited another day. Even veteran, hard-bitten sailors were reluctant to begin a journey—any journey—on a Friday the thirteenth. But it was widely understood that HMS *Winchelsea*, the destroyer designated to lead the Royal Navy escort for the *Benares*, had a date in the mid-Atlantic with an incoming convoy. Typically the naval escorts worked this way—leading outbound liners for several hundred miles, then turning to meet important inbound ships and guide them safely to Britain. HMS *Winchelsea* had just such an appointment to keep—a rendezvous in five days with HX71, a convoy bringing critical supplies from Canada. Sailing any later would jeopardize that arrangement—and the *Benares* needed the *Winchelsea*'s protection.

Friday the thirteenth it would be.

DEREK CAPEL HAD NOTED THE date—and decided he did not mind at all. His heart thumped with excitement, and little Alan Capel—the lucky shard of shrapnel still bulky in his pocket—had reminded his older brother: Thirteen was their lucky number. As far as the Capel boys were concerned it would actually be a *good* day to set sail.

That morning, as the *City of Benares* idled, Gussie Grimmond had posted letters home—not only her own, but also short missives she had ordered her sisters Violet and Connie to write to their mother and father.

"I hope you are all right, we are all right too," Violet Grimmond reported. "We have good food. We have a play room to play in. We have life [sic] practices in case our ship got sunk. We would put lifebelts on and jump into our lifeboats."

Her sister Connie, nine years old, filled most of a page with "X" marks for kisses, leaving space for only a few words:

I hope you are all right. Me, Gussie and Violet feed the sea gulls with bissets [biscuits, presumably]. When Lenny went on deck we saw seagulls swimming in the water and fighting. When we was having milk the bells went for every baby [every body?] to go and put on lifebelts. I bet Jimmy and Jerry [their younger brothers] miss us.

   Goodbye, from your loving daughter Connie.

Ken Sparks gazed happily at his fellow adventurers on deck, across the bay at the *Duchess of Atholl* sailors, and back at Liverpool port.

He had already forgotten family and home; he had forgotten the bombing. Sparks saw *Benares* crewmen holding young children by the hand. He saw several elegant-looking adult passengers at the other end of the deck. He looked up at the ship's smokestacks, hulking twins, her mast looming tall behind them. They were moving steadily now, the engine rumbling. Liverpool began to fade in a twilight mist.

Ken Sparks caught himself grinning at the water. He was thirteen years old. He had never been to sea in anything larger than a rowboat.

CHAPTER 4

"Ease and
Refreshment"

The *Benares'* convoy partners mingled near Rathlin Island, in the North Channel between Scotland and Ireland, eighteen civilian vessels—liners and freighters, tankers and smaller craft—all waiting for the "Commodore," or flagship, to arrive. By the fall of 1940, large liners sailing to or from Great Britain traveled almost exclusively in convoy and the SS *City of Benares,* with her undeniably precious cargo, would be no exception. Later it would become clear that the term "convoy" and the government pledges of a naval "escort" had been poorly understood by the children's families. In no small measure this was because they had been poorly explained.

Maritime convoys had been employed for centuries to guard against piracy, and Great Britain had formally adopted a convoy system at the outbreak of World War II. Convoys ranged in size from a half dozen vessels to flotillas of fifty or sixty, liners and smaller commercial craft that moved deliberately and kept a collective watch for enemy planes or submarines. The convoys were led and protected by Royal Navy "escorts"—typically destroyers equipped with heavy guns, antisubmarine depth charges, and state-of-the-art radar systems. In the event of a U-boat attack, the destroyer would attempt to obtain a sonar "fix" on the submarine, and either fire her guns or drop depth charges. If the submarine had gone, the destroyer would move to rescue survivors.

But when the CORB gave written pledges to "convoy" the evacuee children and promised that convoys would be "escorted" by the Royal Navy, one critical fact was omitted: The children were to be convoyed and escorted only so far as longitude 17 degrees west, which, along the *City of Benares'* route, would have amounted to roughly five hundred miles out into the Atlantic. This was regarded as the approximate boundary of the maritime war, and the logical point at which escort warships would turn about, to safeguard incoming supply ships. Once the destroyer was gone, the outbound convoy would disperse; each vessel would sail the remaining swath of the Atlantic alone and unguarded.

Throughout the summer of 1940 the system had been largely effective, but by September the parameters of the U-boat war had changed, handing enormous new advantage to the German Navy. Hitler's submarines were now hunting in groups, or so-called wolf packs, compounding the threat. The latest U-boat designs had also allowed for heavier fuel loads and therefore more distant forays into the Atlantic. But most important, and most ominous for Great Britain, was the buildup of a formidable U-boat presence at the newly occupied French ports. Working from France's northern coastline, rather than Germany's own Baltic ports, the U-boats' range was improved by several hundred miles. On August 19–20, a U-boat sank a pair of four-thousand-ton merchant vessels—the *Kelet* and *Taira*—west of longitude 20 degrees west. Before August's end, seven more ships were torpedoed and sunk beyond that same marker. It would have appeared that by mid-September, 17 degrees west was an arbitrary boundary.

As the sun fell on Friday, September 13, outbound Convoy 213—OB213 to the crews and land-based radio operators—was aligning itself in nine columns, each two vessels deep, the entire group stretching three miles across the ocean. The *City of Benares* would soon join the convoy and occupy the center front position.

Completing this choreography, roughly three miles ahead, were OB213's naval escorts. HMS *Winchelsea* was a World War I–era destroyer that had distinguished herself during the evacuation of British forces from Dunkirk, three months before. Now she would lead, employing constant lookouts and radar detection to sweep for submarines. More than anything, *Winchelsea* and her four-inch guns were acting as a deterrent.

Two Royal Navy corvettes flanked the *Winchelsea*, while a Sunderland flying boat, armed with submarine-killer depth charges, watched over them all from the air. Altogether, the *City of Benares* and her child evacuees would be shielded and shadowed by twenty-one vessels and one aircraft.

The *Benares* met this group at dusk, under a bleak sky, on Friday, September 13. A steady rain turned to sleet as the convoy pushed northwest, plodding at eight and a half knots through the North Channel, sailing deliberately for the Atlantic Ocean.

· · ·

THE CHILDREN'S ONBOARD ESCORTS HAD been trained to handle boredom and fear, homesickness, and a variety of physical ailments. A handful of their charges wept for parents and siblings that night, but a different challenge presented itself soon after the *Benares* entered the Irish Sea.

The wind had whipped up the water, the waves were cresting higher, and the ship began a slow and steady heave. At first Beth Cummings laughed, feeling the bounce in her cabin. Here was one more exotic twist in a journey that was not yet two hours old. But soon her cabinmates, Joan Irving and Betty Unwin, were queasy and calling for Maud Hillman, their escort. Hillman rushed cups of barley sugar water to the cabin, but by the time these arrived, Beth was ill as well. That first night leveled half the evacuee children, and many paying passengers, too.

Not much fun, Beth Cummings said to herself. Paul Shearing and Fred Steels, seasick in their cabin on the boys' side, wondered how long the turbulence would last. "Maybe," said Steels, "the Atlantic's always this way."

When Saturday morning came, the seas still roiled. Not as bad, but still rough. Hillman and the other escorts made their rounds. Nearly every cabin had at least one child who had been ill during the night.

"Try to eat something," Hillman told Beth Cummings. "You'll feel better for it."

Beth obliged, trying a few morsels of bread and jam at breakfast, but the mere sight of a lavish buffet made her head swim. She could not keep the food down, and in any case soon all the children were being ordered to their cabins: A bomber had been sighted in the skies above the *City of Benares*.

The plane passed and was not seen again. By mid-morning the storm had passed as well.

BY SUNDAY, SEPTEMBER 15, IT seemed that homesickness and seasickness alike had ebbed, defeated by the sun, a calm sea, and a fresh rush of optimism. The escorts busied themselves. Michael Rennie, the Oxford divinity student and rugby star, organized athletic competitions on the *Benares* decks—a tug-of-war, deck tennis, even a lassoing contest. Rennie had borrowed rope from the sailors, and taught his boys to "lasso" deck chairs. Sybil Gilliat-Smith held drawing competitions. Father Rory O'Sullivan found himself busy with "the duties of a nanny," bathing his two five-year-old charges, and "making them see that having a bath was not something to be frightened of . . ." Mary Cornish was appointed "banker" for the children, who carried small amounts of pocket money and were afraid these might be lost or pilfered from their cabins. Word had spread that money could be turned over to Cornish for safekeeping and retrieved when the children wished to buy sweets or lemonade, or other wonders from the ship's canteen. Cornish dutifully recorded "deposits" and "withdrawals" in a small notebook.

Two of the older girls, Rosemary Spencer-Davies and Gussie Grimmond, worked alongside the escorts, looking after the youngest children in a kind of day-care setting on the deck. Older siblings watched younger brothers and sisters—with the exception of Bobby Baker, who had quickly given up looking after his younger brother; John seemed to slip away every chance he got, walking and running along the ship's corridors, drawing gentle warnings from sailors and passengers who told him to stay nearer to the CORB escorts. "The lost boy," one sailor took to calling him. On one occasion John Baker actually found himself in the *Benares'* passenger lounge, in a knot of cocktail-sipping travelers. Somehow John always made his way back—usually just in time for the next meal.

As the *City of Benares* edged into the North Atlantic, routine set in. The children were in bed by eight o'clock, up at seven-thirty in the morning, at breakfast by eight. Reverend William King would lead after-breakfast prayers and then give the floor to the senior escort, Marjorie Day, for announcements about the day's events. These might include a lifeboat drill, a tour with sailors, or school lessons in the nursery. Bess Walder groaned when she heard this last item on the schedule—*Haven't we left school behind?*—but she and her friend Beth Cummings soon discovered the rules were relaxed. No one *had* to go to class.

For the other passengers, there was sport on deck, superb cuisine below, first-rate service from the Indian crew, card games and discussion in the bar and game rooms. More than anything, travelers young and old delighted in what was missing: There were no air raid sirens, no frantic runs to underground shelters, and, of course, there were no bombs.

There were no rations, either. The rules in Britain had allowed eight ounces of sugar and eight ounces of fat per week. Cheese had been limited to two ounces a week, bacon or other meat to eight ounces. Diners aboard the *Benares* could match these levels in a single sitting. Every meal was gluttony. The CORB children in particular were stunned and nearly overwhelmed by what they found in the ship's dining hall. Indian waiters bowed to greet them, escorted them to tables, and pushed in their chairs. Then came the question: "What would little madam like? Little sir?"

Gussie Grimmond, proud and confident in the role of "mother" to her younger brothers and sisters, was nonetheless confounded by the choices and the weight of deciding for all five members of her family. Finally she asked if she and her siblings might have milk, and— Could the waiter please decide the rest?

Bess Walder fidgeted, too, unsure for a moment. "Ham roll," she said at last, and soon Bess had before her a pair of warm, freshly baked rolls, thick slabs of York ham nestled inside. The sandwiches arrived wrapped in lace cloth, on a silver tray. Bess Walder had not eaten ham all summer. She hadn't *seen* ham all summer.

"And what would little sir like?"

Louis Walder had no difficulty with the question.

"Chocolate, please."

Bess told the boy he had to eat a proper meal, and he did, but chocolate came, too. A small box of Cadbury's was delivered on a white plate.

"Chicken!" was Derek Capel's answer, and he repeated it at nearly every meal. Even before the war, chicken had been a rare treat in his household, seen on holidays if at all. Yet here was a lovely chicken breast, served with vegetables and rice and brought by a waiter in a white coat. Then, just as Derek was finishing his last morsel, a plate of fruit arrived—peaches, melon, and pineapple. Fruits had been almost unimaginable treats during the last several weeks in England. *Fantastic,* Capel thought. *It's a Christmas dinner, every meal.*

The children asked for seconds. Some requested thirds. Asked to choose between main courses, several replied, "Both, please." Paul Shearing, shy and reserved though he was, dealt with the dizzying choices by asking for everything on the menu. Finally a waiter suggested, politely, that the boy be a bit more selective. Father O'Sullivan found his most difficult job as escort involved persuading the boys "to have their vegetables *before* their three helpings of pudding."

Few of the CORB children had ever seen such meals, even in peacetime. Certainly they had never eaten this kind of food. Gussie Grimmond labored to restrain her ravenously hungry brothers and sisters, and keep them on their best behavior. When nine-year-old Connie refused a serving, asking for "something else," Gussie pinched her leg under the table. "You'll eat what you're served," she said sternly, "and you'll *finish* it." She chided them for mishandling their forks and knives. Gussie Grimmond not only wanted her siblings happy and healthy; she wanted the Grimmond family well represented on this exquisite ship.

For four days and nights, they ate, played, and lived like kings—and not just the children. The adult passengers walked the decks, took in the bracing sea air, and of course they, too, enjoyed and appreciated the cuisine. The small group of central European refugees may have felt these luxuries most keenly. Rudolf and Ika Olden had been on the run, or in some difficulty, for almost ten years; the *Benares* offered a remarkable freedom from tension. One Czech passenger likened the ship to a rich man's convalescent home.

Bohdan Nagorski felt invigorated from the moment they left Liverpool. He spent as much time as possible outside, reading in a deck chair, soaking in the sun and salt air, a blanket across his shoulders when the winds gained strength. He walked the deck, often in the company of fellow passengers. He remarked to one of them that life on board was "full of ease and refreshment." No *Benares* passenger would have disagreed.

ON SUNDAY MORNING, PASSENGERS, CREW, and nearly all the CORB children gathered on deck. Separate services had been planned for Protestants and Catholics, but Father Rory O'Sullivan, the Roman Catholic priest and one of the children's escorts, had taken ill with a bad case of flu and could not leave his bed.

So Reverend King—"Padre King" to the children—led a joint service instead. The evacuee children stood in rows on the promenade deck, holding hands. The congregation sang "Eternal Father, Strong to Save." Bess Walder listened, tears of joy in her eyes. *We'll be in Canada soon,* she thought. Ken Sparks sang as loudly as he could, all the while staring happily at the sea, picking out convoy vessels nearby. After the service, Marjorie Day read the news from home—which on this day provoked happy whoops and hollers from the deck. The Royal Air Force was claiming fresh successes against Hitler's *Luftwaffe.*

It made for a glorious day. In the afternoon Sybil Gilliat-Smith led another drawing exercise for the girls, Rennie set up new tugs-of-war for the boys, and Ruby Grierson, the Scottish filmmaker, organized a tea party.

Grierson was thirty-six, sister of the pioneering documentarian John Grierson, and an accomplished cinematographer in her own right. Ruby Grierson's most recent work, *They Also Serve,* had been a short but well-received homage to the housewife in wartime England. On board the *Benares,* Grierson was aiming her lens at the children and their escorts, for what would be the first such account of the evacuation program.

Grierson fascinated the children. She was short and slim, wore a beret and slacks, and kept a cigarette dangling constantly from her lips as she worked to frame her shots. She may have been making a film, but to the children Ruby Grierson seemed a film star herself. She took her pictures, and the boys and girls took tea and crackers—delighted at the attention and in some instances trailing after her as she worked. As though the ship were not wonder enough, Fred Steels thought, *Now we shall be in pictures.*

Spirits soared. The children played and sang and daydreamed about movies and games, about good food, and about Canada, that giant unknown land that awaited them. Jack Keeley's little sister, Joyce, was still terribly homesick, and two five-year-old boys—Alan Capel and Peter Short—were in the ship's infirmary with chicken pox, but the eighty-seven remaining children appeared happy and healthy and terribly excited.

Bohdan Nagorski lounged in a deck chair that afternoon and felt the sun and a cool wind on his face. Later he walked to the fence that divided the passenger deck from the CORB-reserved area, and for a while he watched Ruby Grierson and listened to the children. It was hard to imagine a happier sound, hard to recall a more optimistic moment in the twelve and a half months since the war had begun.

THE MOOD AT THAT HOUR was considerably more sober at the captain's station.

Alistair Fairweather, the *Benares'* wireless operator, had received word of a U-boat sighting in the waters near Convoy OB213. Fairweather also reported to the captain's bridge that a Focke-Wulf Condor had been tracked in the skies near the *Benares.* The crew knew well that the Focke-Wulf was a fierce fighter and that it was used often as a "spotter" to pick out targets for German submarines. Harry Peard, a thirty-eight-year-old gunner, one of a handful of Royal Navy men added to the *Benares* crew for this crossing, received word of Fairweather's message and shifted uneasily in his gunner's "nest." He knew that a Focke-Wulf in the vicinity meant a U-boat might be in the neighborhood, too.

The *Benares'* captain, Landles Nicoll, and the convoy commodore, Admiral Edmund Mackinnon, conferred at the bridge. These were the two senior officers on board, and their titles and duties were peculiar features of the convoy system. While Nicoll commanded the *City of Benares,* the overall convoy was the responsibility of Commodore Mackinnon. This division of command was standard on all convoys, but it was not always clear-cut.

A convoy commander's duty was to steer all the ships in unison until dispersal—a step that usually coincided with the turnabout of the escorting warships. Dispersal would allow individual convoy members to choose their own speeds and routes once the protective cordon of Royal Navy vessels had been broken. The duty of the *Benares'* captain was of course quite different: He had to deliver his ship and passengers safely to Montreal.

Edmund Mackinnon was sixty, a career Royal Navy man and decorated veteran of the First World War who had retired seven years earlier. He had silver hair and a strong build, and his "crew" consisted of six Navy gunners and signalers who were part of the subtle militarization of the *City of Benares*. All the ships carrying CORB children had been retrofitted in this way—repainted, a few guns mounted at either end, and a half dozen or so men diverted from Navy duty to help provide a deterrent capacity to what had heretofore been a peacetime commercial liner. On Monday night, Mackinnon radioed the destroyer *Winchelsea* and ordered a series of coordinated zigzag maneuvers. Unless *Winchelsea* could pinpoint and target the U-boat in question, the evasive zigzag was the only defense. Fairweather and the other radiomen received no further warnings that afternoon.

The *Benares* passengers heard nothing about U-boat activity, though the adults at least were certainly aware of the general threat. During those first days on board, many had made a habit of checking periodically with crew members to learn how far the ship had progressed. They knew that each mile lessened the chance of attack; some among them knew that the five-hundred-mile mark was generally considered the outer perimeter of the war theater.

The *Benares* crew ran lifeboat drills daily. The ship's siren would sound, sending passengers of all ages scurrying to their "muster stations," following hallway and stairwell arrows that pointed them to the deck. At Liverpool the ship's chief officer, a hulking Scotsman named Joe Hetherington, had given the escorts special briefings in person and on paper, including typewritten guidelines under the heading "Abandon Ship." The basic counsel was to "see that the children get their life belts and suitable clothing, and proceed to the assembly station allotted to each group." The escorts were instructed to take roll calls and then bring their subjects to their designated lifeboat stations. Ship's officers made sure that passengers carried life jackets at all times and that they knew their lifeboat assignments. The children were ordered to sleep with life jackets over their pajamas, their shoes and overcoats laid at the bottom of their bunks.

Before leaving Liverpool, Zygmunt Gralinski, the Polish diplomat, had asked one of the *Benares* officers about the risks of submarine attack.

"The first two days may contain an element of danger," the officer had replied. "Afterwards we should be quite all right." Gralinski took comfort in those words as he retired Sunday night. When he woke Monday morning, it would be Day Three.

MOST OF THE PASSENGERS NEVER knew it, but the *Benares'* captain was as anxious as anyone on board.

Landles Nicoll was fifty-one, a strong and squarely built man from the small town of Arbroath, along Scotland's northeast coast. He had a high forehead, hair just beginning to gray. Nicoll's Christian name—literally, "Land Less"—suggested a calling to the sea, and Nicoll was in fact a career seaman and navigator. He was also a husband and father, and before leaving Liverpool he had voiced concerns about the trip to his eldest daughter. He would have preferred to guide the *City of Benares* alone, he told her, without the convoy. This would have allowed him to zigzag at his own discretion, and to increase speed when he felt it necessary. The *Benares'* top speed was several knots greater than any of her convoy partners. "If only we could get away by ourselves at sea," he had said, "just the *Benares* on her own, I could employ a zigzag course at high speed and would have a better chance." Even the naval escort, Nicoll feared, offered no guarantee that his ship and all those children would make it safely to Canada.

"I've had a good life," he told his daughter before leaving. "Whatever's in store for me, I cannot complain."

Nicoll was still anxious after forty-eight hours at sea; at the captain's table, Henry and Phyllis Digby-Morton, the young couple traveling to New York for a fashion industry trade show, asked Nicoll whether he had considered sending his three daughters away, as "evacuees."

The captain did not hesitate. "I'd as soon put their hands in the fire."

NO SUCH QUALMS BURDENED MOST of the *Benares* passengers, and by Monday, September 16, "ease and refreshment" really had won the day. The skies were clear. The dining room had been decorated for a children's party. The children themselves were well for the most part, their cheeks reddened by the sun and wind, and their mood first-rate. The Navy gunner Harry Peard came with two of the Navy signalmen for a visit with the children and found them in fine spirits. Derek Capel told Peard he wanted to join the Royal Navy someday. Eleven-year-old Paul Shearing already wished the voyage would last longer. *Why stop at Canada?* he wondered. In a daydream, Shearing found himself leaving Canada aboard the *Benares* for a Pacific crossing. Colin Richardson, the eleven-year-old traveling as a private evacuee, felt he had his run of the ship. When no one was looking, Richardson dreamed up a game in which deck chairs were carried to an upwind position and then slid to the other end of the deck. He found the three Bech children and enlisted them as partners in this mischief. At meals Richardson sat and listened to Englishmen and Hungarians, Poles and even Germans talk about the war. He became a fixture in the lounge, reading comic books and magazines, and after a while the adult passengers took to calling him "Will Scarlet" for the bright red vest he sported. Sometimes they offered him the maraschino cherries from their cocktails. Colin Richardson felt like a child let loose in a grown man's adventure. Like Paul Shearing, he didn't want the voyage to end.

That morning the "news from England" was read again by the chief escort, Marjorie Day, on what happened to be her fifty-third birthday. Her headlines brought more reason to cheer.

The Royal Air Force was claiming 165 successful strikes against German planes in the previous twenty-four hours (in fact the figure was closer to fifty planes—but this was still an impressive turn of events). One English paper was reporting that the latest *Luftwaffe* barrage had been repulsed, its aircraft "heavily engaged over London and all the way back to the coast. The bombers are not able to drop their bombs with any accuracy at all."

To the *Benares* passengers, Marjorie Day's report was another tonic. *It is almost too much good news*, Bohdan Nagorski thought. They were nearly five hundred miles from Liverpool, almost to the point at which the *City of Benares* would be beyond danger. They were almost out of the woods.

Now some on board dared to think Great Britain was, too.

CHAPTER 5

Unterseeboot 48

As the *City of Benares* left her berth at Liverpool, Lieutenant Commander Heinrich Bleichrodt was guiding his submarine several hundred miles to the southwest, off the Atlantic coast of Ireland. Bleichrodt was prowling the shipping lanes, hunting for victims. His was one of more than two dozen submarines enforcing Hitler's blockade of the British Isles.

Heinrich Bleichrodt had taken the helm of *Unterseeboot* 48 just ten days before. U-48 was a Class VII-B submarine, built in 1937 at the German port of Kiel, to the most modern specifications. U-48 was 218 feet long, with a top surface speed of nearly eighteen knots—comparable to a fast commercial vessel. She could also dive to a depth of more than three hundred feet. The class VII-B subs held thirty-three tons more fuel in their saddle tanks than earlier models, allowing for a far greater reach into the Atlantic, and they carried fourteen torpedoes—*aal*, or "eels," the Germans called them—each of which was twenty-three feet long and carried a heavy warhead and state-of-the-art guidance system. The Class VII-B U-boats' mix of strength, speed, and maneuverability made for one of the most threatening elements in the German *wehrmacht*.

U-48's crew typically lived and slept in the torpedo room. It was a tedious and often traumatizing existence, days and nights spent in extremely close quarters with the commingling odors of diesel fuel and men's sweat, and little to break a numbing monotony. Now, on Friday, September 13, Bleichrodt's men were all awake and alert, thirty-eight submariners and one fearsome machine looking for prey.

.   .   .

UNTERSEEBOOT 48 HAD MANY PARENTS, ancestors who had worked for centuries to develop an underwater vessel and weapon, what one historian has called the "wide-ranging highwayman" of the sea.

Legend has it that Alexander the Great descended in a glass barrel to destroy underwater defenses at Tyre; nearly two thousand years later Leonardo Da Vinci sketched drawings for a submersible machine, though at the time he refused to share them. "I do not publish or divulge [my idea]," he wrote, "because of the evil nature of men who practice assassination at the bottom of the sea."

For centuries such "assassination" proved beyond the realm of practical ability, but beginning with the English mathematician William Bourne, who in 1578 drew up the first detailed designs for a below-the-surface craft, a steady evolution was set in motion, from harmless submersible to underwater assassin. In 1623 a Dutch engineer named Cornelius van Drebbel became the first man to steer such a contraption sucessfully; in 1776 the American David Bushnell built the *Turtle*, six feet long and resembling "two bathtubs clamped together," in consultation with Benjamin Franklin and with financial backing from George Washington. Piloted by a colonial army sergeant named Ezra Lee, powered by a crankshaft and carrying a 150-pound explosive, *Turtle* failed in a daring mission to destroy Britain's HMS *Eagle*, which sat moored off Staten Island, just south of Manhattan. It was nearly a century later, during the Civil War, that the cigar-shaped *Hunley*, just five feet in diameter and carrying a nine-man crew, attacked the USS *Housatonic* in Charleston Harbor.

The *Hunley* carried explosives mounted on a fifteen-foot spar that protruded from the bow. Just before nine o'clock on the night of February 17, 1864, a deckhand on the *Housatonic* alerted his crew to a strange craft, something "like a dolphin on the water," heading in their direction.

Within minutes the *Housatonic* was pulling up anchor and sending volleys of small arms fire at the intruder, but they were too slow and too late. *Hunley* rammed her spar torpedo into *Housatonic*'s side, and *Hunley*'s captain, Lieutenant George Dixon, yanked the rope trigger, detonating the torpedo.

The explosion sank *Housatonic* quickly. In the irony of the event, only five of her crewmen died—most were able to climb the rigging and wait for their rescue—while the *Hunley* herself sank as she slipped away, sending all nine crewmen to their deaths. It was never clear why *Hunley* had failed to return to shore, but Horace Hunley's little craft had made history in her short foray from Charleston Harbor. The *Hunley* had become the first submarine to sink

an enemy ship. The fanciful designs of Bourne, Van Drebbel, and the other designers had evolved to produce something very real. As the historian John Stilgoe put it, "Submarine attack forever altered the typical merchant officer's
and seaman's conception of catastrophe."

BY THE OUTBREAK OF WORLD War I, this "conception" was
widely understood, and the submarine had become an essential tool of war.
The sinking of the *Lusitania* in 1915, with more than a thousand casualties, had
erased all doubt of its capability. At war's end, the Treaty of Versailles forbade the
German Navy from obtaining submarines, but the Germans soon acquired a
Dutch shipbuilding company that also happened to design submarines. The
German government could make the technical argument that these craft were
being built for sale to international customers, but it soon became clear that Germany had other things in mind. A young Navy officer named Karl Doenitz was
tasked with developing new submarine designs and war-fighting tactics; two decades later Doenitz was in charge of the German Navy, or *Kriegsmarine*.

In 1935, Hitler formally renounced the Versailles treaty, and in the early
months of World War II, the U-boat became for Hitler and Doenitz the sine qua
non of the blockade of Great Britain. Doenitz had designed his U-boat strategy
around two basic concepts: the "Tonnage War," a simple and brutal plan to sink
ships faster than they could ever be replaced; and the "Wolf Pack," which would
compel a half dozen U-boats to join forces for certain missions. As of September
1, 1940, Doenitz had twenty-seven U-boats on the water, and roughly two dozen
more in various states of repair at ports in Germany and occupied France.

Doenitz and his fleet had been busy during the summer of 1940. The admiral studied British convoys, inbound and outbound, and played a maritime cat
and mouse with deadly efficiency. Doenitz pressed his commanders with questions about their foes: How strong were the Royal Navy escorts? Were aircraft
used? Most important—how far west did the convoys reach before their escorts
turned? Doenitz was an aggressive and restless commander. "If even two days
passed without my receiving reports of ships having been sighted by U-boats,"
he wrote some years later, "I at once ordered a redistribution of my forces . . . I
was most anxious that not one single day should pass without the sinking
somewhere or other of a ship."

The admiral was not often disappointed. In the month of June alone,
U-boats had sunk sixty-three ships in British waters. And in the middle of that
month, Doenitz had been handed an enormous gift. As has been noted, the fall

of France altered dramatically the parameters of the maritime war. Britain would now be forced to rely almost exclusively on transatlantic shipments for supplies and matériel. If Germany could now successfully enforce its blockade of Atlantic commerce, then the British Isles would slowly starve.

Even worse—from the British perspective—the French surrender had given Doenitz the Bay of Biscay, and with it those naval bases much nearer to Great Britain herself. Doenitz took immediate advantage. His U-boat command had kept trains on standby, laden with torpedoes and other matériel, and one day after the French armistice these trains were dispatched to French ports. On June 23, Doenitz himself traveled to France, where he gave his view that the newly acquired ports "could be rendered perfectly suitable" for the *Unterseebootflotille.* The first U-boats reached a French port—L'Orient—on July 7, and later that month the *Kriegsmarine* began their "wolf-pack" operations, dispatching U-boat teams to the busiest British shipping lanes.

Almost immediately, British losses multiplied. It was the beginning of what U-boat commanders would later call their "happy time," and by early August Winston Churchill was complaining to his war cabinet. He wrote to the admiral of the fleet, Sir Dudley Pound:

> The repeated severe losses in the Northwest Approaches are most
> grievous, and I wish to be assured that they are being grappled
> with . . . There seems to have been a great falling off in the control of
> these approaches.

Churchill was worried, angry, and, as ever, impatient. He ordered Pound to study the causes of these renewed attacks, and to find a way to stop them.

HEINRICH BLEICHRODT HAD NEVER DREAMED of being an *unterseeboot* man. He was born at Berga, a small town near Leipzig in eastern Germany, in 1909. His father died young, and Bleichrodt was raised by his mother and older sister. Friends gave him the nickname "Ajax" at an early age; it is not clear why. He was considered something of a rebel as a teenager, though at sixteen he was accepted for training at Germany's selective Finkenwerder Sailors School.

"Ajax" was a stocky young man, pale and handsome, with dark, slicked-back hair, deep-set eyes, and a severe look. He did not smile easily, or often. Bleichrodt was outgoing and a heavy drinker, and in 1933, after several stints with the Merchant Marine, he joined the German Navy. Six years later, just shy of his thirtieth birthday, he made his first tour in a submarine, and for the first time colleagues and superiors noticed Ajax's gifts as a leader, a clearheaded thinker, and a man who won easily the respect of his fellow sailors.

On September 4, 1940, Heinrich Bleichrodt took command of a submarine for the first time. Early on the morning of September 8, Bleichrodt and his crew led U-48 away from L'Orient. Two minesweepers worked the waters ahead of them, and when they parted ways one of the minesweepers radioed a simple message: "Good luck, and good hunting."

AJAX COULD HARDLY HAVE ENJOYED a more auspicious debut. On Saturday, September 14, in the early evening, U-48 picked up the contours of a convoy off northwest Ireland. Bleichrodt tailed this group of merchant ships for a while, and just after midnight he ordered torpedoes fired.

The first volleys sank the *Empire Soldier* and *Kenordoc*, a pair of midsize merchant vessels that went under in a matter of minutes. Smelling blood, Bleichrodt ordered the stern tubes reloaded, and two minutes later U-48 hit the escort sloop HMS *Dundee*, inflicting heavy damage. Later, after a crash dive to evade detection, U-48 returned to the surface and attacked two more members of the ill-fated convoy. *Alexandros* and the *Empire Volunteer* were sunk in the early hours of the morning; five of the thirty *Alexandros* crew were killed, as were six of thirty-nine sailors aboard the *Empire Volunteer.*

Bleichrodt's officers told him they believed the remaining ships in the convoy had begun tracking U-48, so they dove again. By the time U-48 resurfaced, Ajax and his men had lost track of the convoy.

Still, it had been by any measure a brutally efficient beginning, a series of attacks carried out precisely as Karl Doenitz had envisioned for his U-boat men, inflicting damage and terror in the heart of the British shipping lanes. These were also the opening salvos in a career that would make Heinrich Bleichrodt a highly decorated commander, and U-48 the most accomplished German submarine of the Second World War.

THAT NIGHT THE *CITY OF BENARES* and Convoy OB213 were making their initial push into the North Atlantic. Bleichrodt steered west-northwest, unknowingly making an underwater beeline for OB213.

Bleichrodt was operating with what he believed were unambiguous rules of engagement. The German Naval High Command had authorized its total blockade of Britain on August 1, explicitly allowing U-boat commanders to attack ships without warning and without the approval of superiors. International maritime law prohibited unprovoked attacks on civilian vessels, but that rule had already been broken many times during the war. And any U-boat captain who harbored doubts because of international law—and there is no evidence Ajax was such a man—probably knew the Führer's thoughts on such matters.

Five years earlier Germany had signed a protocol barring "the unrestricted use of submarines as weapons of war." But in Adolf Hitler's view, the actual outbreak of war meant the scuttling of such international agreements and any promises made, in writing or otherwise. Any doubting U-boat captain need only have reminded himself of the blunt battle orders given to Admiral Doenitz and his *Kriegsmarine*: "Fighting methods will never fail to be used merely because some international law forbids them."

CHAPTER 6

September 17

They woke Tuesday under a menacing sky, heavy dark clouds buffeted by a strong wind. Mid-morning brought sleet, and by noon it was hard rain. Visibility was uneven, and a light chop on the water became a rough sea. For the second time in five days, heavy swells rolled the *City of Benares*.

The children—though clearly reinvigorated after three days of fresh air and ample food—came to breakfast that morning with little appetite. Captain Nicoll reported a Force 5 gale—roughly twenty- to twenty-five-mile-per-hour winds—and forecast rougher weather for the afternoon. It would be a difficult twenty-four hours, but Nicoll and his crew told passengers not to worry; the *Benares* could handle much worse.

Passengers spent the better part of the day inside, reading and napping and playing cards. The children remained below deck in their cabins or in the *Benares'* fancy playroom. Bess Walder read a book and tended to cabinmates Ailsa Murphy and Pat Allen, both of whom were seasick again. Colin Richardson had found a tiny ball bearing and put it in the drawer of his bedside cabinet. When the seas were calm, the drawer was quiet; now it rattled loudly, the ball bearing ricocheting inside. Derek Capel peered out the porthole of his cabin, trying to pick out ships from the convoy. It had been easy the day before, and Capel loved the game of identifying convoy vessels—Navy corvettes, small boats, and freighters. Now Capel had to strain and stare to find the masts of a solitary freighter. She was the only vessel he could see, and she slipped in and out of view in the gray, wet gauze of early afternoon.

Capel's escort, the Reverend Rory O'Sullivan, had seen that the boy liked to read, and he had given him a gift of *The Wonder Book of Empire*, an illustrated hardcover that celebrated the glory of the British realm, and with it a small talisman that O'Sullivan promised would bring good fortune. The latter was a tiny plastic lamb meant to be worn about the neck as a pendant. Capel thanked O'Sullivan, who was still sick with the flu. He pocketed the little lamb and curled up with the book.

Few passengers were aware of a development far more significant than the inclement weather: The naval escort had left the convoy in the middle of the night.

At one o'clock in the morning, HMS *Winchelsea* and her accompanying sloops had turned to meet HX71, an inbound convoy from Halifax. To the *Benares* crew this came as no surprise; it had been the plan all along. OB213, the *Benares'* convoy, was now more than five hundred miles northwest of Liverpool, beyond the supposed frontier of the U-boat war. But *Winchelsea*'s turn raised several questions.

Hitler's navy had never formally recognized a western limit of operations. As has been noted, U-boat attacks beyond longitude 20 degrees west had been rare but not unprecedented. It is not known whether Captain Nicoll, Commodore Mackinnon, or the CORB senior executives were aware of the late-August U-boat strikes west of this position; if not, one could fairly ask, Why not? There had been nine such attacks altogether. Certainly there was ample information available to a British commander to suggest that the westernmost boundary of the maritime war had been extended.

Winchelsea's departure was all the more puzzling given that the *Benares'* wireless room had continued to receive warnings of U-boat activity up until and after midnight, as September 16 gave way to September 17.

The families of the evacuees—all those mothers and fathers who had agonized over the decision to send their children—had been told in no uncertain terms that their boys and girls would travel to Canada under Royal Navy protection. The precise language from the CORB, given in correspondence to the children's families, had been unambiguous: "The ship in which your child is to sail will be convoyed." Later it would become clear that no parents had understood the fine print, or the absence thereof; the letters did not say "convoyed *to Canada*" or "convoyed *for one week*." It had seemed a straightforward statement: Ships carrying child evacuees "will be convoyed." Parents had probed no further. After all, as one historian would write years later, "the average parent is not a naval tactician."

With the naval escort gone, there remained the question of the next move for the *Benares* and her civilian partners in Convoy OB213. The evidence suggests that after the *Winchelsea* turned, Captain Nicoll and his crew grew jittery, anxious for the entire group to disperse.

It would have been the logical step. Dispersal would have allowed Nicoll to sail faster and more freely. It would also have given him the chance to take evasive maneuvers without involving eighteen other ships in the decision. Without the *Winchelsea*, the convoy was almost wholly unprotected. As the historian Ralph Barker put it, a "convoy without the escort of warships, and therefore without ASDIC [the premier submarine detection system of the time] was easy meat for any patrolling U-boat that might pick them up . . . Strictly speaking, it wasn't a convoy at all."

The signaler Johnny Mayhew, one of the six Royal Navy men sailing with the *City of Benares*, could not understand. *It isn't right to sit here like this*, he thought, *without the warship*.

Mayhew was not alone in his worries. In the early afternoon of September 17, the *Benares*' second engineer, John McGlashan, conferred with chief engineer Alex Macauley.

"Why don't we cut and run for it?" McGlashan asked. With the destroyer gone, he said, they might as well sail alone.

The decision to disperse could only be made by the convoy's commodore, Admiral Mackinnon. Mackinnon had planned from the start to break up OB213—not just the naval escort but the whole convoy—at noon on September 17. It is not clear why he chose not to do so when the moment came. It may have been his judgment that the weather would make dispersal difficult, or that Mackinnon considered a U-boat attack exceedingly unlikely in such rough waters. Both explanations were plausible: The orderly breakup of a nineteen-vessel convoy could be complicated in such seas, and a storm would indeed make it difficult to fire a torpedo with any accuracy.

It is also not known whether Captain Nicoll pressed the matter. Years later a survivor would recall Mayhew saying Nicoll had been angered when no dispersal order came—but this account could not be corroborated. Nicoll's comments prior to departure certainly suggest that his own preference would have been—to use McGlashan's words—to "cut and run for it." Whatever the case, Admiral Mackinnon elected to wait. In early afternoon, he gave the order for a midnight dispersal of OB213.

·   ·   ·

AT NOON THAT DAY, HEINRICH Bleichrodt was at the conning tower of U-48. Swells rose high, and it was difficult to see, but through his attack periscope Bleichrodt could make out a few distinct, slow-moving vessels. Drawing nearer, he found more ships. Bleichrodt watched for a while, then ordered his crew to swing a wide circle around the scene. From his perch he was soon able to estimate the size, position, and speed of his target.

Here was a sizable convoy, much larger than the one he had discovered and attacked three days before off the Irish coast. These ships were sailing westward, in a slight zigzag pattern, at no more than seven or eight knots. And there were at least a dozen of them, fat targets on the choppy water.

Bleichrodt trained his eye on the convoy's center position, and the broad outline of what appeared to be its lead vessel. *That's a big one*, he thought. *Probably a passenger liner.* Concentrating his focus, Bleichrodt could see guns mounted on the liner's deck.

Heinrich Bleichrodt conferred with his officers. It was an inviting target to be sure, almost too easy, were it not for the turbulent seas. They were puzzled by one thing, one critical element missing from what they had seen through the periscope: Where was the escort vessel?

U-48's men had never seen such an impressive collection of vessels sailing naked, as it were, without some cover from the Royal Navy. Rolf Hilse, one of the submarine's wireless operators and keeper of Bleichrodt's logbook, wondered whether there was something different about this particular group of ships. *There is no escort*, Hilse said to himself. *She is sailing alone.* The sight of the convoy broke the day's monotony and piqued curiosity on board U-48. "It makes no sense," Hilse told a fellow crewman.

Ajax wasn't sure what to make of it either, but he chose not to dwell on the question. Heinrich Bleichrodt harbored no doubt about one thing: The ship was a legitimate target. She was sailing in convoy, she was armed, and she was clearly the convoy's prize, long and tall and perched as she was at the lead. To Bleichrodt the missing naval escort was a curiosity—nothing more.

These were the snap judgments of the U-48 crew, though in fact a more basic principle overrode them all: Hitler's unequivocal support for attacks in the North Atlantic, with or without provocation. U-48 was here, and so was the convoy. Ajax was watching his prey, not some line of longitude or latitude. He believed it was his duty to sink that ship.

So the discussion on board U-48 settled quickly on what sort of attack, and when. When to fire the torpedoes? U-boat commanders could elect to attack from above or below the surface, depending on the prevalent conditions.

Above-water attacks were more accurate, but they also risked betraying the sub's position. A submerged attack, by contrast, was safer, but far more difficult. For the moment, the seas were too rough for an underwater attack, and the visibility still good enough to make a surface strike dangerous. U-48 might be seen and herself become a target; the *City of Benares* had guns that could reach Bleichrodt's position. And rough seas could throw off a torpedo's trajectory. In any event, Bleichrodt reflected, there was no reason to rush. So Ajax set a west-southwesterly course, pulling U-48 past the *City of Benares*, and he waited for calm. And for night.

The convoy lumbered on, oblivious and without protection, on Bleichrodt's starboard side, still very much in view.

BY THE DINNER HOUR THE rain had stopped, and the winds had eased somewhat. The dipping sun made an appearance and a rainbow showed itself briefly, delighting children who had been below deck all day.

At the ship's main bar, paying passengers bought rounds, toasting one another and the departed storm, and considered their future in a new world. The BBC's Eric Davis found himself in conversation with a French aviator, a Hungarian journalist, and a Czech who had escaped Nazi Germany. Davis felt privileged to be included in such an eclectic group.

"To Canada!" they toasted, and a small "hurrah" followed. Someone raised a glass to "Will Scarlet"—eleven-year-old Colin Richardson. Richardson, still wearing that scarlet-colored life vest, looked up from his magazine and smiled.

The Hungarian publisher Ernest Szekulesz, an incurable pessimist by nature, mentioned at the bar that there had been whispers about U-boat activity in the area. His remark stopped conversation for a moment, but it was soon quashed by the revelers around him. "Can't be," one passenger said. "The escort's gone."

In other words, if the Royal Navy had withdrawn its protection, then *surely there was nothing more to worry about.* Why on earth would the Navy leave them at risk? They must be beyond the danger zone. There could be no U-boats this far out. By week's end they would be in North America.

From the captain's bridge, Landles Nicoll dispatched men to warn passengers that the storm's lull would be temporary. Still heavier winds lay ahead; rough waters would rule the night. Indian crewmen informed the children's escorts that there would be no after-dinner deck games; the boys and girls were to play in the nursery room or in their cabins. They also delivered a more pleasant message: For the first time since the *City of Benares* had left port, the children were free to retire in their pajamas, without their bulky life vests. *Have them near at hand,* the children were told. That would suffice.

"It's great news," twelve-year-old Derek Capel told nine-year-old Billy Short. "We're in the clear."

The record does not show when precisely this life vest rule was relaxed, or who it was who made the decision. In retrospect it was a highly questionable judgment, given other information reaching the *Benares* telegraph room as night fell. The radio operators Alistair Fairweather and John Lazarus had decoded fresh warnings from Western Approaches, the chief radar station in northwest England. There was a submarine prowling somewhere near the *City of Benares.*

"One probably still far out in Atlantic," came the message, "west of 20 degrees west, probably between 57 and 59 degrees north." This was imprecise information, but it meant that a submarine was operating no more than one hundred miles from the *Benares'* position, and quite possibly closer than that.

There had been other warnings, but as yet no submarine sightings by any of the convoy vessels. Fairweather informed Captain Nicoll and Commodore Mackinnon. The *City of Benares* sailed on.

LANDLES NICOLL HAD BEEN RIGHT about the weather. At a little after eight o'clock, the winds rose suddenly and violently, pitching the *Benares* and ending abruptly the children's post-supper fun and games. The escorts girded for another night with seasick boys and girls, but as they tucked in their subjects they found them cheered and relieved by the no-life-vest provision. Mary Cornish felt relieved as well. "We're safe now," Cornish told the chief escort, Marjorie Day. The children said prayers, asking for calm in the morning. Rory O'Sullivan, still exhausted and flu-ridden, prayed for the ship's safe arrival in North America. Some of the older children read in their bunks. The younger ones drifted to sleep.

The winds rose to a Force 8, more than thirty miles per hour, and a heavy rain slashed the *Benares'* decks. Nicoll and Mackinnon now feared a collision with one of the other convoy vessels more than they did an enemy attack. Indeed, the other ships were having a hard time sailing in place. Dispersing the convoy in these tempestuous waters would have been dangerous.

The *Benares* lookouts were busy monitoring their partner vessels in Convoy

OB213. The third and fourth officers, W. J. Lee and Ronnie Cooper, kept watch from the captain's bridge. Harry Peard crouched in his gunner's nest at the aft end of the ship, wind and sleet hitting him hard. *Couldn't shoot a thing in this weather, even if I had to,* Peard thought, laughing to himself. Two Indian sailors manned the forecastle and crow's nest. The last thing any of these men thought was that a submarine would try an attack in such conditions.

Just before nine o'clock, the gauges recorded a Force 10 gale—fifty-five miles an hour. An officer aboard one of the convoy partners, the *Richard de Larrinaga*, noted in the ship's log: "Wind WNW. Force 10 . . . whole gale. High precipitous seas. Shipping heavy seas fore and aft. Laboring heavily. Fierce squalls."

Admiral Mackinnon ordered the convoy vessels to halt their zigzag patterns. The *City of Benares* slowed significantly and straightened her course. The priority now was to ride out the storm.

GLASSES TOPPLED FROM THE BAR. Waiters struggled to steady themselves. Colin Richardson left the lounge and returned to his cabin. His unofficial guardian, Laszlo Raskai, stayed behind at the bar.

Letitia Quinton and her fifteen-year-old son, Tony—another of the children traveling outside the CORB program—found comfort in a pair of cushioned chairs in the lounge. Tony did not mind the turbulence. He was deeply immersed in *So Great a Man,* David Pilgrim's historical novel about Napoleon. Quinton was an erudite child and he loved history; the book was providing an excellent diversion. He was an only child, stout and energetic, and his mother was a Canadian woman whose English husband had died five years earlier of tuberculosis, when Tony was only ten. Letitia Quinton had not wanted to leave England, but when the war began, her mother had sent a persuasive cable from her home in Victoria, British Columbia. "You and the boy are of no use there," she wrote. "You're dead weight."

Now they were on the first leg of the long trip to Victoria—Letitia Quinton chatting with fellow passengers and Tony buried in his book.

After a rough half hour or so, the storm lagged again, the moon shone intermittently, and Bohdan Nagorski suggested to Zygmunt Gralinski that they take a walk on deck. Given what the crew had been saying, Nagorski knew it might be a while before they would have another spell of calm. They were joined by an Indian medical student and by the British parliamentarian James

Baldwin-Webb. Farther aft, Mary Cornish and two of the other women escorts—Sybil Gilliat-Smith and Marjorie Day—had the same idea. Together they finished their coffee and went up for a stroll.

The women were exhausted but happy. The journey's first days had presented problems large and small for the escorts—nausea and homesickness, fear of bad weather, and fear of lost pocket money—and they had beaten each one back without much trouble. They had found the children to be brave and great sports, and now these three women allowed themselves to feel hopeful and a little proud. Gilliat-Smith felt relaxed enough to actually contemplate what lay ahead.

"I'll be having Christmas in Canada," she mused. So would ninety very fortunate boys and girls.

The women broke into song—"Greensleeves," because the girls had been demanding it constantly, then a run of Christmas carols, because Gilliat-Smith had just put the holiday in their minds. Never mind that Christmas was one hundred days away.

Mary Cornish smiled and said good night. It was a few minutes before ten o'clock. The winds had receded and the evening was quieter now, save for their songs and the steady rumble of the ship's engines. Looking to the stern, the women were once again able to make out other convoy vessels, black shapes that inched along in the moonlight. Peering ahead, they saw nothing. Only the darkness, and an occasional sliver of moonlight.

THE VIEW FROM *UNTERSEEBOOT* 48 was suddenly clearer than it had been all day. The seas were still rough, but clumps of clouds drifted past the moon. The submarine glided closer to OB213.

Heinrich Bleichrodt had been patient. He had shadowed the *City of Benares* and her partners for the better part of nine hours, ample time for a commander to consider the conditions and plan an attack. Bleichrodt had decided to wait for the cover of darkness, and then for the first break in the storm. If and when the storm eased, he would bring U-48 to the surface and take aim at one of the convoy vessels.

Now—at ten o'clock—Ajax sensed his opportunity. U-48 sat roughly half a mile off the *Benares'* port bow. The winds had subsided. The conditions, and the angle of approach, appeared optimal.

Bleichrodt ordered two torpedoes fired from their bow tubes.

.   .   .

THE TWO POLISH FRIENDS TURNED at the end of the deck. Zyg-munt Gralinski suggested they retire, but Bohdan Nagorski was enjoying the walk, and a stiff breeze. It was at this moment that Nagorski made his remark about a U-boat attack.

"Might as well stay here," he said. "Better to be on deck, close to the lifeboats, than undressed, in our beds."

Gralinski laughed. Like so many of the 406 people on the large and elegant liner, these two men were convinced they were out of danger. The crew had said as much. They were now 630 miles from Great Britain.

AJAX HAD MISCALCULATED, JUDGED HIS angle incorrectly. The two torpedoes whistled quietly passed the *City of Benares*, unnoticed by the ship's lookouts. They flew through the water, long and fast but ultimately harmless, and plunged to the seabed.

It was a mistake, a bad one in Bleichrodt's view. You didn't just waste torpe-does like that. Bleichrodt consulted his officers, and adjusted course slightly. At 10:01, U-48 unleashed a third torpedo.

"We'll risk this one," Bleichrodt said. "No more."

Ajax sat back, and waited.

CHAPTER 7

10:03 P.M.

Bleichrodt's torpedo was in the air for one minute and fifty-nine seconds. It was a five-hundred-pound, acoustically guided missile, packed with TNT and a second explosive called HND, short for hexanitrodiphenylamine. The torpedo pierced the side of the *City of Benares* at three minutes past ten, tearing through the number five hold, directly beneath the children's quarters.

The closest convoy partner at that hour was the seven-thousand-ton cargo ship *Clan MacNeil*, sailing roughly three hundred feet off the *Benares'* port side and two hundred feet behind her. From his lookout perch an eighteen-year-old cadet named Edward Smith saw a flash, a yellowish burst through the dark and rain. The sound reached him a moment later. *God*, Smith thought. *Those kids.*

The *City of Benares* shook and shuddered. Alarm bells rang. The lounge swayed. Many of the evacuee children were thrown from their beds. Bunks splintered and fell, wardrobes were crushed, walls cracked, and pipes burst open, spouting small fountains in cabins and then streams of water in many parts of the ship. Fragments of wood and glass and then a fine dust sprayed across cabins and corridors. A gash opened on the promenade deck, above the number five hold.

The torpedo had struck far aft, on the port side. It had exploded directly beneath a row of bathrooms one level below the children's cabins.

The tremor was most violent in the middle twenty or so children's cabins, where eleven-year-old Fred Steels had been sleeping when his bunk came crashing down on him. A few doors down, the same thing had happened to Billy Short.

Short was nine years old. In his case the top bed's wooden slats had come to rest at a steep vertical angle, the lower ends settling just a few inches from his face. The top bunk was his little brother Peter's, but Peter was in the infirmary now, one of the two confirmed cases of chicken pox. Billy Short's other room-mate, Terrence Holmes, was in the other bed, a single. Now that bed was broken, too.

Holmes crawled about, away from the bed. He cried out in pain.

"Can you manage?" Short hollered.

After a few moments Holmes replied, "I can manage."

There was no light in their room, only the misty blue of the emergency lights streaming in from the hall, casting an eerie glow along the floor. The boys headed for the corridor.

Another cabin down, Derek Capel's bed was intact, but his dresser had fallen over between his bunk and the door. Thick chunks of debris blocked Capel's way out. Water lapped at his ankles. The room was dark.

Feeling his way, Capel soon discovered a small opening in the wall between his room and the corridor. The dresser had probably cracked open that hole as it came down, he thought. Capel found a piece of wood, a chair leg, and began banging at the wall. Soon chunks of plaster were breaking free, and the hole had grown considerably larger.

"Got it!" Capel cried. He slithered through.

Now Steels, Paul Shearing, Capel, Holmes, and Billy Short were united in the corridor, a long, narrow space that divided the boys' and girls' cabins and led in either direction to stairwells. Rivulets of water ran past. The emergency lights flickered; the boys could see little more than an arm's length ahead. Paul Shearing caught the sharp smell of burning metal. Capel noticed the distinct slope of the water, like a gentle waterfall. The *Benares* was already angling down, to the stern.

Then Derek Capel heard a soft cry and a thumping sound. He inched forward. *Thud, thud.*

The cry came louder. The *thud-thud* repeated itself. Capel heard a voice, shouting now, from the same spot.

"Out! Out! Need to get *out* . . ."

The voice was familiar. Capel and Billy Short approached, hugging the corridor wall.

More banging. "*Here!* Need to get *out . . .*"

"It's *O'Sullivan!*" cried Derek Capel.

The escort and priest Rory O'Sullivan had been flung from his bed and left to grope in a dark and twisted mess of wreckage. "Get me *out!*"

The boys found a door handle, heard the voice much louder now, and together they pulled, hard as they could.

After a minute or so the door gave way. Out tumbled Father O'Sullivan. He stood with some effort and thanked the boys. O'Sullivan was weak and disoriented, still sick with flu.

"Come on, lads," he said softly. "Got to get ourselves to deck."

The other boys had gone ahead to the stairs. Capel and Short wanted to fetch their brothers, Alan and Peter, whom they had not seen in nearly two days.

O'Sullivan promised to help find the younger boys, but he knew they were in the infirmary and he believed it would be folly to go there now.

"They'll get to deck all right," O'Sullivan told Derek and Billy. "They're with nurses. Can't go wrong."

And then he said it again: They had to get themselves to deck. To Lifeboat 12. O'Sullivan wanted to convey calm, but he also believed they needed to hurry. "It's the same as one of the drills."

EIGHT-YEAR-OLD JACK KEELEY HAD DRIFTED easily to sleep, helped by pleasant thoughts of how distant the war now seemed. To think! Less than one week before, they had slept in those crowded halls at the Sherwood's Lane School, heard the bombs crashing down on Liverpool. Now, more than six hundred miles out, Jack Keeley had calmed himself and even managed to reassure his homesick sister. On this Tuesday night he had happily traded day clothes for pajamas, well aware what the change in rules really meant.

It meant the threat was no longer considered serious.

It meant he and all the other children would be safe.

It meant that, soon enough, they would all be in Canada.

It meant—really!—that the war was just a memory.

The explosion ripped into Jack Keeley's dreams.

He sat up. He heard the alarms, saw and heard a shower of glass, saw that his door had broken open. He saw those weird blue lights, dancing along his cabin floor. Then Keeley saw bits of glass, floating in a shallow pool of water.

"We've been *torpedoed!*"

. . .

JOHNNY BAKER ASSUMED IT WAS a test.

They had repeated the exercise on the *Benares'* decks at least once a day, and all the children—youngest included—knew "the drill": Leave your cabin; walk the corridor to the stairwell; and take the stairs to your "muster station," or gathering point. From there you would be brought to the lifeboats.

The overriding instructions had been simple: Stay calm. Do not panic. Look after the youngest ones.

Johnny Baker was seven years old. A rumble had gone through his cabin, but there was little damage and a faint light still glowed, helping Johnny as he moved about sleepily, rousing the other boys. Stepping into the corridor he found water—and then he found his older brother.

In four happy, hectic days aboard the *City of Benares*, Bobby Baker had spent a great deal of time chasing after his peripatetic little brother. Now he had found him—one more time.

"Come on," Bobby told him, "it's another test. Hurry along."

They held hands and walked slowly toward the staircase. The corridor was dank and dark. Occasionally they heard a cry from an anxious or injured child. Otherwise it was quiet.

At some point during this subdued procession Johnny Baker began to wonder: *Why are we having a drill during such rough weather?*

And why are they doing it in the middle of the night?

KEN SPARKS WOKE TO FIND water coursing into his cabin. The cabin door and part of the outer wall had been shattered. At least he would have no difficulty getting out.

Sparks was thirteen. He had three cabinmates, between nine and eleven years old. He felt it his duty to get them to the deck.

"Let's go, lads!"

Just like a boat drill, he said to himself, but he knew it was no such thing.

Sparks herded the boys out, to the corridor and up the stairs. An officer waved them along, and told them not to bother with the nursery—their "muster station." They were to proceed directly to deck instead.

"Yes, sir!" Ken Sparks replied.

He led the boys to their lifeboat stations, feeling a surge of adrenaline and not even a trace of fear. This was still an *adventure*. Just one more chapter.

Then Sparks headed for his own lifeboat station, on the starboard side of the deck. He was marching along when a sailor took him by the arm.

"Here now, son, there's room in this boat."

Sparks followed the man back to port side, to the station for Lifeboat 12. Here he found Derek Capel, Billy Short, Paul Shearing, Fred Steels, and the escort Rory O'Sullivan. A few Indians had gathered at this station as well, but the sailor had been right: There would be ample space in the lifeboat.

DAMAGE TO THE GIRLS' CABINS, on the *Benares'* port side and directly above the ruined number five hold, appeared extensive. Several girls had been thrown from their bunks. As they struggled to right themselves and reach the corridors, the girls caught the smell of cordite, the whiff of explosives thick and powerful all around them.

Beth Cummings was shouting for her cabinmates, Joan Irving and Betty Unwin. She groped for the light switch, found it, and then discovered that it was not working.

Next she called for Maud Hillman, her escort.

Nothing. She tried again, louder. No reply. Then she hollered again for the two girls.

There was a moan from Unwin. No answer from Joan Irving.

Beth found her coat and pulled it over her life vest and nightgown. Then she stepped nearer to the door. Water was seeping from her cabin to the corridor.

Her friend Bess Walder was in the next cabin, but she had almost no freedom to move. Bess had never been a sound sleeper, and she had sat up with a start as her dresser crashed across the cabin doorway. Water ran around it, puddling up her cabin. There was a decent-sized gash in the door, but it lay behind the dresser and seemingly beyond reach.

How would she get there? How would she pull herself through?

Bess pounded on the wall and set about pulling on clothes, all the while crying for help. "In *here*!" Bess realized that she was wearing a bright green dressing gown, and she remembered suddenly her mother saying how shabby and old the gown was. "You mustn't take *that* . . ."

Well, take it she had, and now she was wearing the thing as she prepared to leave her cabin and evacuate the ship herself. *So be it,* Bess thought. *Mum would understand.* Bess pulled her life vest, big and bulky, over the green gown, and edged toward the door, still not sure how she would escape. There was so much broken furniture blocking her way.

Where are the other girls? Bess Walder wondered. *Where are Miss Hillman and the other escorts?*

Suddenly Bess heard a knock, then a banging against her cabin door. Before she could reply, an arm had thrust forward, pushing through that break in the wall. It was a man's arm, thick and strong, and it startled her.

Bess seized the arm, and almost instantly she was pulled free, over the dresser and into the hallway.

"There's two more in there."

The man tried, in the dark, to reach the other girls. He succeeded with one, the twelve-year-old Patricia Allen.

"Go on," the man said. "Get up the stairs. Get up to deck."

Off they went. In the darkness and confusion, Bess Walder never saw who it was who had rescued her, or what had become of her other cabinmate, Ailsa Murphy.

A large group of children filled the corridor now, some two dozen boys and girls moving slowly for the stairs. It was just as it had been during the drills, the girls thought, only dark and cold, with water at their feet and that acrid smell filling the hall.

Beth Cummings found Bess in the hallway and tapped her shoulder. "We've got a job with Joan," she said.

Beth's roommate Joan Irving was hurt. They couldn't be sure what had happened, only that the girl was moaning and could not walk. They saw no blood. Joan was fifteen. She had been seasick for much of the journey; now she was wounded.

Beth and Bess dragged and then carried Joan forward. The *City of Benares* seemed to sway as they went; it was difficult for the girls to keep their footing. They took short steps, moving toward the stairs.

Then the staircase collapsed.

The girls stood there, staring for a moment. *Could it be?* Bess wondered, realizing the answer almost immediately. Yes—the stairs were gone. The three girls turned without a word and headed in the opposite direction, to the next set of stairs.

MARY CORNISH HAD LEFT FELLOW escorts Sybil Gilliat-Smith and Marjorie Day at about a minute before ten, after their stroll on the promenade deck. She had just reached the end of the companionway on what was known as the "shelter deck," two levels below, when the torpedo struck.

She teetered, grabbing a stair rail. The corridor went dark.

Cornish held the rail, gripped it with both hands. *Please*, she thought, *tell me that wasn't what I think it was.*

She heard water coursing somewhere, powerful as an open faucet. It took a moment, but as her eyes adjusted to the darkness, Mary Cornish realized she was staring into a hole, a black abyss at the ship's center. A wide gash had opened where a bathroom had been. *A torpedo*, she thought. *It must have passed through there.* The slosh of water sounded near.

She felt herself shaking. *The children...*

They were sleeping somewhere, just below the wreckage that lay strewn before her eyes.

How do I get from here to there?

The hole was filling with seawater.

Later Mary Cornish would think, *It's a miracle, really, that the missile missed the children's cabins. It could have killed them all, just like that.* For now, Cornish had to find the girls—*her* girls—fifteen children entrusted to her by the government of Great Britain. There were the Grimmond sisters, and twelve more, all her responsibility. Fifteen daughters of anxious families.

Cornish's path was blocked by a tangle of wood planks, splintered glass, and ruined furniture. Water pooled around it all, over her ankles now. A sailor appeared at her side, and together they pulled at the pieces, scraping and bloodying their arms, working in almost total darkness. Finally, three or four long minutes later, she eased through.

Water streamed through the space they had made. There, on the other side, she found the New Zealand escort Lillian Towns and several of the evacuee children. One of the girls was unconscious, but otherwise Cornish was heartened to see them unscathed, and—for the most part—unafraid. Many of the girls were only half-dressed. The Grimmond sisters were there. Gussie—in charge as always—was leading Violet and Connie down the corridor.

Other girls found Mary Cornish and tugged at her shirtsleeve.

"Auntie Mary, what's happened?"

"You all right, Auntie Mary?"

It was the name they had used almost from the moment they met Mary Cornish at Liverpool.

"It's only a torpedo," she told them, calmly as she could. And then she instructed them to proceed to deck. There was no point, she reasoned, in stopping at the "muster stations."

The girls did as they were told.

Only a torpedo. The line worked well enough so that "Auntie Mary" repeated it several times along that black corridor and then on deck, whenever a
child showed signs of distress.

Marjorie Day had ventured below deck, too. She reached her cabin, stepping through puddles to grab a coat and life jacket. Day found the CORB doctor, Margaret Zeal, in the hallway, and together they navigated a similar mess
of glass and wood fragments and found some of their young charges.

"Get up! Up you go, now!"

Most of the children were wearing their life jackets. *They've paid attention*,
Marjorie Day thought. A ship's nurse tended a wounded girl. Then she told
Day and Zeal that a boy in a nearby cabin had been killed.

The news was delivered matter-of-factly. It was hardly a surprise, given the
thunder and trauma of the U-boat's torpedo. Probably many more people had
died on impact. Still, confirmation of a death sobered the children's escorts. *A
boy has been killed*. Things had seemed relatively calm and orderly in the dark
but quiet procession from the cabins. Now someone was dead.

Day, Zeal, and about a dozen girls found the stairs and took them quietly, a
sober, single-file march to deck.

It was ten minutes past ten. Seven minutes after impact.

THE PAYING PASSENGERS HAD BEEN more scattered when the
torpedo struck. At ten o'clock in the evening few among them had retired for
the night.

The British travel executive William Forsyth was pouring drinks in his
cabin for himself and the German baroness, Amelie von Inglesleben, when
one of the walls disintegrated. Forsyth and his guest were unhurt, only showered in a yellow-white dust. *Could use a drink*, Forsyth thought—but his bottles had been shattered, too. Now he and the baroness gathered themselves and
headed for the promenade deck.

Arthur Wimperis, the screenwriter, had been reading in bed, one cabin
away. He heard a crash, but damage was light in his quarters, other than the
darkness that came as he collected his thoughts. Wimperis felt for his raincoat
and life jacket, his pipe and tobacco. He knew precisely where to go: Lifeboat
number 9. Starboard side.

Other passengers had been relaxing in the ship's library and game room, or
in the lounge. This was where the teenager Tony Quinton had been, happily
devouring the novel about Napoleon. At three minutes past ten, Quinton felt a

powerful jolt and noticed dust lifting, a quick and curious *poof* from the lounge's thick carpeting. A glass fell. Plates rattled. The boy returned to his reading.

But after a minute or so alarms were ringing and the ship's tilt was evident. Tony Quinton laid down his Napoleon book. Letitia Quinton seized her son by the arm and together they rushed to their cabin. She was a quiet but headstrong woman, and she worked quickly to stuff her handbag with jewelry, money, and their passports. "It's sinking, apparently," Letitia Quinton told her son.

Tony Quinton followed his mother, but he could not imagine that the ship would actually go under. For one thing, the atmosphere along the corridor and here in their cabin appeared altogether too serene. He and his mother headed back up to the lounge.

Barbara Bech had been reading in bed when she felt a *whump.* Nothing fell or broke in the cabin she shared with her eleven-year-old sister, Sonia. It was more like a tremor, a gentle one. It jostled them, and nothing more.

Barbara was fourteen, the eldest of Marguerite Bech's three children. The Bechs and the other children traveling as paying passengers were accommo-dated in the forward part of the *Benares*, farther from the torpedo than the child evacuees had been. So while they felt the impact and heard the alarm bells, their dressers, beds, and washbasins remained intact. They slept in single beds; there were no bunks to collapse. And for the moment at least, their lights were still working.

Still, Barbara Bech thought, *That's trouble. Better get dressed.* She shouted to her sister, "Up you go!"

Their mother was two doors down, with nine-year-old Derek. He had been seasick for much of the afternoon. Now his mother was having difficulty rous-ing the boy.

Marguerite Bech was a practical woman, as ready for this moment as any passenger on board. She had a "survival kit" close at hand, a bag that held her jewelry box, the family's passports and papers, money, a bottle of water, and a bottle of rum. She had put Derek to bed in his school uniform, a cap and rain-coat hanging nearby. Sonia and Barbara were outfitted in shorts, cardigans, brand-new duffel coats, warm socks, and shoes.

Within minutes this exquisitely prepared foursome had arrived at the lounge.

Here they found a quiet, dimly lit room, full of men and women playing cards, smoking and drinking, and talking about what had happened. Some snacked on crackers and cheese; others sat on comfortable sofas and easy chairs. Barbara Bech saw nothing to suggest urgency or tension, no sign that this was the gathering point for passengers on a mortally wounded liner. There was only the glimmer of the floor emergency lights, and a few candles flickering from tabletops and the bar. Barbara noticed the candle wax dripping oddly, to one side.

It's calm, Sonia Bech said to herself, with some relief. *Whatever has happened, we shall be all right.*

Marguerite Bech wanted to make one last trip to her cabin to fetch a few more things, but an officer took her by the arm. "No," he said. "You must stay here for now."

So she stayed, her son and two daughters close. The minutes passed.

Why, Marguerite Bech wondered, *are they not telling us what to do?*

ANNIE RYAN, A *BENARES* STEWARDESS, had just enjoyed a bath. She was pulling on a pair of pants when the jolt knocked her to her knees. Her colleague and cabinmate Margaret Ladyman screamed.

Together they scrambled in the dark, gathering clothes, passports, and other papers. As the two women prepared to leave the cabin, Ladyman took Ryan by the arm. She handed her a small package. "Will you look after this for me?" Ladyman asked. She had two sons in the Royal Air Force, she said. "If anything happens to me, would you see that my sons get it?"

The request puzzled Annie Ryan. Why should *her* chances of survival be any better? But Ryan did as asked, taking the small package and cradling it in her arms. Then they walked down the corridor together to fetch blankets from a storage room.

A crew member stopped them.

"Christ—you can't go down there," he said. "It's *flooded.*"

BOHDAN NAGORSKI WAS THROWN TO the deck at the moment of impact and separated from his friend, Zygmunt Gralinski. He heard glass breaking somewhere, felt the ship heave. Others below deck would move quickly upward, to the lifeboat stations; Nagorski righted himself and headed *down.* He believed he had time to collect some of his things.

When he arrived in his cabin, Nagorski was wistful but matter-of-fact. He had escaped from Poland almost precisely one year earlier, along roads bombed by the *Luftwaffe.* In the summer of 1940 he had fled Nazi-occupied

France. The time had come again, he thought, to abandon his belongings and "leave them to the enemy." How many more times would it happen?

The difference now, of course, was that he had to flee a sinking ship, not an aerial bombardment or invading army. And then he would have to hope that someone would come for them. It was remarkable, Nagorski thought, how tranquil and undisturbed his cabin was. No visible damage, no holes in the cabin walls. Perfectly peaceful, really. They had not lost power in this section of the ship; Nagorski's table lamp still glowed. His trunk and suitcase still sat stacked neatly in a corner. It was the same suitcase he had carried from Gdynia, on the Baltic Sea, during his seventeen-day journey south to Romania, the same suitcase he had carried from Bordeaux months later as the Germans advanced. Staring at the luggage now, he felt profoundly sorry. More sad than afraid.

He picked up his coat, his homburg hat, and a diplomatic pouch he was carrying for the Polish Embassy in Washington. This time, he decided, the suitcase would have to stay.

Many passengers were making similar snap decisions about what to retrieve from their cabins. The German doctor and refugee Martin Bum had lost most of what mattered to him when the Nazis ransacked his home, but he had salvaged a small collection of antique books and drawings. "My treasures," he called them, and he had kept them wrapped in paper and string in a small cube-shaped package. Bum shuffled slowly down a staircase, against the grain of people heading for the decks, making his way to his cabin. He held tight to the stair rail, feeling the slight tilt of the ship. Within minutes Martin Bum was in the lounge, clutching his "treasures." He settled in a plush chair, happy for the moment. There he awaited the call to the lifeboats.

Retired Navy Lieutenant Commander Richard Deane hurried from the lounge to rouse his wife—one of the few people who had actually slept through the attack. Deane was fifty-six, and having volunteered for the war effort, he had been asked to aid with military training in Canada. Deane helped his wife into a heavy coat, pulled his own coat on, and pocketed only one other possession—his service revolver. *Might prove useful*, he said to himself.

Jimmy Proudfoot knew instinctively what he would carry to the deck. Proudfoot, a lanky young man from Glasgow, was one of the *City of Benares'* bartenders. After the torpedo struck, Proudfoot picked up some glasses and bottles that had fallen, and poured himself a shot of whiskey. As he left the bar, he grabbed a full bottle and made his way to the station for Lifeboat number 11.

WATCHING FROM LESS THAN ONE mile away, the crew of U-48 was euphoric. They did not yet know what ship they had struck—only that it was a large liner. Hilse, the wireless operator, turned to Heinrich Bleichrodt and said, "It's a hit."

THE SHIP'S MAIN LOUNGE DOUBLED as a "muster station" for paying passengers, and the crowd there was growing rapidly. At about five minutes past ten, the ship's purser, John Anderson, arrived in the lounge and took charge. Anderson had been in his cabin preparing transfer schedules for U.S.-bound travelers when he felt what he thought was the jolt of a collision. *We've hit one of the other convoy ships,* he thought. He collected his papers and made for the corridor. There an assistant told Anderson the jolt he had felt was probably a torpedo's impact; he threw on a life jacket and headed for the lounge.

Any experienced sailor knew the importance of an orderly procession to deck. In the hours ahead, calm and discipline would be qualities as essential to survival as bravery or stamina. Anderson was favorably impressed by what he observed in the lounge; dozens of people had assembled, with no outward signs of tension. "We are to stay here," Anderson told passengers in the lounge, "until all the children have been mustered and placed in the boats."

They all knew this meant the evacuee children—not the three Bech children, Colin Richardson, Tony Quinton, or the five other sons and daughters of paying passengers. Anderson's order seemed reasonable. No one in the room objected.

The BBC correspondent, Eric Davis, was in the lounge, and he watched, thoroughly impressed, as fellow passengers collected in small groups according to lifeboat assignments. Some left for final visits to cabins, returning with what seemed to Davis to be the right gear and—more important—exactly the right attitude. *There are no tears,* he thought. *There is no panic.* People appeared confident that the lifeboat drills had prepared them well, and that the convoy vessels, so near at hand, would make rescue almost routine.

If these people can be so calm, Eric Davis said to himself, *then so can I. There is nothing really to fear.*

. . .

RICHARD DEANE'S WIFE WAS NOT the only passenger to have slept through the explosion. At the *Benares'* bow, far from the point of impact, the ship had sustained minimal damage, and the rumble had been softer, like distant thunder. Colin Richardson, the child they called "Will Scarlet," never felt the torpedo's strike and might have gone on sleeping had the alarms not rung loudly and repeatedly at his end of the ship.

Richardson had dozed while reading a comic book. He was wearing the scarlet life vest over his pajamas. The alarms roused him, and in an instant Colin grabbed his raincoat and balaclava cap and hurried to the hallway. Immediately he sensed the odor of explosives and quickened his step. *Like the bombs,* he thought, remembering the scent in the air that followed a heavy pounding from the *Luftwaffe.* As he neared a stairwell, someone told him he could relax and return to his cabin; the ship would be fine. Colin Richardson did not believe it. He ignored the advice and climbed the stairs.

Within minutes he had arrived at the correct boat station, number 2. There he waited, scanning the deck for his friend and guardian, Laszlo Raskai.

Raskai had left the bar at 10:03. While other passengers descended directly to their own cabins, the Hungarian journalist had gone instead to the evacuees' quarters and helped extricate children from the most badly damaged parts of the ship. After ten minutes or so he had worked his way forward to the paying passengers' quarters, to Colin Richardson's cabin.

The boy was gone.

BESS WALDER AND BETH CUMMINGS had found an officer to help them haul Joan Irving to the deck. Betty Unwin and Ailsa Murphy were close behind. It was raining and confusing, and when they came to their station Bess thought to herself, *There should be more girls here. There aren't enough girls.*

Their boat was number 5, preparing for deployment along the starboard side. Near the lifeboat station Bess and Beth found several of the youngest evacuees, waiting and shivering. Beth, too, was struck by the calm. *All these little ones. You'd think they'd be berserk.* But Bess believed some of the children looked scared. *Cold,* she thought, *and scared.*

"It's all right, don't worry," Bess told them. The wind had gained strength, blowing rain across the deck. "Everything shall be all right." Then she heard a voice. A familiar voice, soft and encouraging.

"We'll be picked up," a girl was saying. "It'll be like before. You'll see."

The voice belonged to her cabinmate Patricia Allen, the twelve-year-old who had survived the attack on the *Volendam* barely two weeks before. Allen had recognized instinctively the tremor in her cabin. *Fancy*, she thought, *it's happened again.* But while she knew this was another attack, she also showed no signs of fear. Every child on board the torpedoed *Volendam* had been rescued and brought home safely. They had suffered no injuries. Patricia Allen understood she might never reach Canada now, understood they would probably be turning back for England. Again. But she did not for a moment believe that her life or any others were in danger.

Bess Walder felt a similar confidence, listening to Allen and watching as the other girls filled an orderly queue at Lifeboat station number 5. The sea was rough, and the wind had gathered strength, but crew and children alike appeared calm. *We shall be all right...*

Then, quite suddenly, Bess was seized with a fresh shock and fear: *Louis!* Where was her little brother?

"Look after that young man," her mother had said, parting words that Bess Walder had not forgotten. It was her one job, the single demand her parents had made.

Bess felt suddenly sick. *Where is Louis?* How could she not know?

LANDLES NICOLL ARRIVED AT THE captain's bridge at about five minutes past ten. He dispatched crew members to assist passengers and assess damage, began dictating distress messages, and demanded updated weather forecasts from his senior officers. He could see for himself that the weather had worsened again.

Nicoll kept an even demeanor as he considered his ship's chances. He knew how difficult it would be to launch lifeboats under these conditions. The rains had returned, the seas were rough, the moonlight intermittent at best. As for the *Benares* herself, she was listing to port side and tilting down at the stern; put differently, she was at risk of going under at one end, or tipping over on her side. Landles Nicoll doubted his ship would last more than an hour.

The chief officer, Joe Hetherington, a strapping, square-jawed, six-foot-four sailor, reached the bridge, breathless and in search of direction.

"Go aft," Nicoll told him, "and find the extent of the damage."

Hetherington had been in his quarters at 10:03, roused from sleep by the explosion. Now he saluted Nicoll and took the steps down from the bridge.

Arriving at the aft end of the boat deck, Hetherington discovered that the torpedo had shattered the number five hold. Beams and hatches had been blown to pieces. There was damage to the number four hold as well. *It's bad,* Hetherington said to himself. *Worse than I'd thought.* Descending further, the chief officer found that the force of the blast had blown through the water-tight door leading to the *Benares'* engine room, damage that took no lives but that opened a path for water to flood the room. This was the ship's heart, as it were, and if water came it would produce steam explosions as the cold Atlantic met the hot steel tubes. Pumps would fail, and the *Benares'* "heart" would cease to function. What Hetherington saw led him to believe the ship would not last long.

Only one thought heartened the chief officer, and it came to him as he climbed his way back to the bridge. Wherever he encountered passengers, he found a disciplined procession to the lifeboat stations. People seemed to know where they were meant to be and how to get there. There was no clamor in the dark corridors and stairwells, no squabbling at the lifeboat stations, not even a crying child to be found. The younger officers seemed calm and in control. The lifeboat drills, Hetherington thought, had been worth the effort.

From the bridge, Captain Nicoll rang the engine room, and thus learned what Hetherington had discovered on his fast tour below deck. Chief Engineer Alex Macauley reported to Nicoll from the engine room platform that water was above ankle level and rising fast. Only a few minutes later the water was at Macauley's belt, and he was on the radio again. He told Nicoll his situation had deteriorated.

"We're up to our waists," Macauley said.

"Right," said Nicoll. "Get everybody out, and go to your boat stations."

In these first ten minutes, no good news came to Nicoll and his officers apart from the calm and order at the lifeboat stations. Otherwise the reports were a barrage of bad bulletins. Together they confirmed the captain's worst fears.

Landles Nicoll stared at an unforgiving sea. There was strangely little to be done. It would be a brutal night, he thought, even if they made it. He looked to the stern as the *Benares* dipped again, bending more steeply forward.

"Lower the boats to the embarkation deck," Nicoll ordered. "Prepare to abandon ship."

TO SOME PASSENGERS IT SEEMED a bleak, too-pessimistic command. At this point they were still convinced the *City of Benares* could survive.

Many people were still waiting in the lounge, nursing coffee or after-dinner drinks as they discussed the situation. The absence of any orders led passengers in the lounge to believe the *Benares* would somehow remain seaworthy.

Another prevalent view was that if the ship did go down, one of the other convoy vessels would soon pluck them to safety. Landles Nicoll and his men knew better. Most important, they knew that the convoy ships were shields, and nothing more. In fact those ships' captains were under strict orders *not* to attempt rescue unless an attacking U-boat had been chased away or destroyed. The fear—real and justified—was that a prowling U-boat would pick off any civilian craft that lingered near the scene of an attack. There is no record of any discussion within the admiralty of amending this rule for a convoy that was carrying child evacuees.

Indeed, Heinrich Bleichrodt and his crew had not held fire following their attack on the *City of Benares*. At seven minutes past ten o'clock, Bleichrodt had spent another torpedo. This one struck the five-thousand-ton freighter *Marina*, a smaller member of Convoy OB213, one of the eighteen ships that had sailed with the *Benares* from Liverpool. The *Marina* carried a crew of thirty-four, and she sank almost instantly. Her own two lifeboats were lowered quickly to the water.

At about a quarter past ten, the convoy finally dispersed.

The storm picked up, lashing the waters.

The *City of Benares* was suddenly very much alone.

BY NOW THE *BENARES* DECK was crowded. Hetherington joined Second Officer Hugh Asher, Third Officer W. J. Lee, and Fourth Officer Ronald Cooper supervising the loading and lowering of the boats. Passengers milled about, some waiting for family and friends, others moving slowly to their designated stations. They were like guests at some macabre dinner, waiting to be seated.

By now all the children's escorts had reached the deck. Maud Hillman had collected about twelve of her fifteen girls, and Sybil Gilliat-Smith had all her group assembled at Lifeboat 8. Gilliat-Smith had also adopted the three Grimmond sisters, originally from Mary Cornish's contingent. The rest of Cornish's group were either with Day and Towns at the station for Lifeboat 10—or missing. Michael Rennie had gathered all his boys, Father King was still missing a few, and Father O'Sullivan had only six of fifteen.

O'Sullivan was worried. He imagined some of the boys had gone to another station, but he also knew it was possible that some had been killed on impact. There had been severe damage along the corridor between his battered cabin and the nearest stairs.

The half dozen boys he had brought to deck were an orderly group. O'Sullivan found them prepared and well behaved and remarkably unafraid. Paul Shearing was not scared, but he could not shake an image, something that had caught his eye during his march to the station. Following O'Sullivan across the deck, he had seen clearly the gaping hole where the number five hold had been. A few sailors were there, standing guard, seeing to it that no one fell in. Shearing caught a good look at the glow of a small fire below, wisps of smoke rising from it. He was amazed that a weapon had been able to tear up the deck like that.

Ken Sparks had seen it, too; twenty-five feet across, he guessed. The emergency lights showed the damage—smoke and some flames and all manner of charred and broken metal. Steam hissed from the hole. Ken Sparks turned his head as he passed. *Wish I hadn't seen that.*

Rory O'Sullivan's greatest difficulty lay in convincing Derek Capel and Billy Short to leave the ship, without knowing for certain that their little brothers, the boys with chicken pox, would be all right.

"Shouldn't we fetch them?" Capel asked again.

O'Sullivan laid a hand on the boy's shoulders. "I am sure they're taken care of, Derek."

Alan Capel and Peter Short were in fact on the opposite side of the deck, at boat number 9. They had been led there by the CORB nurse, Dorothy Smith. These youngest of the child evacuees had been quarantined for two days, but suddenly Smith understood that chicken pox was a trifle. They could infect the whole boat, for all she cared. *We need to get off this ship.*

This was Reverend King's lifeboat station. He and a ship's officer were counting heads. The boys called him "Padre King," their term of affection for the Protestant minister from Canada who had struck many of the boys as the "more fun preacher"—more entertaining, in other words, than the Catholic priest Rory O'Sullivan. It was hardly a fair comparison, of course; O'Sullivan—a sober man to begin with—had been in bed with flu for much of the journey. He hadn't had much time for "fun."

King counted a dozen children and three adults—the screenwriter, Arthur Wimperis; the travel executive, William Forsyth; and the German baroness, Amelie von Inglesleben. Wimperis was helping wrap the children in blankets and carry them to the bow of the lifeboat. Forsyth told King he thought the children were very brave. Then he stepped over the ship's rail and into the boat.

More children appeared. Rex Thorne came, having raced from one lifeboat station to the next in a frantic search for his younger sister. "Have you seen Marion Thorne?" he cried. "Sometimes they call her Mary for short!" Thorne arrived at the station for Lifeboat 9—alone. Soon Reverend King flashed a relieved look and a thumbs-up sign to the chief escort, Marjorie Day. He had all his boys. Lifeboat 9 was full.

They were ready to leave the *City of Benares.*

IN THE AREA SURROUNDING LIFEBOAT 5's station, the emergency lights had failed. The escort Maud Hillman asked crew members for flashlights and additional blankets. Her girls were cold and wet, every one of them dressed in a nightgown or pajamas and not much else. "My God," Hillman said to Hetherington, "the one night we send them to bed without their warm clothes..."

Hetherington took Maud Hillman aside. He had no lights to share, he told her. As for blankets, each lifeboat would have an ample supply. "You needn't worry."

Bess Walder and Beth Cummings were in Hillman's group. They held hands, for comfort mostly, but also to keep their footing. The *Benares* was listing sharply now. Gazing across the sloping deck, Bess looked at the youngest children, standing there shivering and waiting patiently to board the boats. There were some who could not have been more than five or six years old. *How brave they are!* Bess thought. *And how little they understand.* Beth and Bess were, at fourteen and fifteen, among the older evacuees. That meant they were stronger physically, but it also meant they *knew* more. They knew, for example, that they would soon be on the cold, rough water in the middle of the night.

Marjorie Day, the chief escort, hustled down the deck, checking children at the stations against her own lists. She and Hetherington had helped many boys and girls navigate dark stairwells and blocked passageways, and when necessary they had helped find detours to the deck. In a few cases they had carried children to the boat stations.

Day was satisfied that they had done their best; nearly all forty-four girls had been accounted for. She had worked to keep spirits high, and in this she had for the most part succeeded. But when the emergency deck lights came back on, they illuminated a terrible ruby red blot, a growing circle of blood trailing from a nurse and child who sat huddled near the station for Lifeboat 10.

Children nearby began to cry. Marjorie Day nudged them, tried to steer them away. She took two girls by the hand and walked them to their lifeboat. Looking back, Day saw that the nurse was cradling one of the youngest girls, who already had a thick and bloodied bandage around her head.

LIFEBOAT NUMBER 9 WAS TAKING on passengers when Johnny Baker suddenly shoved his brother and wriggled free of the group. "I forgot my life jacket!" he cried, and with that little Johnny Baker ran from the lifeboat station.

His brother hollered after him, "No, you don't!"

The younger Baker was a strong boy. Strong-willed, too. But Bobby was twelve, five years his senior, and he caught his brother and managed to hold him by the arm until "Padre King" came to assist. They were walking the boy back to the ship's rail when Bobby had an idea.

He removed his life jacket and handed it to Johnny.

"There you are."

Johnny Baker slipped the jacket on. Somehow he did not realize whose it was or where it had come from.

THE MINUTES PASSED. THE SEA grew more violent.

Chief Officer Hetherington left the deck for a final survey of the children's quarters. He had been told at various lifeboat stations that children were missing, and indeed he found another dozen or so boys and girls below deck, a short column led by escorts and nurses.

"Hurry," Hetherington advised, but he kept a measured tone and he was still favorably impressed by the order and organization. *Discipline is complete,* he thought. His principal concern was that so many children were in their pajamas. Many had no coats or hats. Some did not even have shoes. *God, they'll be cold.*

On his return to deck, Hetherington passed the children's playroom. It was meant to have been a muster station for the evacuees. He paused here. The room was deserted. Through a dim light he could see toys and games scattered about the floor. It was not clear whether this was the torpedo's work, or the leftovers from some busy play session. Then Hetherington saw a fat, jagged hole, running like a fault line across the floor and up the side wall. The torpedo had passed just a few feet beneath the playroom.

SUDDENLY THERE WAS TROUBLE OR confusion at nearly every station.

Richard Deane and his wife boarded an already-crowded Lifeboat 7 and helped haul in the Navy signalman Johnny Mayhew, the French agent Herve de Kerillis, and four or five Indian crewmen. As an officer called for the boat to be launched, several more Indians rushed the ship's rail. Deane felt for the revolver in his coat pocket and resolved to use it if any more men tried to board.

Calm was slowly deserting Mary Cornish, the even-tempered music teacher who scrambled across the deck, searching for familiar young faces. She was still missing at least three of the fifteen girls in her group. Surely it was a dream, she thought. *Please God, let it be a dream...*

She was preparing to descend a set of stairs when an officer stopped her.

"Right, miss, time to go. Need to get to the nearest boat."

Cornish protested briefly before following the order. She arrived, badly rattled, at Lifeboat 10.

Where are the other ships? Mary Cornish wondered. She and her colleagues had watched them less than an hour before, counted all those comforting shadows at the bow while they chatted and dreamed of Canada.

Where are those ships now?

And if they are gone, then who shall come to our rescue?

Cornish found it impossible to remain at the lifeboat station. She asked fifteen-year-old Rosemary Spencer-Davies to watch the other girls. Spencer-Davies was the most responsible of the evacuees, Cornish thought. *She's as good as any of us.* Mary Cornish's conscience would not let her board the boat without a final search of the children's cabins. Even if the risk was great, even if the officers said no. Even if all she found were dead bodies.

At least then she would *know*.

This time no one stopped her. She never heard the officer's cry, "All clear below!" It was the call for her boat, Lifeboat 10, to be lowered to the water.

The *City of Benares* was in profound decline. It was difficult to walk below deck, along dark, waterlogged passageways that sloped precipitously as Mary Cornish neared the children's cabins.

She found nothing but mangled wreckage and water, much more water than she had seen on her last tour less than ten minutes before. Then she met a sailor, emerging from the children's quarters.

"Please go to deck, miss."

"But I—"

"I've just been through there. There's nobody left. Please go on deck."

Mary Cornish wasn't sure she should believe him, but she nodded and turned for the stairs. At least now she had *tried*.

TO THIS MOMENT, THERE WERE few known casualties. Two Indian crewmen from the engine room were missing; so was one of the ship's stewards. One child was known to have been killed; at least four more were hurt. One girl—the one who lay crumpled on the deck—had been gravely injured. Such numbers were heartening, really; on a liner with 406 people on board, a U-boat's torpedo could have done much worse. This still seemed, as one sailor put it, "a survivable incident."

And yet, at twenty minutes past ten, people up and down the deck were beginning to have doubts. The weather had worsened again; Hetherington noted that the winds were back at "Force 6, with squalls of gale intensity, hail and rain and a confused sea presiding." Tensions had mounted at the lifeboat stations, and now confusion and unease were building in the lounge. Roughly fifty people still waited there, and most were continuing to obey purser John Anderson's command. It was the only instruction they had been given: to wait while the evacuee children were brought safely to the boats. They could not know that many other passengers had bypassed the muster stations and gone directly to deck, or that some crew members were actually already boarding boats. In the lounge they had agreed: The poor evacuee children should go first. Even Marguerite Bech, waiting with three children of her own, had understood this and waited patiently.

Still, the wait—more than fifteen minutes now—had seemed to many passengers to be agonizingly long. The "blackout curtains" mandated to block even the faintest light had remained closed, keeping passengers from looking outside. As the time passed, questions nagged at them: Should they stay in the lounge, as ordered? Or should they follow their instincts and head for the boats? Surely the children had reached the lifeboat stations by now . . .

For his part, the British parliamentarian Baldwin-Webb believed the time had come to move, no matter the orders.

"Look here, nothing seems to be happening," he said to Letitia Quinton. "We had better go to the boat."

Moments later he spirited Quinton and her son Tony from the lounge, up a staircase, and to the station for Lifeboat number 6. It qualified as an act of rebellion, a small one, but Baldwin-Webb's anxiety would prove well founded. As they arrived on deck, they discovered that their designated lifeboat was already taking on passengers.

An elderly Dutch couple, Hirsch and Emma Guggenheim, was being helped aboard. Just two hours earlier, the Guggenheims had impressed Letitia Quinton at supper with their voracious appetites and loud conversation. She found it strange to see them, bon vivants both, struggling like this. Several Indian servants were in this boat; so was the Hungarian publisher Ernest Szekulesz, already grumbling about the *Benares* crew, and what he believed were very slim odds of rescue. There were no child evacuees in Lifeboat 6. The only children were Florence Croasdaile's Patricia, nine, and Lawrence, two. Croasdaile was the American woman whose English husband had been taken prisoner by the Germans. She and her children were paying passengers.

Baldwin-Webb took charge, guiding them over the rail, one after the other. "I'll join you in a moment," he told Szekulesz.

Then Baldwin-Webb was gone, off to help another boat. The convoy leader, Admiral Mackinnon, stepped in. More Indian crewmen came over the rail. Finally the orders were given: Lower the boats.

Down they went.

THE *BENARES*' TWELVE LIFEBOATS HAD a capacity of five hundred—roughly forty-two passengers per boat and nearly one hundred more spaces than would be required even if every passenger and crew member were to reach a lifeboat. The boats ranged in size—thirty, twenty-six, and twenty-three feet in length, able to hold sixty, forty, or thirty passengers, respectively. Each boat was three and a half feet deep, and packed with containers of food and water and a variety of gear, including a canvas tarp and rolled-up sail. They hung from modern Welin davits—known for their ability to lower boats quickly, largely because less manpower was required to bring them down. The Welin davit had been one of the few success stories of the *Titanic* disaster, allowing her lifeboats to launch rapidly to the water.

To land a lifeboat requires great skill, or good fortune—even on a sunny day, in placid waters. Darkness, a turbulent sea, and a dying ship will conspire to make the task vastly more difficult; too often the fall ropes drop unevenly, not unlike the sides of an unwieldy Venetian blind. The *Benares'* tilt meant that her lifeboats would have to compensate on one side, and take care not to land just as angled as the ship herself. Descending too slowly risked the boat being indundated with high waves and loading it with water. A lifeboat that came down heavy with water would face a serious disadvantage from the start.

Even the seasoned chief officer, Hetherington, found himself thinking: *Landing a boat in such conditions will be an awesome task indeed.* Hetherington had given a dozen sailors the jobs of launching lifeboats—one man per lifeboat station. These assignments had been made before the *City of Benares* left Liverpool; every designated "lifeboatman" had been given a Lifeboat Efficiency Examination, admistered by the British Board of Trade. The launch was to proceed in stages, each of which demanded not only skill but keen decision-making on the part of the officer in charge. Eight of the twelve boats were tethered to the boat deck; these had to be lowered one level to the promenade deck, where passengers awaited. The remaining four boats hung from davits at either end of the promenade deck itself. Next would come embarkation, to last until each officer believed he had either filled his boat or could find no more passengers. The lifeboat would then be lowered to the water.

More than anything, what mattered in this process was that the boat stayed level, and that the falls and ropes that held it on either end did not slip or become entangled. Crew members could maneuver these falls, but it was imperative that they do so in something approaching unison. Once the boat was safely on the water, the lifeboatmen would shimmy down by rope ladder to their respective boats. Finally, the falls would be unhooked, like umbilical cords to the mother ship, clipped, and tossed away. Then each lifeboat would be on its own. Every step in this choreography had been practiced carefully and repeatedly in boat drills during the *Benares'* first days at sea.

The drills had been carried out in near ideal conditions from a level ship; in such conditions a launch might have been completed in three minutes. Between ten and ten-thirty on the evening of September 17, 1940, in the North Atlantic, conditions were of course hardly optimal. The *Benares'* severe list meant that port-side boats hung out over the water, dangling in the wind, while starboard lifeboats were pinned awkwardly against the ship. All the boats—like the *Benares* herself—were angled down toward the stern.

The historian and author of *Lifeboat: A History,* John Stilgoe, has written that discipline is often the most important commodity aboard any lifeboat, and that it is too often nowhere to be found. "No one knows," he writes, "how to

toss discipline aboard lifeboats lowering." Calm and discipline are also rare, al-most unnatural qualities when night, shipwreck, and rough seas join forces to challenge a lifeboat passenger. Now, as the first lifeboats prepared for launch, calm—such a welcome, critical commodity in the early minutes—began to desert the *City of Benares.*

Lifeboat number 8 was among the first to load and begin a descent. The es-cort Sybil Gilliat-Smith was on board this boat, together with all her girls and another half dozen from Mary Cornish's contingent, including the three Grimmond sisters. Marion Thorne—Rex Thorne's little sister—was here. So was Jack Keeley's six-year-old sister, Joyce. The CORB doctor Margaret Zeal joined Lifeboat 8, as did the Scottish filmmaker Ruby Grierson.

At about ten-twenty-five, the order was given to launch. Several British and Indian sailors joined in the job of lowering Lifeboat 8 from its davits. The boat tipped slightly; then one end fell with a violent jerk. It hung there, horribly, for a few moments, and then a tower of a wave hit the side of the boat.

Shrieks sounded from the lifeboat, from free-falling passengers, and from the deck, as those boarding other lifeboats saw what was happening below. Lifeboat 8 had dropped to a near vertical position. The boat's dive and the force of the wave pitched more than thirty people—mostly children—to the water.

They fell roughly thirty feet into a loud, swirling sea—all those who had boarded in such orderly fashion, just minutes before. Then the lifeboat itself fell, a straight and violent plunge to the water.

Just like that, Marion Thorne was gone.

Joyce Keeley was gone.

Connie, Violet, and Gussie Grimmond—all gone.

In a single week the Grimmond children had lost their home, raced to enlist in the evacuee program, traveled at the last minute to Liverpool, and won the admiration of children and adults alike on board the *Benares.* Gussie Grim-mond had charmed virtually everyone she met in that short, eventful time.

Now, in a few awful moments, Gussie, Constance, and Violet Grimmond had been thrown into the North Atlantic and washed away.

MARJORIE DAY WATCHED IN HORROR as the bodies flew from Gilliat-Smith's boat. It had happened in plain view, not ten yards from where Day stood. *It cannot be . . .* She stared, her face frozen. All those girls were down there, lost somewhere in the water.

It was almost impossible to fathom. All the preparation! All the care they

had taken to help these children . . . The government of Britain, the staff at Sherwood's Lane School, the crew of this lovely ship, and all the escorts like herself—they all had shared the common aim: They were going to help free these children from the bonds of war. They would offer the sons and daughters of England a better life.

Somehow Marjorie Day had never imagined, even after the torpedo struck, an end like this.

John McGlashan, the *Benares'* second engineer, had seen it, too. One huge swell had knocked the lifeboat forward. *They're done for*, McGlashan thought. *My God . . .* The happy dreams of children, families, escorts, and crew had been ravaged in an instant, swept away in the open water. Searching for some other task, some distraction, McGlashan turned away, to the other end of the deck.

WITHIN MINUTES, BEFORE MARJORIE DAY could collect herself, it was her turn. Her lifeboat, number 10, was being lowered. There were thirteen girls on board—most from Mary Cornish's group. Rosemary Spencer-Davies was here. So were the escort Lillian Towns, the stewardess Annie Ryan, and Ryan's friend Margaret Ladyman. Cornish herself had been left behind.

Lifeboat 10 descended slowly at first. Gently, too. But then the boat swung wildly, out to the sea and back against the hull, beginning what one passenger called its "drunkenly" fall to the water. Marjorie Day seized the two children nearest to her. *God, it's happening to us as well . . .*

Roughly halfway down, Annie Ryan's first aid kit flew from the boat. This was a particularly grave development; Ryan had two injured girls at her side. Some other belongings were lost, but Lifeboat 10's occupants held fast. The boat leveled soon after it touched the water and then it pitched and rocked, like nearly all the others. They had made it to the water, but Marjorie Day had little hope.

We will not last long, she thought. *Not like this.*

Lifeboat 10 bounced in a sea of backwash, perilously near the *Benares'* hull.

AT THE OTHER END OF the ship, Lifeboat 2 made its descent. Laszlo Raskai had helped bring young Colin Richardson and several women aboard, including a ship's nurse who settled in next to Colin. When a sailor extended a hand for Raskai, the Hungarian balked.

"Women and children," he said tersely, though there were already men in the boat.

Angus MacDonald, the ship's carpenter and the sailor in charge at station number 2, gave the order to launch.

Lifeboat 2 made it to the water, but it landed hard, in a fierce swell. Waves seemed to come at the boat from every direction. MacDonald ordered everyone on board to bail water. They did as they were told, thirty-eight people put to work with a pair of pails, but mostly with bare hands. It was a hopeless effort. Within minutes the bow and stern were the only parts of the lifeboat above water.

To Colin Richardson, it seemed they weren't in a boat at all—more like a large, crowded cold bath. Perched there in his homemade life vest, he found himself struggling to keep from floating free of the lifeboat and being carried off by the current.

MARY CORNISH RETURNED AT LAST to her lifeboat station. In less than half an hour she had conducted two tours of the children's quarters, never getting as far as she had hoped. Now she arrived at the ship's rail, and for a moment she thought she was lost. Rosemary Spencer-Davies was gone. Lillian Towns was gone. The other girls were gone. Wasn't this where she was supposed to be?

In a horrible instant she realized the truth. Lifeboat 10 had been launched without her.

"*Miss!*"

Mary Cornish spun around.

"This way, miss!"

Here was Hetherington, the chief officer, still calm, though his voice was firm and his orders came louder now. He directed Mary Cornish to Lifeboat 12, one station away. "It's all right, miss. They've plenty of space there."

The fourth officer, Ronnie Cooper, was holding Lifeboat 12, waiting for it to fill. Cornish went there, dazed and frightened. The scene played in surreal, sickening slow motion.

It's a dream, she thought. *It must be...*

At the lifeboat station she found Bohdan Nagorski, perhaps two dozen Indian crew, a half dozen of the evacuee boys, and their flu-ridden escort, Father Rory O'Sullivan. None of the CORB girls were there. No girls at all. No women, either.

I am safe, Mary Cornish told herself. *There is space in the boat. Soon it will be lowered. The ship is going down* . . . But again she wondered: How could she leave the *Benares*? How could she step into a lifeboat without the children she had sworn to protect?

NOW THERE WAS HORROR ALL around. Virtually every lifeboat was in trouble.

Fall ropes snagged. Lowering gear jammed. Waves of water smashed the listing ship, knocking some lifeboats against the *Benares'* hull and filling others with water. People reached for thwarts and ropes, and for one another. Many lost their grip. The *Benares* travelers—a relatively confident group as they assembled on deck, just minutes before—found themselves suddenly dumb with fear and terror. It was awful—all order gone, and chaos and death in its place—but there was no alternative; the *Benares* would not last long.

"Nothing strikes panic into the heart more surely than the disarray of broken gear and a loose tangle of rope spread over the deck," Frank Mulville would write years later, in his account of the 1970 wreck of the schooner *Integrity* in a winter storm and the subsequent rescue of her passengers. "It is frightening when the order and logic of a boat are torn to pieces, suddenly and irrevocably, and replaced by chaos." Mulville might as well have have been describing the scene on the doomed *City of Benares.*

Lifeboat 5—Bess Walder's and Beth Cummings' boat—began a steady, slow descent, with roughly twenty others on board. The girls had a close look at passengers leaping from the deck to already-launched lifeboats. They saw people hit the sides of boats and others land far off the mark, lost to a raging sea.

Now Lifeboat 5 found trouble all its own. It seemed to go down level, but this was an illusion; in fact the boat was "level" with a badly angled liner. Lifeboat 5 was nearing the water when it lurched, tossing a dozen people to the waves. *Like a bunch of flying fish,* Bess thought, holding desperately to the side. Then Lifeboat 5 was on the water.

Lifeboat 9 began well enough, lowered neatly and evenly until one of its davits jammed. The boat dipped suddenly and then a wave came and smashed its lower end.

Little Johnny Baker was at the high end, the bow, still suspended in air. He held fast for several seconds, and then he was catapulted to the sea. So was his brother, Bobby. The lifeboat lurched forward and back.

Johnny Baker tried, gamely, to tread water, but he was a seven-year-old, and even if he could stay afloat, this sea would soon whisk him away.

A rope ladder was thrown from the deck. Baker saw it come, but he also saw the side of the *City of Benares*, this lovely ship now rearing like an angry stallion, its hull "soaring like a cliff face" not twenty yards from where he splashed and bobbed on the water. There was no way he was going to reach that rope line, he thought, no way he would make it back to deck or to his lifeboat, which hung there, near-horizontal and empty.

But fortune had touched Johnny Baker in one way. He had come to deck with no life jacket, but now he had one, an oversized kapok vest that was keeping him afloat. Suddenly he realized the truth. *It's Bobby's!* His brother had handed him the vest only a few minutes earlier, as they gathered at the lifeboat station. Now, as Johnny Baker thrashed about, his brother's vest was keeping him afloat and keeping him alive. He came finally, somehow, to the rope ladder.

"*You!*"

A sailor was shouting from above.

"You—up this ladder!" he cried. The voice was loud and strong. "Climb up here! Do *not look down*!"

Johnny Baker had no interest in looking down. He took the steps slowly, staring at the ship's side. It seemed forever, but then he was on deck again, and some of the others were, too, soaked refugees of Lifeboat 9. Crewmen were working to winch the boat back to something approximating its launch position.

Within minutes they were boarding again. Someone grabbed Johnny Baker by an arm and practically threw him into the boat. There was urgency now. Baker sat up and huddled with Alan Capel and Peter Short, the "chicken-pox boys." The escort "Padre King" was here, and so were the nurse, Dorothy Smith, and two paying passengers—the screenwriter Wimperis and the businessman William Forsyth.

Bobby Baker was nowhere to be found.

Lifeboat 9 was lowered—again.

Eight-year-old Jack Keeley had been thrown from this same boat—and never made it back. He was still thrashing at the waves, struggling to keep his head above water; his life jacket was not enough with swells this high. Finally Keeley paddled to a rope ladder, grabbed it, took a deep breath, and began climbing. No one had called to him; no one shouted instructions. Jack Keeley had found the rope on his own, and he knew what to do. The wind felt like ice against his soaked clothes. A few rungs up, Keeley discovered a sailor, moving slowly enough so that every few minutes one of his boots came down on Keeley's fingers.

"Relax and let me go!" the sailor hollered to Jack Keeley, when he realized what he had been doing. "You put your hand where my boot has just been—and you'll be all right."

Keeley did as he was told, climbing slowly. He was grateful for the sailor's advice and for the good hold he had on the ladder. Soon he was up and over the deck again.

"Why don't we get you a blanket?" the sailor asked.

Jack Keeley's teeth chattered so hard he could scarcely speak. His lifeboat had gone. He was wearing a thin shirt, a kapok vest, a life jacket, and pajama bottoms.

"Th-th-thank you, sir," he said. He was freezing.

ON BOARD THE STRICKEN LINER, there was still activity below deck, a world away from the lifeboat stations.

Jimmy Proudfoot, the barman, was surveying the aft cabins. He had gone initially at Mary Cornish's request, to be sure that no evacuee girls were stranded below deck. He went as far as he could—blocked as Cornish had been by severe damage along one end of the corridor. On his way back to deck Proudfoot stopped at the lounge.

He was stunned by what he found.

Dozens of people sat there, waiting. It was as though there were no danger, no anxiety at all. Some passengers nursed drinks. Apparently they were still expecting a formal call to the boats.

Dr. Martin Bum was here, still clutching his package of old papers. Marguerite Bech waited in a corner, anxious now, desperate to know what to do with her three children. It was about twenty-five minutes past ten.

The ship's purser, John Anderson, remained effectively in charge of this group, though he had left the lounge and gone in search of direction from senior officers. He wanted some official order to move people to their lifeboat stations.

Anderson found Second Officer Hugh Asher in the hallway, rushing for one of the staircases. He asked whether they were ready on deck to accept more passengers.

"My God!" Asher cried. "Are they still in the *lounge*?"

They were, Anderson told him.

"Direct them to the port-side boats."

Anderson did as he was told. Bum and the other all-too-patient passengers in the lounge headed for the deck.

Anderson's long wait in the *Benares'* lounge—for an order that might never have come—was a bad mistake. It was true—the evacuee children were meant to go first—and it was also true that some senior crewmen should have given the order to move to the boat stations. But officers could be forgiven for neglecting such an announcement, and there is no indication Anderson aggressively sought information about when the passengers should go.

And yet fate would deal with people unevenly, and illogically, on this awful night. Many who made poor or impractical decisions—staying on in the lounge, for example—would be saved; many more who did the "right thing"—reaching their correct lifeboat station, in swift and orderly fashion—would perish nonetheless.

Anderson felt a pang of remorse and rushed back to his office. He opened the ship's safe and withdrew three sealed packages. Two had been left with him by the BBC correspondent, Eric Davis; the third was the screenplay for a film written by Arthur Wimperis. When Anderson returned to the lounge, Davis and Wimperis had gone, but more passengers had arrived. This time the purser told them in no uncertain terms that it was time to leave.

SOME OF THE EARLY DEFECTORS from the lounge had by now made their way to Lifeboat 6. The British parliamentarian, James Baldwin-Webb, was rounding up people there—passengers, evacuee children, British and Indian crew—for a boat that still held vacant places. The Hungarian publisher, Ernest Szekulesz—dour demeanor notwithstanding—found himself filled with admiration for Baldwin-Webb and his take-charge manner. Here was a real general, in a moment when generals were required. Baldwin-Webb had in fact been a major in the First World War; he had fought at the Battle of the Somme. Now he looked tousled and dirty, blood running along one cheek. But he was filled with energy and resolve. People were listening to the man, and following his lead.

As Szekulesz stepped into the boat, Baldwin-Webb was urging Ika Olden to board. The woman was frantic. Her husband, the Berlin lawyer and writer Rudolf Olden, was missing.

Baldwin-Webb took the woman's hand. There were two possibilities, he told her. "Either he is in one of the other boats," he said, "or he'll follow you in a minute."

They both knew there was a third possibility—that Olden was dead somewhere below deck—but this went unsaid. There was no use waiting, Baldwin-Webb told her, adding gently that further delay might prove disastrous for them all. At last Ika Olden relented. She stepped into Lifeboat 6.

It was a horror from the start.

The lifeboat falls slid out of alignment, and the boat dropped into a steep angle, tossing several Indians overboard and sending a heavyset woman crashing into a fellow passenger.

That passenger was fifteen-year-old Tony Quinton. For a moment the woman pinned Quinton in a way that actually made it easier for him to remain in the boat, even as he hung there, dangling over the water. But then he fell, too.

Already badly bruised, Quinton landed on wreckage and other bodies on the sea. For a time he treaded water, frantic. Waves cascaded over him. Tony Quinton was not a strong swimmer. He gulped water.

Well then, the boy thought. *This is it.* Drenched and confused, and nearly choking, he let the swells take him and carry him as he prepared to die. It would happen fast . . .

Then Tony Quinton had a sudden and simple epiphany: *I am wearing a life jacket.* It was an obvious thing, really, but he had forgotten. He felt the jacket's buoyancy and the power of the current. *I'm not done for yet.* Quinton was pulled away from the *City of Benares*, and when the sea lifted him he was afforded a spectacular view of the liner, bent steeply and listing in his direction. Her emergency lights still shone.

A minute passed. Then a single voice rose above the screams and shouts and the roar of the water. Tony Quinton recognized it immediately.

"Mother!"

Letitia Quinton had somehow held her place in Lifeboat 6 as it came crashing down. She sat there now, some twenty to thirty feet from the spot where her son bobbed on the water.

"Come *on!*"

Tony Quinton gathered his strength and made for the boat. He swam the crawl, flailing and making scant progress, but then a gift came, in the form of a heavy wave at his back. He made it easily. *Strange*, he thought—*that she is here, and that the water has brought me to her.* Tony Quinton's mother pulled him in.

Lifeboat 6 was badly waterlogged; only its opposite ends were above water. Roughly a third of the boat's passengers had been lost and all the others were soaked through, having been forced to swim back to the boat. Letitia Quinton noticed that Admiral Mackinnon, the retired Navy hero and commodore of the convoy, was no longer with them.

MARGUERITE BECH HURRIED TO HER lifeboat station. She could not believe they had waited so long. Only fifteen minutes, twenty perhaps, but it had seemed an eternity. And now she was convinced: Those lost minutes had doomed them all. *Why did we not leave earlier, on our own?*

The deck sloped dangerously. Marguerite Bech held Sonia and Derek by the hand and searched for their boat station. Barbara Bech, the fourteen-year-old, followed behind them. An officer directed the family to Lifeboat 4. "There's not many left, ma'am."

She was desperate now. *They've forgotten us.* She was also wracked by second thoughts. Why hadn't she taken her children to the deck? Were her son and daughters any less precious than the child evacuees? *Why did I wait?* They were making their way to the boat when Marguerite Bech tripped and fell. Her jewelry box pitched forward. Rings and pearls and everything else she had in the small container spilled with a clatter on the wet and slanted deck.

Derek Bech stared as his mother scrambled to gather up a ring, a gold watch, and a pearl necklace. Derek was not afraid, still confident even, sure that they would soon be rescued. But he could not help but feel sad and worried to see his mother this way, flustered and kneeling on the wet deck. Someone retrieved Marguerite Bech's locket and brought it to her—whatever else was in the case had been lost. Bech gave the jewels she had recovered to her younger daughter Sonia, who had zippered pockets. The jewelry might stand a better chance with her.

Then they assembled at the station for Lifeboat 4, only to find that the boat had already been lowered. Marguerite Bech, a model of order and calm to this point, stood at the rail, trembling. Derek Bech clutched her hand. Sonia Bech stared at her mother. *What are we to do now?*

Sonia's sister, Barbara, the eldest of the three children, wondered how they had arrived at this moment. They had been so organized, their mother so well prepared, and they had followed every order given. Yet here they were, staring at the sea, their lifeboat already descending to the water.

Derek, the nine-year-old, peered down. *It's a long drop,* he thought.

Then a sailor was at their side, shouting instructions. "Now, listen!" he cried. "Are there any among you who can climb rope?"

Immediately Barbara Bech raised a hand. "I *think* I can, sir."

Marguerite Bech turned to her daughter. "Could you really?"

Barbara was a determined girl, strong and lithe and self-assured. "I think I can," she repeated.

There was no time to deliberate. There were no good alternatives, either. The sailor came to Barbara Bech and helped lift her to the rail, and to a heavy rope ladder.

Over she went. She was an athletic fourteen-year-old and she took the steps easily.

Mustn't let go, she thought. *And mustn't look down*. Before Barbara Bech knew it, there were new voices, people calling to her from the lifeboat.

"That's it, young lady . . ."

"Come on, then . . ."

"In you go!"

"Jump!"

Barbara hung there for a moment, clinging to the ladder, no more than five feet above Lifeboat 4. She wanted to be certain that the boat was really *there*.

Then she let the ladder go. And just like that, she fell in. The boat's passengers caught Barbara Bech, cheered and embraced her. There were thirty-three people in the lifeboat, mostly members of the Indian crew. The man in charge was the *Benares'* carpenter Ewan McVicar. They cleared a place for Barbara and threw a blanket over her legs. She drew her coat collar up, and looked up at the *City of Benares*.

There was Derek, over the rail now, taking his first careful steps down.

The boy had been heartened by what he had seen, his sister taking confidently to the ladder, arriving as quickly and neatly as she had to the boat. Derek Bech came down slowly, pausing at every rung. He was almost certainly the best-dressed boy on board the *Benares*, sporting a school cap and blue blazer. The sailor who had helped Barbara followed a few feet behind.

They were halfway down when a huge swell came, a thundering wall of water that smashed the ship's hull, drenching the sailor and Derek Bech. The boy nearly lost his hold on the ladder.

The wave receded. Derek rubbed his eyes.

"It's all right!" the sailor cried. "Keep to the ladder! All right. Now back up! Back up a step!"

The child froze for a moment. Perhaps ten feet above he could see his mother, staring down, calling to him from the rail. He wanted to follow her advice, but he couldn't make out what she was saying. Was he to go up, as the man said? Or should he keep moving down? He wasn't sure. He felt unsteady now. Unsure, and unsteady.

Turning to the water, Derek saw that Lifeboat 4 had drifted slightly, edged away from the *Benares*. More strong swells were hitting the ship just a few feet below. In that moment Derek and the sailor both knew that Lifeboat 4 was no longer an option.

"Back up, then!" the sailor cried. Derek Bech turned his gaze back to the deck.

Up they went, very slowly now, the sailor and the boy at his heels. When they reached the rail, Derek Bech was hauled over, wet and shivering. *Like a sack of potatoes*, he thought. For a moment he felt relieved, thrilled to see his mother and his sister Sonia, happy to be free of the ladder, and that awful, frightening sea.

But he soon understood that the alternative would be no better. The Bech family had been preoccupied for only two or three minutes with this aborted effort to reach Lifeboat 4, but in that time it had become apparent that the *City of Benares* was near her end.

Far below, Barbara Bech sat cramped in her lifeboat, felt the current carrying them away. The boat was dry and she was almost comfortable there, huddled between two women, the close contact and wool blanket keeping her warm. It had been quite a feat, really, her gymnastic descent to the lifeboat. But Barbara Bech was also mystified, and she was heartbroken. Where was her family? She had left her mother and siblings behind. *What has happened up there?* Barbara wondered, trying to fix her gaze on the sloping decks of the ship. *Where else could they have gone?*

THE LAST OF THE LOUNGE passengers had reached the deck, and found all the lifeboats gone. Only one boat still hung from its davits, and it was already about two-thirds of the way down.

These late arrivals were a well-heeled group: the fashion-industry couple, Phyllis and Henry Digby-Morton; the lumber company executive, Tom Hodgson, and his wife, Margaret; and a woman from Wallasey named Alice Bulmer, traveling with her fourteen-year-old daughter, Pat, and Pat's school friend Dorothy Galliard. By now the *Benares* was beginning her final slide. Seawater sloshed up and down the deck.

Peering down from the rail, Phyllis Digby-Morton could see the lifeboat. It was just about to touch the water. She and her husband understood there was only one thing to do. They consulted with the others, and then one by one they dove. All seven in this group made the plunge, and every one of them landed near the lifeboat. They had barely begun making for the boat when another heavy wave came, sweeping over them all, and turning the lifeboat upside down.

They were fortunate to be near yet another boat, whose occupants saw what had happened and steered as best they could for the new group in the water. This was Lifeboat 2, with Angus MacDonald in charge and young Colin Richardson trying desperately to hold the gunwale and keep above water. The Digby-Mortons managed to reach the boat, and were followed soon after by Margaret Hodgson, thirty years old and a strong swimmer.

Another minute passed before Phyllis Digby-Morton was startled by the sight of a girl splashing wildly, just a few feet off the stern.

"Help! Help!"

This was the teenager Pat Bulmer. With the help of her husband and an Indian sailor, Phyllis Digby-Morton hauled Bulmer in.

They settled in, ice-cold even under blankets, water still coursing over the lifeboat. Margaret Hodgson kept a vigil, staring out from the bow, but it was not long before she and the Digby-Mortons realized the truth: The other three in their party—Tom Hodgson, Dorothy Galliard, and Alice Bulmer—had been lost.

FIVE ELDERLY WOMEN APPEARED ON deck, astonishing Hetherington and the second engineer, John McGlashan. Where had *they* come from?

Distress flares streaked across the sky—trails of amber, red, and white. The moon still threw an occasional glow over the water, as did the powerful emergency lights from the *Benares* herself. It was enough to put the horror below on bright, awful display.

Suddenly there was a new flash of light—blinding, almost. One of the elderly women gasped.

"Look! There's the boat that's come to rescue us!"

The others turned. John McGlashan sighed and shook his head. "That is the U-boat that torpedoed us."

McGlashan was right. The flash had been thrown by U-48's searchlight, whipping across the water.

Heinrich Bleichrodt had lingered. His men were taking turns in the conning tower, watching their victim slip to the sea. U-48's radio operators had picked up the distress signals and heard the name of their prey. Bleichrodt himself had checked for *"City of Benares"* in his Lloyd's Shipping Registry, and learned that he had sunk an eleven-thousand-ton passenger liner.

Marvelous, the wireless operator Rolf Hilse said to himself. They had taken out a very large ship, and then the smaller freighter *Marina* just minutes later.

A very good night, Hilse thought.

JOE HETHERINGTON GUIDED THE FIVE women to the stern, where a half dozen of the ship's twenty-two rafts were lashed to the ship. They were all the *City of Benares* had left. He ordered McGlashan to accompany the women and to begin releasing the rafts. With an Indian sailor's help, Hetherington tossed several buckets to the water, so that lifeboat passengers might have a better chance to bail. Then he retreated to a stairwell. It was time for a final survey of the ship.

Hetherington visited the engineer's quarters and the public rooms, and then he descended toward the engine room. Hetherington felt strangely removed from the chaotic scenes on deck and in the water, the cries and the rain, the battered boats and all those people in distress.

Water had reached the top stairs, slowly drowning the engines. The chief engineer, Alex Macauley, was here, as was the *Benares'* captain, Landles Nicoll, grim-faced and wearing a life jacket.

"You cannot do any more," Nicoll said to Macauley. "You'd better look out for yourself."

"What about you, Captain Nicoll?"

"Save yourself, Mac."

Hetherington concurred—the time had come. He knew it was no good for a ship's officer to survive when her passengers did not, but he also believed there were almost no passengers left to assist. It was madness to remain there, he thought, as the *Benares* met its demise.

"I don't think there's anything more to be done," he said to Nicoll. "There's a raft on the lee side. We can make that all right."

"I think the high side is safer," Nicoll replied.

Hetherington stared at his captain. Landles Nicoll was a wonderful leader, and an unflappable man. Even now he wore a stern look, almost without expression. The journalist and historian Ralph Barker has written that Nicoll probably knew by this moment—if not sooner—that he would go down with his ship. It was, as Barker put it, "not a scenario that any captain of Nicoll's time could contemplate surviving," a "scenario" in which four hundred others, including one hundred children, faced the prospect of awful death in the North Atlantic.

The two men shook hands. The tall, hulking chief officer and the stolid captain. Then Hetherington climbed back to the deck. Nicoll returned to the bridge, where he found the purser, John Anderson. Having canvassed much of the ship, Anderson now gave his last report to the captain.

"All cabins and public rooms are clear. There are still a few passengers on board, but we'll get them away on rafts."

Nicoll thanked him.

"We'd better leave soon," Anderson said.

"It's my duty to stay."

Nicoll shook Anderson's hand, and wished him good luck. Then he returned to the bridge.

CHAPTER 8

S.O.S.

Almost immediately after the torpedo struck, the *City of Benares'* wireless operators, Alistair Fairweather and John Lazarus, were busy in the ship's radio room, tapping out an S.O.S. Fairweather, the *Benares'* first radio officer, may have been the calmest man on board. He drew on a cigarette as he worked out the signal. To his deputy Lazarus and the other men in the room it was as though Fairweather had no idea how grave the situation was; as though he were sending some banal greeting, and not a desperate cry for help.

The distress call was received at the Lyness Shore station in Scotland at six minutes past ten, three minutes after the attack. Twenty-three minutes later, at 10:29, the commander-in-chief at the Office of Western Approaches had the decoded message in his hands.

Western Approaches was run from a nondescript building near the Liverpool waterfront, but its work was vital to the war effort. The office served as the central observation post for a vast rectangular patch of the North Atlantic, reaching several hundred miles west and running north–south from Ireland's northernmost edge to northwest France. Western Approaches logged positions for every convoy, Royal Navy escort, and air patrol in the area, and it was a clearinghouse for all data—however fragmentary—regarding U-boat activity.

The Fairweather-Lazarus message gave the Office of Western Approaches a clear and urgent mission on an otherwise quiet Tuesday night. They were to identify the ship that could reach the *City of Benares*—or her lifeboats—as soon as possible.

. . .

THE OBVIOUS CANDIDATES—TO THE *Benares* passengers at least—were those eighteen commercial vessels that had sailed with the *Benares* in Convoy OB213. Cornish, Nagorski, and the others who had taken an after-coffee stroll on deck had noted the outlines of at least two of the convoy partners, visible despite the darkness and the rain. Probably a half dozen of the OB213 vessels were within a two-mile range at that hour; none of the eighteen were more than ten miles from the scene. Every *Benares* passenger known to have given an opinion on the matter believed the rescue would take only so long as it would take for one of those ships to come to their aid. Bohdan Nagorski assumed that one of those silhouettes he had seen on the water just a half hour before would come soon for them.

What they could not know was that another convoy member—the freighter *Marina*—had been torpedoed just five minutes after the attack on the *Benares*. They were also unaware of the fact that there had never been any real consideration given to deploying these vessels in a rescue mission. The working assumption for all convoys was based on the "fish-in-a-barrel" principle: An attacking U-boat was *expected* to linger, to hunt for precisely such a sympathetic convoy partner. Any who came near would likely be met with torpedoes.

So while it may have shocked the *Benares* passengers, the truth was that at the Office of Western Approaches they were not even considering the *Benares'* partners in Convoy OB213. They were looking for the Royal Navy.

The nearest warship was HMS *Winchelsea*, the destroyer that had led the *Benares'* naval escort before turning nearly twenty-four hours earlier. She was sailing to the east, perhaps two hundred miles from the scene. But *Winchelsea* had new and urgent business. She was operating now as lead escort for the inbound convoy HX71, which was carrying critically needed supplies from Halifax to Britain. Withdrawing the *Winchelsea* would jeopardize not only the ships and crew that made up HX71, but also the supplies they carried. The *Winchelsea*'s departure might actually have endangered even more lives, indirectly, than those that hung in the balance near the stricken *City of Benares*.

The next best option was a Royal Navy ship that was leading an outbound convoy, another collection of vessels heading from Great Britain to Canada. Convoy OB214 was at that moment moving some three hundred miles southeast of the *Benares'* position. The warship in the lead was the destroyer HMS *Hurricane*. And she was considered more "available" than HMS *Winchelsea*.

Within the hour the night officers at Western Approaches had made their decision, and transmitted a brief, dramatic message to HMS *Hurricane*: "Proceed with utmost dispatch to position 56.43 N 21.15 W, where survivors are reported in boats."

Lieutenant Peter Collinson was the *Hurricane*'s surgeon and also her code officer. He was twenty-eight, a physician whose skills had scarcely been tested at sea, given the ship's contingent of largely young and fit sailors. Now Collinson decoded the message and brought it immediately to the ship's captain, Lieutenant Commander Hugh Crofton Simms.

"Utmost dispatch?" Simms remarked, reading aloud to Collinson. The commander assumed that women and children must have been on board a wrecked liner that size—though there was as yet no such specific reference.

It was an awful night, and the weather due west would be worse still. *Hurricane* would have to move quickly on a sea utterly unsuited for speed. Hardly a night for "utmost dispatch."

"We'll do our best," Simms said tersely to Collinson.

CHAPTER 9

Heroes

At latitude 56.43 north, longitude 21.15 west, the elements raged. The winds were back at Force 10, more than fifty miles per hour. Foam-capped swells rocked the lifeboats, and a powerful current tore through a channel between the boats and the *City of Benares'* sinking hull.

Air and water temperatures were not officially recorded, but passengers guessed the former to be roughly fifty degrees Fahrenheit, and average water temperatures for September in this part of the Atlantic were fifty-five degrees. The *City of Benares* had been struck in an extension of the Gulf Stream known as the North Atlantic Drift Current, which kept waters slightly warmer than other parts of the North Atlantic. By comparison, water temperatures around the ill-fated *Titanic* were reported in the high thirties. But fifty-five-degree water and roughly fifty-degree air temperatures were a recipe for hypothermia—particularly if passengers were actually immersed in such waters, or if they lacked blankets or coats or other sources of warmth. The U.S. Coast Guard has estimated that "an average-sized person wearing light clothing and a life jacket may survive up to two and a half to three hours in fifty-degree water." Anyone who has dipped a toe in a fifty-five-degree sea can imagine the effect of sitting in a pool of such water for hours on a cold night.

All twelve of the *Benares'* lifeboats were on the water now, and nearly all were in distress. Ten of the boats had plunged violently to the sea; at least two had overturned. Most of the others had landed wildly enough so that they set off dangerously burdened with seawater. As fast as passengers could bail water, the heaving ocean seemed to throw buckets of it back into their boats. People were wet and cold—in particular the children, many of whom had come to deck wearing only pajamas. Several children were already fighting to stay alive.

The waves swept oil and wreckage from the *Benares* against the lifeboats. The ocean carried people, too; a dead child bobbed here; a survivor struggled there, shouting to be heard over the roar of the waves.

Lights blazed on the water. The radio operators Fairweather and Lazarus, still busy on board the ship, were firing flares from the deck. The moon sent its occasional shimmer, a glow amplified by the phosphorescence of so many life jackets that dotted the water. The entire ghastly tableau was further illuminated by the slanting, giant *Benares* herself, emergency lighting still strong as she began her final slide to the sea.

THIRD OFFICER W. J. LEE'S BOAT —number 11—had been last to launch. It had descended cleanly at first. Lee thought it might actually touch down relatively dry inside, which would have made this boat a success story, an enormous improvement on its predecessors.

Then, close to the water, one of the falls had jammed. One side of the boat dropped, sending more than half its occupants over the side. Fifteen children were thrown to the sea.

The young escort Michael Rennie had held on, and once the boat was free of the *Benares*, Rennie cried out, "There's *children* in the water!" No one seemed to be listening. They were busy caring for themselves or for those next to them in the boat. Then Michael Rennie dove over the side.

Rennie was a powerful swimmer and a strong-minded young man. He was, at twenty-three, the youngest of the CORB escorts, and perhaps the most gifted. Certainly he was the strongest physically. It was Rennie who had run most of the children's games on board the *Benares*; now he was watching those same boys—his partners for tag and lassoing contests and tug-of-war—as they fought a desperate battle to survive.

Rennie's first dive yielded instant success; he powered his way back to the boat, employing a one-armed crawl, a young boy cradled under the other arm. He returned the child safely to Lifeboat 11.

Then Michael Rennie spied another child and dove again. Back he came, lifting the child to waiting arms in the boat.

And then he did it again.

And again.

Rennie repeated the feat a dozen times, a frenzy of diving and swimming that stunned the other passengers. Officer Lee struggled to keep the lifeboat steady and close to Rennie; other adults worked to warm the children Rennie had carried back to the boat. At one point Michael Rennie was warned to slow down. "You'll exhaust yourself," someone said. "We'll need your strength." And in any case, they reminded him, the children wore life jackets; they would presumably be plucked at some point from the sea.

But Rennie believed, correctly, that the current was far too strong to justify such optimism. The boys were like "corks on the water," he said, and he was sure they would be swept far from the boats if he did not reach them soon.

So Michael Rennie dove and dove, delivering more young souls back to Lifeboat 11. It was a harrowing and ultimately spirit-lifting quarter hour. Rennie hauled thirteen of fifteen boys back in this way, wresting them from the water, and from the precipice of death.

OTHER HEROES WERE MINTED ON the waves in the half hour after the *Benares* was hit.

Arthur Dowling, a thirty-three-year-old Australian, followed Rennie's example, diving after children who had been thrown from his lifeboat. Dowling stood a little over six feet tall, and he was an athlete, too, a well-known golf and cricket player from Melbourne. He brought half a dozen boys and girls back to the boat, and refused to reboard until there were no living children to be found in the waters around them.

Laszlo Raskai, the journalist and Colin Richardson's guardian, made his mark as well, swimming with a child clinging to his side, ultimately bringing the boy back to his lifeboat. Soon Raskai was attempting another rescue, diving from the boat as the sea swirled around him. Minutes passed. They called his name, hoarse shouts from the lifeboat, cries drowned by the roar of the water.

In less than a minute they had lost all contact with Raskai, their cries going unanswered and no sign of the man on the waves.

Laszlo Raskai was gone.

In Lifeboat 9, William Forsyth and Arthur Wimperis discovered the boat's container of woolen blankets and began the job of swaddling the children. They ran out before they came to Johnny Baker, so they wrapped the seven-year-old in heavy canvas sheeting instead, and tied the bundle to the thwarts. Baker was terribly uncomfortable, but this arrangement made sense, considering the conditions and also the boy's personality: There would be no chance for him to wriggle free this time.

Marjorie Day's lifeboat came upon a child paddling furiously against the waves. One of the boys in her boat, a thirteen-year-old evacuee from Sunderland named George Crawford, had seen the child first, a head bobbing suddenly to the surface. He saw it was a boy, and then he saw a pair of skinny arms.

Crawford edged forward, leaning out over the water.

The boy was gulping for air. Crawford leaned farther, within inches now. It was not enough. The child splashed madly. Crawford edged out farther still, someone holding his legs as he stretched perilously far, his waist now well beyond the lifeboat's side. Eleanor Wright, also thirteen and also from Sunderland, stared at the gunwale, watching George Crawford reach for the water. She was paralyzed by fear and anticipation. Of course she wanted them to save that boy in the water—but she also feared for George. *I know that boy* . . .

Finally George Crawford corralled the child and pulled him with all his strength.

The boy was Louis Walder, Bess' little brother.

He clambered into the boat, gasping and shivering, and was wrapped instantly in a blanket. Then a heavy wave struck the boat.

George Crawford lost his balance and toppled over headfirst. For a few moments he struggled gamely to stay near the boat, as other passengers reached for him. A man stood to dive, but then another great wave clobbered the lifeboat, knocking the man off his feet and smacking the boat down against the water. The passengers managed to hold on, but they had lost their chance to reach George Crawford. He was washed away.

CHAPTER 10

Farewell

The *City of Benares* was sinking stern first. This lovely eleven-thousand-ton liner was about to disappear. Having watched the sea for four days from the safe vantage points of the *Benares'* deck, passengers now faced the waves from a strange and frightening perspective, gazing up as the swells rose ever higher. The children in particular could not believe that the ship was about to disappear. "Our home!" Paul Shearing said to Derek Capel, at the bow of Lifeboat 12. "She isn't going to last!"

Remarkably, there were still people alive on the *Benares'* deck and at the captain's bridge. Ernest Szekulesz, the dour Hungarian, looking up at the ship from Lifeboat 6, saw a man staring down, his head over the rail. He was tall and heavyset, an older man. Szekulesz squinted in the rain. He thought the man looked familiar. Then he knew. It was James Baldwin-Webb, the member of Parliament.

Baldwin-Webb had been as active as any sailor or officer since the torpedo's strike, directing passengers to lifeboat stations and helping crewmen load and launch the boats. He had refused repeated offers of a place in the lifeboats. Now Szekulesz realized that Baldwin-Webb had never made it off the ship. He appeared to be alone, gazing out at the water, immobile and silent. Szekulesz could not understand why he had stayed behind.

Then Szekulesz saw Baldwin-Webb stepping forward, over the rail. *He is going to jump.*

When Baldwin-Webb landed on the water, it sounded to Szekulesz like the loud slap of an oar. The brave parliamentarian surfaced, and struggled for a minute or so, all the while drifting farther from Lifeboat 6. Tony Quinton thought he saw the man smile for a moment. Then Baldwin-Webb's body lay motionless on the waves; in an instant he was carried away.

THE LAST STRAGGLERS ON BOARD were in search of miracles. Little Jack Keeley, eight years old, had actually climbed *back* to the *City of Benares.*

As he walked gingerly on the slanted deck, he saw sailors tossing rafts off the stern. Keeley tried to move faster but the decline was severe, and the boy slipped and fell. Before he could regain his footing, Jack Keeley found himself sliding down the slippery deck. It was like suction, Keeley thought, a force that pulled and kept him down. He tried to stop, to get a grip or to stand, but it was no use. He tumbled to the sea, losing his boots along the way. The new pair his parents had bought for his journey to Canada.

Jack Keeley cried hard, tears of sadness and fear. Here he was, only his neck above water, barefoot and cold and no lifeboat to go to. And he had no idea where his sister was. Staring back, Keeley saw the steep incline of the deck. To his left he could make out a raft with someone aboard, bobbing on the waves. He hollered as loud as he could, but the raft drifted away.

MARGUERITE BECH WAS WITH DEREK and Sonia at the bow, the high end of the *Benares.* They stood there, aimless, still without a plan. Then a man called out from the lower end of the deck.

"Follow me, ma'am! I know where there are rafts."

The voice, deep and strong, belonged to Eric Davis, the BBC correspondent. Davis was thirty-two, a globetrotter and journalist who had seen his share of adventure before this night. Canada was to have been a stopover, the beginning of a journey that would take him ultimately to Southeast Asia. In the twenty minutes since the U-boat attack, Davis had already guided many women and children to lifeboats, refusing on several occasions to take a place for himself. He had worked with *Benares* crew members, tossing rope ladders to flailing passengers in the water and when possible steering people back to their lifeboats. For a time he had felt like a puppet handler, working the ropes toward the bodies, then leading them over the waves like so many marionettes. Now Eric Davis was looking for a way to save himself and this family he had seen at the higher end of the deck. He knew the rafts were their only chance.

The Bechs moved slowly down toward the stern. It was slippery, the rain heavy now. The *City of Benares* seemed about to go. As they approached Eric Davis, the Bechs heard and felt a loud explosion.

"Probably the boiler," Davis shouted over the rain and the wind.

On they went.

The rafts were fastened by heavy rope to the *Benares'* side. There were twenty-two in all, fat eight-by-eight-foot wood squares, with oil drums lashed underneath as ballast. The rafts were meant primarily to be used by sailors, who would presumably be the last to leave the ship.

At the stern, behind Davis, Chief Officer Joe Hetherington was loosening the rope ties, unleashing the rafts as quickly as he could. Hetherington figured he should free them all before the *Benares* went under. Perhaps some of those poor souls in the water would be fortunate enough to find one. The second engineer, John McGlashan, stood at Hetherington's side.

Perhaps thirty feet away, Eric Davis was trying to save the Bech family. He motioned for them to follow him down the sloping deck. They could all feel the ship slipping strangely beneath their feet. The released rafts floated on waves just beyond the stern. McGlashan made the short leap from the deck and swam hard for one of the rafts. He took hold of it and beckoned to Eric Davis.

Davis saw blood running down McGlashan's forehead, streaming over the rest of his face. *He's been wounded*, Davis thought. The officer was squatting on the raft. Waves rolled over its sides. Then Davis saw McGlashan tie a handkerchief around his head.

Now Davis and the Bech family faced the sea, no good options in their sights. Davis figured he might reach John McGlashan's raft, but that would mean a dive and a difficult swim. It was hard to see how Marguerite Bech and her children would make it. Davis elected instead to find and free another raft himself, and he was beginning this effort when they heard a shout from below. "Down! Down here!"

Marguerite Bech turned her gaze, trying to find the man who was calling them.

"*Down!* Go down the rope! There's a raft at the bottom."

A strong-looking young man sat astride a raft. He wore a sailor's uniform. There was a woman with him. "Down here!" The man was the *Benares'* seventh engineer, Tommy Milligan, a nineteen-year-old from Scotland. The woman was an Australian nurse named Doris Walker. Waves were breaking over and around them. Milligan was beckoning to Marguerite Bech.

Bech was a sensible woman, and she was desperate now. Logic and common sense told her that at this juncture a raft and a strong young sailor were godsends, really. They ought to say a prayer of thanks, and jump to the water. But not long before, Marguerite Bech had sent her eldest child down a ladder, only to lose the girl in a matter of moments to a lifeboat she could hardly see. Just like that, the family had been broken apart.

Where was Barbara now? she wondered. *Where would she end up?*

Then another question, real and awful, crept into her mind: *Shall I never see my daughter again?*

Marguerite Bech resolved that whatever came next, she must never part with her remaining children. Not for an instant. It was her lone wish now— that they endure the night together. Come what may, she had to keep Derek and Sonia close, and she had to find Barbara.

But then her practical nature revealed itself once more, as the liner slid further and that voice cried again from the water. *"Here!"* She nudged Derek and Sonia, telling them they were to go to the man with the raft. *We must live.* So Derek and Sonia jumped without hesitation. They reached the raft relatively easily.

Now Tommy Milligan waved for Marguerite Bech.

"Jump!" he cried. "Come on!"

Jump she did, a short, feet-first leap that left her alongside the raft. A half hour earlier, this would have been a forty-foot plunge. Now, with the ship bent so low to the water, it was a ten-foot drop at most. Milligan pulled Marguerite Bech on board.

It was an untenable situation—five people on a single raft, a tired and drenched pile of human beings holding fast to a few slats of wood. Milligan and Eric Davis understood this, and almost in tandem they slipped off the raft and dropped to the water. If the raft could really hold only four people, then let it be these four, Davis decided. He and Milligan were determined to save them all, two women and two children they did not know.

They began paddling to get clear of the *City of Benares* before the ship went under. They knew that at such close range the suction would almost certainly overwhelm them. As he and Milligan tugged the raft, Eric Davis shouted to Marguerite Bech. They were going to "swim them away," he said. They would drag them as far as possible from the ship.

Eric Davis pulled the raft, and with it the Bech family, crawling and kicking at the water as hard as he could while one arm held the raft. Tommy Milligan pushed from the rear, swimming behind them. Milligan was slender but strong, tall and sinewy, and as he guided the raft, eleven-year-old Sonia Bech found an incongruous thought sailing through her mind: *Gosh, he's handsome.*

Milligan pushed. Davis pulled. The current helped. They drifted away from the *City of Benares.*

Then fate smiled, ever so faintly, on Eric Davis. Here was another raft just a few feet ahead, with a lone man aboard. Having done more than could possibly have been expected of a passenger on a doomed ship, Eric Davis left the others and swam for his own life now. He reached the raft and found the ship's second engineer, John McGlashan, still bleeding from the head but holding steady. McGlashan waved to Davis and pulled him in without saying a word.

AMONG THE LAST CREWMEN TO leave the *City of Benares* was the purser, John Anderson. After his final report to Captain Nicoll, Anderson had left the bridge and found the ship's baker, Archie McAlister.

"Come on," Anderson said, "hurry up or we've had it." Together they hurled themselves to the water. McAlister leaped from the port side and made for what he thought was a lifeboat. He swam well, cutting through the swells, and soon he reached Lifeboat 4, the boat that had taken in Barbara Bech as its last passenger. The passengers pulled McAlister on board.

John Anderson was a weak swimmer by contrast, and his dive had not taken him far. A single wave threw him back within a few feet of the *Benares.* Anderson gave up flailing, and let the water carry him back until his feet felt the hull. He then shoved away, like a mighty push against the wall of some giant swimming pool, using all the leg strength he could muster. He dog-paddled and treaded water for an agonizing time before arriving finally at a raft. When he did, he found that the man stretched across it was the *Benares'* chief officer. *That's a break*, Anderson thought. You could do far worse than find yourself alongside big Joe Hetherington, smart and strong and levelheaded.

Hetherington had dived from the *Benares'* promenade deck, aiming for one of the rafts he had freed just moments before. Now he summoned all his strength and pulled his comrade John Anderson onto the raft.

NOT FAR AWAY, JACK KEELEY had been paddling wildly for several minutes, pleading for help. Time and again he cried out, trying desperately to capture someone's attention, someone in a lifeboat or someone aboard a raft. A small square of driftwood struck his chest and the boy seized hold of it, a flimsy lifeline that carried him along. Keeley spent several minutes this way, clutching the wood plank and riding the waves.

Then he found something else.

A raft, and two men aboard.

Eric Davis had seen the child tossing about on the water, and he and Mc-Glashan tried to maneuver their raft toward him. Davis knew he would need to swing very near if he was to bring the boy on board. A well-timed wave helped; suddenly Jack Keeley was close. Eric Davis seized the moment, pulling Keeley up and over the raft.

Davis and McGlashan slapped the child's back and took him in their arms. Keeley's teeth still chattered, violently now. Here was an eight-year-old boy, thin and wearing soaked-through pajama bottoms, a long-sleeved shirt, two life jackets, and no shoes. And he was choking on seawater. The men cradled him, rubbed his arms and legs hard. Finally Jack Keeley, still gasping, blurted a few words.

"I say! I say—thanks very much!"

Waves battered the raft, keeping them in almost constant peril. They laid Keeley in the middle, the safest and warmest position, though warmth was hardly the right word. After a while Keeley's shivering subsided and he began talking excitedly about his time in the water and the prospects for rescue. Davis talked, too, eager to engage the boy in conversation, trying to keep him lucid and awake. It seemed a good sign that the child still had his wits.

Jack Keeley was worried primarily about his sister. He had last seen Joyce at dinner the night before. She was only six years old. He asked his new companions about her. Was Joyce Keeley all right? "Wasn't she with Auntie Mary?"

Eric Davis had no idea. He had not known Joyce Keeley. And the name "Auntie Mary" meant nothing.

"Your sister'll be fine, I'm sure," he said.

MARGUERITE BECH HAD BEEN EUPHORIC for a moment, a thrill that came once they were all hoisted safely onto the raft. She was relieved to be clear of the *Benares*, to be out of the water, and of course she was elated to have two of her children so near. For their part, Sonia and Derek had kept their spirits up, the boy going so far as to quip that the *Benares'* loss would be "a waste of perfectly good ice cream." But gradually the hopelessness of their circumstance washed over them like one more heavy wave. Marguerite

Bech lay across her son, hoping to shield him from the water, and the cold night. Sonia lay alongside, a once-happy eleven-year-old in pigtails who had gone numb with shock and fear and cold.

This cannot last, Marguerite Bech thought.

THE *CITY OF BENARES* WAS still there, still throwing brilliant light from her decks. To some lifeboat passengers it was almost as though the ship were on fire. It seemed a bizarre show of life from the doomed and all-but-deserted liner.

At about half past ten, there was another small explosion on board. Derek and Sonia Bech looked back and saw the ship standing nearly vertical. Bohdan Nagorski watched from Lifeboat 12, catching a clear view of the deck shimmering in light. The bow lifted. *Like a living thing*, he thought. Joe Hetherington had an uncomfortably close look from the raft he had found only minutes before. He saw the *Benares* rise as if to announce her departure, to command the attention of her former passengers. The liner's lights bathed Hetherington and Anderson and their little raft.

Then the ship went quickly.

In Lifeboat 4, Barbara Bech heard someone say, "She's going..." Thirty-seven heads turned to witness the final moments. People in the boat gasped and cried. Billy Short, perched near Nagorski in Boat 12, saw the lights vanish "like a torch extinguished." Eric Davis watched the *Benares* slide under the waves, heard banging and then a loud groan. That was all. The captain's bridge was the last thing he saw.

And then the *City of Benares* was gone, and with her all that light was gone as well. The ship's departure blackened the night.

Nothing, the chief children's escort, Marjorie Day, thought. *There's nothing left.*

Colin Richardson stared from Lifeboat 2. *Amazing*, he thought. There went the place that had been his home for five days at sea. Vanished. *Just like that.* The boy wondered how deep the water was, how far the ship would plunge before touching the seabed.

Young Derek Bech noticed the silence. All the noises had gone—the shouts, the engine's rumble, the machinery, the clatter of deck chairs and breaking glass—everything that had contributed to the last half hour's awful cacophony. All had fallen silent now. There was only the roar of the waves, his mother's moan, and the occasional faraway cry from some other raft or lifeboat. The ship's flotsam bobbed on the water, deck chairs and broken wood and bodies, too.

FROM HIS CONNING TOWER THE U-48 commander, Heinrich Bleichrodt, watched the *City of Benares* disappear, and he made note of the time. Thirty-four minutes past ten. Rolf Hilse made the following entry in the commander's logbook: "*Der Passagierdampfer sinkt uber das Heck.*" Literally, "The passenger-steamer has sunk by the stern."

The *Benares* had gone under in thirty-one minutes.

CHAPTER 11

Death in the Night

In one respect the *City of Benares* did not go quietly. As the ship went under, she shook the sea, eleven thousand tons of water displaced in a matter of moments. Tall waves rose in her wake, a new roller coaster of water for the already-battered lifeboats.

The first victims were the dozen or so people in Lifeboat 5. The teenage evacuees Bess Walder and Beth Cummings had watched the *Benares* sink from the thwarts of this boat, which had already lost passengers in a rough descent. Those who remained had spent their energies clinging to the gunwales, up to their waists in water and unable to do anything to guide their boat clear of the ship.

Less than a minute after the *City of Benares* disappeared, two enormous swells scored a direct hit on Lifeboat 5, flipping it instantly, and leaving its passengers in a furious fight for their lives.

Well, Bess Walder thought, *here we go. We're done for.*

Bess had seen horrors in the last five minutes that she had never imagined, not in her most fantastic nightmares about war. And yet she had never suspected her own life might be in danger. She and Beth had made it through those dark corridors and up damaged staircases to the *Benares'* deck—and then they had weathered their boat's initial plunge to the water. Bess had believed their harshest tests had passed. Now she felt herself lifted off the water and thrown back down.

Perhaps twenty feet away, Beth Cummings swallowed seawater. The waves were driving her under. It was as though a strong hand were at her back, pressing downward.

I am going to die.

Moments later Beth surfaced. She thrashed at the sea, a fourteen-year-old girl who had never learned to swim, and then she felt the life vest doing its work. She bobbed along, and after a minute or so, something hard knocked her knees and chest. It was a piece of driftwood, swirling in the water. Broken furniture, perhaps. Beth grabbed it and held on.

Her friend Bess had only recently learned to swim. Bernard Walder had taught his daughter that summer. More than that, he had imparted a particular lesson, specific advice about what to do in the event of shipwreck. Now, tossed by the waves, Bess remembered; her father's words came back, dreamlike, ringing in her mind as the water raged mercilessly around her. "You will go down, down, down," he had said, "and when you do, you will then come up, up, up, because people are like corks. And it is when you come up like a cork that you must begin your work, and swim."

Bess understood now. *How strange that he told me those things*, she thought. *And now they're all happening.* She was a "cork," just as her father had put it. She was to waste no energy until she emerged from the sea. Until the "up, up, up" was complete.

So Bess Walder let her arms and legs go limp. For a few seconds that seemed like minutes, she expended no effort, allowing the swells to beat her body down. She just waited to rise, one battered human cork, to the sea's surface.

Soon enough the water surged, rocketing the girl through the surf. She gasped, drawing in the cold air, and began paddling in the waves.

Then Bess saw the boat, bobbing strangely, no more than ten feet away. Almost within reach. Coming nearer, she could see that it was *her* lifeboat. Lifeboat 5. She knew it was hers because it was upside down and because Beth Cummings was there, clinging to its side.

"Hullo, Bess!"

Bess swam for the boat, aiming for the keel. Soon she felt it, sharp, metallic, and cold. Another wave came, throwing her against the lifeboat's side. Bess reached higher, pulling herself so that her upper body at least was above the waves.

There she found a grip, and there she stayed. Hanging on.

"You all right, Bess?"

"All right, yes! You?"

"All right, thanks!"

They held the keel, each girl grateful for the other's company. *Well, Bess is there. I'll be all right,* Beth thought.

The sea raged, the upside-down boat rocked. The girls hung awkwardly from the keel. And yet it seemed a victory.

FOR ALL THE CHAOS OF the launch—the swinging boats, the terrible angles, and the tidal surge brought by the *Benares'* sinking—most of the lifeboats were right side up and well equipped to fight a rough sea. Each boat was double-layered in high-quality timber, heavily built for precisely this sort of moment. "The average double-end lifeboat, in good condition, is exceptionally seaworthy," Phil Richards and John J. Barnigan write in *How to Abandon Ship.* "It is far better-equipped to fight a storm than you are." It would take an exceptional swell to flip a lifeboat—but in the hour after the *Benares* went under, such swells came often. Several of the *Benares* officers were making use of sea anchors—bulky funnel-shaped canvas bags meant to sink beneath the waves and drag the bow of the lifeboat. The effect was to minimize tossing; a sea anchor could keep a lifeboat reasonably steady in rough weather, easing seasickness and buying time for lifeboatmen as they tried to ride out a storm.

The *Benares* lifeboat crews had three options when it came time to propel their craft: Each boat carried a sail, two pairs of oars, and built-in iron handles known as Fleming gear, which were pushed and pulled to turn a propeller under the boat. But in many of the boats the oars had already been lost or broken, the Fleming gear were underwater, and as for the sails, none were raised during this nasty night. The Fleming handles could push the boat only to two to three knots, but they had this advantage: Anyone could use them. They required no expertise—only energy and effort.

Twenty-five-year-old Angus MacDonald was skipper for thirty-eight people in Lifeboat 2, and already they had water at the gunwales. MacDonald was a carpenter by trade, and a reserve in the Merchant Navy. He had always loved the sea—his home was a hundred yards from the water, on the Isle of Lewis—and now he had the sea all around him. MacDonald and his passengers had to struggle to keep above water, or even to stay in the boat, to avoid being carried away. The waves, the water level, and the buoyant life jackets kept conspiring to wrest them from the boat. The smallest passengers especially.

Colin Richardson felt this tug of the waves and struggled to hold fast to the gunwale. It occurred to the boy that he was fighting for the privilege of sitting in a traveling ice bath. Colin thought of his mother, all her exhortations about that red life vest. *You must wear it, night and day.* Colin was grateful now, not just for the vest but also for the gloves he had discovered in one of the pockets. He hadn't known they were there.

The Canadian professor J. P. Day sat behind Richardson. He had made it to Lifeboat 2 after falling from a rope ladder to the sea. A week shy of sixty, Day was one of the oldest people on the water, and he was generally not an athletic man. But he was a fine swimmer—Day had taken his holidays in southern England in part because he loved swimming off the English coast—and he had swum strongly to reach the lifeboat. The lounge stragglers Margaret Hodgson and Pat Bulmer had made it, too, after their own lifeboat capsized. These two were cold, and they were already grieving. Hodgson's husband, Tom, had not resurfaced; nor had Pat's mother, Alice Bulmer, and her friend Dorothy Galliard.

From his perch at the stern Angus MacDonald hollered at his freezing, tired group: "Keep hold to the boat!" Then, moments later: "Keep *moving!*"

He knew the cold water and the icy air would kill them. They would have to generate warmth of their own.

NOT FAR AWAY, THE CHIEF escort, Marjorie Day, was struggling to keep a large contingent of children alive. She was in Lifeboat 10, with thirteen girls from Mary Cornish's group.

What has happened to Mary? Day wondered. Last she knew, Cornish had gone to look for the children. By then the ship had been in a bad way already. *Probably she has died, somewhere below deck,* Day thought. She tried, unsuccessfully, to drive the thought from her mind.

Rosemary Spencer-Davies, the oldest of the evacuee children, was in Day's lifeboat. So were the *Benares'* stewardesses, Annie Ryan and Margaret Ladyman. They were tending to a badly injured girl who had begun to slip in and out of consciousness. They cradled the girl and comforted her sister, who sat nearby, but Ryan and Ladyman found they could do little more to help. Soon after the *Benares* went under, the child died.

Like so many of the lifeboats, number 10 was dangerously waterlogged. Much of its gear—ration boxes, first aid kit, and buckets for bailing—had been lost in the descent. Passengers found themselves throwing out water with cupped hands. The escort Lillian Towns was using her hat. It wasn't much good. Lifeboat 10 plodded along, so heavy it hardly moved on the waves.

After a while they heard a desperate cry from several yards away. It was a call for help, from another boat.

"Lifeboat ahoy! We are swamping! Will you please come over?"

The voice belonged to the *Benares'* second officer, Hugh Asher. His lifeboat, number 3, had taken on so much water that it could no longer hold its passengers.

Soon Asher and two others had come alongside Lifeboat 10. Marjorie Day was thrilled to rescue anyone, and when she saw that the men were sailors, she felt a surge of hope. Three strong seamen might be an enormous help. But Day soon realized how weak Hugh Asher was, and how dejected he looked when he saw the condition of his new lifeboat. Asher had merely transferred from one drenched and battered boat to another.

Marjorie Day was welcoming Asher aboard when she heard a cry from the stewardesses. A second girl had died. The sister of the first.

THE RAIN BEAT DOWN HARDER. The wind stirred again, and the choppy waves became a furious sea. Waves crested in tall peaks, crashing down on the boats, dumping what seemed like huge buckets of heavy water on the passengers. For an hour in the early morning of September 18, every lifeboat seemed in peril, every passenger in danger of being washed away. Water had so overwhelmed some of the lifeboats that to the screenwriter Arthur Wimperis it appeared that people were not *in* the boats at all; they seemed instead to be *sitting* on the waves.

Whenever the sea spray cleared, Bess Walder and Beth Cummings stole glances at each other, and at their upturned boat. About ten people had grabbed hold of their lifeboat, but the girls saw no other faces, only a collection of hands and arms wrapped over the keel, holding on just as they were, only from the opposite side. For a while Beth Cummings fixed her gaze upon one pair of hands, bony yet elegant, ten slim fingers only a few feet away. An older woman, Beth thought. She had no idea who the woman was, but her eyes were drawn to the jewels—one diamond ring in particular—small and dazzling and utterly out of place, it seemed, a bizarre glimmer of beauty amid the horror and the storm.

Mostly the two girls stared at each other. Occasionally they cried out—

"Hang on!" and "Help's coming!"—but more often than not it was impossible to hear. Nearly every cry was muted by the ocean's roar. There were no signs of help, only chaos and this boat, wrong side up, a few pairs of hands gripping its keel in the dark and cold Atlantic.

FROM LIFEBOAT 6, TONY QUINTON stared out at the water, counting the other boats. It provided something to do, an activity for the mind that involved neither death nor loss. Quinton tallied nine boats, maybe ten. He could not be certain. Then he counted the passengers in his own lifeboat. He looked around him, at the bobbing, bouncing figures. There were twenty-two other people on board.

Szekulesz was there, the inveterate grumbler, at this moment complaining about how little help they were getting from a half dozen Indians in the boat. Monika Lanyi—daughter of the writer Thomas Mann—was crying, grieving for her husband. There was a man near Quinton with a Yorkshire accent, wearing an elegant tweed suit, with a cap and pipe. Tony Quinton thought the man appeared remarkably collected, and that he bore a resemblance to the essayist J. B. Priestley. So he gave the man that nickname. "Priestley" he would be.

Quinton invented names for others in his boat. He eyed a tall and vigorous-looking Indian sailor and named him "Gunga Din"; a more solemn Indian would be called "Basil Rathbone," for the "aristocratic sneer" Quinton detected in the man's look. He kept these names to himself.*

Taking this quiet measure of his fellow passengers, Tony Quinton had one overriding impression: His mother stood out, a wonder and a model of good sense and stoicism. Letitia Quinton never complained during a long and awful night on the unforgiving sea.

In Lifeboat 2, passengers and sailors kept up a near-constant bailing, but young Colin Richardson still found himself waist-deep in water. He had to stand when a wave came, to avoid being swept clear of the boat. During the first hours, as they maneuvered slowly from the scene, the ocean smashed Lifeboat 2 time and again. Passengers shifted their weight, rocking the boat purposely, trying to throw excess water overboard. But the merciless Atlantic kept pouring in. At times the sea reached Colin Richardson's chest.

---

*Tony Quinton is to be commended for identifying the Indians, if only with these invented names. Much of the literature about the attack and sinking of the *City of Benares* omits full names of the Indian crew, though there were heroes among them and they certainly bore their share of the tragedy.

Still the boy kept his cheer, on into the blackest part of night. His fellow passengers thought Colin Richardson had the physical and mental stamina of a veteran seaman.

Across this dismal patch of ocean, well past midnight now, the lifeboat passengers battled as best they could. Nearly all the passengers believed they needed only to last a few hours in the boats; surely a convoy partner or warship would be there soon. Ken Sparks rallied the other boys in his boat for a chorus of "Roll Out the Barrel," his favorite song. Wimperis and Forsyth tried valiantly to keep another group of children warm, embracing and massaging them whenever possible. As night deepened, so did the predicament of all these cold and wet refugees of the *City of Benares*. Already some were dying of exposure. They needed a miracle, and—watching the storm pour forth seemingly limitless rain and send gale-force winds against the boats—they believed they needed it soon.

ALL THROUGH THE NIGHT BETH and Bess subsisted on adrenaline, a rush that seemed to shut out the cold, fatigue, and physical pain that grew as the hours passed. Every now and then a fresh blast of cold air would come, whipping their faces like so many bits of ice. They were perhaps ten feet apart. By now they knew to wait for a quiet, windless moment before expending the energy needed to holler a message across the water.

"You all right?"

"Yes! You?"

"Yes!"

"Hang on…"

Bess Walder began to wonder which enemy—cold or exhaustion—would take them first.

Bleak as their situation was, they held certain advantages over the other evacuee children. Straddling the overturned boat meant that they were never immersed in water the way so many others had been; there could be no "ice bath" in an upside-down boat. And the effort of holding the keel served at least to keep them alert. It may also have helped keep the blood flowing, and warmed them ever so slightly. At least they were *doing* something. Finally, the girls had on their side the fact that they were both heavyset and strong, stubborn and strong-minded. Several of their companions were weaker, mentally and physically; some had already surrendered. Bess watched in horror and helplessness as a set of fingers slid back, disappearing from view. She saw and heard nothing more. *A life gone*, she thought. *Just like that.*

Bess wanted to cry. She wanted to help the others whose hands were still curled over the keel. That woman with the diamond was still there. Her fingers were blue.

Hope hung like a ghost in the cold air. They were clinging to the top of an overturned lifeboat in the North Atlantic, a gale churning the sea around them. They had no food and no drinking water, and in any event they had no free hand with which to eat or drink. And they were more than six hundred miles from land.

Occasionally the girls shifted their grip, trying always to raise themselves a little higher, to keep their feet above water. Beth had found the rope that girdled the boat; it made for a better hold than the keel itself. When the sea calmed slightly, the girls were able to climb atop the boat's bottom, allowing for some precious moments during which their bodies were entirely free of the cold water.

At one such moment, Bess looked at her friend and mustered a message.

"Someone will come," she said, loudly as she could.

Surely it was so, Beth Cummings thought. Her friend had to be right. *Someone must come.*

But questions raced through their minds. Both girls wondered, *Where are all those other ships?*

Where is the Royal Navy?

Beth glanced at the other side of the boat, for a look at those lovely jeweled fingers.

They were gone.

THE BECHS LAY DOWN ON their raft to rest. Somehow Sonia, the eleven-year-old, had managed to fall asleep. Marguerite Bech still lay draped over nine-year-old Derek, shielding him from the wind and rain. She was riven with anxiety about her oldest child; none of them had any idea where Barbara Bech was. They had watched her descend to a lifeboat, then seen huge swells carry the boat away, pulling Barbara and the others free of the *City of Benares.* It seemed so long ago.

Marguerite Bech could not keep the scene, and the questions, from her mind.

Is Barbara dead in the water, one more child tossed from her boat? Or is she in the warm confines of a rescue ship, somewhere far away?

In fact, neither scenario was accurate. Barbara Bech was at that moment alive, packed snugly on a thwart in Lifeboat 4. Hers was that rare thing on this foul night, a lifeboat in fairly good condition. The seamen McVicar and McAlister had launched the boat relatively neatly, the Fleming gear had worked, and they had even managed to dole out milk, biscuits, and brandy from the boat's storage lockers. Barbara Bech had one of the boat's fifteen blankets across her legs. The tragedy of Lifeboat 4 was that not one of the evacuee children had been directed to the boat, this rare success, where thirty-two adults and Barbara Bech now enjoyed at least a modicum of comfort and warmth.

As they searched for signs of a rescue vessel, Barbara Bech relived the last moments with her family. Again and again she saw Derek climbing back to the deck, their mother peering out over the ship's rail. Barbara could not believe that they were dead, that Sonia was gone. However gloomy that last haunting image was, it was not possible to fathom that they had been lost on the water. *It cannot be.*

Barbara Bech was not a religious girl, but surely, she thought, *If they have died, then I should feel their spirits, floating around us.* She sat there, disconsolate, staring at her fellow passengers and then the black sky. *Where are they?*

In fact, the rest of Barbara Bech's family floated roughly a mile away, struggling terribly but still alive. They continued to hold fast to the raft, though their hands and fingers ached to the bone and waves still crashed over them.

When one of the waves came, Sonia Bech lost her grip. She scrambled back, only to slip again. This time the girl somersaulted off the raft.

Marguerite Bech screamed. The sailor Tommy Milligan reached over the side. Sonia flailed, choking and feeling for the surface. She wondered what God would look like. *I am going to see Him.*

Reaching far over the raft's edge, Tommy Milligan grabbed Sonia and held her above the water in his powerful arms. She coughed, water pouring from her mouth. Then Milligan hauled the girl back onto the raft. There was no time to give thanks, to God or to Tommy Milligan. Marguerite Bech and her two children buried their heads in the slats of the raft, and waited.

BESS WALDER HAD NEVER BEEN awake through an entire night. This one seemed the equivalent of two nights, or three. Her arms ached from the cold, and from the effort spent reaching for the keel.

Wreckage drifted past. Sometimes clumps of wood knocked against their legs. At one point Bess saw a raft idling nearby, and she could make out familiar faces. There was Maud Hillman, their escort, still alive but wearing a vacant look. Then Bess saw two children huddled near Hillman. She recognized them, too: the Spencer siblings, Joan and James. *Little ones*, she thought. She remembered them from the games on the *Benares'* deck. Joan was nine, James five. They were sitting up, but Bess could see that their faces had gone strange—frozen and listless. No expressions at all.

The faces of death, Bess thought. *If they are not dead now, they soon will be.*

On Bess and Beth's upside-down boat, nearly all the hangers-on were gone, save the two girls and two of the Indian crew, four brown arms draped over the other end of the keel. From time to time Bess heard them, loud cries in a language she did not know.

The rain came as sleet now. Bess Walder's spirit dragged dangerously. What was the use? It would be so easy to let go, and drift away . . .

IN THE DEEPEST, DARKEST PATCH of night—some five or six hours now since the attack—the air and sea felt perceptibly colder. If the temperature at sunset had been around fifty degrees Fahrenheit, now it probably hovered closer to forty. When a gust of wind came, it tore at cold and tired faces. Body warmth drained away. Children huddled close, longing for a few consecutive minutes of calm, a chance to warm themselves ever so slightly. Such moments were rare. More than one lifeboat passenger noticed the bizarre pleasure that came when one among them urinated. It warmed the water, however briefly.

In Lifeboat 2 the teenager Pat Bulmer was crying. She had lost her mother, and her friend Dorothy. Phyllis Digby-Morton held the girl close.

"We'll be rescued," she said.

Pat Bulmer looked up.

"On your honor," she asked, "do you believe it?"

Digby-Morton had no idea what she believed. Her mind reeled. People were dying all around them.

"Yes," she said to Bulmer. "Yes, I do."

Colin Richardson sat at the opposite side of the boat, up on the gunwale, still doing whatever possible to remain above water. At some point during the night he had remembered a promise his mother had made. "If the ship is torpedoed," she had said, "the Royal Navy will come for you . . ."

He let the words play in his mind, again and again. They gave him comfort. "The Royal Navy will come . . ."

The sleet fell hard now, pelting the boats. The Indians in Richardson's boat were chattering loudly. Suddenly one of them fell off the side, "dribbling and incoherent." A second soon followed suit. The Indians had come to the lifeboats in their cottons and sandals. Within another half hour four of these men were dead.

Colin Richardson helped Angus MacDonald ease the bodies overboard. Professor Day, the Canadian economist, found himself too weak to help. He held one of the thwarts and watched, and took notice of how Richardson handled this awful, macabre task—an eleven-year-old treating death with dignity and respect, Day thought, and without a trace of fear.

One of the *Benares'* nurses had been helping the Indians, and their deaths sent her into a paroxysm of fear, and then madness.

"Lift my head!" she cried to MacDonald. "I'm going! I'm *going*..."

Angus MacDonald could do nothing. He sat at the opposite end of the boat, bailing water and helping care for other passengers.

It was Colin Richardson who held out his arms, embracing the nurse. The woman twisted in the boy's grasp. *"I'm going..."*

It became difficult to hold her steady, but he managed, cradling her head, keeping it clear of the water. When possible, Colin Richardson caressed the woman's forehead.

"They'll be a boat coming soon, ma'am. It won't be long now."

The nurse moaned. Her head rolled back. Richardson lifted it again and held her near.

"I think I see a light, ma'am. It could be a ship."

In truth Colin Richardson had seen nothing. But he believed the lie might help. After a while he repeated it. "I can see something. Might be a ship, ma'am."

Soon the sleet had turned to hail, and it hammered them. Richardson shielded the woman's face. "It's all right, ma'am."

Professor Day watched all this with reverence, and awe. *If the night has a hero, here he is,* Day thought, this stoic child, so kind and gentle and so unafraid. And so unwilling to waver. *Please God,* Day said to himself. *Don't take this boy...*

"Good-bye," the woman was saying now. "Good-bye. I am dying..."

She lay still in Colin Richardson's arms. The boy wasn't sure what to do. After a few minutes she raised her head once more. "Are the children all right?" she asked.

Dawn's first light was showing itself, a grayish haze on the horizon, when the nurse stiffened and said no more.

"Colin, she's dead," Angus MacDonald said gently. "You must push her overboard now."

The boy glanced down at the figure in his arms. She lay still.

"I can't do it," he said.

"You did it with the others, Colin. You've done all you can for her. It can't be helped. There's just nothing more you can do."

MacDonald assumed the child was too frightened or traumatized to relinquish the body, and he began coaxing him gently. In fact Richardson's refusal had nothing to do with emotion; he was simply too weak to move. His arms had cramped. No matter what the adults said, he could not lift the woman over the side. Those closest to him were of no use either. Finally Angus MacDonald came to help, sloshing from one end of the boat to the other. Together they lifted the woman and laid her on the water.

NOW, AS THE BLACK NIGHT met the dawn, people were dying in nearly every boat.

The chief children's escort, Marjorie Day, turned to one of the *Benares'* sailors and said, "We mustn't let them sleep." She wanted the children to move and to talk, to remain engaged and embrace whomever sat nearby. She knew how exhausted the children were, but she also knew that in these circumstances sleep could prove fatal.

In Day's boat, the stewardesses Annie Ryan and Margaret Ladyman, together with the fifteen-year-old Rosemary Spencer-Davies, massaged the younger children's arms and legs. When necessary they lifted a child to keep him or her above water. For all the efforts, children were slipping from consciousness. Lives were ebbing away.

A lifeboat passed, a small group of survivors who called out to say they had brandy on board. Perhaps it might help the children? There was probably enough, someone said, so that each child on Marjorie Day's lifeboat might have a taste.

They drew alongside and took the bottle. For a short while the drink seemed a lifesaver, warming cold bodies and lifting exhausted spirits. More than one child rose from a trance-like state to a strange and animated conversation. A drop of brandy could of course have a profound effect on small children.

But alcohol of any kind is a dangerous thing in such circumstances, quickly dehydrating the body and dulling the mind. In Lifeboat 10 the spirit's powers faded rapidly, and so did the children's. To Marjorie Day it seemed that the children were merely drifting to sleep. Some were smiling. But they were not asleep. They were dying quietly, within minutes of one another. In the end, if the brandy did nothing else, it eased death's arrival for a dozen children who left the world in that cold and dreadful hour. At least one adult in the boat wondered whether the brandy had killed them.

As dawn approached, Rosemary Spencer-Davies and Eleanor Wright were the only children alive in Lifeboat 10. Spencer-Davies had lost her brother, John, had seen all her work with the boat's other children do nothing more than extend life by a few hours. All through the night Wright, thirteen, had brimmed with optimism. "Don't worry," she had said, over and over. "The British Navy won't let us down . . ." Now she and Spencer-Davies huddled on either side of Marjorie Day, hoping that daybreak would reveal a British warship and hasten their salvation.

Breaking a spell of quiet, Ladyman turned suddenly to Annie Ryan.

"You'll contact my sons, in the RAF?"

Ryan said she would, and repeated the promise she had made several hours before.

Moments later Margaret Ladyman breathed her last, as though her colleague's pledge had made death possible.

Three of the Indians went next, decidedly *not* in peace. They writhed and cried out, loud and wrenching appeals for help. There was nothing anyone could do.

In Michael Rennie's lifeboat, the *Benares'* barman Jimmy Proudfoot held Rex Thorne, thirteen years old and failing. Thorne was bone cold. His mind was drifting. In lucid moments he grieved for his sister Marion, a seven-year-old who had been in Sybil Gilliat-Smith's boat, number 8, one of the first to be thrown wildly from its davits. Rennie tried to rally Thorne and the rest of the group in song, but he found few takers. The boys were weak and shivering. Rex Thorne's teeth chattered so hard he could not have sung even if he had been so inclined.

Proudfoot embraced the boy, tried to warm him, and told him not to worry. He drew the whiskey bottle he had taken from the *Benares'* bar and gave Thorne a drink. Then he passed the bottle.

The alcohol helped at first, as it had in Marjorie Day's boat. It revived the children. *Marvelous*, Rex Thorne thought. He had never tasted spirits before. The whiskey gave Rennie a much-needed lift as well. He was cradling a small boy in each arm, two of the children he had rescued from the water.

They talked for a while. Rennie said he thought the dawn would come soon. The bottle was passed again. Rennie and Proudfoot assured the boys that a ship would find them once daylight revealed their location.

But then, not long after everyone had taken his sips of whiskey, Proudfoot looked at Michael Rennie and was startled by the change. The young man's head nodded and his eyes had gone glassy. He still held the boys, but he seemed on the verge of sleep. Or worse.

Martin Bum, the doctor, asked Rennie if he was all right.

Rennie nodded. But then he said, almost under his breath, "I am afraid I can't do much more."

The seas had calmed a little. They sat silent for a time, small waves lapping at the lifeboat. Rennie looked at the German doctor and said, "I'm so glad to have you in the boat."

Suddenly Martin Bum cried out, *"Look!"*

While they had been staring at Rennie, one of the boys had lost his grip and actually floated free of the boat. He was barely alive. Bum tried to stand, but found he could not move his legs. He shook Michael Rennie, but Rennie's strength, on such magnificent display some hours before, had been sapped completely. Bum looked at the Indians, a half dozen of them sitting like statues in the boat, the water at their waists. Then Dr. Bum threw his precious package to the water, the papers he had guarded so zealously through the night. He summoned a reserve of strength, and leaned out over the side. He would need free hands to reach the child.

Martin Bum managed to grab the boy's shirttail and drag him back to the boat. With Proudfoot's help he pulled him over the gunwale, and then both men held the boy close. He was still alive.

But within minutes, more waves came. Twice more, Bum and Proudfoot lunged to pull boys back on board. And then death arrived in Lifeboat 11.

Two boys died first. One was the youngster Bum had just rescued. Not long after, an Indian crewman fell over the side. The surf carried him away.

The cruelest blow came next.

Michael Rennie had recovered, it seemed. If anyone was to last in Lifeboat 11, if just one life would be spared, surely it would be Michael Rennie's. This strong and intelligent young man had been a powerful presence on board the *Benares* and then a stalwart in Lifeboat 11, a brave soldier through this terrible night. In the last hour he had begun to speak again, using clipped and rapid-fire language, even before Jimmy Proudfoot had shared his whiskey. Then, quite suddenly, his fast talk had slurred to nonsense. His expression had turned trance-like.

Perhaps a half hour before the dawn, Michael Rennie died.

The surviving boys in Lifeboat 11 had been stoic to this point, brave and optimistic to a fault. The loss of this courageous young man crushed them, cast doom over those who remained in the boat, and by all accounts it shredded their own resolve. "No!" Louis Walder, ten, cried out. "*No!*" Children who still had their senses broke down and cried. They had loved Michael Rennie—even before he had risked his life to save theirs.

Now they would have to manage without him.

TONY QUINTON FOUND IT STRANGE that death could come so easily and gently, in such terrible circumstances. He had known death in a different guise, seen the ravages of tuberculosis take his father at the tender age of thirty-six—but this was something altogether different. Quinton watched a young boy slump quietly, then a second who shut his eyes and rested on the other child's shoulder. They lay there awhile, across from Quinton and his mother. Then a *Benares* sailor, perhaps watching Tony Quinton's expression, leaned close and told him the children were dead. Quinton stared across at the boys. *It's as though they're just going to sleep . . .*

A few feet away, Florence Croasdaile had slipped into madness. She was sailing to America to be with family while she waited for news of her husband, the soldier and prisoner of the Germans. Now, as the new morning broke, Croasdaile had become convinced that her children had been taken from her, and she moaned and mourned their loss.

In a sense Croasdaile was correct. One of the *Benares*' sailors was bouncing two-year-old Lawrence Croasdaile on his knee, while Ernest Szekulesz did the same with the girl, nine-year-old Patricia. They *had* taken the children, but they had done so because they believed it was the only way they might save Florence Croasdaile herself. They did not want her to know that both her children were dead.

TWO MEN IN LIFEBOAT 9 had battled valiantly to keep fellow passengers alive. The screenwriter Arthur Wimperis and businessman William Forsyth had bailed water, sung to the children, and rubbed their cold limbs, but now, in the night's final hour, Forsyth found himself fighting back tears. He thought he could not bear any more horror, or any further loss. He had seen so much death in so short a time.

His fellow passengers had begun to die in the heart of the night, at perhaps two or three in the morning. Forsyth had felt it necessary to count, taking a grim tally as one after another child and adult passenger wilted and left the world. It was an awful business, he knew, but Forsyth could not help himself. He wanted to *know*, and he did not want any death to go unnoticed or unrecorded. By now he believed that sixteen people in the lifeboat had died.

Harry Peard, the strong-willed, wiry naval gunner, had dived from this boat to rescue a child and not been seen since. The children's escort William King—"Padre King"—was gone. Several Indian crewmen had died. And the boat had lost at least a half dozen children. Exposure had killed them all. Forsyth was not a religious man, but in the night he assumed Reverend King's job, ministering to the dead and delivering bodies to the sea. He would kneel beside each boy and recite a few words of a burial prayer, as much as he could remember. Then, with Arthur Wimperis's help, he would ease the child gently over the side.

Mostly Forsyth spent his night fighting a rising fury, as he bade solemn farewells to children, eleven by his own count. Eleven young boys he had never really known.

LITTLE JOAN AND JAMES SPENCER died on a raft in the arms of their escort Maud Hillman. They were already gone when a wave wrested them from Hillman's grasp. Hillman herself was disoriented and exhausted. When the Spencer children slipped away, Hillman reached for them, only to be washed off the raft herself.

As it happened, the raft carrying Chief Officer Joe Hetherington and the purser, John Anderson, was close at hand. They had picked up a German woman a few hours before, and the three of them lay huddled together, waiting desperately for daybreak.

Now the two sailors found Maud Hillman, barely conscious and barely alive, and they raised her from the water.

Hetherington knew the woman would not last long. Together he and Anderson shook and rubbed Hillman's arms and legs, tried everything they could to warm her body. In the meantime Hetherington kept watch for a light, for ships or for other boats. *We need someone to come,* he said to himself. *And we need them soon.*

But Joe Hetherington saw no lights. No ships. Only an occasional lifeboat, drifting in the distance. And the weird gray light of the approaching dawn.

Wind and high swells still battered their raft. *Madness,* John Anderson thought. *This cannot last.* He and Hetherington kept Maud Hillman and the German woman in the middle, sandwiched between them. They did not speak much, though at one point the German, a refugee of the *Reich,* sat up and challenged the chief officer.

"Where is your famous British Navy?" she asked Hetherington. "Why haven't they come to rescue us?"

Hetherington looked away. It seemed a strange time for such a statement, and strange to hear it from the lips of a citizen of Germany. In this cold and horrible hour, the question stung Joe Hetherington.

"What happened to your *German* Navy?" he snapped. "Why didn't they obey the code of the sea? And care for survivors?"

BESS WALDER AND BETH CUMMINGS had stopped speaking. It was not just that the effort tired them; they had also discovered that an open mouth tended to fill rapidly with seawater. Time and again their overturned boat rose high, lifting both girls and both Indian men with them, and jolting them all back against the lifeboat's underbelly. The life jackets served as a kind of padding, but their bodies took a battering every time.

All that sustained these two teenage girls now was the understanding that if one were to abandon the boat, her departure would kill the other. They *knew* this. *If I go, she'll go,* Beth Cummings thought. Beth had her mother to think of as well. Anne Cummings was a widow with two sons already at war. *I have to live,* Beth thought. *Mustn't leave my mum alone.* But mostly she looked at her friend Bess, not ten feet away and fading fast. Each girl felt responsible for two lives, not one.

The Indians mumbled loudly. To Bess Walder it seemed like prayer.

Bess prayed, too, for herself and for her friend, for her brother, Louis, and for her parents, for all the beaten and bedraggled souls she could not see, the children especially, struggling somewhere on the water. *What's happened to all those people?*

If only we can last the night, Bess thought, *then we shall be found, and rescued.*

In the faint gray light, she saw Beth's bruised and exhausted face. With great effort Bess pulled herself up and mouthed the words, one more exhortation: *"Hang on..."*

CHAPTER 12

First Light

At last, a welcome sight: not a boat, or a ship—just a faint ribbon of light. The first real glimmer of dawn. Pitiful though it was, cold and gray and flecked with sleet, here was a beginning.

A new day.

For the *Benares* survivors it meant the lifting of an awful darkness, a curtain of horror that had draped itself over every raft and lifeboat on the water. Dawn offered at least momentary solace to roughly one hundred fifty withered souls, men and women and children who had lasted the night. Some were unconscious, some lucid, some had ice chunks in their hair, and some were wrapped warmly and almost comfortably in blankets or canvas sheets.

Whatever their disposition, each one of these people understood a basic fact: They should have died in a night such as that. That they were alive as the light of the day showed itself over the water was remarkable. It meant they had a chance.

We shall be warm now, eight-year-old Jack Keeley thought. *Soon the sun will come. And then the rescue ships will find us.* Colin Richardson watched the horizon and said to himself, *We shall live.* Marjorie Day, chief children's escort and a frostbitten passenger in Lifeboat 10, was reassured by the sight of other lifeboats, distant but visible. It brought the comfort of shared experience.

They felt they had won a small victory, a battle with the longest, most terrible night they had ever known.

.   .   .

"VICTORY" WAS SHORT-LIVED. AS the dawn rose, and that ribbon of light stretched the length of the horizon, a fuller measure of the disaster became apparent. The scene stunned the survivors.

A ship carrying more than four hundred people had left twelve lifeboats, about ten rafts, and a mess of wreckage on the water. The boats had scattered, drifted apart. Many carried corpses. Three of the lifeboats were upside down. Soon after first light, the weather worsened. Sleet turned to hail yet again, and the hail came hard, *pop-pop*ping on the boats.

If the vast and barren sea brought gloom, so too did scenes in the lifeboats themselves. Passengers examined their immediate surroundings and saw haggard, wind-beaten faces, shivering children, and strange, vacant expressions. Wood planks and deck chairs bobbed on the water around them. In many places the sea was slick with oil. Bodies, young and old, floated past. The old rocking horse from the *Benares'* playroom nodded gently on the waves.

They had waited so eagerly for daylight, but when the day's full light came it revealed only the grim-looking sea, still-choppy waters under a slate-gray sky. There were no planes in the air, no ships on the water. A gull hovered here and there, leading some to think—incorrectly—that they were close to land. The noises of the night had subsided, and now there was only the lapping of the water, and the occasional whimper of a survivor.

The *City of Benares* seemed a distant dream, a lovely home they had left long ago.

BESS WALDER WATCHED THE YELLOW streaks of light cut across the eastern sky. She lifted her head from the keel to look for the other boats, but all she saw was water and sky and what looked like bits of furniture floating past. Bess and Beth still clutched the keel of Lifeboat 5. They were grateful to be alive.

The girls had left the *Benares* with roughly twenty others in their boat, including eight of the evacuee children. Now only Beth and Bess and the two Indian sailors remained. One of the Indians was delirious, laughing loudly. The other lay sprawled across the rudder. Bess saw the second man's contorted face, wide eyes frozen in a frightened look.

Then she realized that he was dead.

The girls could hardly speak. Their throats were parched, lips swollen, sea salt

Eddie Grimmond (*far right*) and Hannah Grimmond (*second from left*)
stand in the rubble of their home on Lilford Road in London
after a bombing on September 9, 1940.

Front row: Bess Walder, Louis Walder, and Beth Cummings

Peter and Billy Short

Alan and Derek Capel

Rosemary Spencer-Davies

John Spencer-Davies

Fred Steels

John and Bobby Baker

Ken Sparks

Barbara, Sonia, and Derek Bech

Colin Ryder Richardson

Girls' escort
Mary Cornish

Boys' escort
Michael Rennie

The SS *City of Benares*

Landles Nicoll
Captain, SS *City of Benares*

John Anderson
Purser, SS *City of Benares*

Joe Hetherington
Chief Officer, SS *City of Benares*

Heinrich Bleichrodt
Commander, U-48

caked around their eyes. The cold seemed to have fastened their hands to the keel. Their legs had been thumped incessantly against the boat. Waves still worked them over, the salt stinging their cuts and sores. Bess assumed death was near.

ACROSS A WIDE PATCH OF water near the *Benares'* resting place, dawn was a time to count the living and the dead. And to nudge corpses to the sea.

The ship's carpenter, Angus MacDonald, had fourteen people still breathing in his boat. He had begun the night with thirty-eight. Soon after daybreak a young man lost his mind, shouting wildly at the others. He threatened to throw people overboard. MacDonald did not know the man's name. He tried to calm him but it was no use. After a final shower of cries and epithets, the young man threw himself to the sea.

Colin Richardson was still alive in this boat, his blond hair matted down, his scarlet vest a spot of brightness in the gray morning. The boy had lost feeling in both legs. Peering up over the gunwales Colin could make out a few other lifeboats, though not well enough to recognize their occupants, or even to know whether they were alive or dead.

MacDonald rummaged in the two feet or so of water to find a food locker under the boat's thwarts. He opened the locker—cutting his hand in the process—and passed biscuits, canned beef, and rum around the boat. Margaret Hodgson felt the spirit warm her. Pat Bulmer, fourteen, was terribly hungry, but when the food came she found her lips and tongue too swollen to take it. The professor J. P. Day had fastened his leg to one of the iron Fleming gear handles, to keep from being washed away, and at a crewman's urging Pat Bulmer had done the same. The tactic had worked—Day and Bulmer were still in the boat—but the skin around Bulmer's knee had been scraped nearly to the bone.

The morning was also a time to consider strategies for survival. For a time they sang songs—"A Long Way to Tipperary," for starters—but their voices were weak. Colin Richardson listened while the others sang, concentrating all the while on one thing: *I must not sleep.* He had seen too many people close their eyes during the night, seen their heads droop, and watched them slip quietly from sleep to death.

In Lifeboat 7, the retired Navy man Richard Deane had gathered up fat planks of driftwood from the water and laid them across one end of the boat. Passengers could sit atop the wood, providing themselves a perch well above water, or they could crouch beneath the planks when a heavy swell came. This simple structure had probably kept at least a few of the boat's passengers alive.

Deane was angry with himself for having had the idea only in mid-morning, several hours after his wife had succumbed. They had buried Dorothy Deane at sea, just as daylight came.

When dawn came to Lifeboat 6, the Hungarian Ernest Szekulesz still cradled Florence Croasdaile's dead children, Patricia and Lawrence, afraid of what their mother would do if she knew they were gone. Szekulesz pretended to feed the children, caressing them now and then. "Here you are, young lady . . ."

For a time this well-intentioned ruse had the desired effect, but ultimately it made no difference. Florence Croasdaile never knew what had become of her children; by mid-morning she was dead as well.

From the beginning Szekulesz had forecast gloom, much to the annoyance of Letitia Quinton, who sat nearby and wished the Hungarian man would keep quiet. *We've pessimism enough*, she thought, but as she watched Szekulesz now, up to his chest in water and holding two dead children in his arms, she felt a rush of pity and admiration for the man and realized he may have been right. Gloom seemed the correct forecast.

On Joe Hetherington's raft they were using the escort Maud Hillman as a shield. Hetherington had rescued her during the night, pulled her from the raging sea, but Hillman had breathed her last just before dawn. Now her corpse offered shelter from the wind and hail.

They lay there freezing—Hetherington; the purser, John Anderson; and the German woman, who had grown increasingly irritable in the night. They did not know her name. Hetherington and Anderson had worked hard to keep her on the raft, and they had talked openly about the effort this entailed for a woman who could be so unpleasant in return. Several times during the night she had chastised them. And the Royal Navy, too.

Awful as it was, the thought had occurred to both men: *We could just let her go . . .*

Hetherington eyed the woman's tartan scarf. It was the only bright-colored object on the raft. *Might make a good signal*, Hetherington thought, and in a ghoulish joke he whispered to Anderson, "She's worth saving for that scarf alone."

At any rate, by daybreak the woman had mellowed. As they watched the dawn, she suggested quietly to Anderson that they meet the morning with prayer.

"Me?" the purser replied wearily. "I wouldn't know what to pray about."

So the woman began alone, in a heavy accent. "Our father, who art in heaven, hallowed be thy name. Thy kingdom come . . ." The men joined in. They were reduced to whispers by the time the short prayer was finished. "Amen."

Suddenly Joe Hetherington rose to his knees, unsteady on the raft. He pointed at the water.

"A *ship*!"

Anderson looked up. The two men held each other, trying to keep steady, and together they stared at the ocean.

The German woman frowned. "Where?"

"I saw a *ship*!" Hetherington cried again. He waved a handkerchief at the sky. But there was nothing. Only the bleak, blank horizon.

"You're seeing things," said Anderson.

THE HAIL AND SLEET PASSED, and in late morning the sun appeared. The sea was considerably calmer now, and those who could summon the strength made forays into the lifeboat lockers. The lockers had been drenched, but most of the stocks they held had been well protected. The *Benares* survivors found cans of condensed milk, corned beef, ship's biscuits, and sardines. There were flasks of rum, jugs of water, and a stash of gray blankets.

In Lifeboat 11, several lockers were underwater. Third Officer W. J. Lee found that the blankets were soaked through. He laid them out along the gunwales. Lee had better luck with a tarpaulin, which he draped over one end of the boat, where the German doctor Martin Bum was trying desperately to keep the boat's surviving boys warm. He would do whatever was needed, he told himself, to be sure they did not die.

Once the storm abated, and the waves weakened, Lee and Jimmy Proudfoot managed to raise a wooden container, only to find that it could not be opened. Lee used a hammer from the supply box to smash open the container, which was filled with cans of condensed milk. Improvising further, Lee poked holes in the milk cans by pounding them against the nails that protruded from the box. Lee and Bum passed the cans around the boat; Lifeboat 11's passengers enjoyed some sweet milk.

Bum still had two boys huddled close. After a while Officer Lee looked at the doctor and nodded gently. Finally he felt it necessary to tell Bum that both boys were dead.

Martin Bum was devastated. With these two gone, he and Lee counted seven children lost, and seven Indian crew as well. Fourteen deaths, in a lifeboat that had been launched with twenty-one people aboard.

Thirteen-year-old Rex Thorne was still alive, though he said nothing and stared in the same vague, slightly frightening ways the other boys had, before they took their last breaths.

Terrible questions hung over the boat, and they wracked Officer Lee's tired mind:

How long can we last?

How many shall we lose?

Will someone come for us?

And if so, when?

THE RAFTS HELD SUPPLIES, TOO, one small watertight locker for each. Eric Davis dug into his stash and prepared breakfast for himself and his two passengers, John McGlashan and the eight-year-old evacuee Jack Keeley. They would share biscuits, condensed milk, and a few sliced peaches from a can. *If only we could know how long we will have to last,* Davis thought. *It might ease the mind.* As it was they had no idea. When would their rescuers come?

As he passed this small meal around, Davis noticed that McGlashan was unresponsive. He still had a strip of towel wrapped around his forehead, bloodied and matted down. This thickly built, athletic man was silent now and barely conscious.

By contrast, little Jack Keeley remained his garrulous self. He asked Davis whether McGlashan was all right; Davis nodded. He thanked Davis loudly and profusely for the food and drink; the milk in particular had gone down well. Then Keeley began asking questions.

"Which way are we going?"

"That way," said Davis, nodding to the east. "The wind is blowing us that way."

"Yes, but which way is that? Are we still going to Canada?" Keeley strained to look. "Or are we on our way back to England?"

He's got a lot on his mind, this boy, Eric Davis thought. *Talkative, too.* Davis took a moment before answering.

"Back to England, I should think."

. . .

LATE MORNING FOUND BESS WALDER and Beth Cummings still alive, still holding on, numb now from waist to toe. Each girl alternated her grip, holding the keel or the rope that ran around the boat's exterior. They spoke sparingly. "Here's a wave!" one of them would cry softly.

"Here's another!"

"Look out!"

"Hang on!"

At one point the girls saw an object approaching, something larger than the other flotsam on the water. As it came nearer, they realized it was a lifeboat. A boat with empty places. A boat floating right side up. It was no more than thirty yards away.

Is it real? Bess wondered. *If so, then it is our best hope. Our only hope, perhaps.* A lifeboat, dry and right side up, while no guarantee of rescue, would offer at least a place to sit and wait, and warm themselves. There might be food and water, too.

Bess tried calling out to her friend. No sound came. The girls' throats were coated with salt. Their voices had been ravaged by the elements, and by so much hollering in the night.

The lifeboat they had seen was number 4, with the *Benares'* carpenter Ewan McVicar in charge. McVicar and fellow crewman Archie McAlister saw the girls, tethered, it seemed, to the keel. McVicar got his boat's Fleming gear working and tried hard to reach Bess and Beth, and their upturned boat.

Crouched low in Lifeboat 4, fourteen-year-old Barbara Bech watched and saw the overturned lifeboat, saw that people were hugging its sides. As they drew near she had a better look at the two girls—*alive,* she thought, but barely moving. *Look at them, hanging like that on that upside-down boat.*

How could they possibly be alive? Barbara Bech wondered. *Have they been like that all night?* It had been hard enough in an upright lifeboat. *How could they hold on so long, in such cold and rough waters?* It made Barbara believe her mother and siblings must be alive, too. *If these two can survive . . .*

Suddenly the seas rose yet again. The harder McVicar and McAlister worked the Fleming handles, it seemed, the heavier the swells beat back at them. They worried about capsizing. For a brief spell they were forced to abandon the Fleming gear and lie low in the boat.

A minute passed. Soon Bess and Beth realized, dumbfounded, that the lifeboat was retreating. It would not reach them, at least not now. The sea was tossing their boat, and the other one, too. Bess saw the shape receding, fading quickly, until their saviors were just another speck dancing on the waves.

No use crying, Beth Cummings thought. *There will be other boats. And I haven't the energy to cry, anyhow . . .*

Odd thoughts crowded Beth's mind. It occurred to her that at that very moment classes at her Liverpool school were in session. She felt a strange sensation, dreamlike, as though she were there, perched at her desk. Beth imagined she heard her teacher; she closed her eyes and summoned the smell of the classroom.

Her friend was daydreaming, too. Bess Walder had her mind fixed on Louis, her little brother. He was dead, she thought, somewhere in these waters. Bess imagined a return to her home in Kentish Town, and Louis not there with her. *What'll I tell Mum and Dad?* The question brought fresh torment, worse than any physical pain.

Louis Walder was ten years old. Their parents had implored Bess to watch over him. *Poor Mum and Dad*, thought Bess. *They've lost their only son.*

The awful thought redoubled her resolve. Her parents would need her now, more than ever. *I must hang on . . .*

COLD, SOAKED, AND CLINGING IMPROBABLY to a small raft, Marguerite Bech was abandoning hope. If there was to have been a rescue, she thought, it would have happened by now. The Navy would have come.

Sonia and Derek were still with her, still alive, but the canisters under the raft—the containers that gave it buoyancy—had come loose. For several hours Marguerite Bech's hands had been pounded and pinched as those canisters banged against the raft's underside. Her fingers were cold and bloodied, her knuckles rubbed raw. She wanted desperately to let go, but how could she? Relaxing her grip, even for an instant, might spring her from the raft. Which, in turn, might kill her children.

The time dragged. Marguerite Bech felt her concentration ebb, her mind wander. Any remaining strength seemed to be floating off, like so much flotsam, in a peaceful yet palpable way.

In this trancelike state Marguerite Bech turned to her daughter. "Sonia, darling, I think we'll just take off our life belts, and go to sleep in the water." It was a remarkable thing to say, a mother's invitation to die, spoken in a soft and serene tone. "We'll just go to sleep . . ."

Sonia Bech sat up, startled, and seized her mother's arm.

"No!" she cried. "No, Mummy, *don't! Don't do that!*"

Her mother stared, sleepily.

"*Don't!*" Sonia shouted again. "*Please!* I'm sure we'll be picked up soon."

So Marguerite Bech kept her eyes open, though it seemed a mighty struggle to do so. She kept her life vest on and held fast to the raft. Only minutes later a boat slipped into view, sails up.

It's a yacht, Marguerite Bech thought. Sonia waved wildly. *Is it real?* she wondered.

It was no apparition. It was also not a yacht, or a lifeboat from the *City of Benares*. What Marguerite and Sonia Bech had seen was a smaller lifeboat belonging to the freighter *Marina,* the second ship struck by U-48 during the night. The boat was drifting closer. Soon there was no question. It was coming for *them.*

The man at the helm of this lifeboat had lived his own adventures during the night. Leslie Lewis was the *Marina*'s second officer, and he had leaped overboard after U-48's torpedo struck his freighter. A lifeboat had found Lewis, and he and nine other sailors had watched the *City of Benares* go under—"sitting on her tail, an awesome sight"—as they moved away. Then Lewis and his men had waited out the long, cold night.

At sunrise Leslie Lewis had hoisted his sail. They spent an hour debating a plan, electing ultimately to head southeast, for the north coast of Ireland. A six-hundred-mile trip, Lewis guessed. It might take a week to make land. It was mid-morning when they found Marguerite Bech and the others. Lewis maneuvered expertly to their side.

What he found was a raft that was breaking up, its slats knocking against one another. Lewis saw two children, one of whom appeared half-asleep, or catatonic. Or both. This was the nine-year-old, Derek Bech.

Lewis and his men pulled five soaked people aboard: Marguerite, Sonia, and Derek Bech; the nurse Doris Walker; and the *Benares'* seventh officer, Tommy Milligan. It was not rescue really, but relief. Five people had been granted an upgrade from wretched raft to small lifeboat. And a relatively dry one at that.

A short while later they came upon two more rafts, carrying three Indians who were in even poorer shape. Leslie Lewis brought these men aboard. He now had eighteen people in his boat, matching exactly the small lifeboat's capacity. Ten *Marina* crewmen and eight survivors of the *Benares* huddled close. Lewis set his course for Ireland.

Marguerite Bech was handed two blankets, one each for her son and daughter. They shivered and said nothing, but they were warmer now. Safer, too, she thought. Slowly, Marguerite Bech allowed hope to return.

The idea of a week-long journey home, across six hundred miles of ocean, seemed almost unimaginable, and to think of traveling anywhere without her daughter Barbara was too much to bear. But at least they were in a boat now. It was an obvious improvement.

OTHERS WERE STILL RELEGATED TO rafts. By midday Eric Davis was seeing things. He looked up at clouds and thought they were ships. He tossed biscuit crumbs to phantom gulls. Davis, Jack Keeley, and John McGlashan still held fast to their raft, no lifeboat, plane, or ship in sight.

Davis was determined to keep Keeley busy. He asked him questions, implored him to lift an arm or flex a leg, anything that might occupy the child's mind or warm his limbs. *Whatever happens*, Eric Davis repeated to himself, a numbing speech that kept his own brain occupied, *I must not let the boy die*.

Crouched behind Davis, John McGlashan writhed about. He was losing his mind.

BESS AND BETH SAW APPARITIONS, too—icebergs, huge flying fish, and birds the size of dinosaurs. Beth saw an enormous green monster jump the waves, watched it and yet knew somehow that the thing did not exist. Then both girls saw the *Benares'* rocking horse, that lovely creature from the ship's playroom, bobbing perfectly alongside some deck chairs.

Bess stared and wondered: *Is this a mirage as well?*

Their reveries were broken whenever a big wave hit, drenching them yet again. *A million waves*, Bess Walder thought. *How long can this go on?* When would it end? More important—*How* would it end? The surviving Indian lay motionless between them, eyes wide and wild. Occasionally he cried out, shouting to the sea. Surely, Bess thought, their savior was near. A ship, or the good Lord. One would come for them, and soon.

For the moment they looked out at the sea, that vast and bleak horizon. Bits of flotsam were carried past, and a few rafts and lifeboats idled, far away. Otherwise, nothing. Only the occasional mirage, and a dead man. And a madman.

. . .

NOW DEATH WAS AT HAND in nearly every lifeboat. It stalked Bess Walder and Beth Cummings. It came in late morning for Rosemary Spencer-Davies, who had been so admired on the *Benares* and so brave in the lifeboat. It moved in the water around Colin Richardson. This courageous boy was having doubts now, expending so much energy to stay in the boat, and fend off the cold. *I am freezing . . .*

And now, at the midday hour, death took direct aim at John McGlashan, Eric Davis, and Jack Keeley, on their little raft.

Keeley's mind was drifting. "How do you stop these things," he asked Davis, "when you want to get off?"

Davis said nothing. The boy was talking nonsense now, he thought. *I don't have the strength to answer.*

Then Jack Keeley bolted upright. He grabbed Davis by the arm.

"Look!"

Davis stared back sleepily.

"Get him! *Quick!"*

Suddenly Davis saw. John McGlashan was sliding off the raft.

It had happened in an instant. Together Davis and Keeley crawled to the raft's edge and grabbed hold of the engineer. They hooked their arms under McGlashan's armpits and began hauling him back.

John McGlashan was a big man—he weighed more than two hundred pounds—and his body did not come easily. But Davis and the boy threw all their strength into the effort, and slowly they brought the engineer back onto the raft. Eric Davis shook McGlashan and slapped his cheeks.

"C'mon, man!" Davis bellowed. "You all right?"

McGlashan nodded. He spat some seawater and lay on the raft, and said nothing. More waves came, coursing over the three of them. Eric Davis shook off the water, looked at Jack Keeley, and thought to himself: *That boy saved his life.*

SINCE SUNRISE, THE CHIEF CHILDREN'S escort, Marjorie Day, had been counting boats. The exercise allowed her to focus on something other than horror, and loss. It kept her mind at work.

She had seen a lifeboat with no one on board, another two that were upside down. She counted a few more that were no more than tiny spots in the distance. Twelve in all, she thought. Twelve dots on the water. Marjorie Day could not be certain; perhaps she had counted some boats more than once. Some of them were far away.

In fact Day had counted correctly. But what she could not have known, from a distance, was that not every boat she saw belonged to the *City of Benares*. One of the twelve was Leslie Lewis' lifeboat, the boat from the freighter *Marina*. So there were only eleven of the *Benares'* boats in the area.

One lifeboat was missing.

CHAPTER 13

Miracles

Bess Walder leaned forward, catching the glazed eyes of her friend. A large wave came, the water lifting them high, then higher still, and then the familiar fast crash down. Bess' legs smacked the keel yet again. The wave receded, and Bess looked for Beth Cummings, as she had done after every large swell, all night and through this long and miserable day.

Beth lay there, shaking off water, looking exhausted and confused. They had now been together on the keel of their overturned boat for eighteen hours.

And then Bess looked at Beth Cummings and mouthed a single word.

"Ship."

It came like a croak, an animal's sound. Beth heard it, barely. She stared at her friend and attempted a reply—a gesture, a shake of her head. But Beth felt too weak even to bring a simple expression to her face. What she wanted to convey was *No, Bess dear. There is no ship. You are imagining things.*

Bess knew she had seen fantastic things on the water. She knew her mind was not working well, any more than her arms and legs were. Things were not *clear.*

And yet surely it was there, that black speck, a vague smudge on the water. Surely she could see a cloud of smoke, small but rising. A speck on the horizon, though now—wasn't it so?—the speck loomed larger, gaining form, becoming a thing of substance. Bess wanted to say so to her friend, but no words would come. At any rate, she thought, *Either it is a ship or it isn't.*

I don't need to tell her. Soon we will know.

. . .

HMS *HURRICANE* HAD BEEN ON a maritime sprint. The first orders had come just after midnight, and the ship's commander, Hugh Crofton Simms, had faced immediate questions: How fast could *Hurricane* move in these seas? When would they reach the site of the attack? Would it be in time to make any difference?

By Simms' own assessment, he and his crew of 110 men had begun 301 miles from the scene, taking *Hurricane* directly "into the teeth of a gale." A Force 8 gale, to be precise, raising a heavy swell. *Hurricane*'s maximum speed was thirty-six knots, but in such seas even half speed would be a dangerous adventure. Simms and his crew were veterans of several rescue operations, and they could imagine the scene at 56.43 north, 21.15 west. The *City of Benares'* lifeboats had languished in just this sort of gale, in the dark. "Survivors in the water," the wireless had said. "Proceed with utmost dispatch."

Hugh Crofton Simms was thirty-three years old, already a fifteen-year veteran of the Royal Navy. He had captained several warships before *Hurricane*, including a stint as skipper of HMS *Scout*, which had been moored at Hong Kong before the war. HMS *Hurricane* was a new destroyer, christened that June at Barrow-in-Furness. Simms' wife, Joan, had broken the champagne bottle on the hull. *Hurricane*'s motto was simple: "Strike Hard."

At the moment the distress message arrived, *Hurricane* had been sailing at twelve knots. That speed would get them there after dark the following day— nearly twenty-four hours after the torpedo's strike. Simms was a practical skipper, not given to extremes, but having read the S.O.S. and conferred with his officers, he dismissed caution and pushed his destroyer to fifteen knots. He told his men they must reach the site before nightfall.

Hurricane hurtled forward, leaning one way and another, an eighteen-hundred-ton destroyer bouncing, it seemed, on the water. It was a punishing pace. Leading Seaman Albert Gorman, tough, hardbitten, and at twenty-seven years old a veteran in his own right, shuddered below deck. *If this continues,* Gorman thought, *we shall need rescuing ourselves.*

By eight in the morning, the storm had abated. The seas were still choppy, but Simms responded to the improved weather by spiking his speed to twenty-seven knots. *Hurricane* bounded along. The atmosphere on board was electric; by now nearly every crewman was aware of the circumstances. Shipwrecked survivors awaited them, another two hundred miles ahead. At some point during the night Simms had learned that the *Benares* had carried evacuee children, and by now word had reached his crew; the men had heard that there were children at the scene, suffering in the water. In her first months at sea, *Hurricane* and her sailors had saved a life here and there, but it had been, in Albert Gorman's estimation, a "boring, tiring, and frustrating time." Now they were racing to rescue dozens of English boys and girls.

At 10:00 A.M., Simms huddled with his navigational officer, Patrick Fletcher. He had ordered Fletcher to study the winds and the spare information from the Lyness station in Scotland and the Office of Western Approaches, and to take these data and map a "box search" around the *Benares'* last known position. Long before the advent of global positioning and other satellite technologies, the "box" had been a common and time-tested method of mapping a search area.

Fletcher reported his findings to Simms. Together they agreed on a "box" that would commence some thirty miles east-northeast of where the *Benares* had gone down. Fletcher had calculated that this was as far as the winds could have carried lifeboats by mid-afternoon. *Hurricane* would start her search there, beginning a twenty-square-mile canvass to the southwest. With some luck and efficient seamanship she might complete the job by nightfall.

As Fletcher and Simms knew well, the box search was inexact science. In the case of the *City of Benares,* Fletcher had been overly generous in gauging the wind's effects. Specifically, he had not considered the possibility that lifeboats had been heavily weighted with water, or too damaged to have hoisted a sail. He could not have known it, but these were precisely the circumstances afflicting nearly all the *Benares'* boats.

Hurricane reached the edge of Fletcher's box earlier than anticipated, at a little after one in the afternoon. They had made remarkable time. Simms slowed his ship dramatically, and ordered every available crew member to deck. Telescopes and binoculars were passed around. The destroyer's siren blasted over the water.

Their search began at a deliberate pace. *Hurricane* moved twenty miles due west, turned to port, and then steered due south for one mile. Then she turned to starboard and tracked another twenty miles east, and so on, one mile over, twenty miles across. As one sailor put it, "We did not intend to miss an inch of it."

For a time they saw nothing. No boats. No rafts. Not a shred of wreckage. HMS *Hurricane* plodded along, but excitement drained a little.

Where were all those children?

And then, at about one-thirty, one of Simms' lookouts saw a sail.

. . .

IRONICALLY, THE FIRST BOAT *HURRICANE* found did not carry survivors from the *City of Benares;* it belonged to the freighter *Marina.* Officer Leslie Lewis' lifeboat was sailing with its eight refugees from the *Benares* and nine others from the *Marina* herself.

The sailors hurled ropes and scramble nets from *Hurricane*'s deck. The *Marina*'s survivors climbed the ropes easily; the small group from the *Benares* required help.

Cheers went up from the deck of the warship. *Hurricane*'s sailors were heartened by what they had found: children, alive; no serious injuries; and eighteen people in all, elated and grateful to see the destroyer. The fact that most of them were from another ship went unnoticed. The fact that only two on board were children hardly seemed to matter—in fact, it only reinvigorated the *Hurricane*'s sailors. Now they would have to find more children on the water.

Considering their ordeal, these *Benares* survivors were in remarkably good shape. In Derek Bech's case his survival had everything to do with his mother's ceaseless efforts to shelter him. During their agonizing hours on the raft, she had draped herself almost constantly over her son, shielding him from the wind and rain, and the slashing sea. Derek's feet were numb and his entire body ached, but he was conscious and able to thank the *Hurricane* sailor who hauled him up in a ship's net. Marguerite Bech, in turn, had lived because her daughter Sonia had convinced her not to relax her grip at the moment when she had all but surrendered to death. And Sonia Bech had Tommy Milligan to thank. The strong young sailor had pulled her back to the raft just as she began to inhale Atlantic water.

Milligan and the Bechs owed their lives to Eric Davis, the BBC man, without whom they might never have left the *Benares* safely in the first place. They had no idea what had become of him. They were also indebted to Lewis, the *Marina*'s second officer, who had steered expertly to their raft and offered every available space in his boat. Lewis had risked his own life and the lives of his crewmen by bringing the *Benares* refugees aboard. Had they been at sea much longer, Lewis would have had eight more stomachs to fill and thirsts to slake.

They were all carried below *Hurricane*'s deck, given clothing and blankets, rum, and a piping hot vegetable soup. Derek and Sonia Bech were brought large cups of warm milk and shown to hammocks in the mess hall. Soon they were asleep.

Their mother could not rest. She had a single, overriding concern and she raised it with every crew member she met in the warm warrens of the destroyer: Had they seen another young girl? A fourteen-year-old? Blond?

"Have you seen a girl called Barbara Bech?"

They had not, they told her. And they had other pressing business at hand.

HURRICANE LABORED ON. SIMMS KNEW that the *City of Benares* had carried more than four hundred crew and passengers. However uplifting the experience of finding the one lifeboat, the fact was that they had collected only a small fraction of the *Benares* survivors. The ocean ahead—the next swath of the box search—appeared barren indeed. Surely there were more people alive, somewhere on these waters?

On they went, mile after mile of Fletcher's box. Enthusiasm waned. *Where are the people?* Albert Gorman wondered. It was at a quarter past three, nearly two hours after the first rescue, that a *Hurricane* sailor spied a group of rafts, dots on the water, bunched close together.

Drawing near, the ship's lookouts saw that there was a single passenger on each raft; nearer still, they could make out a dark-skinned turbaned man, sitting cross-legged on one of them. Soon they found that the other three were Indians as well, members of the *Benares* crew. Every one of them was near death.

Heavy swells came as they threw down bowlines for the Indians. For each man, they had to pass a line around his chest and then lift him as gently as possible to the *Hurricane* deck. All four were saved, but the effort took half an hour. *Precious time*, Simms thought.

It was three fifty-three in the afternoon.

Where were the children?

THEY WERE EIGHTEEN PAINSTAKING MILES into the twenty-mile grid when Simms heard a cry from one of his lookouts.

"Boat right ahead!"

The commander ordered maximum revolutions in the engine room. *Hurricane* flew ahead, and within minutes, Hugh Crofton Simms had found what he had been looking for. Here were lifeboats, and rafts. And here were people, many people, and many children among them.

As they approached, *Hurricane*'s sailors crowded one side of the deck, angling for a look. It became clear that they would have to hurry. Among other things, Simms realized he would have to put Albert Gorman to work.

Gorman was a twelve-year Navy veteran, who sensed on this afternoon that he might be part of the most important mission of his career. Gorman had been handed a new assignment before the *Hurricane* left Liverpool: He was to captain the ship's whaler. It had not seemed a particularly glamorous or even important promotion at the time, given *Hurricane*'s fairly uneventful summer patrols in the North Atlantic, but now, at four o'clock in the afternoon of September 18, Albert Gorman sensed the job was about to take on much greater significance.

Simms' every stop in the search box presented a potential test of seamanship, the work necessarily delicate, a hulking warship sidling close to a boat or raft with passengers who might be near death. A sharp motion or too-rapid approach could produce a fatal swell; on the other hand, lingering too long would mean precious minutes lost. It might also invite U-boat interest, presenting a large and idling target.

With all this in mind, Simms dispatched Gorman's whaler and a larger motorboat to the water. It would fall to these small craft and their navigators to conduct the actual rescues.

GORMAN AND A JUNIOR SAILOR sped for a lifeboat, saw it was upside down and abandoned, and veered sharply away. The whaler hopped on the waves, speeding for another boat. This one was at least bobbing right side up. The sailors arrived, brimming with adrenaline and excitement. Gorman slowed his craft, and the younger sailor tied a rope to one of the lifeboat's oarlocks.

Their enthusiasm receded instantly.

Gorman counted twenty people in the lifeboat. Most appeared to be dead. Immediately his eyes were drawn to a child—an infant, eighteen months old, he thought, maybe two years—who lay in the boat's midsection. The younger sailor stepped around the bodies. He lifted the baby, held it in his arms. Then he turned and cast a horrified look at Albert Gorman. He started to say something, but no words came.

"We are looking for the *living*," Gorman said sternly.

The sailor looked away, trembling. Then he laid the child down. Moments later he was violently ill over the side.

Albert Gorman stepped gingerly into the boat. *There's one,* he thought. *Look at her...*

A young woman—twenty years old, Gorman guessed—sat on a thwart, her head nodding. *She's trying to say something...*

He clambered over the corpses. Albert Gorman was a rough-hewn sailor, but he had never seen anything like this. The woman had nothing on but a frock and stockings, both of which were badly torn. Blood ran from a knee. Gorman saw a ruby ring and a wedding band. "Here—" he began, extending a hand.

Then Albert Gorman saw that the woman was dead, too. She nodded again, but at close range Gorman realized that this was not a sign of life but merely the sea's effect, each wave lifting her gently, bobbing her head up and down.

Gorman turned away. He felt a rage building as he moved among the bodies. The young sailor watched him.

"Don't stand there," Gorman said irritably. "Come and help." He drew a deep breath. "This," he said to the sailor, "is where youngsters turn into men."

But there was nothing either man could do. They stepped awkwardly in the boat. All twenty passengers were dead.

Gorman cupped his hands and yelled up to *Hurricane*'s deck. "Should we find I.D.?"

"No," came the answer. "Come aboard." Gorman took a last look at the young woman with the rings. Then he stepped into the whaler.

Normally they would have checked for identification and held proper burial services for the woman, the child, and all the others in the boat. But Simms and his crew were convinced there were still people alive in the other boats, still chances for rescue in what remained of their search box. So they pressed on, leaving the lifeboat behind.

LETITIA QUINTON LEANED OVER THE gunwale of Lifeboat 6.

"Look!" she cried. "A *ship*!"

Her son, Tony, turned slowly.

There she was. Unmistakable. Tall, long, and gray. *Lovely!* Letitia Quinton thought. A run of waves came, clouding their view for a moment. But when the waves had passed, they saw it again. More clearly now. *A warship,* Tony Quinton thought.

Ernest Szekulesz, ever the pessimist, still had doubts.

"They haven't seen *us*," he said weakly. "They will not come for us."

"Nonsense!" Letitia Quinton said. She had grown weary of Szekulesz's talk.

Then one of the Indians on board—the well-built man Tony Quinton had taken to calling "Gunga Din"—said it emphatically: Without question the ship was coming for *their boat.* They were about to be rescued. Letitia Quinton glared at Szekulesz and tried to imitate the Hungarian's accent. "Yes, yes!" she said loudly. "You see? Big ship come!"

And yet for the moment, Szekulesz's pessimism was warranted. The ship's motorboat gunned its engine and a sailor called to Lifeboat 6. "Back for you shortly!" They were going first to pick up people from rafts.

The motorboat whizzed past. Szekulesz groaned. "That is what they *say.*"

IT WAS ABOUT QUARTER PAST four. On his small raft, Eric Davis feared he had doled out supplies too liberally. He had fed young Jack Keeley several beef-and-biscuit sandwiches, and he and Keeley had both drunk two cans of condensed milk. Davis had never considered saving any stocks, never thought they might be abandoned so long, and he had been certain that the elements would kill them well before they ran out of provisions. Now he noticed that the raft's supply of milk was down to two cans. Surely, Eric Davis thought, they would be found before nightfall?

Their one fellow passenger, the *Benares'* second engineer, John McGlashan, had scarcely moved in nearly twenty hours. He had wrapped his strong arms around a corner of the raft, the sea drenching him and pushing his body this way and that. Otherwise McGlashan had kept still. On several occasions Davis and Keeley had assumed their companion was dead.

But now, in this late and dreary patch of afternoon, John McGlashan stirred. He raised himself slowly, lifted his bandaged head. It was enough to startle Jack Keeley. *He's seen something,* the boy thought.

McGlashan whispered a single word. *"Destroyer."*

Then Keeley and Davis saw her, too. She was still far off—Davis could never have guessed what sort of ship. But John McGlashan was sure. Then they heard the siren. A long, shrill blast. All three of them were watching now. Davis sat up and hollered at the horizon.

Probably, he thought, *they cannot see or hear us.*

And then, as suddenly as they had seen her coming, they saw the ship turn away.

God no, thought Eric Davis. *That would be too cruel.*

In fact HMS *Hurricane* was merely executing one of her final box-search turns, tantalizing two men and a boy on an eight-foot-square raft. After a quarter hour she had turned again and was nearly upon them, gray and glorious and easily the most impressive thing Jack Keeley had ever seen.

It would be no easy rescue. Even at minimum speed, the destroyer made swells that would rock a lifeboat; with a raft *Hurricane* would have to approach gently indeed. The ship edged near, and again Albert Gorman was sent to fetch the men, but somehow the destroyer herself wound up closest to the raft. Sailors threw ropes to the water; the first fell wide of their mark, and then one clipped Eric Davis on the head, knocking him back. He recovered, and quickly grabbed the rope.

The sailors' first priority was the boy. Jack Keeley was too weak to stand. Sailors moved down bowlines, close to the water, and scooped Keeley up in their arms. He was light and came up easily. But another of *Hurricane*'s movements had whipped up the sea again. Suddenly, moments from their salvation, Davis and McGlashan were washed off the raft. After all those hours spent battling the sea, the two men nearly drowned just a few yards from the hull of HMS *Hurricane*. Without hesitation three sailors dove after them and managed to carry John McGlashan and Eric Davis to safety.

McGlashan was brought immediately to *Hurricane*'s surgeon, Peter Collinson. Jack Keeley was carried to the engine room, the warmest place on board. Davis joined him there soon after. They were given sailor's clothes, blankets, and plates of hot food. Someone handed Eric Davis a glass of rum. He looked at Keeley, this eight-year-old wonder, still shivering, teeth chattering, a perplexed look across his round face.

Davis' hand shook as he poured half his rum into the child's cup of milk. "Try a drop of this."

Jack Keeley lifted the cup to his cold lips, spilling much of the drink as he did. A single sip sent a surge of energy through him. "I . . . I . . . say," Jack Keeley stammered. "I say! Thanks very much!"

SUDDENLY IT SEEMED THAT BOATS and people loomed everywhere *Hurricane* looked. The destroyer's challenge was to find survivors as quickly as possible—without abandoning the methodical pace of the box search. The last thing Simms wanted was for his ship to hurry past a raft or lifeboat and inadvertently leave someone behind.

At about four-thirty, *Hurricane* came as promised for Lifeboat 6. This boat carried Letitia Quinton and her son, Tony, and the doomsaying Ernest Szekulesz. When all was said and done, many passengers had high praise for the Hungarian. He had been a tough and practical presence in the lifeboat. Szekulesz in turn was effusive in his thanks for the efforts of parliamentarian James Baldwin-Webb, the man who had helped so many people move from the *Benares'* deck to the lifeboats, only to miss his own opportunity for rescue.

Next *Hurricane* put down bowlines for Lifeboat 7, where the retired Navy Lieutenant Commander Richard Deane and fifteen other adults were huddled, still alive. They had begun the night with thirty people; as the averages went on this wretched day, those were not terrible numbers. Deane himself had probably saved many of Lifeboat 7's passengers by constructing his simple driftwood "seat" and shelter. Sadly, no children had embarked to Lifeboat 7. Deane landed on *Hurricane*'s deck in a cauldron of emotion—thrilled that he was alive, furious at the *Benares* crew for the way the lifeboats had been launched (a misplaced anger, all the evidence would later suggest), upset because the Fleming gear had not functioned in his boat, and above all anguished because his wife had died during the night. Dorothy Deane was fifty-five years old.

Another few minutes later, and *Hurricane* was bearing down on W. J. Lee's lifeboat, number 11. Here sailors found fourteen survivors in a boat that had set out with thirty-four people on board. This was Michael Rennie's lifeboat, the one that had seen so much heroism and tragedy in the last eighteen hours. Rennie was dead—as were most of the children he had labored to save. Of fifteen children who had left the *City of Benares* in Lifeboat 11, only two still breathed: Louis Walder, Bess' little brother, barely clinging to life; and Rex Thorne, the boy from Wembley whose sister, Marion, had been lost as the lifeboats were launched. Thorne had blacked out in early afternoon. As they were brought up to the *Hurricane*, Officer Lee and the *Hurricane* sailors assumed the boy was dead.

IT WAS NOW NEARLY FIVE in the afternoon. The sun lay low on the horizon. *Hurricane* was embarking on the last mile of her box search in the last hour of daylight.

Derek and Sonia Bech were sleeping on board the ship. Their mother, Marguerite, was still weak, but she had recovered well enough so that she could now help tend to new arrivals. For three hours she had been the only adult woman on the warship who was physically able to help. She cared for other female survivors, massaging feet and rubbing listless, frozen faces. And at every chance, she approached a crew member of the *Hurricane:*

"Have you seen my girl? Have you seen a teenage girl, a girl named Barbara Bech?"

The answer was always "no," but the fact was they *had* seen Barbara Bech. They just hadn't known it was her.

From the captain's bridge, Hugh Crofton Simms and his officers had spied Lifeboat 4 at about three in the afternoon, and judged its passengers to be in much better shape than the others they had encountered thus far. So Lifeboat 4 had endured an extra wait, nearly two more long and agonizing hours. Had Marguerite Bech known, she would no doubt have protested furiously. But she did not know, and it proved to have been the correct decision.

Hurricane saved at least a dozen people in the intervening hours, several of whom would probably have died had Simms not initially bypassed Lifeboat 4. The evacuee boys Rex Thorne and Louis Walder, to name two, might well have been counted among the dead. When *Hurricane* returned finally for Lifeboat 4, she found all thirty-three of its passengers still alive. The only tragedy here—and it was significant—was that this successful boat had carried not one of the child evacuees. Its only child passenger was Barbara Bech, who was hauled to deck in a scramble net and brought to a room that hugged the ship's funnel. She was lying on a cot, wrapped in a blanket, when a sailor appeared in the doorway.

"Is there anyone here called Barbara Bech?"

"Yes," she said. "I am!"

"Well, young lady, your sister and brother are here, and your mother, too. All safe."

The girl's heart leaped. She sat up and tried to say something, but no words would come.

"Your mother's been worried sick about you," the sailor said.

Barbara Bech gave a faint reply. She had been worried, too.

They were reunited below deck, where Marguerite Bech was busy bathing a fellow survivor. By now she had heard several terrifying accounts of the *Benares'* last minutes; and begun to doubt that she would ever see Barbara again. Certainly Barbara Bech—recalling the scenes on the *Benares'* deck—had imagined the worst for her mother, sister, and brother. She shrieked with joy when her mother was brought to her room; Marguerite Bech wept and held the girl close. "Derek and Sonia are sleeping, darling," she said, sobbing. "You should do the same."

Hurricane's small craft moved rapidly now. They came next for Alex Macauley, whose crowded lifeboat had been reduced to a complement of four men: a Jewish refugee from Germany, two Indian crew members, and Macauley himself. Four more bedraggled souls, beaten, but alive.

BY NOW BETH CUMMINGS COULD see that Bess had been right. A ship was coming . . . Better still, it appeared at last that the ship was coming for *them*, and for the Indian seaman who still breathed, straddling the keel between them.

A miracle! Bess thought, and then she lapsed, her vision gone blurry and her thoughts badly clouded. Slowly she slipped from consciousness. Somehow her fingers still held the lifeboat's keel, but the concentration and discipline of mind that both girls had displayed for so long seemed to desert them now. Minutes later—how long she could not be sure—Bess came to, in a hail of shouts and cheers. Someone was yelling, above the waves. *"Come on, girls!"* The voices came loud and strong and . . . *in English!* There was no mistake. *Listen!* Bess thought. *They're Brits!*

"Hang on, dears, hang on! We're coming!"

It's no dream.

Still Beth Cummings refused to believe the best. *Probably a German ship,* she reasoned. Wasn't it too convenient for a ship filled with British sailors to materialize just now, so soon after she and Bess had prayed and hallucinated and prepared to meet their maker? *How can we be sure?* In any case they could hardly see—Beth's sight was blurred, too, her eyelids rimmed with salt.

Bess was convinced the ship was British, but she had a different worry: that the ship might steer right past them. They were in no position to cry out or signal in any way. Their hands remained locked, frozen to the keel.

THE NEXT THING THE TWO girls knew, the whaler was bearing down on them, and then a pair of strapping, happy sailors were at their side, offering outstretched arms. More whoops and hollers rained from the *Hurricane* deck. *It's like a rugby match,* Bess thought. *And they're cheering for us.*

Beth squinted at the destroyer, made out "H06" painted white on her side. She saw the whaler, heard the voices, and her doubts and suspicions slipped away. *Thank God,* Beth Cummings murmured to herself. Then she passed out.

Hurricane's sailors had poured oil overboard, to calm the waves around the upturned lifeboat. Albert Gorman piloted his little craft alongside. *Pitiful,* he thought, looking at the girls. *But at least these are alive...*

"Come on, darlings," Gorman said. "Let's go." Neither child budged.

He edged closer to Bess.

"Let's go, now!" he shouted. "Come on, dear."

He reached to the boat and asked again. "Come on . . ."

Nothing. No reply. The two girls lay there, wrapped around the keel. It appeared that both were unconscious.

They'll die here, Gorman thought. For a moment he wasn't sure what to do. "Come on, girls . . ."

Albert Gorman realized that force would be required. He would have to pry their hands from the keel. Finally Gorman dislodged their fingers, one at a time, as carefully as he could. Skin broke off. Their hands were bloated and soft, like jelly. The girls did not cry. They did not say a word.

Then Gorman and the other sailor lifted Bess Walder and Beth Cummings to the whaler, covering them in blankets. Gorman took the surviving Indian next, his body rigid. He, too, said nothing; yet he, too, was alive.

Gorman spun his craft around and sped for the *Hurricane,* three inert clumps under blankets in his boat. *Please God,* he said to himself. *Let them live.* As he pulled up to the destroyer, there were more roars of approval from the deck.

WHEN BESS WALDER CAME TO, she was in a bunk, wrapped in two thick blankets. Opening her eyes, she saw gray walls, a half circle of sailors, and her friend Beth sleeping in a large cushioned chair nearby. The room spun strangely. Two sailors were staring at her, trying to tell her something.

"Have some, dear."

"Here you are."

The men had cut loose their clothing—Beth's dress and Bess' bright green nightgown—and taken them to dry in the boiler room. They had brought cups of hot soup, but the girls could not swallow what they were given. Their throats were raw; sores had opened inside their mouths. Albert Gorman told them they could wait; perhaps after the soup cooled it would go down all right. "In the meantime we'll fetch you something else."

One of the sailors left and returned minutes later with sugar water and rum, and this the girls managed. After a while they were given warm baths— painful at first to soft, raw skin. Beth found herself momentarily frightened by the water. *I could do without seeing water ever again.* But then it was fine; the bathwater soothed. Afterward they wrapped Beth Cummings in a thick towel. She was dizzy and exhausted, sharp pains shooting down from her knees and bruises dotting her entire body. Bess felt weak and feverish. Neither girl could walk without assistance.

But Albert Gorman and the surgeon Peter Collinson believed the girls were out of danger. *They will make it,* Gorman realized, and he felt a touch of pride at the thought. What Gorman could not understand was how they had lasted so long. A miserable night, and a long day. How was it, Gorman wondered, with all the death he had seen on the water, all the people who had died in the upright boats, that these two girls had survived on a boat turned upside down?

IT WAS GETTING LATE. HMS *Hurricane* had made her last turn in Patrick Fletcher's box. A dozen men with binoculars watched the water. The sun lay low on the horizon.

Just before six o'clock, they discovered two more lifeboats, each carrying a single survivor. The Dublin businessman Maurice Maher was rescued here, as was a Royal Navy signalman named Michael Goy. The other signaler, Johnny Mayhew, had not been found. Minutes later *Hurricane*'s men found another boat, this one abandoned. *Hurricane* had now located nine lifeboats inside the twenty-square-mile box.

The destroyer inched ahead. The men scanned a hazy, darkening sea. Five hours into their search, they were not yet finished.

ONLY ONE CHILD BREATHED IN Lifeboat 10. Eleanor Wright was an energetic thirteen-year-old, one of the girls the escort Mary Cornish had been looking for as the *Benares* went down. Wright had been brought aboard this boat by the chief escort, Marjorie Day, nestled at the stern, and warmed snugly in a wool blanket. She and Day had watched, horrified, as one after another of the children slipped away. At midday Eleanor Wright had taken the escort's hand.

"The Navy won't let us down, Miss Day."

It had seemed a remarkable opinion, expressed by a remarkable child, as spirits and bodies failed all around them. *Why does she say that?* Day had wondered. *What does she know?* It may not have been the Navy's fault—but *some-*

one surely had let them down. Fourteen children were gone. The Navy had been no help to them.

In mid-afternoon, crewmen in Lifeboat 10 had used the pajama shirt from a dead child to fashion a flag, tying it around the top of an oar. Eleanor Wright had volunteered to hold the makeshift flag—"I can do it," she told them—and she shared the task with one of the sailors. They kept the oar raised for a while, until a strong wave struck.

Eleanor Wright was knocked down hard. She felt a sharp pain in her leg, and cried out. *God, no,* thought Marjorie Day. *We cannot lose her.*

Now, as HMS *Hurricane* slowed for Lifeboat 10, it appeared that Eleanor Wright would be the boat's lone child survivor. They had not lost her. Marjorie Day looked at Wright, who was back under a blanket now. *Why,* Day wondered, *has this girl outlasted all the others?*

Eleanor Wright was unconscious when the *Hurricane* arrived.

It was twenty minutes to seven.

NOW *HURRICANE* CAME FOR ANGUS MacDonald's boat—Lifeboat number 2.

MacDonald, the *Benares'* carpenter, appeared to be the only one in his boat with any energy left. He had opened a gash on his hand as he fished for one of the supply lockers, but otherwise he was in remarkably good shape. Like the crew in Lifeboat 10, he, too, had tied a piece of cloth to an oar and held it aloft for much of the afternoon. For hours MacDonald had been imploring the others not to abandon hope. "They'll come for us," he promised. "I can assure you, they'll come."

From the *Hurricane* deck, Seaman Reg Charlton saw what looked to be a beaten, bedraggled group—and then he heard a sound, faint but unmistakable. "Rule Britannia . . ." *God,* Charlton thought. *They're singing.* MacDonald shouted to the deck, but Charlton had already fixed his eye on a blond child in a red life vest, a thin figure perched in the middle of the boat. Colin Richardson was shivering uncontrollably.

"Get the *boy*!" Reg Charlton cried.

They threw bowlines down. "Up you go, young man!"

Colin could hear them but he could neither move nor speak. His hands hung limp at his sides. Though his legs shook with the cold, Colin felt nothing below his waist. Albert Gorman's whaler was in service again, and as he pulled up to Lifeboat 2 he called to the deck for another rope line. Charlton obliged, and then Gorman and his partner fashioned a holster of sorts, slipping it under Colin Richardson's arms. Gorman flashed a thumbs-up to several sailors on the *Hurricane* deck.

"One, two, three, *heave now!*" the sailors cried. "Come on, lad! Up you go!"

But Colin Richardson was a statue. This boy who had been so stoic and brave in the night was bone cold and catatonic now. It was another several minutes before they were able to raise him to deck, a slow and painstaking ascent, as though they were lifting some fragile and precious package. Reg Charlton doubted the child would live.

The sailors unwrapped Colin Richardson and hurried to retrieve the other passengers. In an unfortunate moment of overzealousness they rushed off together, leaving the boy standing on the deck. He crumpled instantly, hitting his head hard. Colin was rushed to the engine room and wrapped in blankets. His condition was grave.

Others in Lifeboat 2 were not faring much better. For hours fourteen-year-old Pat Bulmer had watched MacDonald care for others, watched him raise the flag, always feeling that she ought to have been helping—and always physically unable to budge. She shook uncontrollably in a sailor's arms and felt a sharp sting in her throat as she swallowed some sips of tea. J. P. Day had spent more than twelve hours with his legs jammed under the lifeboat's mast, in his effort to avoid being washed away. When *Hurricane* came, Professor Day was still wedged in, only now he had lost consciousness. Day was extricated with some difficulty and brought on board. Trying desperately to revive the man, *Hurricane*'s sailors pried open his jaw, held his mouth open, and poured rum down his throat.

The professor coughed and spat the rum, but his eyes opened and scanned the surroundings. He quickly recovered his senses and blurted a question.

"Is Colin all right?"

"Yes, sir."

"He'll live?"

"Believe so, sir."

John Percival Day let out a sigh. He managed a weak smile. "That," he said, "does me more good than anything. Even your *rum!*"

THE LAST LIFEBOAT WAS FOUND just before seven.

By now William Forsyth had buried more than twenty people on the water, most of them children. They had left the *City of Benares* with thirty-two passengers; eight were still alive. All day Forsyth had prayed for an ever-shrinking group of boys in his boat; together with the German doctor, Martin Bum, and the screenwriter, Arthur Wimperis, he had struggled to keep these children alive. Now four boys in Forsyth's boat clung to life by the thinnest of threads. None of them was conscious. Forsyth himself was fading.

Johnny Baker was lifted first when the *Hurricane* came; he was still bundled tightly in canvas sheeting. He had been sheltered this way, cocoonlike, almost since the *Benares* went down. The men who had found the sheets and enveloped Baker had probably saved the boy's life, but by now the extroverted seven-year-old had gone mute and blank-faced.

Johnny Baker came to in the officer's mess as sailors gently peeled away the canvas. The men carried him to a chair, and someone produced a glass of warm milk and a pair of blankets. Baker swallowed the milk, and within minutes he was asleep.

The other three boys—Terrence Holmes, ten; Derek Carr, ten; and Alan Capel, five—were carried directly to ship's surgeon Peter Collinson's triage rooms below deck. Collinson had managed to revive thirteen-year-old Rex Thorne, in a lukewarm bath. "That one's a survivor," Collinson told a fellow sailor. Now they had these three new boys, all unconscious. Little Alan Capel would be the youngest survivor brought on board the *Hurricane*.

The oldest survivor happened to come from the same boat. Arthur Wimperis, sixty-five, was carried to *Hurricane*'s deck after all the children had been secured. Wimperis was conscious, and he came aboard fairly bursting with admiration for the boys in his lifeboat and badly shaken by the deaths of so many of the other evacuee children. Arthur Wimperis had helped Forsyth "bury" more than a dozen of them on the water.

Finally William Forsyth himself was lifted by two *Hurricane* sailors. They found him "more dead than alive."

HMS *HURRICANE* HAD COUNTED TWELVE lifeboats on the water. They had brought 115 survivors safely aboard, 105 of those from the *Benares*. Peter Collinson had spent a long afternoon treating survivors, dressing wounds, and doing what little he could to soothe a profound trauma.

It was nearly seven o'clock. The sun was showing its last red-orange glow, a lovely orb sinking low on the horizon. *Hurricane* had combed all twenty square miles, and done so with great care. Her crew had exhibited heroism and fine seamanship in every rescue. Exhausted and yet exhilarated, sailors split their duties now, either caring for the survivors or guiding the destroyer. Ever vigilant, Hugh Crofton Simms ordered that the search be continued until the last light had gone.

It was during these final minutes of daylight, shadows dancing on the water, that they came upon a raft, probably slightly beyond the perimeter of Patrick Fletcher's box. Albert Gorman had imagined his day was done, but here were more of the *Benares* refugees, two men and one woman, clinging to life, and to a tiny square of a raft.

The men were two of the *Benares'* senior officers—the purser, John Anderson, and the chief officer, Joe Hetherington. The heavyset woman between them was the German who had chided Hetherington several hours earlier, mocking the slow response of the Royal Navy. Now the Navy was coming for her, and preparing to care for her—and she could neither move nor speak. Her name remained a mystery.

In the last hour, Anderson and Hetherington had made a pact: They would not spend another night this way. If sundown arrived before a rescue vessel did, Hetherington had suggested, they would simply allow themselves to slip off the raft. Anderson had voiced no dissent. Such a plan seemed not only sensible—at this stage it seemed almost appealing. Other *Benares* survivors would probably have understood: If the alternative was another night spent hewed to a near-frozen square of wood, with no shelter from the elements, then death might actually have appeared the more palatable option.

"Remember what you said," Anderson said to Hetherington now, his voice a scratchy whisper. The two men repeated their pledge: At nightfall, they would release their grip. They would go to their deaths quietly and simultaneously. Joe Hetherington was drowsy, senseless nearly, but in the waning minutes of daylight he could see that Anderson had lost his resolve.

"Wait awhile longer," Hetherington told his colleague. "Think about your wife and girls."

Anderson tried, but he found his mind would not cooperate. He stared weakly at Hetherington. Suddenly John Anderson's eyes widened. "A *ship!*"

Only a few hours before, Joe Hetherington had said precisely the same thing, having imagined a warship on the horizon.

"Nonsense," Hetherington replied now. "Forget it."

What John Anderson had seen was the distant frame of HMS *Hurricane*. *Hurricane*'s sailors were still on an all-points lookout, and somehow a sailor had made out the tiny raft's outline, in the half-light of dusk. Later Albert Gorman would wonder how they had found this minuscule object on the water. The sun was all but gone when the ship approached. *Hurricane*'s bow wave rocked the water, enough to pitch the raft and send the German woman to the sea.

Hetherington found enough voice to yell to the *Hurricane* deck: "Get the *woman* first!" Two crewmen dove—about a twenty-foot plunge—and in less than a minute they had corraled the woman and lifted her above the waves. She was alive. One of the sailors who had dived was Lieutenant George Pound, son of the British admiral Sir Dudley Pound. He and a fellow crewman tied a bowline around the woman and began performing artificial respiration.

"*Danke, danke,*" the woman said finally.

She came to on the *Hurricane* deck.

It's odd, thought Albert Gorman. *Us English sailors, saving Germans off the water.*

So Joe Hetherington and John Anderson, who had been among the last to leave the *City of Benares*, would be the last people collected by HMS *Hurricane*. The last of 118 very fortunate souls.

They were brought to the captain's cabin, and a short while later Hugh Crofton Simms found the two men wrapped in towels, still shaking. He congratulated them both and told them they must ask for anything they wished for on the destroyer. Then Simms had a question.

"Gentlemen, what's your tipple?"

They answered together. "Whiskey!"

HURRICANE TURNED, HER MISSION COMPLETE. Returning to a more conventional pace, she would have a two-day journey to northwest Scotland.

The day's last light flickered on the water. The first stars showed themselves in a nearly cloudless sky. The sea was still. Albert Gorman watched from the deck as *Hurricane* swung about, preparing to leave the scene. He could still make out a few lifeboats and rafts drifting about, and he thought how strange it was to leave them all, ghosts and shadows on the water. Some lifeboats still had dead people on board. Gorman could not shake the image of that one awful boat he had visited, and he wondered how long it would last like that, bobbing meaninglessly, until it was swallowed and smashed up by the sea.

Hurricane's crew felt a stew of pride, revulsion, and fury at what they had seen and done in the North Atlantic. Earlier in the day, Seaman Reg Charlton had imagined himself steeled for whatever he might discover at the scene. Charlton had known he might find himself face-to-face with some of Hitler's victims on the water, but he had never imagined this. That night *Hurricane*'s sailors cursed the Germans. Some of them broke down and wept.

Meanwhile the beneficiaries of their courage and kindness rested in bunks and hammocks, in mess halls and officer's cabins, or in whatever makeshift recovery rooms the ship's crew could offer. Letitia and Tony Quinton found themselves on a pile of sacking in the ship's storeroom, not sure who had put them there. Tony's back ached and his mother had suffered bruises and scrapes up and down her legs—but these were relatively minor injuries. The boy took comfort in the news that among the other six survivors in their lifeboat had been the men he had christened "Priestley," "Gunga Din," and "Basil Rathbone." *Perhaps,* Tony Quinton thought, *I shall one day know their proper names.* Letitia Quinton, who had never wanted to leave England in the first place, looked at her son and said, "Well now, that's that. We're not doing *that* again."

Hurricane's men had by now shifted their efforts from rescue to relief and emergency care. The ship's officers had surrendered their cabins to the survivors; sailors offered their own hot meals and clothing. Most of the women and children suffering from exposure and shock were quartered in a twenty-foot-square wardroom, laid out on ship's blankets and kept under constant watch. Roughly a dozen more serious cases were billeted in the captain's quarters and other rooms nearby. Peter Collinson was making rounds in all these places, quiet corners of the destroyer that had been converted to triage wards. Collinson had tended to little more than minor illness as the *Hurricane*'s chief physician; in his parallel role as cipher officer he had decoded messages and censored sailors' outgoing mail. Now Collinson was working to save lives, tending wounds and battling infection, wrapping frostbitten limbs and seeing to it that sleeping children were not drifting into comas. At one cot, Collinson administered mouth-to-mouth resuscitation to revive Terrence Holmes; at another, he and a petty officer tried to feed soup to a catatonic Colin Richardson. Collinson dressed Beth Cummings' bloodied and frostbitten ankles, and he made a splint for Eleanor Wright's leg, which had been fractured during the fall she had taken, in her last hours on the water. Nearly all the survivors were suffering from frostbite and what Collinson termed "immersion foot," a less serious form of trench foot but still terribly painful and damaging to the skin. Collinson had these patients sedated, their legs elevated on pillows.

While he worked, Peter Collinson had an offer of help from a tall, attractive woman wearing a sailor's pants and sweater. "Can I be of assistance?" she asked. Collinson refused politely, and returned to his patients. After a while he noticed that the woman was still there, watching him tend to children, and he saw that she had gone pale.

"Mind if I lay down awhile?" she asked.

"Of course not," Collinson said apologetically, and he prepared a cot.

The woman was Phyllis Digby-Morton. Her husband was recuperating in a cabin. She lay down on Collinson's cot and slept until morning.

Later that night, after food and a few hours of rest, several of the children began asking after siblings. Jack Keeley had no idea what had become of his sister. Johnny Baker, though profoundly weak, called out to every sailor he saw, asking for news of his older brother, Robert. "Bobby Baker's his name," he would say. "Y'know him?" Remarkably, this same seven-year-old who had run free of his *Benares* lifeboat station did the same thing here, leaving a bed only hours after his rescue. Once again the boy lost himself on a ship, this time navigating the warrens and corridors of a Royal Navy destroyer. But this time Johnny Baker was not running around on a lark. He was limping badly, and he was on a desperate mission to find his only sibling. One of the sailors ran into Baker near the mess room and brought him to the ship's captain. Unabashed, Baker pressed the captain directly. "Have you seen my brother?" he asked Hugh Crofton Simms.

Simms had not realized that Baker had a brother, or that the brother was not among the survivors. He took the question lightly and replied with a smile, "When you speak to me, address me as 'Captain.'"

Johnny Baker did not miss a beat. "Captain, sir, have you seen my brother?"

But Simms had not seen Bobby Baker. Nor had anyone else.

Most of the survivors were too drained to talk, or to move about the ship. Bess Walder rested in the captain's quarters. Peter Collinson had told Bess that she would face a lengthy recovery, but a recovery it would be. He was certain of that.

As she lay there, in the early hours of night, sleep would not come. A familiar dread had crept into her mind.

Louis...

Where was her brother? How was she to return home without him? Without even a body? "Look after that young man," her mother had said. She could not have been clearer. Bess felt she had failed her family.

She told Collinson of her fears. How, she asked him, would she explain the loss of her only brother?

"You shouldn't worry about that," Collinson told her. "They'll be so pleased to have you. Some mummies and daddies won't have anyone." Then the surgeon was off to tend to more seriously injured survivors. Bess Walder fretted awhile longer, now worried not only about Louis but also about these "mummies and daddies" who might find themselves with no children at all. Finally she slept.

The next morning one of *Hurricane*'s officers was leading a tour for the few boys who had survived and could still walk. They stopped for a visit to the ship's boiler room.

Suddenly one of the children cried out, "That's my *sister's!*"

A few articles of clothing were drying on lines, children's clothing mostly, hanging in the warm boiler room. The boy was pointing to a girl's green dressing gown. "That's *hers!*" he said. "I *know* it is!"

The officer was skeptical. "How do you know?"

"Because," the boy said, "it's the gown we had a row about."

Within minutes, this news had reached the destroyer's senior officers. Soon, Hugh Crofton Simms was banging on the door of the captain's cabin, *his* cabin, which was for the moment occupied by two teenage girls named Beth Cummings and Bess Walder.

"Sit up, miss!" Simms ordered.

Bess edged herself up in the bed, with pain and with great difficulty. *After all*, she thought, *you do what the captain says*.

Simms had a hand behind his back. "I've got a present for you."

Then Bess Walder watched, incredulous—*sure* she was hallucinating now—as the captain swung an arm around.

From behind him there appeared a frazzled little boy in oversized sailor's clothes.

"LOUIS!"

FOR BESS WALDER IT WAS a second miracle, a pair of wonders she would never fully comprehend. Somehow she had been given the strength to grasp the keel of that wretched boat, and then the gift of a friend at the boat's opposite end. Somehow the Royal Navy had fetched them both, in what would almost certainly have been their final hour. Somehow, in the heart of an awful, deadly night, her little brother had surfaced, literally, plucked to safety by a thirteen-year-old boy named George Crawford, who had died from the effort only moments later. And somehow Louis Walder had survived in Lifeboat 11, one of only two children from a group of fifteen who was still alive when *Hur-*

ricane came. Of twenty-three sets of siblings in the group of evacuees, Louis and Bess Walder were the only ones to have been brought on board the warship.

The Bech family had cause for wonder, too. In a tragedy that had shredded families, all four of them had been spared. As Marguerite Bech helped *Hurricane* sailors tend to the wounded, she began to comprehend the enormity of the disaster and the miracle of her rescue. Once it became clear that *Hurricane* would find no more refugees of the *City of Benares*, she asked herself, *How is it that all of us—four souls who arrived on deck too late for the boats—are still here? Why have we survived?*

The two surviving children's escorts, Lillian Towns and Marjorie Day, were asking themselves the same questions, and agonizing over what had happened to so many others. The escorts had left Liverpool with a profound sense of duty and responsibility to ninety boys and girls, and to the children's families. Marjorie Day believed they also had made a solemn promise to their nation to see these sons and daughters of Britain to safer shores. *Why had we been sent,* Lillian Towns wondered, *if not to save these children?* It seemed altogether wrong, she thought, that they would soon be back, alive, on British soil, without the boys and girls entrusted to them.

Collinson and the other sailors found the adults generally more traumatized than the boys and girls, who recovered quickly and took an instant interest in their new surroundings. Jack Keeley was cold and sore for hours after his rescue—but he was alive, and ecstatic to be on a ship filled with English sailors.

ALBERT GORMAN, WHO HAD HOISTED an even dozen survivors from the water that afternoon, experienced new adventures in the night and day that followed. He was almost an elder statesman in the *Hurricane* crew, and it was with this in mind that Simms summoned him to the captain's deck on the night of September 18. It was the eve of Gorman's twenty-eighth birthday.

"I know you're a married man, Gorman," the captain began. He then asked him to help bathe and dress some of the older female survivors. Gorman did not care for this latest assignment, but he did as he was told. He began by bringing one woman a pair of sailor's pants.

"These have a hole in them," the woman said with a smile.

"You shouldn't be surprised," Gorman replied. "We are built differently."

The woman laughed. Gorman smiled. They had not heard much laughter since the first survivors had been brought aboard.

Gorman was called next to assist a heavyset woman who was still in her soaked clothes, and feeling ill. He drew a bath, helped her to a nearby stool, and suggested she get in the tub. Then he left, to afford the woman her privacy and to tend to other women in need.

Fifteen minutes later Gorman returned, knocked on the door, and found the woman where he had left her, still perched on that stool. Her face was gray.

"There, dear. Into the bath . . ."

At which point the woman leaned forward and vomited.

Gorman cleaned up after her, gave her a cup of water, and again he suggested that a bath might help. The woman nodded, but it was clear she would need help getting out of her clothes.

So it was that Leading Seaman Albert Gorman found himself struggling with a corset and a line of knotted lace that seemed terribly tight and impossible to untangle. He worked at them with his fingers, growing exasperated and a little embarrassed. Finally Gorman drew his sailor's knife and began cutting the bottom of the lace.

Soon, as Gorman described it, "there was a sound like a piano wire, and the corsets parted and fell, onto the floor. And so, if I may be so bold, did most of my friend."

And so the woman had her bath.

PROUD, DRAINED, AND PROFOUNDLY ANGRY, Commander Hugh Crofton Simms drafted a brief report of the rescues late that night and sent it by signal to the commander in chief of Western Approaches. "Investigation required on arrival," he wrote. "Commodore of convoy and captain missing. Most women and children saved are without husbands, parents or money."

There were, Simms added, "no other survivors alive from *City of Benares.*"

He was a steely veteran captain, but until this day no one who knew Hugh Crofton Simms had thought of him as a particularly rough or vengeful commander. Later that night Simms recorded this blunt threat in his diary, as his ship made for Scotland:

"Pity the poor Hun who meets the *Hurricane.*"

.   .   .

THURSDAY, SEPTEMBER 19, 1940, DAWNED bright and clear over the North Atlantic. It was a beautiful morning. Some of the crew had enjoyed their first sleep in more than forty-eight hours. Then, soon after breakfast, sailors and survivors alike received a terrible blow.

Three children had died during the night. The ten-year-olds Derek Carr and Terrence Holmes and the five-year-old Alan Capel had all come aboard unconscious. Holmes had been revived—but only briefly. The others had never awakened.

Simms called passengers and crew to the quarterdeck later that morning and read burial services for these latest young victims of the attack. The boys represented all the others, Simms said; this was to be a service meant for every man, woman, and child lost from the *City of Benares*. Hymns were sung, and then the bodies of Holmes, Carr, and Capel—three boys from Middlesex— were each draped in a Union Jack and lowered slowly to the sea.

"And we therefore commit his body to the deep," the *Hurricane*'s chaplain said, once for each child. "God rest his soul."

Sailors and survivors alike were overcome. Many who witnessed the ceremony—including some whose naval careers would stretch for several years—would later call it their most profound memory of the war. They cried for these lost boys and for the others, all those taken by the U-boat's torpedo or by the unforgiving sea. And they cried for families who had proudly dispatched sons and daughters to what they had believed would be a safer future.

The bodies slid from under the Union Jacks, into the North Atlantic.

THE *BENARES* SURVIVORS SPENT A day and a half on board HMS *Hurricane*. Many remained shocked and sick. Sailors found some of their new charges huddled close, pale and frightened.

For the most part, the children proved the exceptions. Colin Richardson had recovered remarkably after a single night's sleep. He was sore and woozy, but that afternoon he and Derek Bech played on *Hurricane*'s deck, gazing in wonder at the ship's guns and depth charge cannon. Jack Keeley and Rex Thorne were tired, and Thorne had difficulty walking, but together they trailed happily after sailors, pretending they were sailors, too. All the children had been outfitted with warm and wildly oversized crew pants and sweaters. Checking on Beth and Bess on the afternoon following their rescue, a weary Peter Collinson warned the girls to expect the ship to shake, sometime within the half hour; *Hurricane* was preparing to drop depth charges. "Now, you mustn't worry, girls—but we've reason to think there's a sub in the area." They were too tired to worry, even when the ship heaved profoundly as the charges were dropped. "Everyone all right?" Collinson asked with a smile as he made rounds a short while later. The girls assured him they were.

At eleven o'clock on the morning of Friday, September 20, HMS *Hurricane* pulled into Prince's Pier at the Scottish port of Greenock. It was one week since the *Benares* had left Liverpool. A crowd of several hundred had gathered at the Greenock docks, including the shaken architect of the children's evacuation program, Geoffrey Shakespeare.

A few survivors bounded off the warship, after a fond farewell with the crew. Most left HMS *Hurricane* more carefully. Bess Walder and Beth Cummings had to be carried off on stretchers, though even from their horizontal vantage points they thrilled at the scene.

Albert Gorman watched this procession, and he saw two ambulance drivers with a stretcher bearing a blond girl wrapped in blankets. He recognized the girl—she was Eleanor Wright, the thirteen-year-old from Sunderland.

Later Gorman made these notes in his diary:

> I stood and watched ambulance men bring down the girl with the
> broken leg. On a stretcher. As they were about to pass me, she asked
> the ambulance men to stop. They stopped and she beckoned me to her.
> I bent to listen. She kissed me softly and said "Thank you."
>
> Everyone saw this. I was full up and then knew that I was not as
> tough as I thought.

Hugh Crofton Simms penned an angry letter to his wife and mother, a lyrical account that acknowledged the heroism of his men and finished with a profound set of memories from his time covering Patrick Fletcher's search box:

> I remember as we approached, three men singing "Rule Britannia."
> Two girls on the bottom of an upturned boat. The dead white staring
> faces in each boat. They lie there still. The way no one thanked anyone,
> as they couldn't speak . . . The Doctor bringing four children back to
> life. Three of them dying. Conducting a majestic burial . . . George
> Pound leaping in to save a woman washed off a raft. This woman being
> a German. Giving away all my clothes. Everyone giving away every-
> thing. The peace of that night. Tiptoeing down to the cabins to whisper

Hallo. The next morning, sunny, bright, too late. The awful feeling that
I might have missed someone . . .

"I do not know how I managed to survive," William Forsyth said as he
stepped gingerly onto the pier at Greenock. "But the memory will haunt me
all my life."

"It is a miracle that we lived," Bess Walder told a reporter. "I owe everything to my friend Beth." Beth Cummings said almost the same thing, from
her bed at Smithston Hospital: "I should not have made it, were it not for that
girl."

It seemed—late that morning on the twentieth of September—that the
story of the *City of Benares*, with all its horror and wonder, was over.

BOOK TWO

LIFEBOAT 12

The most important thing for any lifeboatman to do, is to school his own mind … Make up your own mind not to get excited, and stick to it. Don't say you won't be afraid, for you will. When the torpedo explodes you will get a sinking sensation in the pit of your stomach, and your knees may become a bit weak. The best cure for this is action.

—B. A. Baker
Third Officer, *Prusa*
Quoted in *How to Abandon Ship*

Lifeboat 12

The officers of HMS *Hurricane* were distressed by news that reached them half the distance back to Great Britain: They had missed a lifeboat.

It had been Hugh Crofton Simms' fear, an "awful feeling that I might have missed someone." He and his men had performed magnificently; they had rescued more than one hundred people and accounted for twelve lifeboats at the scene, and they had assumed they were finished. After all, the *Benares* had carried exactly twelve lifeboats. But during that chaotic afternoon and early evening the fact that one of these boats had borne passengers from the torpedoed freighter *Marina*—a fact known to several of *Hurricane*'s sailors—had not been recorded. Or, more likely, its significance had escaped notice in the rush to save and care for survivors.

They had combed Patrick Fletcher's search box with great precision. No survivor had mentioned the other boat, but then no survivors had really been keeping track. The sick bay and surgery ward on board *Hurricane* were hardly the places for that. Survivors were too exhausted, sailors too occupied tending to scared and wounded refugees from the *Benares*. In any event, no one survivor knew the full picture of which boats and which passengers had been brought on board.

So Simms and his men were saddened and puzzled to learn that one *Benares* boat was unaccounted for. Nevertheless, they did not believe there could be any more survivors at the scene. Having seen the terrible detritus of the *City of Benares*, they were unanimous: This twelfth boat, wherever it was, was surely beyond hope.

A few passengers shared memories of their final moments aboard the *Benares*, struggling to recall whom they had seen and where they had seen them last. Chief Officer Hetherington believed the missing boat was number 12, and he remembered seeing Father Rory O'Sullivan with several of the evacuee boys at that lifeboat station. One of the two surviving children's escorts, Marjorie Day, reported that "of Father O'Sullivan I know nothing but Miss Cornish was in that boat [number 12]. I imagine they were swamped but no one knows." If they had survived, Day thought, perhaps another ship would find them.

The fact was that no other ships were looking. HMS *Hurricane* had been a one-vessel search party and her work was done. But the question lingered, and Hugh Crofton Simms assumed they would never know the answer.

Where was Lifeboat 12?

RONNIE COOPER, A TWENTY-TWO-YEAR-OLD SCOTSMAN, was the *Benares'* fourth officer. He had been off-duty and asleep when the torpedo struck, but he had come to his senses in a hurry and hustled to his designated lifeboat station—number 12—within minutes of the explosion. And he had guessed immediately what had happened.

Several Indian crewmembers had already congregated at Cooper's station by the time he arrived. They queued for a place, offering to help Cooper lower the boat. Soon Rory O'Sullivan was here, having brought five of his boys to deck—Billy Short, Fred Steels, Howard Claytor, Paul Shearing, and Derek Capel. A sixth evacuee, Ken Sparks, had been steered here by another officer. The children stood there, patient and quiet—like waiting for the cinema, Paul Shearing thought. Also at this station were Bohdan Nagorski and the escort Mary Cornish, who had been directed to Lifeboat 12 after missing the launch of her assigned boat. Cooper's was now a crowded station.

Nagorski had grown increasingly anxious since leaving his cabin. He feared for his friend Zygmunt Gralinski, unseen since the immediate aftermath, and for children he knew were missing. There had been many more boys than this during the lifeboat drills. These thoughts were racing through Nagorski's mind when Officer Cooper began barking orders. "Clear away," he called out. "Stand by for lowering."

Nagorski and O'Sullivan protested, urging Cooper to wait. Was there not still space in the boat? O'Sullivan, weak though he was, insisted that more children were coming. They *had* to be on their way to deck. "Must have just had a rough time below," he said. Nagorski found the ship's assistant steward, George Purvis. Had the order been given to come to deck? he asked Purvis. Were there not more people waiting at the muster stations?

The order had been given, Purvis assured, and then he added, "Sir, the ship may sink at any moment."

Cooper told O'Sullivan there were officers below deck looking for the children, but then he relented. The launch would be delayed.

Nagorski hurried across the deck, looping around the destroyed number five hold, on a last search for his friend. He did not find him, and he saw none of the missing boys. At the launching station for Lifeboat 11 a sailor stopped him, taking him by the arm. There were vacancies in the boat, he said. In the commotion, someone was offering Bohdan Nagorski a seat.

Nagorski declined. "I am assigned to Lifeboat 12," he said, and with that he retraced his steps and found a place in Cooper's boat, number 12. It was a life-or-death decision, made in an instant.

THE WINDS WERE STRENGTHENING, THE *Benares* listed steeply, and Ronnie Cooper felt he did not have much time. Together with Purvis and the Indians he began to guide his group over the ship's rail and into the boat.

Lifeboat 12 swung out and back, buffeted by the winds as so many of the other boats had been. Passengers had to time their step carefully, in some cases leaping to land safely in the boat. When the boys' turn came, Cooper and a fellow sailor practically threw them aboard.

Sitting in the boat as it rocked in this way, Billy Short heard the awful sounds—shouts from the deck and frightened cries from the water. Short was nine years old, the youngest of the group in Lifeboat 12. He was too small to see what was happening. Sea spray washed over him. *Wasn't like this during the drills,* Billy Short thought.

Now Officer Cooper told the group to prepare for the descent to the water. One last time Cooper heard an objection, this time from Mary Cornish. Cooper and Purvis nudged her toward the rail, but she remained torn and anguished. Though she had conducted a below-deck search of her own, Cornish still believed she was abandoning her charges.

"There are no more children coming to deck, miss," Cooper said gently. "We can be certain of that."

Then Nagorski and O'Sullivan were back. Ronnie Cooper persuaded Cornish at last that her life was now the only one she could actually save. More than that, he said, there were young boys in the boat who would require her help and attention. He did not say it explicitly, but Cornish thought she understood the implication: *It would be good to have a woman on board, to help care for these boys.*

Just then eleven-year-old Fred Steels was gazing out at the water, trying to see over the gunwale, and he heard a cry from the opposite end of the boat. He turned just in time to see a nearby lifeboat dropped from its davits. It hit the sea with a huge splash. Steels had a good look as the boat fell; he wondered what had happened to the figures he had seen. *I hope they'll manage*, he thought. *Hope they can make a swim back to their boat.*

From the *Benares*' deck, someone flung a raft and then life vests over Lifeboat 12 and down to the water. Mary Cornish watched these objects fly overhead, from her place in the lifeboat's midsection. She felt physically sick. She also felt helpless, and terrified.

Finally Ronnie Cooper gave the order. "Stand back!" he called to the other sailors. "Man the falls and reels!"

Lifeboat 12 was lowered to the sea.

It was one of the last boats to go, and it dropped fast, the boys hanging on. *Like monkeys*, Ken Sparks thought. For a terrible moment the stern fell, dropping awkwardly, the bow left high, the top end of a dangerously steep angle. The roar of the sea lifted, close now. To O'Sullivan it seemed they were riding "a badly adjusted elevator." But then Cooper had the falls back in alignment and the lifeboat leveled. Not one of his charges was thrown to the water.

What mattered most was how the boat would land, and this Cooper managed adroitly, letting out rope in slow and steady increments, adjusting the boat's angle several times as it neared the water. The trick was to come down level, though the *Benares* herself was leaning profoundly to the stern. Cooper succeeded where most others had not, and his passengers held on. Lifeboat 12 touched the water relatively gently and evenly.

Once the boat was down, four more Indians came down the ladder, followed by the ship's steward, George Purvis. With twenty-seven Indians, six boys, O'Sullivan, Cornish, Nagorski, and Purvis, there were thirty-seven people on board Lifeboat 12.

The last to descend was Ronnie Cooper. He looked about the *Benares*' deck and saw fellow officers Joe Hetherington and Hugh Asher working to free rafts at the stern. *At least they will try*, Cooper thought. *They will have a chance.*

The *City of Benares* was sloping dangerously now. *God help them*, Cooper thought; then he seized the rope ladder and stepped down to Lifeboat 12.

THE SWELLS RAN HIGH, BUT landing cleanly meant that Lifeboat 12 had not been inundated with water. They had heavy sprays to contend with and they immediately set about bailing, but while passengers in the other boats found the sea almost immediately at waist level or higher, this group had only a few inches of water to contend with, shallow pools that sloshed about their feet.

They also had several able seamen on board. Cooper and Purvis were young but highly regarded members of the *Benares* crew. So was one of the Indians on board, a strong young general servant named Ramjam Buxoo. Ramjam had helped board the six boys, helped bail once they hit the water, and instructed his compatriots to assist as well.

Then, within minutes of launching, Lifeboat 12 found more recruits. Cooper carried out a series of daring rescues, five "stops" on the raging sea that brought eight more crewmen into the boat. The rescues were technically difficult—Cooper had to steer toward flailing swimmers, then hold the boat steady while Ramjam, Purvis, and the others dragged bodies on board—and to some passengers it seemed both a risky endeavor and a dangerous overload. Built to hold forty people, Lifeboat 12 now carried forty adults and six children. But Cooper and Purvis were determined to save anyone they could. They could not have known it at the time, but their courage and selflessness in these early moments would reap great dividends. In the span of perhaps five minutes, Cooper and Purvis had snatched up people who would prove immensely valuable in the ordeal that loomed.

They were pulling away when Billy Short saw the *Benares* tilt high, her deck lights washing over the water, a momentary glow that nearly reached Lifeboat 12 itself. They were perhaps three hundred feet from the ship, and they watched together as the *City of Benares* went under, her lights shining brightly until she vanished.

Majestic, Billy Short thought.

"Farewell," Mary Cornish whispered.

LIFEBOAT 12 WAS ALREADY FAR enough from the *Benares* so that it hardly suffered from the undertow created by her sinking. They had worked the Fleming gear hard to get themselves clear. But the seas still ran heavy, and the overall picture was still dreadful: a lifeboat jammed with people; the flu-ridden Father Rory O'Sullivan, in pajamas and coat, barefooted and violently ill; Mary Cornish terribly frightened, staring up at waves that looked to her like "black mountains"; more than two dozen Indians dressed in light cottons; and six young boys, seasick, confused, and cold.

Fred Steels watched as a wave socked a low-lying lifeboat, nearly tipping it over. Paul Shearing heard a cry from the water—some poor soul he could not see was calling for help. Shearing did not hear the voice again. So much around them seemed to spell doom. Time and again the waves lifted Lifeboat 12 high and dropped it down. The boys screamed each time, though they felt a thrill more than they felt any fear. Derek Capel marveled at the ocean's power. One moment it seemed he was atop a church tower, looking down; the next, he was at ground level, the same tower rising high above. As the swells pummeled the boat, Bohdan Nagorski turned up his coat collar and said to himself, *We will not make it. We will not last until morning.*

And yet, as the hours passed and these peaks and valleys repeated them-selves, making for a seemingly endless seaborne roller coaster, Nagorski no-ticed something else: They were holding their own. They had witnessed many of the other lifeboat horrors—people tossed in midair, boats upended, children whisked away by a fierce current—and as yet none of these things had hap-pened to *them.* Lifeboat 12 was tossing violently, but by the early hours of morning fear and fatalism began to lose their grip. The children even struck up a round of "Roll Out the Barrel." Certainly the night was awful, but at least they were right side up. Cooper passed word to his passengers: Do not worry—this boat is sturdy and will not be easily overturned. If anyone wished to help, he said, they might bail water; otherwise he told them all to try to rest. Pre-sumably they would be found and rescued after daybreak.

Bohdan Nagorski revised his assessment. *We can make it,* he thought. *This boat is strong.*

"LIFEBOATS ACQUIRE CHARACTER WHEN SHIPS sink," the Harvard professor John Stilgoe writes in *Lifeboat,* a history of shipwrecks and lifeboat journeys. "Shipwreck confers on every lifeboat individual identity and significance beyond measure." As the terrible night stretched, the *Benares'* Lifeboat number 12 was acquiring her own identity and character, every wave a contribution, every hour a challenge to her crew and passengers.

Purvis, the steward, scrambled at the stern, struggling to keep his balance as he searched the lifeboat stocks for torches and flares. Finally he found a packet of torches and managed somehow to light one over the rolling waters, producing an eerie red glow that illuminated Purvis' face and threw sparks at the waves. Now and then they could see similar lights from the other boats. Purvis also found a container that held a stash of fifteen heavy woolen blankets, dry and neatly folded. He passed these to the bow—the children would be as warm as he could possibly make them.

The lifeboats all held sails stashed below boards. Purvis and Ramjam freed Lifeboat 12's sail, but Cooper judged the seas too rough to raise it during the night. Instead he and the other crewmen worked the Fleming gear, the steering devices built into all the boats. There were five sets of the Fleming handles, the stubby iron struts that jutted up from the boat's bottom and ran along its midsection. Pushing and pulling the handles turned a shaft, which in turn spun a propeller under the rudder. The Fleming gear had been broken or submerged in most of the other boats, but in Lifeboat 12 the iron handles were working. Soon Cooper put a Fleming "crew" to work, christening a rotation that would include not just sailors but also Nagorski, Cornish, and the children, too. The levers' value as navigational tools was perhaps eclipsed by the warming effect they had and the enthusiasm they generated in the children, who pushed and pulled with vigor, singing songs and cheering one another on.

"Pull harder now!" Fred Steels hollered.

"We're 'avin' an *adventure*!" cried Ken Sparks.

The one quiet child was Paul Shearing, eleven, the boy who had wanted to leave England to escape the taunts and teasing of schoolmates. Shearing passed much of the night cowering at the bow. He thought of joining the other boys, but his shy nature still showed, even in these circumstances. He lay there, cold and badly cramped, and listened.

The other five boys were upbeat, enthusiastic even. They bailed water and worked the Fleming handles, all of them feeling like proper sailors, important players in a wild, middle-of-the-night wartime drama.

An adventure, Fred Steels thought. *I wonder what'll happen next.*

THE NIGHT HOURS PASSED, THE cold working into their bones, fatigue setting in, the rough seas keeping them drenched and occasionally seasick. In the last hours of darkness Cooper noticed that they were away from the other lifeboats, but he kept his Fleming "crews" working, as much for the distraction and exercise as anything else. Then, as the black night showed traces of gray light, Cooper thought he saw something. A glimmer on the water. Cooper dared for a moment to believe this was a rescue vessel and he tried to maneuver his boat toward it.

Soon they saw that the light was being thrown off by a pair of torches, not from a rescue ship but from another lifeboat. This one looked considerably smaller than theirs.

As they came near, they heard a voice.

"What ship are you?"

"The *City of Benares*. And you?"

"*Marina.*"

Cooper and his fellow sailors in Lifeboat 12 had not known the name *Marina;* nor had they known that another vessel in Convoy OB213 had been torpedoed. *Marina*'s captain, R. T. Paine, was at the helm of this lifeboat, one of two that ship had put to water (the other was Leslie Lewis' boat—the one that would later collect Marguerite, Sonia, and Derek Bech along with two others from the *Benares*).

Cooper came alongside the *Marina* boat and asked who was in charge. Then he explained Lifeboat 12's circumstances to Captain Paine.

Paine's boat was crowded, too; he had sixteen merchant sailors on board. Paine told Cooper he planned to remain near the scene of the attacks until daybreak at least. By then, he believed, a rescue vessel would come. He also suggested to Cooper that their boats stay close together. Two lifeboats would be easier to find than one, he reasoned. Cooper agreed to keep his boat near.

STILL SCAVENGING BELOW BOARDS, GEORGE Purvis discovered a flask of brandy. As dawn neared and the seas mellowed, he passed tiny cups around the boat.

Without prompting, the boys started another chorus of "Roll Out the Barrel." They took turns on the Fleming gear and talked about the effects the handles were having on their hands. It was terribly cold now. The sleet beat hard, and bits of spindrift flew at their faces. Somehow the boys took no notice. They had not slept, yet they did not feel tired. Their stimulant was the powerful pull of adventure, and even Paul Shearing felt it, wary and shy and jammed though he was with Mary Cornish at the bow.

Lifeboat 12 was faring well. Having taken on less water, the boat was significantly lighter than the others, and Ronnie Cooper had steered it cleanly through the high waves. His passengers were consequently at less risk of expo-

sure, their mood was relatively good, and—most important—they had yet
experience the trauma that so many others had suffered: the shock of seein
anyone among them die.

DAWN ARRIVED, REVEALING A BARREN, hail-dotted sea.

Cooper and Purvis, unflappable in the night, were stunned to see how alone
they were. Lifeboat 12 bobbed on the waves, only the *Marina*'s little boat
along for company. There was no rescue vessel, no other vessel at all. Nothing
but waves and gray sky on the horizon.

Mary Cornish had hoped to see other boats, or a ship, and she had been sure
the morning would offer some visible reminder of the tragedy. But morning
brought no such thing; where Lifeboat 12 drifted there were no bodies, no
rafts, not even any wreckage. There was just the sea spray and the hail, the
Marina's lifeboat and the waves.

Officer Cooper scanned the sea and tried to guess at where they were. *How
far have we gone?* Probably three or four miles from the scene, he surmised, but
they could not be sure. At about seven o'clock, the *Marina*'s Captain Paine
came alongside and informed Cooper he had decided to make for Ireland. He
had deliberated with his crew for much of the night, and in so doing he had
considered circumstances quite different from Lifeboat 12's. R. T. Paine carried
a small complement of highly experienced seamen—sixteen of them—and no
other passengers. Lifeboat 12—while better off than other *Benares* boats—was
crowded with forty-six people, only a handful of whom were sailors. Paine calculated that if the westerly winds prevailed he might make landfall in a week;
Cooper and his men believed their "cargo" to be too heavy and that Lifeboat 12
would never be able to match such a pace. For the moment, in that morning's
ugly mix of hail and sleet, they could not even raise a sail.

So the two boats parted company. Cooper wished Paine well.

About an hour later, the storm blew past, and Ronnie Cooper and Ramjam
Buxoo dug into the lifeboat lockers for badly needed sustenance. Bohdan
Nagorski sat up, cold but optimistic. He imagined that the destroyer *Winchelsea*
was racing for the scene.

Thirty-nine men, one woman, and six boys waited quietly for their rescue.

IT WAS ONE OF THE many cruel ironies of that long night and th
new morning, Wednesday, the eighteenth of September: Lifeboat 12 was pe

forming *too well*. Its frame undamaged, its interior dry, and its passengers relatively strong and in good spirits, the boat worked up a decent pace as it drifted to the east.

Cooper and the others could not have known it, but their good fortune and fine seamanship were conspiring to ruin their chances of rescue. The eleven other *Benares* lifeboats were moving slowly, near the scene of the attack. Waterlogged, overturned, and in some cases badly damaged, their heavy weight and limited mobility had left them well within the confines of HMS *Hurricane*'s search box.

Lifeboat 12, by contrast, was propelling itself out of the box. Unencumbered by water, pushed along by Cooper's Fleming crews, Lifeboat 12 slipped from the scene. To little Billy Short it seemed they had a current all their own.

CHAPTER 15

Taking Stock

There is an illustration in the World War II–era pamphlet *Safety for Seamen*, a coproduction of the U.S. War Shipping Administration and the United Seaman's service, that aims to advise the survivors of a shipwreck. The drawing shows a half dozen men in a lifeboat brandishing small wooden bats against a group of demons on the water. The latter are caricatured as seaborne devils, each with a label: "Fear," "Anxiety," "Loss of Faith," "Anger," and "Over Fatigue."

These were among the enemies arrayed against the *City of Benares'* Lifeboat 12 as it drifted eastward. Taken together with the more obvious deficits of water, food, shelter, and warm clothing, the boat's passengers faced formidable obstacles. They were cold, tired, terribly cramped, and already they were hungry and thirsty. A majority had been ill during the night, and some were still nauseous.

By mid-morning, the seas had calmed considerably, and rays of sunlight angled through clouds. The temperature may have reached fifty degrees; Cooper and his mates worked to raise the sail, a job made difficult because it was so hard to avoid nudging or stepping on their fellow passengers. Forty-six people took stock of their supplies, their circumstances, and their surroundings.

The lifeboat itself was twenty-six feet long, eight feet three inches wide, and curved into a high point at either end. With floorboards in place, the boat's depth was three and a half feet. The lifeboat was a sturdy and seaworthy mix of timbers, built to British Board of Trade specifications that emphasized "increased buoyancy when water-logged." As has been said, these were hardly flimsy craft. In calm waters, a man could walk in a Board of Trade lifeboat and it would scarcely move.

British lifeboats were also crammed with supplies—the assumption being that any shipwrecked traveler might require sustenance for several days. (A parallel assumption was that no lifeboat would be stranded for much more than a week; presumably a ship would radio for help, and given how crowded shipping lanes were in the Atlantic in late 1940, some craft would reach the boat before long.) Virtually every square inch below boards held a watertight container, and the *Benares* officers had been drilled on precisely what they would find in the event of shipwreck, and where they would find it. In his job as assistant steward for the *Benares*, Purvis had monitored pro- visions of food and drink, and helped supervise cooks and barmen and gen- eral servants. He now took on the job of opening Lifeboat 12's lockers and itemizing its stocks. George Purvis would in effect act as "steward" for Lifeboat 12.

Purvis and the other sailors rummaged through eight metal lockers and found that none had been damaged during the night. Each container mea- sured roughly two feet by three feet, with a depth of about eighteen inches. They held cans of salmon, sardines, and corned beef, smaller cans of pineapple and peaches, and several boxes of ship's biscuits. There were cases of con- densed milk in small cans and two large metal canisters filled with water. The latter interested Purvis most; before he doled out a drop of water, he wanted to know precisely how much he had to work with. Moving carefully about the stern, Purvis began calculating how much water each passenger ought to have when their first meal was served.

In a separate stash Purvis discovered a kind of grab-bag survival kit. There was a rudder and tiller, a bucket for bailing, a pair of water dippers, two small axes, an oil lamp, oil, a box of lifeboat matches (made to light even after ab- sorbing water), a sea anchor, and a thick canvas tarpaulin, which Purvis and two of the Indians put to use early that first morning, constructing a hood over the bows. The tarpaulin became a small tentlike shelter, a taut waterproof hood under which two adults or three or four children could crouch at any given time. Purvis had already found the wool blankets during the night; these would have to be carefully divided. Most of the passengers were dressed for a brisk autumn day at best, and the Indians were particularly ill equipped, in their loose-fitting cottons and life vests. Under her life vest Mary Cornish had only a thin shirt, silk blouse, and cotton jacket. She had no coat. Rory

O'Sullivan wore a coat, but had only pajamas underneath, and no shoes. Bohdan Nagorski was perhaps best off, in a heavy coat and homburg hat, but from the first morning he volunteered the coat as a blanket or wrap for the children. The sailors had their peacoats.

The boys were almost all underdressed; three of them were barefooted. Fred Steels and Ken Sparks wore duffel coats, and Billy Short was still wearing the cut-down fur coat his aunt had "downsized" for him. Howard Claytor, Paul Shearing, and Derek Capel had no coats at all.

Purvis' search of the boat's stocks yielded another piece of disheartening news: The lifeboat's compass had been irreparably damaged, he reported to Cooper, and he had found neither a radio nor sextant anywhere below boards. Cooper nodded, as though he had expected as much, but the boat's ranking officer must have been crestfallen to learn that his lifeboat was beginning its journey deprived of these basic navigational tools. Cooper and his men would be forced to rely on more primitive forms of navigation—namely, the sun and stars—provided the weather improved enough to see them.

Finally Purvis found a can of grease under the boat's floorboards. Father Rory O'Sullivan, still seriously ill, stared with macabre interest at this last item. He remembered suddenly that Columbus' crewmen had been reduced in their most dire days to eating the soles of their shoes. A nightmarish vision came to the frail priest, of himself and the others in the boat, several days on, consuming the grease from Purvis' little can.

LIFEBOAT ACCOUNTS ARE REPLETE WITH reminders that discipline and camaraderie are critical commodities on the open water—and that, unfortunately, they are not all that common. In the cramped and unpleasant confines of a typical boat, "Propinquity remains a problem, and great efforts of self-control are required to avoid serious disagreements—quarrels, even." So wrote Jean Merrien in *Lonely Voyagers*, his collection of stories about small-vessel ocean voyages. One of the better-known of history's lifeboat survivors, First Mate Owen Chase of the ill-fated nineteenth-century whaleship *Essex*, wrote in his journal about the value of discipline and optimism among a boat's passengers:

> There were with us many whose weak minds, I am confident, would
> have sunk under the dismal retrospections of the past catastrophe, and
> who did not possess either sense or firmness enough to contemplate our

approaching destiny, without the cheering of some more determined countenance than their own.

The absence of faith and discipline ("firmness," as Chase put it) could have punishing consequences—not just "quarrels" but violence and cannibalism as well. "There is something peculiar in a small boat upon the wide sea," Joseph Conrad wrote in *Lord Jim*. "Trust a boat on the high seas to bring out the irrational that lurks at the bottom of every thought, sentiment, sensation, emotion."

The lessons were simple: Strength of character and a positive outlook were vital; and it mattered who you had at your side in the boat.

It was perhaps too soon to gauge such qualities in Lifeboat 12—though the crew had certainly shown resolve and noble character, and the children had been undeniably brave and enthusiastic through the night that followed the U-boat's strike. As a group, the occupants of Lifeboat 12 could also boast that thus far there had been no outward signs of disagreement, or negative outlook, anywhere in the boat. One could say there was no Szekulesz—the ill-tempered Hungarian—aboard Lifeboat 12.

While George Purvis and Ronnie Cooper organized provisions, the people on board took quiet measure of one another. The boat's passengers and crew were English, Scottish, Indian, and Polish, and they ranged in age from nine—Billy Short—to forty-nine—Bohdan Nagorski. They were forty-five men and one woman, the children's escort Mary Cornish. Among the men, thirty-two were Indian crew and servants, led by the general servant Ramjam Buxoo. Cooper had plucked six of the Indians from the water after launching; all six knew they were incredibly fortunate to have seats in the boat. Throughout the night Ramjam had asserted himself among his compatriots; now they turned or sat at attention whenever he spoke. Cooper detected immediately that to the other Indians Ramjam was a figure of some authority. He also appeared to be one of the few who spoke English. Several of the Indians were Muslims, and their routine included bowing to Mecca at least three times daily—rinsing their mouths and washing their faces before chanting prayers in quiet unison.

Among the *Benares'* British crew, the acknowledged leaders were Purvis and Cooper, who had supervised the launch and navigated superbly during the night. Ronnie Cooper had commanded respect, even awe, in those awful first minutes on the water. He had saved eight men and done so almost matter-of-factly, as though it were just what any young sailor might have been expected to do in a similar situation. He was twenty-two, at five-foot-six a strong and stocky man from a seafaring family in Dundee, on Scotland's east coast. Though he had been a vocal presence on the *Benares*' decks, supervising lifeboat drills and then the real thing on the night of the seventeenth, Ronnie Cooper was essentially a shy and reserved sailor. He rarely spoke unless spoken to.

George Purvis was twenty-three, like Cooper a Scotsman, born and raised in Glasgow. Purvis had a high forehead and a long, angular face. He had spent the quarter hour after the attack racing to bring children to deck, including an injured girl whom he carried from her cabin to a lifeboat station. Purvis was a cool, unflappable man, of unfailing good temper, and unlike Cooper he was a voluble character. The boys called him "Georgie-Porgie," and they loved him from the start.

Doug Critchley and Johnny Mayhew were two of the sailors Cooper had hauled in during the night. Critchley was twenty years old, a cadet from Cheshire who had learned to sail as a child and wanted to join the Royal Navy for as long as he could remember. Critchley had signed on with the Merchant Navy as a teenager, expecting to transfer later; this was only his second voyage.

On board the *City of Benares,* Critchley had covered twelve-to-four-o'clock shifts, afternoon and early morning, and he had therefore been asleep when the torpedo struck. After impact he had hurried to one of the *Benares'* five-inch guns, anxious to locate the U-boat and return fire. He never found the sub, and minutes later the call had come to abandon ship. Critchley had reached his lifeboat station too late and dived from the deck, only to find his lifeboat dangerously waterlogged. Critchley had treaded water for nearly half an hour before Cooper found him and pulled him over the gunwales and into Lifeboat 12. Doug Critchley was a lightly built but strong man, and he brought to Lifeboat 12 his own considerable gifts as an amateur yachtsman.

Johnny Mayhew was a Royal Navy signaler, one of the small contingent of Navy men assigned to the *Benares* for the voyage. He had spent an anxious Tuesday afternoon on or around the captain's bridge, wondering why the liner had not been permitted to race ahead of the convoy. Since the U-boat attack, Johnny Mayhew had been in two lifeboats already, tossed from both as the sea heaved in the night. Lifeboat 12 would be Mayhew's third try.

Then there was Harry Peard—"Gunner Peard," as they called him. Peard was another Royal Navy man, and he had passed the previous four days watching for submarines and aircraft from a gunner's nest recently affixed to the

Benares' stern. The nest, the half dozen gunners and signalmen, and a coat of dull brown paint had represented the *Benares'* makeover from commercial liner to evacuee transport ship. At thirty-eight, Harry Peard had been one of the oldest sailors on board the *City of Benares.*

Peard had never gone to deck or to any lifeboat station. He had been at his position when the torpedo struck and the impact had thrown him straight to the sea. Peard was a small man, at five-foot-three barely taller than the oldest children in Lifeboat 12, but he was a barrel-chested figure, wiry and strong. He swam for nearly half an hour in the swirling ocean, and twice he helped pull children to lifeboats, calling "Take them!" from the water. The *City of Benares* had already gone under by the time Ronnie Cooper found him.

Even on this first morning, it was apparent that Harry Peard would stand out. In the cold, cramped boat, where it was difficult even to shift in place, Peard seemed in perpetual motion. Nagorski marveled at the man's energy; it was as though the group consisted of forty-five tired, sick, and lethargic souls, and one talkative gunner from the Royal Navy. Peard was also strong-willed—a gruff, foulmouthed character—certainly not one to keep thoughts and feelings to himself. "Right! Chins up!" Peard hollered to the children that morning. "No use sulking, see?" *A rough diamond*, Derek Capel thought. *Wonder what he'll say next.*

Peard's assessment of the situation was simple: He believed there was nothing to be gained by wallowing in the trauma of the event or the difficulty of their circumstance, and he considered it defeatist, even dangerous, to do so. Peard told the Indians—who seemed particularly worried that first morning—that an airplane or a warship would be coming for them.

"They'll be here soon," he assured Ramjam, who translated dutifully. Many of the Indians appeared grateful to receive Peard's message.

To Capel and the other boys Peard was an extraordinary presence, a sailor drawn from picture books and newsreels about the war. Ken Sparks watched him and wondered what it would take to be a sailor someday. *To be just like Harry Peard.*

PROSTRATE IN THE BOAT'S CENTER, too weak to stand and barely able to speak, lay the thirty-two-year-old Reverend Rory O'Sullivan. O'Sullivan was a handsome man with an athletic figure, but now his face was pale and drawn and his body badly weakened. His case of flu, contracted during the first days of the voyage, had not abated. Other passengers watched

O'Sullivan shiver under a blanket on the boat's floor; they were convinced that he would be the first to die.

Rory O'Sullivan was a brave man and no stranger to drama and peril; he had fled Nazi-occupied France earlier that summer. After the U-boat's strike, O'Sullivan had led five boys and carried a sixth to the ship's deck, but he had suffered mightily in the lifeboat. O'Sullivan had taken his turn to row in the early morning—only to collapse after a few minutes spent pulling the Fleming gear. When he came to it was nearly midday, and Rory O'Sullivan found himself staring up at the sky, the legs and feet of fellow passengers all around him. *There cannot be*, he thought, *a less comfortable place to rest.* At one point he heard someone say, "The priest won't last much longer."

MARY CORNISH WAS FORTY-ONE, AND already she had spent twenty years studying and teaching music. She was a gifted classical pianist, trained as a child in England and later at the Royal Academy in Vienna. She had brown eyes, high cheekbones, and dark brown hair that she wore pulled back in a bun. Cornish had a soft voice, but she was a supremely self-confident teacher. A writer said of her first meeting with Mary Cornish that "the impression she gives . . . is that of a woman of great reserve, not self-assertive yet one who clearly knows her own mind on all essential matters."

Cornish had never been on an ocean voyage before this one. Her appearance in Lifeboat 12 had been an accident, a consequence of her last-minute forays below the *Benares'* deck. On Wednesday morning her presence seemed a gift, given that the only other children's escort in Boat 12—Father O'Sullivan— was in no condition to help. Mary Cornish had not even realized the boys *had* an escort on board until dawn came and she recognized the priest laid out on the boat floor.

Cornish resolved to act as Rory O'Sullivan's substitute. *If I am here*, she thought, *then someone else must be watching my girls.* No doubt the girls were safe, she reasoned, in some lifeboat she could not see. It made sense. *I shall care for these children instead.* She would take it as her calling to occupy, amuse, and care for a half dozen restless English boys. The beneficiaries were Fred and Billy, Howard and Paul, and Derek and Ken, six children aged nine to thirteen, who on this bleak morning looked out at the sea and saw not fear but high drama, not danger but adventure, pure and wondrous.

Howard Claytor was eleven, an only child from Middlesex. His parents had warned him expressly about the risks of torpedo attack. He in turn had told them that—risks notwithstanding—he *really* wanted to go to Canada. Claytor had loved the *City of Benares*, and spent hours cavorting on her decks and sprinting along her corridors, building an appetite for those fantastic meals. Now it was different, of course, but to Howard the lifeboat afforded a chance for new thrills, chief among these the close company he was keeping with ship's officers and Navy men. It was incredible, really. *Imagine*, Claytor thought, *what I shall tell my friends!*

Fred Steels was also eleven, a short boy with a round face and a pageboy haircut. Steels was one of five children in a Yorkshire family, two of whom had died before Fred was born. Like the other evacuees, Steels had thrilled at the chance to see Canada—"the cat's whiskers," he said—though he knew next to nothing about the country. In Lifeboat 12 Steels sat at Claytor's side, warm coat draped over his pajamas. Fred Steels came from a family of seamen, and he could follow the finer points of sailing and navigation. He scanned the horizon, looking for the Royal Navy. *Goodness*, he wondered, *what will the warship be like? How big will it be? And how many sailors will come for us?*

Paul Shearing, another eleven-year-old, was easily the quietest in the group, the boy from Bournemouth who had talked his mother into letting him go "to get away from things I didn't like." Though Shearing had cut his foot on a glass shard moments after the attack, by now the cold had numbed the pain. In midmorning he emerged from the shelter at the bow for his first real conversation with the other children. *Nice boys these are*, he thought. *We shall have a fine time.*

Ken Sparks was thirteen, the eldest of six *Benares* evacuees from Wembley and the oldest boy in Lifeboat 12. Sparks had watched the war at close range, seen and smelled London burning, and he had made a hobby of studying the names and contours of German and British aircraft. He had passed hours staring at the sky, trying to match the faint outlines he saw with photographs from newspapers and magazines. Like so many of the evacuee children, Sparks had known a difficult childhood. His mother had died just days after he was born, having suffered complications following a premature birth. Sparks had been raised by his father and a stepmother.

On board the *Benares*, Ken Sparks had spent most of his time playing with a Wembley neighbor, ten-year-old Terrence Holmes. Now, sitting in the cramped bow of Lifeboat 12, Sparks shivered and wondered what had become of his friend. He said a short prayer for Holmes, and then another to thank his stepmother, who had bought the coat he was wearing just days before he left. "You must keep an eye on it!" she had warned, and Ken Sparks had done just that, keeping the coat close at all times and bringing it to the deck after the torpedo struck. Ken Sparks remembered that now, pulling up the collar and feeling almost happy in his place in the boat.

These four boys gave only passing thought to their plight, paused not a moment to consider their mortality. Never did they think they might have been abandoned on the water. "I'll see it first!" Sparks said to Shearing, meaning the ship they both believed was near.

The two remaining children were more subdued—for good reason. Billy Short and Derek Capel had younger brothers whom they had last seen below the *Benares'* deck, before the torpedo's arrival. More than the others in Lifeboat 12, these two needed reassuring. On their first full day together, Capel asked O'Sullivan, Cornish, and Nagorski the same questions: What did they know about his little brother, Alan? Where had he gone? Where was he now? *Me brother's only five*, Derek Capel thought, and he reminded Rory O'Sullivan of this.

O'Sullivan would say only that he was certain the other boys were in good care, wherever they were. Peter Short, also five years old, was brother to Billy, the Sunderland boy with the heavy Scottish brogue. Billy Short had discovered that whenever worry intruded, a wave seemed to splash across the bow, dousing him and returning him to the moment at hand. *Better not think about Peter too much.* It was the one good thing about the seemingly endless swells—Billy Short never forgot his little brother, but those waves also kept reminding him that they were in the thralls of a great drama. He stared down past the Indians to the figure of Ronnie Cooper, perched on the till, quiet and stern and looking out over the water. *I'm on the sea with sailors*, Billy Short said to himself. *Real sailors. It's a grand adventure, is what it is.*

Rounding out the group was the Polish shipping manager, Bohdan Nagorski, the only one in the boat who had been a paying passenger aboard the *City of Benares*. He still had his homburg hat, though his suit was soaked through and he had offered his coat as a cover for the boys' legs. At five-foot-eleven, Nagorski may have been the tallest person in the boat; at forty-nine he was also its elder statesman. The boys assumed, judging by Nagorski's dress and demeanor, that he must be a rich man. Fred Steels told the other boys that the man in the hat was a count and a millionaire.

Harry Peard eyed Nagorski with suspicion. For one thing, he wondered, *How the devil does he still have that hat?* Surely the night's winds would have ripped it free. There were many privately held misgivings and concerns, up and down the boat. Peard distrusted Nagorski; Cooper worried that the Indians might grow unruly when food and water were distributed; one Indian sailor confided to Nagorski his wish that the *Benares'* captain, Landles Nicoll, were aboard. "I do not believe," he said, that "the young officer [Cooper] can get us home." Another Indian complained that O'Sullivan—sick though he was— was occupying too much space on the lifeboat floor. Certainly their collective condition—jammed together like so many sardines—was fertile atmosphere for complaint.

And yet for his part, Bohdan Nagorski felt the tonic of optimism. He looked about in mid-morning and thought, *Perhaps we have a chance. This is a good group. The crewmen are sharp, the children brave.* Maybe, he thought, they would live.

ONE OF RONNIE COOPER'S FIRST initiatives was to reorder the seating. This was not easy; even in a calm sea it would have been difficult to stand or circulate in the crowded boat. As it was, no one could move an arm or leg without disturbing a neighbor. All night Mary Cornish had felt the jab of an iron Fleming handle at her back. She had Nagorski bunched against her left side, Howard Claytor and Fred Steels huddled to her right. *We are like a pile of stones along the roadside,* Cornish thought. *If one of us moves, the rest may come tumbling down.* Cooper laid down an early rule: No one could move in the boat unless there was an emergency. It would be a hardship for all—but especially for six boys who had grown accustomed to an almost itinerant exis- tence in the warrens and corridors of the *Benares.* Now they would sit or squat in a small square of space, wedged against one another, with no room to roam.

Next Cooper determined that he and his fellow British crewmen should group themselves at the stern; it was the natural place for the sailor in command—not just because the tiller resided there, but also because it af- forded a perch from which Cooper and his men could watch over their fellow passengers, and the ocean itself. Cooper would have Critchley, Peard, Purvis, and Mayhew near him at all times.

The Indians—easily the largest contingent—would occupy the middle, what Purvis called the "waist" of Lifeboat 12. Nagorski and O'Sullivan were given the next two spaces; it was assumed these two worldly men would be best suited to "communicate" with the Indians and with each other. This left Cornish and the children at the bow, nearest to the newly built canvas shelter. In this arrangement they would also be far from the salty, all-too-realistic talk of Peard and the other sailors.

It was a strange exercise—like seating guests for a large dinner—and it was difficult to manage, but Cooper believed it was essential to get the details just right. He knew they might be together for several days. They might, for that matter, be together for the rest of their lives.

The steward George Purvis knew it, too, and it was with a long journey in mind that he began doling out provisions at noon. Lifeboat 12's passengers were by now ravenously hungry—they had gone without food or water since dinner on board the *Benares* the night before—and many were preparing for a feast of biscuits, canned fish and meat, with canned fruit for dessert. Above all, they craved *water*. Purvis had been making careful preparations all morning, running the microscopic details of this first meal through his mind and imagining the next several days of life in the lifeboat. If they were rescued on this day or the next, he reasoned, then they would have their feast. For now, however, Purvis began by assuming their voyage would be considerably longer than that. He had thought it through like a scientist, considering not only how long they might be in the boat but also how small the rations could be without risking revolt among the passengers or dangerously depleting their strength. Purvis knew instinctively that any judgments he made on this first day would prove critical.

At noon Father O'Sullivan said grace, almost in a whisper, from his "bed" on the boat's floor. Then, with a sad kind of military precision, their first meal came around the boat. It was paltry and satisfying to no one.

Purvis had counted out ship's biscuits—forty-six of them. He then used his pocketknife to cut forty-six thin slices from a slab of corned beef, and with the help of Critchley, Peard, and Ramjam, these finger-length sandwiches were passed from the stern. The first went to the children. Purvis then counted small cans of condensed milk, which Critchley punctured before distributing. The children in particular enjoyed the milk's thick consistency and sweet taste, and they gulped it down. Fred Steels thought he might break a tooth on the hard biscuit, but with the milk it went down like a rich dessert. This "meal," the painstaking procession and then the consumption of biscuits and milk, lasted three quarters of an hour. Nagorski noted that it was orderly; no one grabbed for the food, and nothing was dropped as the sandwiches were handed down.

Then it was time for water.

Purvis and the other sailors knew that food would not be their primary concern. Healthy men and women could subsist for weeks on very little solid food. The need for calories would be minimal in Lifeboat 12; no one in the boat would be expending much energy on this journey, however long it lasted. Water was the worry, dehydration already a powerful enemy.

These were first orders of business for any lifeboatman: to count food stocks and measure water, and to calculate rations. Like most victims of shipwreck, Purvis suffered for having no precise time frame; he could not possibly know how long his water supply would need to last. A human being in normal conditions is encouraged to consume a minimum of two to three quarts of water in a day; the amount depends on food intake and energy expended, and it is of course greater for someone existing on the open, unsheltered sea. If the Lifeboat 12 passengers had an advantage, it was that they would presumably be exerting themselves only minimally—and eating very little. Digestion requires a great deal of water; the group in Lifeboat 12 would have little to digest. There are accounts of lifeboat passengers in extreme cases subsisting on as little as a quarter pint of water a day, though rarely for more than a week.

It was with these matters in mind that Purvis had been making his calculations. Every assessment was predicated on a worst-case assumption. To start, he considered the very real possibility that a rescue effort might never materialize, or that it might have passed them by. Next he and Ronnie Cooper guessed (correctly) that the lifeboat still lay more than six hundred miles from land. If the winds held steady, if the Fleming gear functioned properly, and if the boat steered clear of storms, then Lifeboat 12 might reach Ireland in eight days.

Might reach Ireland. It was an optimistic forecast. Their ability to navigate— without a proper compass—was compromised. The weather might worsen, which in turn would limit their opportunities to raise the sail. Strength would wane, rendering more difficult the turning of the Fleming handles. Neither Cooper nor Purvis shared these grim prognoses with the others. Ronnie Cooper was not a man for oratory or announcements, and George Purvis was a careful, meticulous character, who in this case had concluded that an open discussion of their situation would only sap morale. They kept these deliberations to themselves.

Checking the boat's water barrels, Purvis discovered they held a total of sixteen gallons. That worked out to roughly 1.4 quarts of water per person in Lifeboat 12, or a shade under forty-five ounces. Purvis understood immediately that unless they were to be rescued soon, these were terrible numbers. One and four-tenths quarts in a *day* would have made a meager allotment; spread over a week or more it was almost unimaginable. For reasons that were never understood, Lifeboat 12 had been stocked with far more food than could have been consumed, given the water supply; if much more than one week passed without rescue, the water needed for digestion would be gone, while salmon, tinned beef, and biscuits remained.

George Purvis settled on a meager ration indeed: He would serve two "dippers" of three ounces each, twice a day. Any less and they might die in a few days, Purvis figured; any more, and the stocks would be gone in less than a week. It is not known whether Purvis measured the overall amount right down to the ounce; if he did, he would have found that three ounces, taken twice each day by forty-six passengers, would mean 276 ounces a day—1,932 ounces in a week. Their sixteen-gallon total amounted to 2,048 ounces; in other words, after seven days they would have only 116 ounces left. Assuming all forty-six passengers in Lifeboat 12 lived that long, these numbers meant they would run dry on day number eight.

It was a pitiful ration, Bohdan Nagorski thought when he first saw Purvis' little metal flask, but he concurred completely with Purvis' strict allotment. It would be very hard, but it was also smart and sensible. Nagorski only hoped it would not provoke a small rebellion in Lifeboat 12.

With help from Ramjam Buxoo, Nagorski explained to the Indians that the servings of water would be very small and that they had to be so. There could be no debate, and no complaints. The Indians were still talking about this when the dipper came around, four or five inches tall and the diameter of a penny. After each serving the flask was returned to Purvis, who poured for the next in line, carefully as possible. Forty-six times he doled out a dipper and sent the little beaker down the boat.

God it tastes good, Derek Capel thought, savoring his first drink in nearly eighteen hours. Capel did not want to relinquish the dipper; he held it longingly after he had finished. Ken Sparks gulped his portion—just two mouthfuls, he reckoned. Sparks thought he would have had no trouble swallowing all forty-six servings. "When'll we have more, Auntie Mary?" he asked. Mary Cornish told him they would all have to be patient.

And so it went, the dipper passed and savored, refilled for the next passenger, and then passed again. It was a careful, almost excruciating ceremony. And then it was over.

Purvis closed up the flask; in six hours they would have another serving. A few of the Indians grumbled, but there were no loud complaints, not on this first day. Purvis took this as a success, and afterward he gave one critical warning to his fellow passengers: Whatever the temptation, do not drink the seawater. This was second nature to the professional seamen on board but perhaps not so obvious to others. Drinking saltwater was dangerously counterproductive. It would upset sodium levels in the blood and lead ultimately to the condition known as hypernatremia—symptoms of which include muscle twitching, seizure, delirium, and ultimately coma. Purvis did not mention such details, saying only, "Don't drink from the sea. It'll kill you."

THEY WERE TIRED THAT AFTERNOON and generally quiet, but personalities were beginning to show themselves. One personality in particular.

Soon after the midday "meal" Harry Peard rose at the stern. He stood there awhile, stretching his arms, flexing, as though he were preparing for exercise. Then he stripped quickly to his undershorts and leaped over the side. The lifeboat shook.

Passengers gasped; someone cried out. A few of the boys stood, nearly losing their balance as they angled for a look. *What's he doing?* Fred Steels said to himself.

A murmur went up from the Indians. *The man is mad,* Nagorski thought.

The water temperature was probably no more than fifty degrees. Peard swam a vigorous crawl alongside the boat.

Mary Cornish did not like what she saw. *Awful example for the children,* she thought. *Now they'll want to do it, too.*

Ken Sparks watched, startled, as Peard splashed about on one side, dipped under the waves, and after what seemed an eternity emerged, laughing, on the other side of the boat.

"Marvelous!" cried Harry Peard.

Sparks and the other boys cheered. Cornish tried to distract them, but they craned their necks, staring at the strange man in the water.

"Come on in, lads!"

Cornish threw Peard a harsh look. She told the boys they were not to listen.

"Hell, you're not *ill!*" the gunner retorted, treading water near the bow. "It's lovely, see? Come on!"

"*Ignore* the man," Mary Cornish said firmly.

O'Sullivan, weary and confused on the bottom boards, concurred.

"You stay here, boys," he said. His voice came faint and raspy.

Harry Peard swam to the stern and climbed back on board. The lifeboat shuddered again. Peard had decided Mary Cornish was a tedious, all-too-proper woman. *A spinster is what she is,* Peard thought. Some in the boat shared that view of the forty-one-year-old music teacher. *Probably not the type to get her fingers dirty,* Derek Capel thought. Nagorski, while irritated by Peard's antics, found the one woman in the boat to be dreary and humorless. He wished she would smile—if only to show the boys she was not without hope.

Whatever the others thought, Mary Cornish was there, jammed like the others in a drifting lifeboat, and she was determined to protect and perhaps even save the children. She might never have dirtied her fingers before (they were, after all, the fingers of an accomplished pianist), but now Mary Cornish would have no choice. When she heard Cooper and Doug Critchley discussing the need for some sort of flag, Cornish quietly pulled a pink camisole from under her dress.

"You can use this," she said.

The men hesitated. Some of the Indians turned their heads. But Mary Cornish insisted and quickly the garment was on its way back to the stern, provoking loud murmurs from the Indians and leaving Cornish in a cotton jacket and life vest. The camisole was tied to an oar. Lifeboat 12 was now in possession of a small, pinkish flag.

JUST AS GEORGE PURVIS HAD carefully counted out provisions, Mary Cornish now busied herself with calculations of her own.

The children were plainly restless. Cornish could only guess how they might be after another day or two on the water. She realized she would need a strategy, some way to keep the boys alert and entertained, their minds engaged. Boredom was really the chief danger, she thought, the lifeboat itself a kind of prison, trapping active and excited boys who had enjoyed races, tugs-of-war, and other games on board the *City of Benares.* Food and drink were simple matters in a way—they would either be there or not. But tedium was different. Mary Cornish believed this was an enemy she could fight, or at least keep in check.

"All right, boys, listen to me . . ."

To start with, they would sing. Cornish asked each child to suggest a tune. Ken Sparks' hand shot up and soon there was music from the bow. "Roll out the barrel, we'll have a barrel of fun . . ." It was Sparks' favorite song. Another boy chose "Run, Rabbit, Run," and a third wanted "Pack Up Your Troubles." Appropriate, Cornish thought as they sang—"What's the use of worrying, it never was worthwhile. So pack up your troubles in your old kit bag, and smile, smile, smile!" By the time they came to "There'll Always Be an England," the sailors in the boat were joining in.

They sang together for a half hour or so. The children brightened. It passed the time and brought smiles to tired faces. When the songs faded, voices gone weak or attention drifting, Mary Cornish suggested conversation. She asked the boys to describe everything they could remember about the *City of Benares.*

Again the boys responded, recalling meals on board and the games they had played. Billy Short said he would never forget the waiters' uniforms. Fred Steels remembered the filmmaker Ruby Grierson, how she had pointed her fancy cameras at them all. "Can't wait to see the movies!" Steels said excitedly. It had not occurred to him that anything bad might have happened to Grierson or her cameras.

On they went. This exercise lasted another hour or so. It was impressive, Bohdan Nagorski had to admit, how the woman engaged the boys. After a while, when the talk veered to the chaos surrounding the torpedo's strike, and the "falling lifeboats," Mary Cornish tried to change the subject.

What, she asked, would the boys eat on their return?

"Roast beef!" came an answer. "Yorkshire pudding!" someone else said. "Sausages for breakfast—maybe on a Swiss roll!" One boy wondered whether they might turn up in Ireland. In which case, he said happily, "We'll have Irish stew, then!"

Mary Cornish rubbed the boys' arms and legs as often as possible. As a music teacher, Cornish had sometimes massaged her pupils' hands in the final moments before a performance. The idea then had been to coax blood to the fingertips. Now Cornish resolved to massage the boys' feet and ankles several times a day, and in particular when they woke during the night.

Dusk approached. Ken Sparks had a question.

"Which would you rather be," he asked Mary Cornish, "bombed at home, or torpedoed in the Atlantic?"

An interesting question, she thought.

"Torpedered," one of the boys replied. Cornish dodged the question and polled all the boys instead. She wanted to be sure that each child had his say. Would they rather be attacked at home, or at sea?

This provoked another spirited discussion. Derek Capel had no doubts: Bombing at home was an awful thing, with nothing like a silver lining. This, Capel thought—this strange journey in the lifeboat—was at least *interesting.*

Even as the sun lowered, waves slapping the boat and another day receding, no rescue ship in sight, six young boys were in agreement: It was better—and it was undoubtedly more exciting—to have been *torpedered* in the Atlantic.

. . .

ON THIS FIRST DAY RONNIE Cooper had been an almost silent skipper. He issued only a few simple commands from the stern, mindful that unease or anger might soon show themselves in the cramped and hungry group. Everyone was to take a turn pulling the Fleming gear, Cooper said, and everyone would keep a lookout watch. Nagorski did a shift that afternoon, leaning out over the gunwale, feeling the wind against his face. Later the boys pulled lookout duty as well, delighted for the chance, gripping the mast as the little boat pitched and shook. Ken Sparks wanted desperately to be the first one to spy a ship.

While they watched and hoped, Cooper called the group to order and gave a curt, cursory statement from the stern. They were, he said, "heading for Europe."

This puzzled many of the others. Father Rory O'Sullivan, still lying on the floorboards, heard Cooper and wondered, *What does he mean, exactly?*

"Have we any idea *where* in Europe?" O'Sullivan asked.

Cooper did not answer. Perhaps he had not heard the question. O'Sullivan asked again.

"Ireland," Cooper replied. "We're headed for Ireland."

Bohdan Nagorski believed that expending effort and energy to head eastward was madness. It would be better, he thought, to remain near the spot where the *Benares* had gone down, and he said as much to Cooper. A rescue vessel was more likely to find them there.

Cooper tried to assure Nagorski that sailing was the better of two difficult options. In fact, Cooper understood the near hopelessness of making for land. Even if they made it, how many of his forty-five passengers would be left after six hundred miles in these waters? But by late afternoon Cooper also believed that any rescue party must have come and gone. Surely they had missed Lifeboat 12.

And if that was the case, then what other choice was left?

Nagorski pressed the matter. He still felt strongly that the scene of the sinking was the only place a search party would know to look. And he found it impossible to see how they would reach Ireland before it was too late. Nagorski stepped carefully over Lifeboat 12's thwarts to argue the point at the stern, with Cooper and his crew.

The annals of lifeboat passage suggest that their disagreement was a common one. In *Sea Survival: A Manual*, Dougal Robertson attempts to settle the matter, writing that "the successful conclusion to the voyage shall always be given priority over the random chance of rescue." In other words: Make for land; do not wait for someone else to find you. This was Ronnie Cooper's point, and he told Nagorski in a polite but firm tone that the accepted practice for any shipwrecked crew was to head for the nearest coast. Moreover, said Cooper, between the extremes of making land and staying put there lay the real chance that they would meet other vessels—a warship, a liner, a fishing boat, even—if they crossed shipping lanes en route to the British Isles.

Finally, Ronnie Cooper shared his belief that any search party had probably missed Lifeboat 12. Nagorski, Cornish, and O'Sullivan had all assumed that the convoy vessels or the departed escort destroyer would return for them. Cooper explained that the convoy ships were instructed never to remain at or return to the scene of a U-boat attack; as for the destroyer *Winchelsea,* Cooper said he believed she had urgent duties that had called her away. In his view, sailing for Ireland was the best in a poor group of choices. They were blessed, he said, to have a fine sailor in Critchley, and solid, good-tempered seamen in Peard, Purvis, Mayhew, and Ramjam Buxoo. They had food stocks to last three weeks if necessary.*

"Understood," Nagorski said. He told Cooper he respected the decision, and he added that he had appreciated the chance to have his own views heard.

The day wore on, light dimming on the horizon. The children quieted again, and the adults fell silent, too. Spirits fell along with the sun. The terrible night and the long day spent staring at the sea had left Lifeboat 12's adult passengers downcast and physically spent. Mary Cornish felt a fresh respect for the vastness of the Atlantic. *Imagine,* she thought, *it is just like this— nothing but rolling water and giant sky—for hundreds upon hundreds of miles.*

Harry Peard chose this dreary moment to venture to the bow. He came, unsolicited, with a message for his fellow passengers. A shipwreck, he insisted, was really no great thing. Part of life at sea, it was. The skies might darken, and bring rough weather. The seas might beat down on your lifeboat. You kept your chin up.

Peard walked the length of the boat, stepping around bodies and carrying a harsh thought for nearly everyone he passed along the way. When he saw Rory O'Sullivan fingering his rosary beads, Peard snickered. "That won't do you any good—not here." Stepping near Mary Cornish, he stopped, nodding to the boys. "Here, what's all this?" He was irritated by the sight of the poorly clad children. "This one's got no blanket on! No wonder he's cold, see? Poor little

*It appears Cooper made no mention of the water supply in this discussion; clearly they did not have a three-week supply on board.

bastard! Come on, son, let's tuck the blanket under—that's the way." He wrapped a blanket more tightly around Howard Claytor's feet.

"Here!" Peard huffed. "This boy's feet are cold, see? Why ain't someone rubbin' 'em? What do you escorts think you're here for?" Cornish *had* been massaging their feet, but she kept quiet. Then Harry Peard made an unfortunate comparison.

"My wife, she's got a way with kids, she has. She keeps 'em fit as fleas, and stands no nonsense, neither. But there, I reckon no woman knows how to look after kids properly unless she's got some of her own."

It was an unvarnished affront, issued after less than a day spent together in the boat. *Well,* Mary Cornish said to herself, *too bad his wife's not here.*

Peard wasn't finished. "Take you, for instance," he said, still eyeing "Auntie Mary." "What do you know about kids? Got one of your own? No. Nor likely to have, either."

Cornish stiffened. "You're right on both counts. And what of it?"

The gunner shrugged. "No offense, of course."

He seemed a boor on that first day, a monster, almost. *A bossy fellow,* Derek Capel thought. Rory O'Sullivan wondered what effect such a provocative and outspoken man might have in the crowded boat if they were to spend several days together. They would have enough demons to contend with without this kind. Perhaps it was best to look away, O'Sullivan thought. *If we ignore the man, then maybe he'll shut his mouth.*

In fact, Harry Peard possessed other, more constructive qualities. He was tireless, for one. He looked as though he'd just returned from a vacation—rosy-cheeked and grinning, never a hint that he had barely survived the night, having been pitched to the Atlantic from a gunner's nest and nearly drowned. Peard showed no sign, either, that he had scarcely eaten for twenty-four hours and gone without sleep for considerably longer than that.

Perhaps most important, Harry Peard was an optimist, through and through. This would prove a common trait in Lifeboat 12, but it ran to extremes in Harry Peard. "Only a shipwreck," he said, time and again.

Peard took up any task Cooper needed done, did his best to cheer the Indians, and every move he made seemed to interest and entertain the children. Billy Short was awestruck from the start. *There will be no defeat with this fellow Peard,* Short thought. *Harry the Gunner.*

Finally, Peard was an experienced sailor and a physically powerful man—though this also led him to assume, eyeing the frail O'Sullivan, that something must be wrong with O'Sullivan's character rather than his body. If he—Harry

Peard—required so little food, rest, or warmth, why then should anyone else complain?

DEREK CAPEL FELT A PANG of loneliness as the light went. They would spend another night in the lifeboat. The realization made him think again of the previous night and his little brother, Alan. *I hope he's safe,* Derek said to himself, and he tried hard to imagine just where on this ocean he might be. It made it harder, not easier, for Capel to find sleep. Paul Shearing wondered how they would sleep, scrunched as they were at the bow.

Jammed between the children and the Indians, Bohdan Nagorski suffered fresh pangs of doubt. Where was the *Winchelsea*? She had left the convoy more than twenty hours before the attack; presumably she had turned and made haste for the scene. Now it was more than twenty hours *after* the torpedo's strike. Had Officer Cooper been right? Nagorski wondered. Had the *Winchelsea* been too busy with her new mission? And if so, who would come for *them*?

The boys harbored no such thoughts. Other than Derek Capel, who had come to know some *Benares* crewmen and may actually have heard about the *Winchelsea*'s turn, the boys did not even know what had happened to the escort vessels. Though cold and dispirited, the boys were unafraid. Not for a moment did they believe they might be doomed on the water. They were having fun. And they were certain their rescuers were coming.

JUST THEN HMS *HURRICANE* WAS nearing the end of her box search, and her sailors were busy lifting the last *Benares* survivors from the water. Lifeboat 12 was moving east, roughly ten miles away. Out of the box.

CHAPTER 16

Life in the Lifeboat

Prayer at sunrise. Morning conversation. Some stretching of achy limbs—with care taken not to jab a neighbor. Lunch at noon. Harry Peard's swim. Stories for the children in the afternoon, then dinner at six. Songs, and more prayer. Near-constant massage for the children's arms and legs—Mary Cornish and Bohdan Nagorski presiding. Sleep—whenever conditions permitted. Slowly, and without ceremony, a routine settled over Lifeboat 12.

Ronnie Cooper and Rory O'Sullivan had the only functioning watches; from the first day they made a practice of checking each other's "times" at daybreak—say, 6:30 and 6:40—and then resetting each watch to an average of the two. There was no breakfast. The day began instead with perfunctory talk about the night, the morning's weather, and whatever could be said about the progress Lifeboat 12 was making. The children took turns napping under Purvis' canvas tarp, two or three of them snuggled close, and when Derek Capel poked his head from under the flap on their second morning together, Bohdan Nagorski remarked, "He looks like a duck, coming out of its hole." From this moment the little shelter at the bow would be known as the "Duck's Hole."

Thursday, September 19, brought fewer clouds and a steady wind, strong enough to fill a sail. Soon Cooper and the young yachtsman, Doug Critchley, had them cutting cleanly through the waves. The boat moved at steady speed.

Cooper had his assigned teams work the Fleming gear, and with Critchley he scheduled the lookouts. The sailors involved the boys as often as possible, even if no additional watches were needed. Periodically one boy would be chosen to join an adult and watch for any shape or stirring on the horizon. When Fred Steels' first turn came, he kept seeing plumes of ship's smoke that were really clouds. Perhaps, he thought after a while, they weren't there at all.

From the start it was clear that the cramped seating would prove a powerful foe. "Crowding precludes any confidential discussions," John Stilgoe writes of the typical lifeboat condition, and "equally so any masking of error." For Mary Cornish it was the "severest trial"; she found herself wedged tightly against the children, the boat's side, and the Fleming gear handles that seemed to press constantly at her back. Close quarters also meant that the lifeboat passengers would require some arrangement for personal hygiene. As tightly bunched as they were, this was no trifling matter.

Nagorski and Cornish had tied a handkerchief to a slab of driftwood; there was no soap, but anyone who wished could dangle the handkerchief over the side, reel it back, and rinse his hands and face. Nagorski had dried an old Polish newspaper; he offered its pages as hand towels. Critchley produced a comb, rinsed it in the sea, and passed it to the boys. They took turns pushing it through their tangled locks, surprised at how much pleasure a comb could bring.

There was of course no privacy in the boat. Many passengers had been violently ill during the first night—at close proximity to one another. This had had the salutary side effect of eliminating instantly any feelings of skittishness or pride.

Without much discussion the crew instituted a simple system: Anyone who needed to "use the facilities" would raise a hand or call out "Bucket!" The boat's pail would pass from Cooper's place at the stern. In heavy seas, passengers would have to wait; the bucket would be required instead for bailing. The only real wrinkle in this arrangement came when Mary Cornish was the one raising a hand. Then the bucket would come with more ceremony, passed via the Indians, who smiled and muttered about the *memsahib*. The boys giggled, but they made a kind of shield around "Auntie Mary." The men turned their gaze.

As time passed, hands rose less frequently. Living as they were on so little food and water, they soon found they had very little need for Ronnie Cooper's bucket.

THE MORNING HOURS WERE LONG. There was little to do before Purvis' "midday event," the elaborate but tiny lunch he drew from the stocks.

It would be corned beef one meal, sardines the next, an occasional small chunk of canned salmon. Each came with a single brittle ship's biscuit. O'Sullivan would say grace as George Purvis gathered the food.

Purvis was deliberate as he served. He was obviously careful not to waste a scrap, but he also wanted to stretch the time. The later the meal was finished, he reasoned, the less time there would be for his hungry passengers to pine for supper.

After lunch on the nineteenth, the boys' spirits sagged once more. *How many hours will it be,* Howard Claytor wondered, *before that thimble of water comes around again?* Derek Capel felt an almost painful urge to get up and run around. Paul Shearing cowered under the Duck's Hole, quiet and cold.

While the other adults rested, chatted, or gazed out at the sea, Mary Cornish watched the boys. On that second afternoon she could see them wilting as Purvis stashed away the food and water. They had tired quickly of songs, and the torpedo-or-bomb questions. Tedium had set in, draped over them like a heavy curtain. She saw Shearing at the edge of the Duck's Hole, saw his stare, vacant and glassy-eyed, and she worried again. The absence of activity, she feared, was proving as harmful as the lack of food and water.

For a while they played "Animal, Vegetable, or Mineral." That knocked away another hour. Then one of the boys suggested the game "I Spy," which began well but fizzled fast. There was too little to "spy" from their perches in the lifeboat, once they were done noting fellow companions, mast and sail, Fleming handles and supplies, swells and sky. "I spy another wave," one of the boys said, but the game was ultimately a stark reminder of the obvious: There was almost nothing around them, a vast and almost blank canvas for their eyes. Nothing to "spy." They were stranded, in the middle of nowhere.

Derek Capel had warmed to "Auntie Mary," watching and listening as she tried all these games and conversations. *She's not boring,* Capel thought. *Not a spinster at all, really.*

That afternoon Cornish had a new idea, a break from the games and conversation. She would tell the boys a story. A great, memorable story. It would be a long tale, something epic, rich in characters and strange settings, loaded with "chapters" and as much suspense as she could muster.

"Are you listening, boys? We're going to have a story now."

Six tired children rallied, eager to know more.

"Ready, Auntie Mary!"

"What sort of story, Auntie Mary?"

"Will it have heroes and villains?"

Indeed it would. "It's a Bulldog Drummond story," she announced, and the boys cheered. From their vantage point, it was as though "Auntie Mary" had brought a new person on board.

Hugh "Bulldog" Drummond was a square-jawed British captain, a Londoner with a valet and a flair for adventure. He was a well-known creature of fiction, invented by the author Herman "Sapper" McNeile in an immensely popular 1920 novel called *Bulldog Drummond.* A dozen more books and then several films had followed, which helped explain why Drummond was a familiar figure to six shipwrecked boys from England. McNeile's Drummond was strong and cunning, a precursor of James Bond, capable of taking on organized criminals and wild gorillas in a single episode. Mary Cornish would fashion her Bulldog Drummond an action hero, clever, tough, and fearless. Useful traits for the boys to consider, she thought. *I'll make him a good example.*

"Ready for the story!" a perked-up Ken Sparks announced, and the other boys laughed heartily. Cornish eased herself to the middle of a thwart so that the boys formed a circle around her.

Her first installment had Captain Drummond embroiled somehow with Nazi agents in London. Before long she found herself talking about secret wireless installations, about Hitler's codes and Churchill's code breakers.

The boys drew even closer, staring up at "Auntie Mary." Lifeboat 12, the turbulent sea, the lack of food, and all their other tribulations seemed to fade away. For a time at least, they were somewhere else, someplace shrouded in mystery. *What is Bulldog doing? How will he escape?*

The initial "reading" lasted roughly half an hour. Several of the Indians edged nearer, too, wondering what it was that had so captivated the children. Mary Cornish had surprised herself. *Where is all this material coming from?* She was an introvert by nature, but she had a rich imagination, and she had a nephew who had given her an idea of the tastes and passions of young English boys. Cornish knew nothing, really, about codes or code-breaking, about the Nazis or the British intelligence services, but she had managed to invent tactics and machines and a parade of eccentric characters. Later she would toss in airplane squadrons, brave parachutists, even a terrible German submarine commander, always improvising on the spur of the moment and never certain where precisely her narrative was leading. She wasn't sure she had her facts in order, either, and she didn't much care.

Mary Cornish knew only this: No matter how severely he was tested, Bulldog Drummond would ultimately win the day; the boys came to understand and expect as much. As important, Cornish determined that Drummond's story would never really end. Like any good serial drama, this one would have installments punctuated with questions, some lingering drama, strands of suspense to guarantee that the audience would long for more.

"What's next?" Derek Capel wanted to know, after Cornish closed her first "chapter" that afternoon. "What happens to him now?"

"Not just yet, Derek," Cornish said softly.

The boys protested

"*More*, Auntie Mary!"

"Please, Auntie. *Please* go on."

But they would have to wait. Cornish was never certain when she would deliver another chapter, or how its plot line might run. But she had decided that entertainment in her corner would be rationed, the tale strung along. The Bulldog Drummond stories—like dipperfuls of water—would be spaced apart.

So began a soap opera, in effect.

"We'll have another chapter tomorrow," Mary Cornish said on September 19, and the boys cheered again, wondering what the next segment might bring.

What was Bulldog doing?

Won't the Nazis get him, next time?

Will he win, again?

SUPPER CAME WHEN O'SULLIVAN AND Cooper made a late-afternoon check of their watches and agreed it was six o'clock. They said grace; more than one of the children observed that the prayer lasted longer than the meal itself. Afterward, George Purvis passed milk tins to the children. Then came the precious dipper. The water was swallowed, the dipper returned, and that was that.

Dusk approached. Their third night in the boat lay ahead. O'Sullivan led the Lord's Prayer—his scratchy voice now barely audible at the twin ends of the boat. "Hallowed be thy name . . ." The boys mumbled along. The Indians said prayers of their own.

Nagorski and O'Sullivan fell into conversation about the torpedo attack, wrestling with a question neither man could answer: What had become of the others? They shared recollections from the *Benares'* deck, the people and the boats they had seen in those final moments. But the fact was that neither man had any real mental picture of what had happened.

O'Sullivan was most keen to learn what had become of his fellow escorts

Michael Rennie and Reverend William King. Nagorski thought of his friend Zygmunt Gralinski and the English member of Parliament, James Baldwin-Webb. He shouted questions to the others in Lifeboat 12, wondering whether anyone else had known those men; they had not. Nagorski replayed the after-dinner walk they had taken with the Indian student, the four men talking and laughing, and then the ship's violent shudder. He remembered other travelers, faces he could not match to names, interesting and intelligent people he had met at meals or at the *Benares'* bar.

Had he been the lucky one? Or was his group the unfortunate minority, stranded after the others had been found and brought to safety? He remembered that night's on-again, off-again storm, and he remembered watching a lifeboat fall violently to the water. Had everyone else been brought back by now, carried home by some ship the Lifeboat 12 group had never seen? Or had there been no rescues at all, only death on the water?

O'Sullivan wondered, too, about the other boys in his group on the *Benares*. He had last seen them as night fell Tuesday, a few hours before the attack. *Had some children died, below deck?* O'Sullivan did not think so. The crew had reported only a few casualties—one child dead, two or three severe injuries. He remembered the mess in his cabin, how it shook on impact and how his dresser had gone crushing into the wall. *Had other cabins been more badly damaged?* It did not help that fever and nausea had made a hash of O'Sullivan's mind, mangling his memory and sense of time.

Now the sun slid low in the sky. The children slipped into sleep. Bohdan Nagorski looked to the east and saw two colorful arcs, bright rainbows on the horizon. They were beautiful, he thought. Like portals opening into another and happier world.

Then night was upon them, like a cold and heavy blanket. Their third night together. The boys shivered in their sleep. Cornish had wrapped them in three pairs, in blankets and plastic sheeting. She had sent two boys to the canvas "Duck's Hole," and every now and then she would rub the boys' feet under the blankets. She was desperately afraid they might die of cold as they slept.

Even the professional sailors, English and Indian, seemed to fade by day's end. Cooper, their steady leader, had given up hope that a search party was coming. Ramjam Buxoo confided to Nagorski that many of the Indians seemed resigned to the prospect of death at sea. In conversation with Nagorski and O'Sullivan, Ramjam sprinkled his talk with references to "Allah the Compassionate," whose good graces would save them if He so wished. There was,

Ramjam said, little any of the others could do. He believed his God "was wise, and would send storms if He thought best."

Nagorski still held out hope for the *Winchelsea*, Mary Cornish was still afraid, and Father O'Sullivan was too sick to contemplate much beyond his own condition. O'Sullivan was fighting for his life, and he knew it. He still lay on the bottom boards between the children and Indians, wearing sandals and pajamas, a blanket across his legs. He considered asking for an extra serving of water, then thought better of it. *It would,* he thought, *be like taking from the children.* But then O'Sullivan felt a wave of sickness, and with it a fresh uncertainty. How mad it would be, he told himself, to die before a ship came! *To become a corpse, one dead man in a boat full of survivors.* Like Bess Walder and Beth Cummings before him, Rory O'Sullivan repeated a single phrase, a hundred times, it seemed: *I must hang on.*

NIGHT BROUGHT MISERIES ALL ITS own.

The boys had worn brave faces by daylight; it was less easy in the night. No matter how tightly wrapped they were, how close together they lay, the boys still felt the winds whistle through their blankets and pajamas, sending fresh chills all around. The nighttime temperature was probably between thirty and thirty-five degrees. Sometimes, deep in the night, a boy woke—roused by the crush of a wave, the wind's whip, or a fresh blast of cold air. Whimpers would come from the bow.

"It's all right," Mary Cornish would say. "That's only the wind in the sail, blowing us home."

At one point all four boys outside the Duck's Hole stirred, crying softly, and their cries drew a visitor and a small stir in the gently rocking boat. Here was the indefatigable Harry Peard, stepping in and around the Indians, on a careful walk from stern to bow, for a middle-of-the-night talk with the children. It was hard enough to travel the boat's length in daylight. Even Mary Cornish was coming to realize that Harry Peard could manage just about anything.

Peard crouched near the boys, and after some amiable chatter he began to ramble about their plight in a raw, emphatic whisper. The gunner's theme remained a grand, overriding optimism. A shipwreck was no cause for alarm, he told them. A brave boy need feel no fear. Most important, Harry Peard promised that when England's sons and daughters were in trouble at sea, the Royal Navy never let them down. "A day or two more," said Peard, "and we shall be found."

His words helped. Howard Claytor felt comforted, hearing an experienced seaman say such things, and say them with such confidence. Some minutes passed. The crying abated. Then Harry Peard spoiled the visit by carrying on with a brutally frank assessment of the situation once he thought the boys were asleep.

"Ought to have been in Ireland by now," he muttered to Bohdan Nagorski, opening a soliloquy about the crew's failings—the Indians in particular. Peard was nearly twenty years older than Cooper and his other British crewmates, and he believed the younger men should have been working the Fleming gear harder. Cooper ought to have pushed them. On Peard went, about the dwindling stocks of water and the thinning chances that any of them would be saved.

Derek Capel lay there freezing, wide awake, listening to Harry Peard, and hating every word he heard.

Nagorski wished Peard would stop talking. Mary Cornish tried in vain to ignore the man. Later, after Peard had retired to the stern, another boy cried and said he was hungry. Mary Cornish found herself borrowing a page from her new nemesis. She said there would be food later—and then she gave an answer Harry Peard might have given.

"Don't you realize that you're the heroes of a *real* adventure story?" she said softly. "There isn't a boy in England who wouldn't give his eyes to be in your shoes."

Her tone was gentler, but the message was vintage Peard. "Did you ever hear of a hero who *sniveled*?"

It seemed rash and out of character. Mary Cornish thought she would never have said such things to a child a few days earlier, but she was learning, toughening her skin. Cornish felt she needed to convince the boys that the adventure would trump any suffering, that they were actually *privileged* to be experiencing such wonders in the North Atlantic.

Would they not, after all, be able to tell friends they had been with *English sailors in a lifeboat?* That they had been given rowing assignments and lookout duty, and the most exciting Bulldog Drummond stories? There was deprivation, to be sure, but there were no chores, no schoolwork, and more important there were no bombs, no screaming sirens, no Stukas in the sky. These six boys had known terror in England, the terror of fear, never knowing who or what might be hit during the night. By comparison Lifeboat 12 made for an almost placid existence.

Derek Capel lay there listening, cold and tired, and he came slowly to believe that Mary Cornish was right: There could be no purer adventure for an English boy. Capel could think of several schoolmates at home who would have *loved* to be here. Fred Steels thought Auntie Mary was right about something else: Heroes *did not snivel*. Bulldog Drummond never would, anyway. So Steels decided *he* wasn't going to snivel, either.

WHEN HE COULD NOT SLEEP, Bohdan Nagorski stared up at the night sky. For a time he counted stars. He tried to catch the outlines of his colleagues in the boat, the lean copper-colored faces of the Indians to one side, the huddled children to the other. Some of the Indians were always talking, it seemed. How, Nagorski wondered, do they have the energy? And what were they talking about, in the darkest corners of the night? Even with their chatter it was quiet enough to hear the sweet rumble of the children's breathing as they slept.

When the night was like this, still and cloudless, Nagorski enjoyed it, almost. He let his mind drift. There was so much time to contemplate the universe, infinite and endless, all those stars above, all the ripples of water on the ocean. The three-quarter moon, lending a shimmer to the sea. He was cold and exhausted and not at all sure they would live—but the night itself was beautiful.

It was a sweet and soulful reverie, though after a while it dampened his spirit. It led him to consider the expanse of the ocean, and in turn the infinitesimal chances of meeting a ship or ever reaching land. Nagorski had listened carefully to the crew, heard their calculations. Now, on night three, Cooper's men were guessing they might need at least nine more days and nights to reach England.

That would make twelve days in the lifeboat. Forty-six people in a twenty-six-foot boat, hardly any food, and those pitiful servings of water. *Can we possibly last for twelve days?* Many lifeboats before theirs had lasted similar lengths of time; John Stilgoe's *Lifeboat* tells the story of the *El Dorado*, which foundered off Chile in 1913, and whose captain led ten men to Easter Island, seven hundred miles to the northeast. They survived the eleven-day journey. But such successes were usually the result of a well-provisioned lifeboat, or a crew comprised wholly of professional seamen.

Bohdan Nagorski was an optimist at heart, and again he recalled his flight from Gdynia, in Poland, and his subsequent race to stay ahead of the Germans as they plowed southward through France. He and O'Sullivan had traced similar paths as refugees. Both men believed they were survivors. Bohdan Nagorski had been blessed, many times over, in the year since the outbreak of war. But twelve days on the sea?

FRIDAY, SEPTEMBER 20, CAME CLEAR and warmer. At last they could dry their clothes, and for the first time the children stood, away from Cooper's shelter and bright-faced in the first truly mild weather they had seen. The winds were strong. The boat made good speed. Cooper believed they could cover one hundred miles on a day like this.

It was one week since the *City of Benares* had left port.

Already thirst plagued the group in Lifeboat 12. The children talked incessantly about the next "meal," but mostly they had water, not food, on their minds, counting the hours that remained until the dipper would come around again. The ship's biscuits—regarded as treats by the boys on day one—had by now become more useful as utensils. The children would hold their sardine or corned beef chunk on the biscuit, and then gave the latter to Cornish for "safekeeping."

Billy Short suffered different torments, still downcast and still worried about his little brother. Short was convinced that Lifeboat 12 would make it, that he and the forty-five others had nothing to fear. But in his mind he could not help but replay that short half hour on board the *Benares*, from the moment of impact to the launching of the boats. He recalled the damage done to his cabin, the other boats' wild descent. *Peter would have been in one of those boats*, he thought. *Unless he never made it to deck.* Such sad and muddled thoughts flew through Billy Short's mind. It became increasingly difficult for him to see how his brother could have survived.

Bohdan Nagorski edged to Short's side and tried to console the boy.

"Your brother might have gone to another lifeboat," he said. There had been eleven other boats, after all. "Probably he is in better condition than the rest of us." Surely, Nagorski added, those other lifeboats had been picked up by now.

While he spoke to Billy Short, Nagorski was thinking again of his friend and compatriot Gralinski, a lovely man who had always said he could trust his instincts in even the harshest circumstances of war. He imagined Gralinski at that moment enjoying the comforts of some other ship, warm and rested, probably with little Peter Short as one of his companions. They would all be together soon, he thought. In Ireland. In Scotland. In London. It didn't matter, really.

He said as much to Billy Short. Your brother is probably with my friend. Soon they would all be together.

BY THE FOURTH MORNING, THEY no longer spoke of ships or rescue. The lookouts had been abandoned. There was a tacit understanding—among the adults at least: No one was searching for them anymore. There was no longer any possibility, Nagorski said to O'Sullivan, of "a miraculous encounter." The children had lost count of the days. The yachtsman, Doug Critchley, had lost a lifelong zeal for sailing. He confided to O'Sullivan that if he made it safely to England he intended to sell his once-beloved boat. Critchley was finished with the sea.

Cooper and his men conferred quietly, guessing the boat's position, their minds focused now on reaching land, not meeting a rescue vessel. In the meantime, all on board craved diversion, and diversion continued to come primarily from one source.

Day and night, Harry Peard annoyed and entertained, irritated and heartened just about every one of his fellow passengers in Lifeboat 12. His every visit to the bow was like a small tornado—exciting, upsetting, often leaving damage in its wake. On the fourth morning, he came to teach the boys a set of cockney songs. He tried a bawdy limerick, but this time a reproving look from Cornish held him back. No matter—by then smiles had already returned to six tired, wind-beaten faces.

At midday, Peard took his swim again, for invigoration and exercise certainly, but also to show the boys how little they had to fear from the Atlantic Ocean.

"Why are you going swimming, mister?" Howard Claytor asked.

"Well, I want to keep in practice, see," Peard retorted, "in case we get torpedoed again."

By now he was the only adult still nimble enough to get around so easily in the boat. Bohdan Nagorski was beginning to recognize Peard's value "as a source of diversion and humor" for the children, even if his particular brand of humor irked him and the other adults on board.

Peard's acid tongue had hardly mellowed. He reproached O'Sullivan—"You pray too much"—and went so far as to suggest that working the Fleming handles would *cure* the priest. And having scolded Mary Cornish earlier for paying too little heed to the boys, Peard now pronounced her "too protective of the children."

As for Nagorski, the respect was not yet mutual. *The man is too aloof,* Harry Peard thought. *And why, for God's sake, is he drying out his bankroll, in full view of the children?*

Nagorski was indeed "drying out his bankroll," laying out pound notes on the thwarts, under the first good sun they had seen. He wanted to preserve what little money he had.

"I intend to use the money after our rescue," he told Peard, and he said it loudly so that the boys would hear. *After* our rescue, he said. In other words, rescue was not a matter of if, but when. The boys could count on it.

Then Bohdan Nagorski handed Peard a one-pound note.

Harry Peard shot him a quizzical look. "What's the use of that here?" Peard asked. "I see no shops."

Nagorski smiled. Harry Peard broke into a broad grin and pocketed the money. Some of the boys laughed. *They're funny,* Paul Shearing thought. They had enjoyed a nice bit of theater, the two men smiling and joking about their money.

One child sat sullen, decidedly *not* amused. The exchange had struck Ken Sparks like a thunderclap. He had remembered something.

What's happened to our money?

They had banked their precious travel allowance with Cornish and the other escorts on board the *City of Benares*. Every child had carried spending money, provided by family or by the CORB itself. It hadn't been much, but it was all they were to have had until they were united with their host families in Canada.

"The money's gone, isn't it?" lamented Ken Sparks.

Indeed it was. *In good conscience I cannot deny it,* Mary Cornish thought. *His money is lost, somewhere beneath these waters.*

The boys had talked about the gifts they would buy their parents when they landed.

"Four-and-eight I had," one of them said. "Four-and-eight. Saved up, it was, ever since Mum said I was to go to Canada. Dad gave me two shillings. I'll never be able to get that much again."

"Four-and-eight!" cried one of the other boys. "That's nothing. Know what I had?"

"I dunno."

"Thirteen bob."

"Thirteen bob!"

"Go on. You never had thirteen bob."

"I *did*! My uncle gave me ten bob for when I got to Canada."

"I had a new coat, but it's gone, too."

"Do you think they'll give us our pocket money back?"

"Mum won't ever be able to make it up."

"P'raps they'll give it back when we get to Ireland."

Bohdan Nagorski heard all this, the boys matching poignant and pitiful stories. It saddened him.

And then it gave him an idea. Nagorski turned to the children, waved for their attention. Six boys shifted in their places, still cramped like sardines. They looked up at the tall gentleman in the homburg hat. He would return their money, he told them. He would give them back what they had lost, once they were home. "You will have your money, when we land."

Derek Capel felt a burden lift. Ken Sparks couldn't believe it. Howard Claytor thought, *What a strange gentleman this is...* All the boys were thrilled about the money. But beyond the promise, they had noticed something else.

It was the one word. *When.* Not "if" they made it home—but "when." Again this well-dressed man, who seemed to know things about the sea and about the world, was making it plain: They would reach land, or they would be rescued on the sea. They would make it home, one way or the other, and once there, they would have their money. There was no longer any doubt—the man with the hat had said it would be so.

Soon they were on to other matters. To their now-familiar questions.

"Auntie, will they take us to Canada after all?"

"Auntie, which would you rather be, bombed at home, or torpedoed in the Atlantic?"

CHAPTER 17

In Memoriam

As Lifeboat 12 struggled with the elements, the meager water supply, and the barren sea, HMS *Hurricane* had roared home, delivering her *Benares* survivors back to Britain.

For a few glorious days in Scotland, they were nursed and feted, the children in particular showered in adulation, their stories lapped up by local authorities and the British press. Newsreel cameras recorded their every move. Newspapers heralded the "Miracle Kids" brought ashore by HMS *Hurricane*.

"The passengers behaved magnificently, particularly the women and children," gushed the businessman William Forsyth to a reporter at Greenock. "The little mites obeyed every instruction." The Canadian professor J. P. Day called Colin Richardson "the bravest and kindest boy I've ever seen." *Hurricane*'s commander, Hugh Crofton Simms, saluted his ship's surgeon, Peter Collinson, "to whose unceasing efforts and medical skills the saving of many lives is due," and after visiting with survivors, the CORB program director Geoffrey Shakespeare praised the heroism of the escorts Marjorie Day and Lillian Towns. "One cannot speak too highly of the conduct of Miss Day and Mrs. Towns," Shakespeare said, adding that "it is astonishing that either one of them is alive."

This was an overriding theme as the story of the *Benares* was told: It was a miracle that anyone had been saved, all those hours later, and in such tempestuous seas. Chief Officer Joe Hetherington wrote a list of people he believed were deserving of official citation: the stewardess Annie Ryan; the wireless operator Alistair Fairweather, for his "total disregard of danger"; and two Indians—

Captain's Boy Abdul Suban and Deck Sarang Raimodur Samsaddoun—for "assistance to passengers during launch, and cheerful willingness in the lifeboats."

Ten-year-old Louis Walder grinned for the cameras and pronounced the experience "not very nice, but very exciting." His sister, Bess, and her friend Beth Cummings were photographed at Smithston Hospital. It was by now five days since their rescue from the overturned boat, and like many of the survivors they were still frail; a medical officer had been so "impressed" by the girls' bruises he had summoned other doctors to see them. In the photographs, Bess and Beth appeared to be forcing smiles from their hospital beds. Doctors watched over Rex Thorne and Jack Keeley in particular, two boys who had nearly died from exposure. Eric Davis had suffered with Keeley but came away remarkably free of injury. "I am perhaps the luckiest of them all," Davis said, "because not only am I alive but I have hardly a scratch or a bruise."

There were fourteen children in the *Hurricane* group—seven evacuees and seven more who had been among the paying passengers. Apart from Bess and Beth, and Thorne and Keeley, all the children were housed at Glasgow's Central Hotel. They were given kilts and keys to the city, and on the night after their arrival the lord provost of Glasgow held a party in their honor.

Colin Richardson, the eleven-year-old hero of Lifeboat 2, darted about the hotel and played in the lobby with the three Bech children. At the Glasgow party Richardson told reporters his "scarlet vest" had saved him; when his mother arrived in Scotland, she made it clear that she agreed. "Thank God I gave Colin a proper life jacket," she said, "and also that he wore it day and night, as I told him to."

Having walked off *Hurricane* in a motley mix of their own pajamas and sailors' pants and sweaters, and without their pocket money, the evacuee children were fitted with new sets of clothes donated by the CORB. Marguerite Bech wanted something more for her children, and having dried her pound notes on the *Hurricane*'s deck she found she still had enough for a small shopping spree. On their second day ashore, she took Sonia, Barbara, and Derek to a Glasgow clothing store and brought a new outfit for each child. Marguerite Bech moved slowly, but her children practically marched along the sidewalks, showing no ill effects from their long night and day on the water.

In a short and cheery newsreel titled "Evacuee Children Still Smiling," the surviving boys and girls were seen in their Glasgow quarters while a narrator bellowed: "Those who were saved are in the highest spirits! You wouldn't think these kids had undergone [an] ordeal!"

If the festive air seemed excessive, for what was after all the silver lining in a terrible tragedy, it was also understandable. The war had produced precious little good news in Britain to date, and the newsreels had made for an almost numbing catalog of bombed cities and casualties and invective about the enemy. Nazi villains and their victims had dominated the fare. So when the *Benares* survivors appeared, unlikely heroes in the maritime war with Adolf Hitler, reporters and photographers trailed after them. And the lord provost of Glasgow threw a party.

THEY REMAINED IN SCOTLAND FOR at least two days. Some stayed longer because their relatives were slow to reach Glasgow; and others in the group remained in the hospital for a week or more following their rescue. While many survivors laughed and celebrated, the horror of the event lingered, still very near the surface. The dour Hungarian Ernest Szekulesz told a reporter he had survived "by a stroke of luck," and then Szekulesz broke down and sobbed. "I did not know," he said, "that women and children could die so heroically."

The survivors—children and adults, even crew members—had assumed there would be others like them, that additional ships must have reached port carrying evacuee children from the scene. If not to Scotland, then Ireland perhaps. No doubt there would be more reunions, in time. But in those first forty-eight hours in Scotland, the terrible word spread: There would be no more arrivals. These reunions would be the last.

The details were learned, and they were crushing: Of the *Benares'* ninety child evacuees, eighty-three were gone. The surviving seven were those boys and girls who had landed at Greenock: Bess and Louis Walder, Beth Cummings, Eleanor Wright, Rex Thorne, Jack Keeley, and Johnny Baker. That was all.

Baker, at seven the youngest in this small group, was still asking after his elder brother, Robert, who had handed Johnny a life jacket moments before they boarded the lifeboats. Jack Keeley was searching for his sister, Joyce. Rex Thorne wanted to know what had become of his sister, Marion. "Mary for short," they had called her.

No one had an answer.

On Friday, September 20, brown envelopes from the Children's Overseas Reception Board—the CORB—had arrived at fifty-nine homes across England. They carried letters signed by Geoffrey Shakespeare, member of Parliament and chief architect of the CORB program:

I am very distressed to inform you that in spite of all the precautions taken the ship carrying your child to Canada was torpedoed on Tuesday night September 17th. I am afraid your child is not among those reported as rescued and I am informed there is no chance of there being any further lists of survivors from the torpedoed vessel.

Like so many other parents you were anxious to send your children overseas to one of the Dominions to enjoy a happier and safer life. You courageously took this decision in the interest of the children, believing that this course was better than continuous air raids . . .

Hitherto there have been no casualties among the thousands of children sent overseas; unhappily the course of the war has shown that neither by land nor sea can there be complete safety. As a parent I can realize the anguish that this letter must cause you.

Lily Shearing found the envelope in her letter box, official-looking and rimmed in black. She knew instinctively what it was, knew her son, Paul, must be dead, and for a moment she considered stuffing the envelope back inside, as if to reverse time, and somehow deny that the letter had ever come. In Hanworth, Elizabeth Capel mourned the loss of both Alan and Derek. "They went away perfectly happy," she told a reporter. "Then came this terrible blow."

Sunderland Mayor Myers Wayman invited Mr. and Mrs. John Short to a public service at St. Thomas Church in honor of their sons, William and Peter, and the eight other Sunderland children lost in the attack on the *City of Benares*.

Terrence Holmes' parents in Wembley received a second letter, from the Navy chaplain serving with HMS *Hurricane*. He described the funerals held for Holmes, Carr, and Alan Capel aboard the destroyer. "One has the faith that in the arms of the Heavenly Father they have already been received with love," the chaplain wrote. "The Navy did what it could for their remains. God give you comfort still." Holmes' mother told a reporter that Terrence's desk at home was "just as he left it—there's the drawing of a ship he made just before he left . . . He was mad about ships and the sea."

Edith Keeley refused to believe the news. If her son, Jack, had survived, if he had lasted twenty hours on a *raft*, through an awful night and day, and during a terrible storm—then surely little Joyce might yet be found? When Mrs. Keeley and Jack were reunited at London's Euston Station, where the children's odyssey had begun two weeks before, she met her son with a long embrace. Then she began asking questions.

When had he last seen Joyce?

Jack Keeley wasn't sure. He had not seen her at the lifeboat stations.

"Could she be on a raft?"

The boy shook his head. No, he said. It didn't seem possible.

"Another boat?

No, Jack said. No chance. Every boat had been found, he told her. Picked up, or left at sea, with no one to rescue.

But could she not be alive somewhere? she persisted.

The boy shrugged. He couldn't say for certain.

His mother paused, looking at her son. Then she began to cry.

SEVERAL SETS OF SIBLINGS HAD perished. The three Pugh brothers of Liverpool; the three Moss sisters from Newport; Phyllis, Vera, and Edna Beasley of London's Winchmore Hill; and James and Joan Spencer, at nine and five the youngest pair of siblings on board the *Benares*. They had died on their raft in the early morning of September 18. It was, for the group at Glasgow, almost too much to comprehend.

More brutal than any other death notice was the one delivered to Lilford Road in Brixton. It had made space for five names: Violet Grimmond, Connie Grimmond, Lennie Grimmond, Eddie Grimmond, Jr., and Augusta—Gussie—Grimmond.

They were all dead.

Gussie Grimmond, eldest of the five, had impressed and inspired many people in a short time. They remembered her well at the school at Fazackerlay, where the children's journey had begun. The Sherwood's Lane headmistress, Margaret Abraham, had implored the CORB authorities to save places on the *Benares* for the Grimmond children. She recalled the mothering Gussie had given to her brothers and sisters, the care she had taken to be sure they presented themselves well.

The news from Scotland left Margaret Abraham shattered.

In less than two weeks, Eddie and Hannah Grimmond had lost their home to a German bomb, and five of their children to a German torpedo. On the day they received the news, they found a separate fat envelope shoved under the door of their temporary home. Inside were scraps of paper covered with drawings and a child's meandering scrawl. These were the letters Gussie and Connie had posted from Liverpool after their first look at the *City of Benares*.

"I wish you were here with us," Gussie had written.

We go into a big room for meals and we have table napkins and three
different kinds of knives and forks. Eddie and Lennie are sharing
a cabin. We have had three practices in life drill in case our boat got hit.

Please Mum, don't worry. There are men to guard us at night in case
our boat was sunk. Please do not answer this letter as I will be in mid-
Atlantic.

Your loving daughter—Gussie

"This is not war," Eddie Grimmond told a reporter in Brixton. "This is cold-blooded murder."

The "good news," limited as it was, was delivered in person. Two bowler-hatted men called on Anne Cummings at Liverpool. "Your daughter's had an accident," one of the men said. "Kindly come to Scotland." An official from the British Foreign Office rang Bernard and Rosina Walder's door in Kentish Town.

"What do you want?" Bernard Walder asked.

"I've come to tell you that your children are safe."

"Thank God," Bernard Walder said. "It's about time." He assumed this meant that Bess and Louis had reached Canada. Instead he and his wife were told to collect their children at Glasgow. It was the first they had heard of the attack on the *City of Benares*.

NEWS OF THE SINKING GALVANIZED a nation already badly battered by war.

"I am full of horror and indignation," Geoffrey Shakespeare told the House of Commons,

that any German submarine captain could be found to torpedo a ship
over 600 miles from land in a tempestuous sea. The conditions were
such that there was little chance for passengers, whether adult or
children, to survive. This deed will shock the world.

Indeed it would.

Now that families had been notified, British newspapers were permitted under wartime censorship rules to print accounts of the attack. In doing so, they let loose a fusillade of invective against Hitler, unparalleled to this point in the war.

It was, the headline writers said, "Murder at Sea," a "Bestial Crime," an example of "Nazi Inhumanity."

"Nazis Torpedo Mercy Ship, Kill Children" ran the headline in the *Daily Sketch.* "Hit Without Warning, 700 Miles from Land," cried the *Daily Herald,* getting the distance wrong but capturing the prevailing sentiment: "Without Warning." The *Daily Express'* edition that day filled its first page with coverage of the attack under a banner headline, "Children's Liner Sunk Without Warning in a Gale—Outrage in Atlantic." The subheadline said, "Sent to Escape the Bombers, English Children Are Murdered." It was, the *Express* correspondent wrote, "a deliberate and sadistic crime for which it is beyond any normal imagination to conceive the punishment."

The *Daily Mail* ran a passionate editorial that used the attack on the *Benares* to build a case for worldwide war against Germany.

> Read the details, dreadful as they are. Let them burn into our minds as proof of the character of the foe we are sworn to defeat. Let them never be forgotten, until the day of reckoning comes.

The relatively subdued *Times* of London inveighed against Admiral Doenitz and his Navy, going so far as to say that "of all the brutalities that have earned Nazism the execration of the civilized world, none will stay longer graven upon the records than the sinking of the *City of Benares.*" The paper had no way to know, of course, what Nazi Germany had in store.

THE NEWS CRUSHED COMMUNITIES ACROSS England. Residents of the northern city of Sunderland, which had sent eleven children on the *Benares,* learned that only one child—Eleanor Wright—had returned. "Hitler and his gang of murderers," declared the *Sunderland Echo,* "must be hung on the lamp posts of Berlin once we have won the war."

Only Beth Cummings had survived in a group of twelve from Liverpool. Twelve boys and girls from Wales had sailed on the *Benares;* all were missing and presumed dead. Eight children had departed from Southall, including the Baker boys, Robert and Johnny. Only Johnny Baker came home.

"We are so thankful we still have Johnny," their mother said as she traveled to Scotland to fetch him that week. "We can hardly believe the Germans would stoop to such wholesale, cold-blooded murder."

At a school in Wembley on Monday, September 23, children and teachers were in a bomb shelter, waiting out what had by then become a fairly routine air raid warning. When they assembled after the all clear, word came that seven of the school's children had perished en route to Canada. Ken Sparks was one of them; Marion Thorne another. Her brother, Rex, was the lone survivor among thirteen Wembley children who had sailed on board the *City of Benares.*

Smaller local newspapers printed lengthy eulogies. Paul Shearing was remembered under the headline "Victim of Nazi Inhumanity." The *Southern Daily Echo* wrote a long piece about Fred Steels under the banner: "Loss in Ill-Fated Children's Ship; Eastleigh Home Saddened." Steels was remembered as a child who had loved sports, and only recently learned to swim. "Fred had been looking forward to going to Canada," his mother told reporters. "He was tremendously keen on the idea. Even now I cannot realize we should never see our boy again."

Mrs. Steels received a condolence letter from the headmaster at the Toynbee Road Council School; in response, she sent her son's toys to the school and asked that they be distributed among his classmates. On September 23, the entire student body stood in silent prayer, in Fred Steels' honor.

THE NEWSPAPERS WERE ALSO FILLED with stories of heroism at sea. Reporters wrote of the escort Michael Rennie's selfless rescues in the wake of the attack, and the courage of the *Benares'* captain, Landles Nicoll. But mostly they wrote about the endurance and bravery of the children. Several dispatches described the odyssey of Bess Walder and Beth Cummings, and nearly every report mentioned Colin Richardson's stoicism and courage on the water.

The *Evening Times* of London cheered the "11-year-old boy, hero of disaster." He was, said the *Daily Mirror,* the "hero of the ship." Richardson's lifeboat companion Margaret Hodgson told reporters that Colin "had gone round trying to comfort passengers in distress," and the *Benares'* carpenter, Angus MacDonald, who had skippered Colin's lifeboat, told the *Mirror* that the boy's

> spirits never went down, and his cheery voice could always be heard above the moaning of the other people suffering from exposure . . . Even when the adults were moaning from the cold and sleet bleating into their wounds, even when the dead were being lowered overboard, young Richardson kept trying to cheer us up. He was magnificent.

As a result of such coverage, telegrams and letters poured in to the Richardson home from family, friends, and perfect strangers, from across Britain, from the United States, and even from South Africa. One British veteran there sent his complete collection of war ribbons. The family that had invited Colin Richardson to America sent a short telegram from New York's Long Island. "Immensely relieved Colin is safe. Our newspapers mentioned his courageous conduct."

ASIDE FROM THE EVACUEE CHILDREN and their escorts, 212 passengers and crew had been lost. Many well-known members of that cosmopolitan group of *Benares* passengers were missing and presumed dead—the filmmaker Ruby Grierson, the parliamentarian Baldwin-Webb, the German refugees Rudolf and Ika Olden, and two well-known sons of Poland, Bohdan Nagorski and Zygmunt Gralinski, to name a few. Eric Davis, the British Broadcasting Corporation correspondent who had been instrumental in saving the Bech family and then lasted so long on a raft with Jack Keeley and the second engineer, John McGlashan, spoke for all the dead in a sober but angry message delivered via the BBC:

> The efforts of every adult within reach are nothing compared with the
> vindictiveness of a harsh sea and a bitter wind, and a merciless
> enemy . . . We were a cosmopolitan company. That torpedo did not
> merely strike at an English ship. It was a blow against all that was free
> and hopeful in Europe . . .
>   There were on board Dutch and Germans and Austrians and Poles, all
> of whom believed, as we believed, that freedom to think and act and to
> bring up young children in security and safety are fundamental to a good
> world order.

In the United States, the attack brought fresh calls for Washington to abandon its neutrality. Iowa Senator Clyde Herring cited the torpedoing of the *Benares* as proof that Hitler was a "mad butcher." Secretary of State Cordell Hull weighed in. "I am sure," he wrote, "there will be no division of opinion in this country, that this was a most dastardly act." The Australian Prime Minister R. G. Menzies decried this "latest exhibition of savagery by the Nazis," and in Canada, the minister in charge of settling the evacuee children called the attack on the *City of Benares* an example of "Nazi fright-fulness." Under the headline "Slaughter of the Innocents," the *Montreal Gazette* editorialized that

> the cowardly spirit of evil and the intense feelings of hatred that Adolf Hitler has let loose in the world were manifest in all their sinister crookedness in one of the most tragic sea disasters that have been recorded in the war.

At the Canadian port of Halifax, where the *Benares* herself was to have made her initial North American landing, the *Duchess of Atholl* docked on September 22. This was the ship that had occupied the berth opposite the *Benares* at Liverpool.

The *Atholl* sailor J. R. Creswell, the young man who had watched the *Benares* children and sung along with them at Liverpool, bought a newspaper at Halifax and saw the headlines.

Creswell had hoped all the way to Canada that the attack he and his fellow sailors had heard about had had nothing to do with that lovely group of children, the boys and girls who had waved and sung from the liner's deck. They had made such a glorious portrait of youth and hopefulness, Creswell thought. He cringed when he saw the front page. Then he threw the newspaper away.

THE FIRST OFFICIAL GERMAN RESPONSE was to deny that anything had happened. Hitler's chief propagandist, Joseph Goebbels, claimed there was no record of the attack, that Germany took care to strike only at clearly armed vessels, and that the German Navy had no U-boats working six hundred miles off British shores. The only plausible conclusion, said Goebbels, was that Churchill had orchestrated an elaborate ruse, concocting the story as a propaganda tool. In a remarkable dispatch on September 23, the German government took aim at the Reuters News Agency, which had published some of the first reports of the attack:

> The Reuters Lie Agency reports with a loud exclamation of pain the torpedoing of an armed British auxiliary steamer . . . according to a time tested pattern of horror, the case is being adorned dramatically.

As accounts of the sinking became public, Goebbels and the German government changed their story. Perhaps the *Benares* had gone down, Goebbels said, but if so it was because the British had blown up the ship themselves to elicit sympathy and perhaps draw the United States into the war.

Further evidence shredded this theory—not least the existence of a communiqué from Berlin that lauded U-48's commander, Heinrich Bleichrodt, for sinking the *City of Benares* and eight other vessels. The September 21 *wermachtsbericht*, a daily combat brief, reported that "the U-boat under command of Kapitänlieutenant Heinrich Bleichrodt sank nine merchant vessels for a total of 51,862 tons." It ranked as one of the most prolific U-boat missions of the war.

Now Goebbels altered his defense once more. If Germany *had* struck the *Benares*, he argued, then the attack must have been justified. He accused the British admiralty of having turned the *Benares* into an armed merchant vessel:

> The device of putting children in auxiliary cruisers and calling them
> children's export ships might be extended to munitions factories; through
> the presence of a few children they could acquire the status of orphanages.

In other words, Great Britain was ultimately responsible because it had placed its children in dangerous waters. "If the ship was really torpedoed with the loss of 83 children," Goebbels argued, "then the murderer's name is Churchill. Nothing is sacred to this monster."

Goebbels was hardly credible, and the epithet he chose for Churchill was scandalous, as were many of the words he chose during the war. If anyone was a monster, it was he. Yet there was at least some reason in this last argument Goebbels made, an argument that would remain the official German position at the Nuremberg War Crimes Tribunal nearly six years later. At the least, the sinking of the *Benares* would leave the British Admiralty open to questions.

Why had the *Benares'* naval escort turned when it did? Why had the slow-moving civilian vessels not departed when the warship left—to allow the *City of Benares* to sail faster and perhaps draw less attention? Why had the children been told it was safe to sleep without their life vests—even as reports of U-boat activity were being received by the ship's telegraph operators? And—had the *Benares'* senior officers and the CORB executives not been aware that U-boats had been active beyond the seventeen-degree-west line of longitude?

The men who might have shed light on these matters—Captain Landles Nicoll and the convoy commander, Admiral Edmund Mackinnon—had gone down with the ship. The other key player—U-48's Commander Heinrich Bleichrodt—said later he was crushed when he learned that his torpedo had sunk a ship carrying child evacuees. He also said he had been operating under simple and unambiguous orders: Find the largest ships you can, and destroy them.

BUT THIS DISCUSSION OF WHO knew what, and when they had known it, would come later. In the raw aftermath of the tragedy, the emotion of the moment was outrage, the chief reflex a raucous call for revenge.

King George VI broadcast a speech to the nation on September 23, a review of the war to date, in which he said of the *Benares* tragedy, "Surely the world can have no clearer proof of the wickedness against which we fight than this foul deed."

Winston Churchill was asked about reprisals. The prime minister ducked the question at first, then replied, "Yes—all in good time." Four days later Churchill wrote to his Chiefs of Staff Committee:

The possibility of our having to retaliate on the German civilian population must be studied, and on the largest scale possible. We should never begin, but we must be able to reply.

Eddie and Hannah Grimmond were not interested in this sort of studied, measured response. They were seized with rage over the attack and the death of their children. "If Hitler thinks he can beat us this way, he's mistaken," Hannah Grimmond said. "This may be his way of stabbing us in the back, but it's not going to work in England."

The following week Eddie Grimmond left his job as a council laborer to join the King's Royal Rifle Corps, the regiment he had served during the First World War. "I'm going to join up and try to get a good frontline job," he told a reporter. "My only wish is to find some way to get back at the Nazis."

THE FIRST MEMORIALS WERE HELD on the weekend of September 21–22.

In Sunderland, they remembered Peter and William Short and the other Sunderland casualties. Samuel Storey, a member of Parliament for Sunderland, sent a telegram to the family. "Mrs. Storey and I are deeply grieved by your great loss, and send sincere sympathy."

At Herne Bay, Reverend Rory O'Sullivan was remembered as a pillar of the local church community and a beacon of strength and wisdom during wartime.

At London's St. Jude on the Hill Church, the life of another escort, Michael Rennie, was celebrated at High Mass. The vicar was Rennie's father, Maxwell, and the principal speaker was Bishop Horace Crotty, who sprinkled his eulogy with examples of the heroism Michael Rennie had shown, diving to pull so many children from the water. Crotty wove these together with verse from the book of Revelation:

There was war in Heaven: Michael and his angels fought against the dragon. And the dragon fought— and prevailed not . . .

Nor shall we fail to think this morning of those young human Michaels, the bearers of his great name, that young chivalry of God who go forth each day to fight by the side of their own great Angel, to subdue that beast that murders little children, and lays great cities low, and ravages and torments with human life.

You of St. Jude's, as well as members of his own dear home, will think today of your own Michael Rennie, who died with the great Michael's spirit surely somewhere near him, guarding God's little ones, when the beast assailed them, succoring and defending them here on earth . . .

Bohdan Nagorski's brother received a message from the *Benares'* parent company. It was sent from Liverpool to Zygmunt Nagorski's London apartment and written in the standard clipped language of the telegram:

Deeply regret inform you vessel by which your brother Mr. B Nagorski was travelling has been sunk by enemy action and his name is not included in list of survivors.

A letter to the same address was posted the following day.

With the greatest regret we found it necessary to telegraph you yesterday conveying the sad news that the vessel in which your brother, Mr. B. Nagorski, was travelling had been sunk by enemy action, and that his name was not included in the list of survivors.

We must now confirm the information then given and in doing so beg to tender our sincere sympathy in the bereavement you have sustained.

Obituary notices for Bohdan Nagorski were published in Canada, Britain, and his native Poland. The September 23 edition of the *Toronto Globe and Mail* led with the news from the North Atlantic: "294, Including 83 Child Refugees, Lose Lives as Canada-Bound Ship Torpedoed . . . Storm-Tossed Boats Are Scenes of Death." The paper carried a dispatch from Greenock that was rich in detail provided by the survivors.

But it was not true that 294 people had died, nor that 83 of the child evacuees had perished. Some of the obituary writers had spoken—or written—too soon.

CHAPTER 18

Whales, Ships, and Phantoms

Father Rory O'Sullivan had been seriously ill for a week. He had suffered almost from the moment the *City of Benares* left Liverpool, and it would have been hard to imagine poorer conditions for convalescence. O'Sullivan had spent most of his time flat on his back on the boat's bottom, lifting himself to a sitting position when the meals came. He had come to consider each morning a blessing, almost a surprise, and he offered prayers of thanksgiving whenever his mind steadied. From their first morning together, several fellow passengers had watched O'Sullivan and imagined they would soon be burying him at sea.

So it stunned many of the others to see Rory O'Sullivan on Saturday morning, the twenty-first of September, standing atop one of the thwarts. He was gaunt and gray-faced, but very much alive. And he was smiling.

O'Sullivan had stood for a reason—he had seen something on the water.

"Look!"

There, perhaps one hundred yards off the bow, the back of a whale skimmed the sea's surface, blue-black and shiny. It hurtled along, obscured now by a wave, then back in view, coming a bit closer. Soon a second whale appeared, further in the distance.

The boys gawked. Paul Shearing thought he was dreaming. Even the sailors were impressed. "They're *huge*!" Doug Critchley cried. Mary Cornish peered at the water, wondering whether the creatures were real or phantoms. *Are these the first signs of madness?*

But soon the whales were nearer, clearly visible, creating a surf all their own as they whipped along, parallel to the boat. If this was madness, then it had afflicted them all at once. The crew took up the Fleming gear, working to steer away from these enormous visitors. Cooper implored the Indians to work the handles, but the men were listless or sleeping, or out cold. Undaunted, Cooper tried a different tactic. He asked Ramjam to tell his compatriots that whales had been known to scratch their backs on the undersides of lifeboats. "For sport," Cooper said.

Ramjam raised an eyebrow, but he passed the message. He and Cooper had established a solid relationship during their time in Lifeboat 12. Now Cooper saw the effect his fable had on the group in the boat's midsection. Soon several of the Indians were up and pulling on the Fleming handles.

For a time Cooper and Critchley were seriously concerned about the "storm" the whales might create if they swam too near the boat. But they kept their distance, like polite guests. They showed their long, smooth backs a few more times, cutting soft arcs on the water, and then they dove and disappeared.

Paul Shearing was sorry to see them go; these elegant giants had provided a welcome and all-too-brief entertainment. Rory O'Sullivan sat down and said another prayer of thanks—this time for the beauty of God's creations.

SUNDAY THE TWENTY-SECOND CAME COLDER than any previous day. Clusters of hail had collected on the gunwales, and Peard and Critchley began the morning trying to break off chunks of the hail and gather them in their milk cans. Several Indians joined in, and after a while everyone had a chance to suck on some salty bits of ice.

Later that day they trapped water in another, more conventional manner. A light rain fell in mid-morning, and at Cooper's direction they laid out the sail, covering the children and many adults but mostly endeavoring to collect rainwater. They did well enough so that before noon Purvis was able to pass small portions around the boat, a welcome supplement to the twice-daily dipper. But Purvis' passengers found themselves quickly disappointed. The water had absorbed the sail's coat of sea salt. It was almost like tasting the Atlantic itself, Paul Shearing thought. Cooper and Purvis admonished the others that this water was probably not fit for consumption, but they noticed several of the Indians were drinking it anyway.

For lifeboat passengers, the temptation to swallow seawater was as common as sunburn or thirst itself, and as has been noted, those who surrendered to it often found the effects catastrophic. A dehydrated person who consumes saltwater is in essence forcing his or her kidneys to extract fluid from the body to help excrete the salt—and the fluids are not there. Cooper, Purvis, and Ramjam were desperately worried that men would die in their boat because they had ignored the warnings.

It was their fifth full day in the lifeboat, and apart from those lovely whales they had yet to see so much as a dot on the horizon. Lips were caked with salt, and mouths had gone dry, nearly free of the saliva needed to moisten food. Chewing and swallowing had become almost impossible tasks. The boat was quiet; only a few Indians talking, Harry Peard whistling a tune, and the mast groaning in the breeze. *Like an old man in pain*, Mary Cornish thought.

In mid-morning George Purvis broke the stillness to report that there would be a noon "treat." It was an announcement meant primarily for the children. Purvis had been fastidious as ever with his supplies, but he was also conscious that the boys' spirits now hung perilously low. It had become difficult for anyone on board to swallow one of the mealtime staples, the ship's biscuit; it was simply too hard and dry for mouths as parched as theirs. The boys had asked Mary Cornish to "store" their portions for later, and her pockets had filled quickly with biscuits, half biscuits, and biscuit crumbs. No child ever demanded his biscuit back, so lunch had been reduced to a slice of corned beef, canned salmon, or sardine—all of which were salty to the taste—together with the few sips of water. Today, Purvis would add a wedge of canned peach.

It seemed a trifle. It did not look like much, either, a single slice per person, perhaps one-eighth of an actual peach. Only a few days before, they had feasted on entire plates of fruit in the *Benares'* dining room.

But when Purvis' "treat" came, Derek Capel thought it was the finest food he had ever eaten. Billy Short believed he had never tasted anything so luscious and rich. The cool, soft fruit watered his mouth, leaving pure sweetness on the tongue. Then it slid like honey along his throat, lubricating all the way. Fred Steels, feeling all the same sensations, wished he could freeze the moment. *It's like candy, is what it is.* He wanted to hold that sliver of peach in his mouth, soft and wet and never to be swallowed. At least not until they were rescued.

Then the dipper of water came. It was almost too much, bliss upon bliss, the moist fruit washed down, a fantastic salve for dry, cracked mouths. The boys licked their lips—in itself something that had not been easy in the last few days. Then they peered at the stern. Was there more?

God, Billy Short thought, *what I wouldn't do for another slice of peach...*

But Purvis was closing up his containers. The meal was finished; there would be no more treats today. In five and a half hours they would have supper.

Watching the boys fade again, George Purvis hollered down to the bow. "Tomorrow," he cried, "will be a good day!" He had nothing in mind to support the promise, but he felt it necessary to make it nonetheless.

THAT AFTERNOON THE SEAS RAN mellow, calmer than any day thus far. They sailed under an azure sky, only a few wispy clouds here and there. The lookouts stood without difficulty at the mast. Cooper put visibility at roughly three miles.

It was one of the children, leaning out over a gunwale, who cried out.

"*Smoke!*"

Heads lifted and spun to the west.

Smoke it was. A small black shroud, far on the horizon.

They had all imagined their rescue, forty-six different ideas and daydreams of how precisely the moment would arrive and the event itself unfold. The boys had dreamed of motorboats and clipper ships, Royal Navy cruisers and liners like the *City of Benares* herself. They would be scooped dramatically from the water, fed and clothed and whisked back home, no doubt to a heroes' welcome. Even now, five days on, Bohdan Nagorski kept expecting the destroyer *Winchelsea*, the *Benares'* lead escort, to appear. He had a vivid picture of the ship fixed in his mind.

Now, at five o'clock on their fifth afternoon, there was what seemed to be a real vessel, a grayish shape with a black plume hovering over it. Both shape and plume were looming larger, and within minutes the boys were on their feet, waving wildly, though the ship—and they were not yet certain it *was* a ship—still sat far off, due west. Cooper guessed its position to be roughly two miles away. Whatever the distance, Cooper knew it would be more difficult for a ship's sailors to see them, given how low on the water the lifeboat was. With this in mind, he and Ramjam raised the oar with Mary Cornish's pink camisole fluttering in the breeze.

For the first time the boys themselves suggested to Father O'Sullivan that prayers were in order. *A fine idea,* O'Sullivan thought, and he began with a plea. "God, let them come our way . . ." Then he said the Lord's Prayer. Soon the adults had joined in—the Europeans anyway—adding prayers of thanks, and prayers of hope. "Please, Lord, let that ship's captain see us . . ."

They stared at the horizon, and prayed.

While they waited, a memory came to Mary Cornish, and it startled her. It was clear and frightening, a scene she had dreamed often as a child, in which she struggled on a murky sea, trying to stay above water, while some huge vessel hovered in the distance.

The ship would come for her, rocking weirdly, and then for some reason young Mary was always in midair, leaping clumsily as she tried to reach the deck. In the dream she had mistimed her jump, landing instead in the waves and discovering—in the hazy trance of sleep—that drowning was not an unpleasant thing. A wall of water would spin wildly—yet harmlessly—all around her. She would wallow in the water, strangely serene, waiting for her ship, and waiting for some resolution—death or life. Neither ever came.

Now it appeared that the first part of her dream—the hopeful part—was coming true. There she was, shipwrecked on the ocean, and a ship was heading in her direction. Surely the resolution—life or death—could not be long in coming.

WITHIN MINUTES THE VAGUE SHAPE had acquired definition. *She's a steamer,* Ronnie Cooper thought. *Medium size. And she's moving fast.* "Merchant vessel," Cooper said matter-of-factly to Critchley and Mayhew, and he asked them to guess her distance. They figured she was now less than a mile away.

The Indians were suddenly alive with excitement, some of the men standing and gesturing to the water. O'Sullivan and Mary Cornish stood, flanking the six boys, who shouted and burst into song. Then they saw the ship take a slow turn in their direction.

My God, that's it, Rory O'Sullivan said to himself. *We are saved.*

They scrambled to prepare for their rescue. Mayhew, the Navy signal man, worked furiously with flags, while Critchley maneuvered the sail, steering Lifeboat 12 toward the ship. Cooper, no longer the quiet skipper, cupped his hands and called his passengers to attention. Then he hollered instructions from the stern. Rescue on the water was no easy thing, he warned his suddenly giddy group. The ship would stand far higher than they were, he said, and each passenger would probably have to be lifted to deck, one at a time. "If you feel strong enough, volunteer to raise yourself," Cooper ordered, explaining that rope ladders would likely be tossed their way for this purpose. Anyone who required help, he stressed, should ask for it.

Next Cooper and Peard ordered the dismantling of any gear that might interfere with the operation. The Duck's Hole awning over the bow was brought down, and the heavy iron stanchions supporting it were yanked from their sockets. This was done to minimize risk to the boys' legs as they stepped from the boat. When the stanchions came free, the sailors jettisoned two of the three sets, tossing them overboard. There was no place to stash these bulky chunks of iron, and no longer any apparent need to have them on board. This gesture won cheers from the Indians, and it thrilled Ronnie Cooper. In his heart he wanted to toss every last thing to the water.

It was a glorious moment, made better somehow by what they saw in the skies behind the steamer: a row of black, angry clouds. The promise of another rough storm. *Our boat will battle that one alone*, O'Sullivan thought. *We shall be gone.*

The boys were still singing. Bohdan Nagorski thought of his wife and daughters. Mary Cornish allowed herself a smile. What they saw next nearly killed them all.

It cannot be, O'Sullivan thought. Fred Steels saw the faces around him, smiles falling away.

The steamer was turning again—this time in the wrong direction. Nagorski saw heavy smoke billowing from her funnel. Then the turn was sharp and unmistakable. The ship pushed away, to the north.

Nagorski could not understand. Was it a German craft? Mayhew still waved his flags. Cooper stared, standing still. Was it simply a case of a ship's crew not paying close attention to the sea?

Several of the boys began to sob and shudder, reaching to embrace O'Sullivan or Auntie Mary. Paul Shearing thought he had never seen so sad a sight as his new friends, the other boys, weeping and huddled with the escorts. Shearing himself felt strangely detached, almost too weak to cry or to absorb the situation around him.

Now Mary Cornish became convinced the whole episode had been a dream—*her* dream, a more cruel version of the nightmare she had known as a child. She was stranded on the water, just as she had always been stranded in her dreams.

Soon there was no doubt. The ship had run what appeared to be a series of tantalizingly slow zigzags, bringing her steadily farther from Lifeboat 12. They had been close enough to see her masts and funnel. Certainly near enough to assume they had been saved. Now the steamer was only a slim outline again. They stared as the shape blurred, shrank, and then vanished altogether. The halo of smoke went last, like a candle snuffed, all their hopes shattered.

In its place the black clouds came—the storm they had figured on riding out from the warm confines of a ship's cabin. For the first time the children cried hard, an awful sound that filled the little boat.

THE DESPAIR WAS TOTAL, ALMOST unimaginable. The Indians reverted to a sullen mass, and the boys became a frightened, whimpering group. Even the ever-cheerful Purvis, huddled with Cooper, Critchley, and Mayhew at the stern, could find no encouraging words.

Rory O'Sullivan struggled more than anyone with the turn of events. *It cannot be*, he thought. The steamer's disappearance had not merely challenged his resolve and his optimism; it was testing his faith. That faith had withstood many challenges in O'Sullivan's thirty-two years. He had already suffered a life's share of trauma and setback, but this seemed different. When one of the boys turned to O'Sullivan and asked, "What's the good of praying, sir, if the ship came so close without taking us?" the priest began an answer. Then he caught himself, his mind weak and his ability to concentrate fading.

It was the sort of question he had been asked countless times, in all manner of circumstances; indeed it was a question he had posed to himself on many occasions—as a child, as a student, and then as a priest. Why did the Lord bring trial and tragedy to pious, undeserving souls? Why did He test his subjects? O'Sullivan had always found answers and explanations which—while never complete and not always satisfactory—had at least helped advance his own understanding of God and of life. On occasion he had allowed himself to believe he had helped his fellow men. Now, for the first time, Rory O'Sullivan found himself unsure, and unable to respond.

He mumbled something to the boys about the need to maintain hope, but his answer was unconvincing and he knew it. Here he was, a man of the cloth and a congenital optimist, a man who could find value and meaning in the most mundane experience, and yet in the aftermath of a simple event—a ship's approach, and subsequent turnabout—he was feeling a profound sense of doubt. O'Sullivan found himself troubled by the facts of the episode—*surely the men on that ship had seen us*—but mostly he worried over what it had done to these sweet young boys. What spiritual lesson were they to derive from such a moment? Rory O'Sullivan believed he understood the tests war presented to all God's children, but the dangling of such hope—to six children in particular—seemed a terrible, cruel tease. It was, O'Sullivan thought, a challenge devoid of meaning.

· · ·

WHEN FATHER O'SULLIVAN GOT AROUND to giving the boys a fuller answer to their question, perhaps a half hour later, he told them that prayer would give them the ear of God, that He would know they were His obedient servants. It was no use, O'Sullivan said, taking on this battle without His help.

As for the facts, O'Sullivan said the steamer had probably been a German ship. And who among us, he asked, would have been happy to be brought aboard such a ship and ferried back to Germany?

The boys shook their heads feebly. None of them would have wanted *that*.

Still they stared at the sea, hoping the ship might turn again.

God, they are brave, Rory O'Sullivan thought. He lay back down in the boat, feverish again. He found himself frightened—and still struggling to understand.*

THE WRENCHING STORY OF THE lost steamer occupied Lifeboat 12's passengers for an hour or so, as long as it took for the storm to roll in. Nagorski believed they had missed their greatest chance for rescue. The boys—so excited at the sight of the ship—lay near Mary Cornish, some of them stunned and silent, others still crying and asking questions. "When's that ship coming back?" Ken Sparks wanted to know.

Critchley and Mayhew worked to refit the Duck's Hole, minus the stanchions they had thrown in the water. Cooper and Purvis sat sullen at the stern.

It fell to Harry Peard to find a silver lining.

"What's the matter now?" he asked, scampering near the children. "Downhearted because she didn't pick us up? *That's* nothing to worry about." The boys said nothing. *He's a proper screwball*, Fred Steels said to himself. For once

*It was never certain what ship it was, or why she had turned. Theories abounded. The steamer's crew might have believed Lifeboat 12 was a decoy; during the First World War the Germans had used fake lifeboats to lure ships into U-boat range. Perhaps the ship's lookout had let his attention falter or—though this seemed hardest to fathom—perhaps the ship had been on a standard zigzag route and one of her routine turns had only appeared to be angled toward the lifeboat.

Much later it was suggested that the ship may have been HMS *Ascania*, an old liner converted recently to armed merchant cruiser. The *Ascania* had been on a return trip to her base at Halifax that afternoon, when one of her lookouts reported seeing a ship's lifeboat; but nothing more was seen and he was told he must have imagined it. *Ascania* steamed on for Halifax.

it seemed Peard's tactics, and his perky optimism, were not enough. "We'll see plenty more ships tomorrow," he assured them, "now that we've reached the shipping lanes."

Paul Shearing stared quizzically at Harry Peard. Then he turned to Cornish. "Auntie Mary, what's a 'shipping lane'?"

Peard's theory was not wholly implausible. Perhaps the sight of a steamer really did mean they were in the shipping lanes. Maybe they would have company in the morning. "There'll be another one along, any minute," Harry Peard insisted.

Ronnie Cooper didn't believe it. He agreed with most everyone else: That little steamer had probably been as good a chance as they were likely to find. O'Sullivan was even more pessimistic; perhaps, he thought, the Germans had overrun Great Britain. Perhaps there were no longer any friendly vessels to be found in these shipping lanes.

In any event, forty-six pairs of eyes now scanned the horizon and found . . . nothing. Only a newly choppy sea, and that angry band of clouds.

DUSK ARRIVED. THE STORM ROSE, and the passengers of Lifeboat 12 lay low and braced themselves. It would be a violent night.

Rory O'Sullivan decided to tell the boys a story. O'Sullivan felt he owed them as much, something more than Bulldog Drummond, and certainly something more meaningful than the flimsy explanations he had offered for what had transpired that afternoon. What he came up with was the story of Rocamadour.

Rocamadour was a small city in southern France, home to a shrine built to honor the saint Amadour in the twelfth century. Following the discovery of Amadour's remains at the site in 1166, the shrine had become an important place of pilgrimage.

O'Sullivan chose Rocamadour now because for centuries the shrine had been a beacon for sailors and voyagers anticipating trouble on the sea, or for those giving thanks for a miracle on the water. Legend had it that sailors had been saved because of vows they made at sea, promises to visit the sanctuary at Rocamadour. The church had recorded sailors' messages of thanksgiving; many men had made the pilgrimage in bare feet. O'Sullivan finished his story by telling the boys about a bell in the church sanctuary that was known to ring on its own, its peal marking the moment a drowning sailor was rescued at sea.

The boys gazed intently at the priest. The story was as far removed from Bulldog Drummond as they could imagine, but it had captured their attention nonetheless. *What's it mean?* Shearing wondered. Expressions returned to vacant faces, and the moment O'Sullivan had finished, the boys wanted to know when they should plan to make their own vows and pilgrimages to Rocamadour. Why, a puzzled Derek Capel wondered, had they waited this long?

The wind was whipping up the water again. The storm would be upon them soon. Father O'Sullivan tried to explain that Rocamadour was in France, which was not only far away but also now in the hands of the Germans. One had to take care, O'Sullivan told the boys, not to make a pledge to God that could not be honored.

Nonsense, the boys replied. Neither distance nor Adolf Hitler would keep them from O'Sullivan's special place. And if they *were* kept away somehow, then they insisted they would make "pilgrimages" to their own churches and give thanks at neighborhood altars. God, they believed, would understand.

Rory O'Sullivan smiled. Again he thought, *They are marvelous, these boys. We must not lose a single one.*

Then he told them they were right—God *would* understand.

Six English boys resolved to visit the sanctuary at Rocamadour. The bell in that church would ring for them all, and then they would make the pilgrimage together, after their own miracles on the water.

BY SEPTEMBER 22, THE TERRIBLE news had reached most of their families in England, and in one way or another they were being missed, or mourned, or memorialized. Ronnie Cooper's brother Ian was one of five sons at sea, and from the Scottish port of Methil Ian Cooper phoned his mother that night. He had just learned that the *Benares* had been sunk. "Ronnie is in danger," he told her, "and in need of your prayers."

Friends and family had no reason to think that anyone not yet returned home could possibly be alive.

Cooper *was* alive that Sunday evening, together with his forty-five passengers aboard Lifeboat 12, but their spirits and physical strength had never been poorer. Optimism was now as scarce as anything else, and more than anything they felt acutely the pain of monotony. Even the most patient adults were now crazy with the ache to walk or run. Bohdan Nagorski had come to understand why Harry Peard so craved his plunges to the water and those round-the-lifeboat swims. But Nagorski was now too weak to contemplate doing the same. Mary Cornish feared she was losing her tether to reality. She felt the presence of demons working around their little boat, beating back every last shred of hope. Together they all worried about the storm that was bearing down on them, a fierce brew that was turning dusk to pitch-black night.

This would be their sixth night in the lifeboat.

Yet again, Harry Peard made the difficult walk to the bow. Perhaps he recognized just how dire things were; perhaps he was simply restless. Whatever the case, as the storm blew nearer Peard lumbered awkwardly forward, scarcely able to keep his balance, carrying his message for the boys: There was nothing to fear, nothing even to be sad about.

Hope and optimism had not yet deserted Harry Peard. "That ship shows we've reached the shipping lanes," he said again. It was in fact a *good sign* that they had crossed her path.

Nagorski had to smile. *Only that man could find good in what we have just seen.*

"How about some more of Captain Drummond?" Peard bellowed.

"Yes!" one of the boys cried. "Yes, Auntie Mary! Yes, for Captain Drummond!" Again they turned to Mary Cornish. A perfect time, they insisted, for another chapter.

Cornish winced. The sea was heavy now. Her vision blurred and her mind swam. She was already finding it difficult to invent more glory for her captain, more adventures for her listeners. Surely their own adventure would suffice for the moment, the waves opening a fresh assault on the boat. But she also felt she could not refuse the boys, and so another chapter spilled out, another collection of enemy agents and temptresses, the hero Drummond navigating expertly through them all.

Strands of her story seemed to veer strangely, like the boat itself, and sometimes the boys could not hear or understand her. After a while Mary Cornish felt faint. Her voice was weak. Each word had become a hardship. She was dazed, worried for own well-being and wondering how to close this installment. Then she looked at her children in the half-light. They were asleep. Six boys dozed, huddled against or on top of one another.

With Nagorski's help she laid blankets over them, and began the job of wrapping them in pairs for the night. The storm was coming hard.

How long can they last? Mary Cornish wondered. She wanted to ask Nagorski his opinion, but the wind and the water roared and superstition told her not to start such a conversation. *Better to concentrate our energies,* she thought, *on lasting the night.*

The skies had gone storm black, and hail twinned now with heavy gusts. It would be a powerful storm. At six-thirty Cooper and Critchley ordered the sail brought down.

. . .

NIGHT FELL VIOLENTLY. THE WINDS reached gale force and the lifeboat rocked. Cooper shouted a reminder from the stern: "Lie low!"

They needed no reminder. The hail came at an angle, slashing hard and cold.

It was their darkest hour yet. Cooper, Critchley, Peard, and Mayhew barked orders. Everyone was to sit still, stay low, and hang on. "Hold anything you can!" Peard shouted.

The boat heaved. Cornish felt one of the boys fall violently against her. The Indians began bailing, but soon the storm raged too powerfully for anyone to do much more than crouch in the boat.

God help us, Rory O'Sullivan said to himself.

The stanchions that had supported the awning were gone. Now, as hail tattooed the boat, lashing at their faces, Cooper's decision to throw the stanchions into the sea looked like a colossal error. The awning had been reduced to a sheet, draped unevenly over the boys. Nagorski and some of the Indians had to sit on the canvas to keep it from blowing away.

They all lay there, clutching the thwarts or the gunwales, or one another. Swells drenched the boat. The boys slept fitfully. No one else slept at all.

Mary Cornish lay on the foresheets, an arm hooked around one of the Fleming handles in a desperate attempt to tie herself to the boat. Cornish listened to the screaming wind and thought she heard a message, a mean-spirited cry: *The cause is lost. You have done well to last this long. But now...*

Her mind wandered now to thoughts of Odysseus, Homer's tireless sea traveler, battling treacherous seas and malevolent gods who had placed so many obstacles in his path. As the wind and waves and rain tore up the ocean, Mary Cornish felt a kinship with Homer's hero. She believed that good and evil were locked in some elemental battle, having it out around their boat. It would end soon, in destruction or salvation. One way or the other, it would end. Forty-six lives lay in the balance.

A dozen times in the night they thought they were done for, the battle lost. The hail became rain, and the rain never relented. The sea made a powerful whirlpool around them. Cooper threw out the sea anchor. Nagorski, Peard, and several Indians took turns bailing, though they made little progress and after a time it became too rough even for Harry Peard. The swells ran at least as high and hard as the night the *Benares* had gone down. The difference now was that they were physically and mentally so much weaker than they had been as passengers aboard the *City of Benares.* Time and again they imagined a wave would spell their end—and each time Lifeboat 12 landed, *thump,* hard but safe on the water. Ready for a fresh onslaught.

It was another storm and another long, wild night that should have defeated the little boat. It should have killed everyone on board.

DAYBREAK SEEMED TO TEASE THEM. A spray of light, then more wind and rain. Bohdan Nagorski had thought the dawn would never come.

Mary Cornish raised herself slowly, feeling a searing, throbbing pain in her hands and legs. The blanketed bundles of children were cold, wet, and still. Cornish fully expected the dawn to reveal death in their midst. But death had not come. The others stirred slowly—all of them. Cooper and his men were alive. Nagorski and O'Sullivan, too. Ramjam Buxoo conferred with his countrymen and found a beaten, badly frayed group—but he reported back to Cooper that every one of the men still breathed.

Mary Cornish could hardly move, but she did manage to sit up and peer under the ruins of the Duck's Hole.

"Hello, boys."

"Hey, Auntie Mary."

So the count was as it had always been. Thirty-nine men, six boys, and the woman they called Auntie Mary.

It's a miracle, she thought. *We are not so easily defeated.*

MIRACLES NOTWITHSTANDING, THE ATMOSPHERE ON the morning of September 23 was palpably, utterly bleak. The dawn was a soup of gray, save for a scattering of whitecaps on the water. Squalls came and went. The boys woke bone-cold, and some cried softly under their blankets. Cornish spent the day's first hours rubbing limbs again as vigorously as she could, enlisting Nagorski's aid. The boys lay there, quiet and shivering.

At least one child still had Rocamadour on his mind. *I'd go anywhere,* Ken Sparks thought, if it would help lead them home. Sparks, the eldest boy in the boat, found it hard now to believe that not long before, he and the others had been so excited, so taken with the "adventure" of living with sailors on an open boat. *I want to be home,* Ken Sparks said to himself. *I want this to end.*

The Indians may have been alive, but they were an almost inert clump of bodies in the boat's midsection—cold, red-eyed, and expressionless. They stirred for morning prayers, rinsing their faces and mouths as always, but many of them were shaking badly, and their collective prayer was reduced to a low murmur. The British sailors feared that some of the Indians had been tasting seawater again, unable to resist that profound and deadly temptation.

A few hours later, when Purvis passed the noonday ration, the Indians' sick and tired eyes fastened on the dipper and followed it, trance-like, waiting for it to come to them. Everyone took the water, but almost no one ate. Their tongues and throats felt dry and crusted with salt; their voices were nearly gone, as was their ability to swallow solid food.

Mary Cornish looked around her. The "miracle" was already a memory. *We shall not last another night,* she thought.

THAT AFTERNOON, A SHOUT WENT up from the stern—one of the sailors had seen something. Bohdan Nagorski strained for a look and thought he could make out a ribbon of gray etched far on the horizon. Once again, all eyes fixed on something vague but interesting. Again, precious mental energies were spent on hope and prayer.

Mary Cornish saw the ribbon, thought its edge too sharp and well defined to be a cloud.

Land, Bohdan Nagorski thought.

O'Sullivan was first to speak the word aloud. "Land?" he said weakly. "Is it? Is it true?"

One of the children shrieked.

Ronnie Cooper believed it *was* land, and he and Critchley guided the boat in that direction, but Cooper also felt he had been cheated by the steamer's visit and her subsequent retreat. Hallucination was possible, too, though for the most part he felt reasonably well. So he said nothing, not even to his colleagues at the stern. Privately he wondered, *What are we looking at? Ireland? Scotland?* The truth was he did not know where they were. And he did not believe they were anywhere near Ireland or Scotland.

Nagorski knew that any land would constitute a sensational victory, a chance at the very least to rest, to dry off, to signal properly for help. He believed their chances would multiply even if all they were doing was beaching themselves on some barren patch of rock.

The sun was falling, drawing a close to their sixth day in the lifeboat. Their seventh night loomed. Would they make landfall? Was it really land anyway?

The ribbon never fattened. As daylight faded, it was still a smudge, something amorphous. Still far away.

Then it was night. Again. A calm night this time, clear, with hardly any wind. O'Sullivan dragged an empty milk can over the side, trying to trap a fish in the little container, and in the darkness he saw something shimmering in the can, occasionally glowing bright, a fire-like sparkle in the water. He had collected scores of tiny fish, every one of which glittered, throwing off a rich phosphorescence from the little cup. As he had done for the whales before, Rory O'Sullivan said a prayer of thanks as he stared at nature's creations. Then he tossed them back to the sea.

Ronnie Cooper ordered a flare hoisted to the masthead. This would be their signal to the coast. If a coast it was . . .

Cooper's flare swung an arc of light around the boat, a strange and intermittent flash in the cold black night.

CHAPTER 19

Last Rites

That night they were awakened by cries from the bow. "Help!" was the only word Mary Cornish could make out. Otherwise it was a trail of gibberish, loud and frightening. Ken Sparks, the oldest of the boys and to this moment among the heartiest passengers in Lifeboat 12, was delirious. Cornish and Rory O'Sullivan labored to calm him, while some of the Indians grumbled, their precious sleep disturbed by the wailing.

Privately Cornish worried that this was the beginning of the end—not just for Ken Sparks but for the five other boys as well, brave young souls who had scarcely complained since the *City of Benares* had gone down. Now all six children were badly depleted, and one of them was losing his mind. Soon, Mary Cornish feared, the boys would fade away.

DAWN CAME, AND FOUND KEN Sparks sleeping soundly. The passengers had waited excitedly for daylight, for a fresh look at the horizon, fully expecting to find further evidence of land. But when the sun rose, they could see no land, no ribbon or smudge, no band of anything to be found. They saw only the waves, and one another. Another hope had been smashed, another dream put down.

This time there was no great discussion about what had been seen, and what might have been imagined. No one had the energy for that, or perhaps they had lost interest in such talk. It was merely one more example of the great ocean's game, the elements toying with forty-six cold and failing souls.

. . .

IT WAS TUESDAY, SEPTEMBER 24. They had been in the lifeboat a week. The sun shone brightly, making for a crisp and relatively warm dawn. The temperature may have cleared fifty degrees by mid-morning.

For the most part these conditions were lost on a sick and dangerously dispirited group. The brilliant sun only made their solitude more plain. None of them—not even Officer Cooper—had any real idea where they were. With no navigational tools, and his mind ravaged by thirst and hunger and fatigue, Ronnie Cooper had begun to lose his bearings, as it were. Were they close to Ireland? One hundred miles away? Two hundred? He couldn't be sure. There was virtually no conversation, and though the sun warmed them, it also seemed to deepen lethargy up and down the boat.

The boys were in particularly poor shape. They ached terribly, from a near-constant contact with the boat boards, and one another. Billy Short felt as though he had been beaten by a paddle. The pain in their mouths and throats had sharpened. All six boys had open sores that made swallowing anything but water not only difficult but excruciatingly painful as well. The sea salt burned their skin, and even their eyes hurt, stung by wind and sun and the lack of sleep.

Mostly they suffered from a dearth of calories and water. Taken together, all the food and drink they had consumed in their week on the water might have equaled two ordinary meals, even for a poor boy in wartime England. And from one Wednesday to the next, each passenger had consumed only slightly more than one quart of water.

How long could this last? A severe form of cotton mouth had come over the passengers, saliva thick and tongues sore and bloated. Fred Steels found his tongue sticking to the roof of his mouth. O'Sullivan had taken to watching the dipper as it was passed toward him—and "with what recriminations and shouts did we greet the unfortunate whose trembling hand spilled even the tiniest drop . . ." What lay ahead as their water stocks dwindled had been described graphically in several lifeboat accounts before this one. The *Essex* leader Owen Chase had found that as his thirst intensified, "In vain was every expedient tried to relieve the raging fever of the throat." Death caused by thirst would bring a particularly horrible end; after the last drops of water were swallowed, the tongue would become "a senseless weight, swinging on the still-soft root and sticking foreignly against the teeth." The throat would swell, and breathing would become almost impossible. They were not at this stage yet, to be sure; but if they were not rescued soon, or by some miracle brought water they could drink, then they would soon die of thirst.

Bohdan Nagorski studied his fellow passengers. The sun had brought them into sharper relief. He found drawn and emaciated faces, bloodshot eyes, gazes blank and wandering. The Indians' cheeks were chapped and scarred; mouths hung open. Ramjam Buxoo was among the few who still spoke regularly, or seemed active in any way. At least one of the Indians was comatose; Ramjam checked occasionally to be sure his compatriots were breathing.

We will lose people today, Nagorski thought. He also wondered, for the first time in a week: *Do I look like the others?* He felt weak but still mentally able to absorb the scene and consider his circumstances. For whatever reason, Nagorski remained hopeful—and unafraid. O'Sullivan had weakened again. His flu may have passed, but he was very frail. So was Mary Cornish. She conserved words, hoping to save her voice and her energies for Bulldog Drummond.

Suddenly, not long after sunrise, the mass in the middle of the boat stirred. One of the Indians rose, pulling off his long cotton shirt. Those around him muttered, their sleep disturbed, and some rolled onto their sides, away from the commotion. Then the man shouted to the sky and leaped over the gunwale.

For a moment it seemed he was taking a dip in the ocean, perhaps mimicking one of Harry Peard's midday swims. But then the man was paddling strangely, a swimming stroke turned frantic wave, far off the stern. Soon he was shouting and thrashing at the water.

And then the man was being swept off by the waves.

It was no midday swim. This was madness in mid-morning, what Cooper and Purvis took to be the result of swallowed saltwater. Ronnie Cooper thought he had seen some of the Indians sipping seawater as they washed in the mornings, or drinking up the salty puddles from the sail. Cooper had seen its effects before.

Nagorski saw the man's head come to the surface once more, but by now he was too far to help. Then a heavy swell came and the man was gone, the current carrying him away. It had happened so fast. No one had managed to stop him; in the first critical moments, no one had seen the need.

The other Indians appeared stunned. The incident roused most of them, and as a group they were suddenly active and talkative again, gesturing to the water. Nagorski thought they looked scared. Ramjam crouched and addressed the men. He was trying to keep them calm. It would be all right, he said. That one had simply lost his mind.

Now they were forty-five.

In truth most of the adults had expected death to come sooner—and more often. Nagorski could not understand how it was that Rory O'Sullivan was still breathing; Cornish had been stunned, after the storm-wracked night, to find all six boys alive. But in the end, the manner in which death came—a dive off the side on a brilliant morning—startled them all. Ramjam told Ronnie Cooper he would assess as best he could the mental state of the other Indians. Cooper did not press the saltwater question, but he implored Ramjam to warn his colleagues again of the danger. They must resist the temptation, Cooper said. Privately he knew they might all die of thirst soon, when Purvis' stocks ran out, but he also believed they would be gone sooner, and faster, if they drank from the ocean.

Either way, Cooper knew, death would revisit his boat. It was only a question of when. And how.

BY LATE MORNING THE INDIANS were disconsolate, pleading to Purvis for water and distraught at the loss of one of their own. Bohdan Nagorski reminded them that there would be water soon; it was almost time for the midday meal.

Then Nagorski tried a novel way to improve the men's spirits. One of the sailors had discovered a bottle of iodine in the boat's medicine chest. It was one of the few supplies on board that they had not yet used. The night before, Nagorski and O'Sullivan had remarked on the horrific conditions of the Indians' feet; many had left the *Benares* in sandals, or without any footwear at all, and now their feet were reddened, swollen, and pocked with sores. O'Sullivan worried they would require amputation if they survived. It was his idea that they use the iodine to help.

So Bohdan Nagorski began tending to the Indians on this bright morning, rolling up their cotton pant legs and "painting their feet," as he put it, daubing them with the iodine, rationing this as carefully as any commodity in Lifeboat 12. Ramjam explained to his curious countrymen that the dark liquid was medicine, and that it would soothe their pain and ward off infection.

The task kept Nagorski busy for nearly two hours. The children watched, fascinated. One by one the Indians who took part bowed their heads and thanked Nagorski, and for a time he seemed to forget the anxiety and foreboding that hung so heavily over the boat. It helped to know that he was still able to do something, and that this "really trifling aid," as he called it, had been so well received.

AT NOON GEORGE PURVIS—NOW scarcely strong enough to stand—began distributing biscuits and sardines. He poured out the water rations and passed the dipper. Nagorski saw that Purvis' hands were trembling.

Purvis had yet to tell the others, but he had determined that this would be their last noonday serving. There was simply too little water left; rations would be halved. From now on water would be served at dusk only.

The boys were advised to suck on shirt buttons or any other plastic that might stimulate what limited saliva they could muster. This instruction was strange and interesting enough to enliven the boys, if only for a while. Billy Short experimented with his coat buttons. Derek Capel used the plastic figure of a lamb that O'Sullivan had given him while they were on board the *Benares*. Capel sucked on the small talisman and found that it brought at least some moisture to his mouth, but after a while the effect subsided, and soon interest in this "activity" waned. A half dozen boys were listless again.

The boat moved slowly, carried by a gentle wind. There was hardly a sound, save for the lapping of the waves. It was hard to believe this was the same body of water that had ravaged them so often during the past week.

Then, after "supper" and the evening's water, as the sun descended yet again, the boys were tugging at Auntie Mary's sleeve.

"Bulldog Drummond, please!"

"Please, Auntie Mary!"

Even Ken Sparks, in such distress the previous night, was adamant. "What's Captain Drummond *doing*?" Mary Cornish didn't know whether to laugh or cry. *Where do they find the energy?* she wondered. And then: *Where shall I find mine?*

Her throat stung, her tongue was swollen, and her mind raced with anxiety. She wanted to dream up another Drummond tale, but she felt she was losing command of her faculties. Questions came to torment her: Which child would die first? When would it happen? And how? These were terrible thoughts, she knew, but there they were in her mind, persistent and unmovable. And then she thought: *Whatever happens, I must not die first. The boys will need someone...*

Odd reveries frightened Mary Cornish, images of storms and people flailing

on the water. Her mind was cluttered with everything, it seemed, save for co-
herent thought.

Somehow she strung a few ideas together, managed to concoct new troubles
for Captain Drummond, the beginnings of a narrative. The effort felt like
plodding through a swamp. Her voice sounded thick to her own ears, and to
the boys she was barely intelligible. Her mind wandered and at times her
"chapter" veered strangely off course. Ken Sparks could see she was having a
difficult time.

But Auntie Mary pressed on, retrieving the story line, straining to bring
Drummond's escapades into some focus. Her motivation was simple: They
were *her boys* now. And Captain Drummond was all her boys had left. Only
this, a few drops of water, and some buttons to suck on.

THE EIGHTH NIGHT CAME. THEY had been sleeping for several
hours when a piercing cry broke the still.

"Drink! Drink! *Please!*"

One of the boys was screaming.

"I am *mad* . . ."

The others stirred, turning to the bow. It was a horrible cry. Cooper felt an
urge to push the length of the boat to the child's side, but it was too dark, the
sea too choppy.

This time the voice belonged to Paul Shearing. His expression contorted as
he cried out—an image rendered more frightening by the spinning flare
Cooper had raised once more to the mast. The boy's face was illuminated every
few seconds. Shearing writhed in pain.

"I am mad," he repeated. "I am going mad. Give—me—a *drink.*"

The light threw strange shadows. Paul Shearing became convinced he was
in a jail cell.

"I am *mad* . . ."

His shouts and wailing rattled Lifeboat 12. O'Sullivan prayed and Cornish
held the child close, singing softly to him. Neither prayer nor song did much
good. At one point Shearing wriggled free and began to lift his shirt, hollering
all the while. It was not unlike the scene played out the previous morning,
when the mad Indian had thrown himself to the water.

The adults managed to hold Shearing down. "It will be all right, son,"
O'Sullivan said. Nagorski threw a blanket over the child's shoulders. Cornish
massaged his arms and legs.

Paul Shearing screamed even louder.

It was a fit of delirium like the one Ken Sparks had suffered, only far more severe and long-lasting. Some of the Indians recoiled, afraid that whatever spirits had seized this child might come next for them. The other boys were afraid, too, watching their friend and boat mate suffer. Would they all be this way—a ball of pain and madness—before long?

Shearing had already suffered more than the others, wracked for days by pain in his legs and feet. Now these pains were excruciating, shooting sensations, some mix of frostbite and trench foot, the condition that comes to those whose feet sit in water for too long. Trench foot had crippled thousands of soldiers during the First World War; Paul Shearing's feet were bloated and dotted with sores. Still, his principal complaint involved thirst; his cries were for water.

O'Sullivan prayed loudly and kept the boy down, while Cornish removed her jacket—leaving her in short sleeves in the cold night—and wrapped it around Shearing's ankles.

"A drink!" he cried again. "Water!"

Then Paul Shearing kicked wildly, throwing off the jacket and sharply jabbing Rory O'Sullivan.

From the stern Ronnie Cooper shouted an impossible request. Could they please keep the child quiet? The Indians had been clearly shaken by Shearing's cries, and Cooper feared a domino effect begun by the commotion at the other end. In the night especially, the specter of unrest frightened the crew. O'Sullivan, Cornish, Nagorski, and even the other children were doing what they could, but there was no quieting Paul Shearing.

Reverting to French—a language he knew the boys would not understand—Rory O'Sullivan turned to Nagorski and said, *"Il va mourir de soif."* He will die of thirst.

Nagorski leaned to the stern, away from the boys, and in a shouted whisper he asked George Purvis: Could one portion of water be spared? "Please," Nagorski implored. "The child is *dying*."

Purvis and Cooper considered the request. It had been an article of faith on board Lifeboat 12: Rules were rules. Rations were what they were, and for good reason. What might have seemed an obvious response in any other circumstance—i.e., give the child his water—instead provoked careful deliberation from the stern.

Purvis feared the Indians might riot if they saw special servings of water passed surreptitiously in the night. The Indians still outnumbered the others three to one, and while there had been no outward sign of racial animosity, in either direction, Ramjam had made it known to Cooper days before that the mere hint of favoritism to any "white" passenger might provoke anger, even violence. It went without saying that a riot in this crowded boat would carry grave consequences. Ronnie Cooper had already warned his fellow British crew that the Indians were restive. And he noticed now that one of them held the boat's last functioning flashlight, and he was aiming it at the boy in the bow. As the Indians complained to Ramjam Buxoo about the loud child, Cooper took the extraordinary measure of passing the boat's small axe down the boat to Father O'Sullivan, with instructions to use it if it became necessary. O'Sullivan and Nagorski were stunned; they had never seen the weapon, and initially neither man understood why Cooper had sent it their way. O'Sullivan laid the axe below the boat boards. He believed that any conflicts with the Indians could be peacefully resolved. Certainly this frail Catholic priest was not going to be the first to use violence on board Lifeboat 12.

Beyond the threat of unrest, Cooper and Purvis had to consider the minuscule stock of water that remained. They were dangerously near the bottom of the second and last cask. Paul Shearing might be beyond hope, or at least beyond the good that one dipper of water might do for him. Were precious drops of drinking water better spent on the boys who still had a chance?

Purvis and Cooper reflected quietly on these wrenching questions, and after a few minutes, Purvis "smuggled" one dipper of water to the boy, deputizing Doug Critchley to carry it as unceremoniously as possible to the place where Shearing lay wrapped in Mary Cornish's jacket. Nagorski thought he heard a distinct grumble from the Indians, but if they were seriously upset, they did not say.

Shearing was still shaking on the boat floor. He took the water and immediately he wanted more. "A drink!" he cried. "I am *mad.*" O'Sullivan held him close again, repeating the Lord's Prayer several times over. He said other prayers, reciting some of them in Latin, and this—together with the sight of the priest cradling the boy—convinced others in the boat that Rory O'Sullivan was in fact reading the child his last rites. Fred Steels assumed Shearing was dying, or dead. So, for that matter, did Harry Peard, and it surprised no one to see Peard rise and begin another middle-of-the-night foray to the bow.

"What's going on now?" he demanded. His voice had gone hoarse, but it was still firm. "What's wrong with the poor little blighter?"

"Water . . ." Paul Shearing croaked the word.

Mary Cornish looked up at Harry Peard. *God*, she thought, *get that man away.*

"Water?" Peard said, in mock disbelief. "Is that all? Of course you want water! We all do." Peard chuckled. "You'll get your water in the morning."

Paul Shearing mumbled again, hardly audible this time.

"Now you forget about it," Peard said sternly. "You'll have plenty of water when we're picked up. And that won't be long now. Is that all that's wrong with you?"

"My feet are cold," said Shearing.

Peard came near, studying the boy and his feet. Then he glared at Cornish and O'Sullivan. "That's a nice way to look after a kid." He rewrapped Shearing's feet with Cornish's jacket, using a length of twine to fasten the clothes to the boy's legs.

"Your feet warm now?"

Shearing hesitated, shaking still. "My feet are cold."

Peard hollered to Critchley, demanding his overcoat. Without hesitation the young sailor removed the coat and passed it to Peard, who in turn tied the coat around Shearing's lower body. "There," the gunner said. "Any better?"

But the boy simply said it again. "My feet are cold."

Bohdan Nagorski noticed hopefully that the child was at least speaking sense. He was sick, cold, and miserable—but the delirium appeared to have passed.

Peard promised Shearing his feet would feel better soon. "They're wrapped properly now, and they'll be warm as toast in half a jiffy." Together with Cornish, Peard rubbed the boy's legs.

Again Nagorski marveled at the strength and resolve of Harry Peard. *It is as if he has eaten three meals a day . . .*

Once more Peard asked his question. "Are your feet warm?"

"Y-yes," Paul Shearing stammered finally.

"Then you'll be all right in the morning."

Shearing nodded weakly.

With that Harry Peard stood and trudged back to the rear of the boat, muttering as he went about boys with cold feet, about women who didn't know how to look after children, and about men who believed prayers would solve everything.

Dreadful, Rory O'Sullivan thought, but he felt powerless to say or do anything about it. Harry Peard had energy, a seemingly limitless store. The rest of them had none.

As for the scene Harry Peard had left behind, it soon improved. Whatever it was—the prayers, the extra clothing, the drops of water, the massage, or perhaps Harry Peard's strange tirade—Paul Shearing quieted. Soon he and the others at the bow were asleep.

MORNING BROKE, FIRST LIGHT COMING roughly an hour after Paul Shearing had settled down. They met their eighth dawn with silence. Strength was gone from all of them, save for the indomitable Gunner Peard. Worse, the will to live was frittering away.

This powerful drive had stayed with them until now, the same force that had saved Beth Cummings and Bess Walder during all their hours spent clutching the keel of an upturned lifeboat. Now the Lifeboat 12 survivors were losing their resolve. O'Sullivan heard one of the boys praying for his father and mother. Most of the Indians had stopped praying altogether. Nagorski saw the boys' faces, wan and idle, eyes seemingly fixed on nothing. He himself felt sore and cold and terribly weak.

Paul Shearing had cheated death, beaten it back in the dark night, but Mary Cornish was sure that death would come again. It might come slowly or rapid-fire, under a storm or on a calm sea, but it would come. And now death had allies: Though they still had a box of canned meat and two or three remaining cans of salmon, and an almost rich store of biscuits, almost no one could stomach or digest solid food anymore. Purvis guessed that they had condensed milk for three more days, but the thick sweet milk no longer appealed. There were three cans of fruit and the fruit juice that came with them.

All these calculations were overshadowed by the assessment Purvis had made about the supply of water. They had only one or two servings left.

CHAPTER 20

A Dot in the Sky

The day had arrived in spectacular fashion, a gorgeous orange-yellow sunrise over a tranquil sea. Lifeboat 12's sail scarcely rippled. The sky was blue and cloudless. Soon the sea shimmered, the sun "overreaching himself in splendor," as Bohdan Nagorski put it. Mary Cornish thought even the saddest spirit would be lifted by such a morning.

Eight days of this, she thought, *and we might have managed quite well.*

This lovely morning—Wednesday, the twenty-fifth of September—was marred by the looming horror in the narrow confines of a small boat, moving slowly eastward, roughly four hundred miles from Ireland. They were a motionless, dying bunch—listless children, sailors too weak to pull the rowing gear, Indians drifting in and out of sleep. Nagorski thought some of the Indians were dead; Ramjam assured him they were only sleeping. In mid-morning Cornish struggled to articulate a request to the crew. Perhaps the tarp could be pulled back so that the boys might dry themselves in the sun? The words came in a broken whisper too faint to be heard at the stern. Her message had to be passed along; no one could speak loudly enough to be heard at any distance.

Cooper and Peard obliged. It was an enormous effort, but the two men walked the length of the boat and unclasped the plastic sheets, stashing them under the bow. Five of the boys were then lifted to the thwarts nearest the stern, and allowed to dangle their feet in the water. This had also been Cornish's idea—anything, she thought, to refresh the children. The sixth child, Paul

Shearing, was still suffering from trench foot, exposure, and a clouded mind. He remained at the bow, wrapped in a coat and blanket.

Then an incongruous moment presented itself against this miserable tableau: Harry Peard prepared for his late-morning swim. It was almost as though nothing had happened, as if they were on some short cruise a few miles from shore. Peard stripped to T-shirt and undershorts and threw himself to the water, rocking the boat as he left it. He splashed about for fifteen minutes or so, swimming and circling Lifeboat 12. Then he was back, grinning and pronouncing himself greatly refreshed.

LIFEBOAT 12 PUSHED LAZILY EASTWARD, still—unbeknownst to its passengers—a good week's sail from the nearest land. Most in the group had long since given up pulling the Fleming handles. Absent a strong wind, they let the boat bob along, without comment or conversation.

The noon meal came and passed without a drop of water. Cooper gave a cursory statement to explain the cut in rations. For all the concern he and Purvis had felt regarding morale and the possibility of anger or violence among the passengers, there is no record of any protest as passengers received this dismal news. Perhaps fatigue was now such that even the prospect of a twenty-four-hour stretch without water scarcely registered.

As for the "meal" itself, it hardly deserved the name. *A farce*, O'Sullivan thought. The ship's biscuits went untouched. Each passenger was given a chunk of canned salmon, but many could not manage this, either, without water to wash it down. Then Purvis delivered another of his "treats," this time in the form of a tiny portion of canned pear. It was all Purvis could offer to moisten the tongue—thin slivers of fruit and whatever juice could be drawn as they went down.

Mary Cornish saw the remarkable effects the small chunks of pear had on the children. They brightened just a little, and it made her wonder: Why couldn't the youngest passengers have *all* the fruit that remained? And all the water?

Let the adults perish, she thought. *The children must live.*

Only one person on board knew the true gravity of the situation. George Purvis had conducted another check of his stocks and estimated that only one full serving of water remained, then perhaps a few individual dippers after that. How these last portions would be shared, Purvis had just begun to consider. Shearing and O'Sullivan would be obvious candidates. Or perhaps all the boys ought to be served. *We should probably save the youngest*, he thought. For

now Purvis focused on the final full ration that would be distributed after supper. He would leave the other decisions to Cooper.

Then they would begin to die. They would succumb to exposure or dehydration, to hunger or madness. They might fail quietly, never to revive, the
way so many passengers had died during the night of the attack. Perhaps that
would be best. Otherwise they might languish in pain, like Paul Shearing. Or
jump over the side, as the tormented Indian had done.

Several passengers were asking themselves the same question: How would
their voyage end? And how, in the end, would they die?

Even Harry Peard would die, Bohdan Nagorski thought, hard as that was to
imagine. *What could possibly defeat that man?* Nagorski had come to admire
Peard immensely, despite all his coarse and crude behavior. Forty-six men like
Harry Peard would have made an untenable mix, Nagorski thought, a gallery
of rogues. But *one* such man, high-spirited, loaded with energy and constantly
cheering on the children—such a man was invaluable.

Nagorski believed Harry Peard had saved the screaming child—
Shearing—during the night. Certainly his ever-positive bearing had kept
hope alive, and not only among the children. Nagorski looked at the gunner
and said to himself, *Harry Peard will be the last to die.*

Purvis informed Ronnie Cooper about the dwindling water supply. From the
tiller, Cooper made a basic, blunt assessment, sharing it only with the British
crew. They had to find land—or a ship—by nightfall. Tomorrow morning, at
the latest.

KEN SPARKS SAT UP WITH a jolt. It was a few minutes after one
o'clock.

What's that? he wondered.

Then he stood. The sea was calm, but Sparks wobbled anyway. He was terribly weak and his legs hurt. The other boys sat still or slept. And then Ken
Sparks shouted, a loud, throaty cry that shattered the stillness and startled all
who heard it.

"Plane!"

For a moment there was no response. Sparks' fellow travelers were too exhausted, too confused, or perhaps too conditioned for letdown.

"Look!" Sparks begged the others. "It's a *plane!*"

Bohdan Nagorski could make out a dark point, high on the horizon. He had
heard the boy, but he did not believe him. It wasn't a plane, Nagorski thought.

A storm cloud, maybe. *The child is seeing things.* This was, after all, one of the boys whose mind had slipped during the night.

But Sparks was insistent. "Plane!" he cried again.

At this point Nagorski thought to himself, *If little Ken can rise to greet this visitor, whatever it may be, then I will rise, too. The poor child...* With pain shooting through both legs, Bohdan Nagorski stood.

A few others followed suit, struggling to their feet.

By now Ken Sparks had pulled off his shirt and was waving it wildly at the sky.

"Here!" he cried. *"Here!"*

Howard Claytor wondered which adult would help quiet poor Ken Sparks.

"Plane!" Sparks shouted again.

Doubt still ruled. There was no sound, no droning engine. The dot was approaching slowly. It was a large bird, surely. Or their imagination . . .

Then it seemed Sparks had won a few converts. Some of the Indians were smiling. Other boys pointed to the sky.

Ronnie Cooper was almost afraid to hope, so he worried instead. Even if by some wild twist of providence this *was* an aircraft, would it see *them?* And if it did see them, could they be sure it was a friend—and not a German? And how could they know that it was a friend with *time enough for them?* Would an airplane bother with a few civilians on the water?

Then Cooper barked an order from the stern: Everyone was to lie down, in the event it *was* a German plane.

Nonsense, Nagorski thought. For the first time in eight days he disagreed sharply with Lifeboat 12's chief officer. *We are done for anyhow. Why not stand and shout, and help that plane to see us?*

Another minute passed. Cooper's order—indeed an odd command from the steady Scotsman—was being widely ignored. Even Cooper's colleague Johnny Mayhew was standing—and signaling. Ken Sparks still stood, still waved his shirt skyward. Once more Mary Cornish's camisole flag was run up the mast.

At last they saw it clearly—a gray and growing shape. And then they heard the drone.

"Plane!" another boy cried, jumping happily at the bow.

"Plane!" Ken Sparks hollered, one more time.

The drone became a roar, the aircraft swooping fast and low, in full view now, a helmeted figure peering from the window. And now they all knew, long after Ken Sparks had made his own determination: It was a plane. And it was flying right for them.

. . .

BOHDAN NAGORSKI COULD NOT BELIEVE it. *Someone has come for us.*

In our darkest hour, Rory O'Sullivan said to himself, *we are saved. By the hand of Providence . . .*

Nearly all the boat's passengers waved now, handkerchiefs and shirts and turbans, a motley collection of tattered, filthy clothing. Everyone who could stand was standing, waving and hollering, like a ward full of patients raised suddenly from their sickbeds.

Johnny Mayhew, the Royal Navy signalman, fashioned a pair of flags, using colorful turbans borrowed from the Indians. Mayhew stood on a thwart with Harry Peard and waved an S.O.S. in semaphore code. They had only to guide the aircraft to their position and to pray that the plane was not piloted by Germans. And to pray that this time, their rescuer would not tease them and turn away.

THE AIRCRAFT WAS A "FLYING BOAT," a seaplane with fighting capability that belonged to the Sunderland Division 10 Squadron of the Royal Australian Air Force. The Sunderland had been a workhorse for the Allies, functioning as an airborne escort for shipping convoys, hunting and depth-charging U-boats they picked out from the air. The Sunderlands also had a good record in aerial combat; they were known to the *Luftwaffe* as the *Fliegendes Stachelschwein,* or "Flying Porcupines." On occasion Sunderlands had been called upon to land and rescue people on the water.

The plane zeroing in on Lifeboat 12 had flown out into the Atlantic to assist the escort of inbound Convoy HX73. It had turned back for Britain earlier that day, and now the pilot and squadron leader, W. H. Garing, and his crew were patrolling for U-boats on their way home. At about 1:45 on the afternoon of September 25, Garing's flight path crossed the meandering movements of a small boat roughly three hundred miles northwest of Ireland.

This remarkable coincidence might not have sufficed to save Lifeboat 12 had Garing not been watching the water carefully on his sub patrol. And Garing *still* might have missed the boat had it not been for a boy who stood near the bow, waving a tattered shirt at the sky.

Garing spotted something on the water. A speck, no more defined to the Sunderland crew than the dot in the sky had been to a teenager named Ken Sparks.

Garing was eager to get home, but he edged nearer to that spot on the waves, and as he did he thought he saw movement, a flicker, some sign of activity.

Someone was waving from the water. Garing decided to swoop down for a better look.

RONNIE COOPER COULD SEE IT clearly now. "Sunderland," he said to Harry Peard, as matter-of-factly as one could say such a thing, at such a moment. Peard was uncharacteristically quiet. For all his unnatural stamina and optimism, all the times he had forecast their rescue when it appeared a fantasy, Harry Peard was skeptical now that the moment had come. He stared at the sky. He wanted to see these saviors up close.

Rory O'Sullivan reminded the boys of a promise they had made. They were to pray if a rescue vessel came. This was a plane, not a "vessel" per se, but that hardly seemed to matter.

The children joined hands. Ken Sparks shut his eyes and repeated to himself, *Please God, let that pilot see us . . .* Then he and the others said the Lord's Prayer. They must have spoken these words a hundred times during their time on the water.

Ronnie Cooper remained his stoic self. He had shown little emotion during the last eight days—not in the scramble on the *City of Benares* deck, not even during the daring rescues he had led from Lifeboat 12 as the *Benares* had slipped under a raging sea. *Marvelous skipper he is*, Harry Peard thought. This was powerful praise, coming from Peard.

They watched the plane circle, banking lower now. Mary Cornish saw the pilot poke his head again from the cockpit, and again she thought, *I must be dreaming*. Then the plane's Aldis mirror lamp began winking a Morse code message.

Johnny Mayhew saw it immediately, and knew this was his moment. It was his *language*. A Navy signalman could go for long stretches without practicing his craft—and when the time came he would quickly become the most important member of the crew. Now Mayhew shielded his eyes and peered at the plane. He read the mirror-light signals and sent answers via semaphore, still using the turbans as his flags.

"C-I-T-Y . . . O-F . . . B-E-N-A-R-E-S," Mayhew flashed, and then he resent the signal, just to be sure.

Within minutes the Sunderland's lamp was blinking a reply. On this clear day, the plane very close now, Mayhew could read the signals easily.

"Cannot land. Too rough. Help coming." A second Sunderland would be there soon.

In fact Garing had concerns beyond the choppy waters. He had seen that there were dozens of people in the little boat, and calculated that he had neither the fuel nor the space needed to rescue them all. The other Sunderland held more fuel; it would either ferry survivors to ships, a few at a time, or call a ship to the scene.

The news flew to the other end of Lifeboat 12.

"It's a *Sunderland*!" Ken Sparks cried. "A flying boat!" Sparks, too, had been quiet for much of the ordeal, and had badly weakened over the previous twenty-four hours. Now he was a chatterbox, a young student of war making a loud display of his love and knowledge of planes and warships. He was proud, fancying himself the boys' resident sailor and military expert. "It's coming for us!" he shouted to the others.

They were almost dancing with excitement now. Cornish, Nagorski, and O'Sullivan were still not absolutely sure, but the Indians appeared to have no doubts. They had been utterly transformed—sullen, near-comatose souls rose up, laughing and shouting at the sky. As for the boys, they had fished out their empty condensed milk cans and were busy clattering them together and using them to reflect the sun at Garing's plane.

"Oh, *boy*!" cried Howard Claytor. "We're going to *fly home*!"

Cooper called his passengers to order. He knew the plane was preparing to leave the scene—and he wanted all on board to understand. Another aircraft would come, he explained. Cooper showed no exuberance; his mood remained guarded and sober. He wanted to *see* the next Sunderland, and to touch English soil—any soil, for that matter—before celebrating. Rory O'Sullivan took to praying again, clasping hands with Billy Short and Derek Capel, asking God's mercy for their brothers, Peter and Alan. "Lord, let us see them soon."

Before leaving, W. H. Garing had dropped a small food parcel that missed its mark, slapping the water some fifty yards away. The wind quickly carried it off.

O'Sullivan watched the parcel fall and vanish. It seemed a bad portent. *Are we dreaming again?* he wondered. *Had the plane really been there? Or are these the imaginings that come in the hours before death?*

They waited. The minutes dragged. The Sunderland's replacement was nowhere to be seen. The children remained buoyant. Now that they could contemplate their rescue, Fred Steels became conscious for the first time of just how small and pitiful their surroundings had been. He had never complained—none of the boys had, really—but suddenly Steels could not fathom spending five more minutes on board this miserable little boat.

FLYING EAST, W. H. GARING RADIOED his nearest squadron partner, Sunderland P9624, led by Flight Lieutenant Ernest "Doughie" Baker and his wing commander, Francis Fressanges. At about two o'clock, Baker flew in low. He swept past, and then back again, completing a wide circle over the boat. He made a rough count, concluding as Garing had that he could not take them all. Baker had also been flying with Convoy HX73, whose lead vessels were now located less than forty miles from Lifeboat 12's position. Rather than land here and attempt to gather up the boat's passengers in a series of flights and sea landings, Baker decided instead to direct the convoy's main warship to the scene. Now Doughie Baker became commander and chief architect of a highly complex rescue operation.

First he ordered his signalman to flash word that a ship was coming. Next he instructed his crew to fill a parachute bag with food, drink, cigarettes, and "smoke floats," as much as they could spare. To this heavy packet they attached a life jacket for buoyancy, together with a more detailed note that Baker himself penned, explaining that a warship was on the way, and describing her position and approximate time of arrival. It would be about two hours, Baker wrote. Finally he instructed them to set off the smoke floats when the rescue ship appeared.

Baker circled once more. A crewman dropped the parcel. This one landed cleanly, within a few yards of Lifeboat 12.

Mayhew and one of the Indians pulled the package aboard, and Mayhew read the message. "Rescue vessel," it read, "approximately 40 miles away."

Finally Baker radioed Lieutenant Commander N. V. "Pugs" Thew, a New Zealander and senior officer of the escort vessel in question, the destroyer HMS *Anthony*. Baker would rendezvous with the destroyer in the event they needed help locating the lifeboat.

Doughie Baker flew east. Before long he was over the convoy. From the air he watched as the *Anthony* turned about. Thew, the commander, raised his pace to high speed. Baker's Sunderland plane shadowed the *Anthony* from the air. After nearly an hour he saw that she was slightly off course.

"Follow me," he signaled.

. . .

THIS TIME THE WAIT—THOUGH considerably longer—did not trouble the *Benares* survivors. The twin visits of the Sunderlands, the clear, specific messages deciphered by Mayhew, and finally the note they received— "warship coming"—had convinced them of two things they needed to know: This was no phantom; and these men in the air were not Germans.

It helped of course to have a new and wonderful gift, courtesy of Doughie Baker and his crew.

The unflappable steward, George Purvis, almost didn't know what to do. Having zealously guarded tiny stocks of salmon and corned beef for more than a week, having rationed those thin slices of fruit and doled out water by the milliliter, Purvis now presided over a small banquet. Here were canned peaches and canned soups, cooked fish and beans in tomato sauce kept warm in a thermos flask. The thing they needed most—water—was not in the bag. But that did not matter terribly. Lifeboat 12's parched passengers drained every drop of juice or sauce from the cans. It still hurt to swallow, but they gorged themselves. Fred Steels emptied the juice from a container of canned pears, and then feasted on the pears themselves. He almost choked. After wolfing down food, several of the adults grabbed for cigarettes.

Someone asked for water from Lifeboat 12's last reserves. Purvis and Cooper consulted briefly and refused the request. Cooper's explanation was simple: We have not yet been rescued.

Cooper was insistent that order and decorum be maintained until they were saved, but his answer about the water enraged several of the Indians, the same men who had grumbled when extra water had gone to Paul Shearing in the middle of the boy's awful night. Suddenly, tension broke the happy atmosphere on board Lifeboat 12. Ramjam Buxoo was again cast as diplomatic liaison between Cooper and the Indians, and he tried to soothe the men by explaining that the officer was taking an understandable last precaution. In all likelihood they would have all the water they could drink in a short time.

But two of the Indians remained livid, and unmollified. After Ramjam's explanation they rose and rushed the stern.

For a few frightening moments a struggle ensued. It was the first real conflict—certainly the first act of violence—in their eight days in the boat. Nagorski and O'Sullivan moved reflexively to guard the boys. Mayhew, Critchley, and Ramjam stood and held the men back.

"We are about to be saved," Ramjam assured them. "We shall have ample water. There is no time for this."

Cooper tried to remember where the axe was—the small weapon he had passed to the bow the previous night. In the same moment he hoped desperately that no weapon would be required. Ramjam stood between the two seething Indians. The men glared, but they retreated. And then they were quiet.

IT WAS A LITTLE AFTER four o'clock. The mood on board—among forty-five people who had lain inert and deathly ill an hour before—had changed in remarkable ways. They were still in terrible physical condition— Paul Shearing, Rory O'Sullivan, and some of the Indians dangerously so—but spirits had soared. A downcast, miserable group had turned festive, almost ebullient.

Johnny Mayhew, having laid down his flags and enjoyed what he considered a superlative meal, fished out a mouth organ. He played, and the other sailors sang. "It's a long way to Tipperary . . . It's a long long way to go . . ."

When that was done, someone started another tune. "Pack up your troubles . . ." They were giddy now. Even some of the Indians sang, laughing and guessing at the lyrics.

Bohdan Nagorski felt a rush of pride as they sang and ate and waited for the warship. Nagorski had never really lost hope, but he had shared neither the unflinching confidence of Cooper and Peard, nor the indomitable faith the boys had shown. It was incredible, he thought, that they were still alive. *We have done something remarkable.*

They sat feasting on the Sunderland's food, eyes glued one more time to the horizon. Now they had something very specific to watch for. At Derek Capel's suggestion they gathered up the remaining cans of condensed milk— "souvenirs for our moms," said Capel. They had been on the water for nearly eight full days. It had been186 hours since the torpedo's strike.

CHAPTER 21

Miracles

They were still eating when the ship slipped into view. At last Ronnie Cooper relaxed, felt a flood of relief come cascading over him. George Purvis passed celebratory dippers of water down the boat. Johnny Mayhew fired the Sunderland's flares. Fat plumes of reddish-black smoke shot skyward.

The children laughed with Mary Cornish at the bow. It was no illusion. This was a *ship*, and no ordinary ship, either. She was huge, or so she seemed to forty-five people who had spent eight days jammed against one another in something akin to a long rowboat. Here was a long, sleek Royal Navy warship, coming fast now.

Cornish had to work to keep the boys from leaning too far over the gunwales. They couldn't believe their eyes.

At a hundred yards the ship slowed dramatically and began cutting a sharp angle toward them. It was four-thirty when she swung alongside in a slow and deliberate maneuver, taking care not to roil the waters. Nagorski stared up at the great gray hull of a destroyer. *A fine feat of seamanship,* he thought.

There was no sign of nationality, no flags or other markings. Only a large "H40," painted black on her side.

Then they saw sailors at the rail. The men were waving and pointing and grinning broadly.

COMING NEAR, HMS *ANTHONY*'S SECOND-in-command, Ronald Brooke, saw a man perched at the lifeboat's tiller—Peard or Cooper, probably—

and he saw a boy waving a shirt—Ken Sparks. Nearly everyone else in the boat was sitting or lying down. Brooke was a first lieutenant and a decorated hero of the Dunkirk evacuations. He and his officers had heard the story of the *City of Benares* in grim detail. Brooke was thrilled at the chance to pluck these people from the water, so many days later. He made a note of their position—54.43 N, 14.20 W—roughly halfway between the site of the attack on the *Benares* and the Irish coast. Then, peering down at the little lifeboat, Brooke had another thought. *My God, they've been sitting like that for more than a week.*

EVEN NOW MARY CORNISH HAD the feeling it was happening to someone else—that she was dreaming again, or watching someone else's rescue. Hearing voices from the destroyer's deck, Cornish became suddenly convinced the sailors were German. Surely she had heard someone say *herren*, the German word for "men"? Rope lines were dropped to the lifeboat. Two men came shimmying down.

Mary Cornish was dizzy; it was all happening so fast. She saw the men up close now, a blur of clean and gorgeous faces. She then realized the voice she had heard belonged to a Scottish sailor, and that what she had heard as *herren* was actually "stern."

They're not German at all.

One of the men had come down next to Rory O'Sullivan.

"Are you British?" O'Sullivan asked weakly.

The man laughed. A loud, hearty laugh. To Father O'Sullivan it was a glorious, unforgettable sound. "Of *course* we are!" said the sailor.

It was almost too much; the enormous ship, this strong and red-faced sailor, the happy cries from the deck. Their senses—deprived for so long—were suddenly overwhelmed. Mary Cornish stared at the side of HMS *Anthony* and thought she would cry.

More rope ladders came dangling down, and then a heavy net. "Up you come!" the sailors hollered, but few of Lifeboat 12's passengers could manage. Every one of the boys had to be lifted gently from the lifeboat thwarts to the net. After a loud cry of "Ready?" *Anthony*'s sailors would order the net hoisted to deck.

The survivors made a pitiful sight. Shearing was semiconscious and shrieking again with the pain in his feet. "I cannot move!" he cried. He tugged at O'Sullivan's sleeve. "I shall be left behind."

O'Sullivan himself, unsure how exactly he would reach the ship's deck, told Shearing they would not be left behind. "I promise you," he said.

Only two or three of thirty-one Indians reached the deck unaided. Even the stalwarts Cooper and Purvis needed help. Harry Peard bounded up the ladder, of course, and embraced the first sailor he met. "Fine job," he said. Mary Cornish *felt* strong enough to grab hold of one of the rope ladders, and a strange elation came over her as she took the ladder's first rungs. Again, it was as though all this were happening to someone else.

Then Mary Cornish collapsed, the moment she set foot on the deck.

Nagorski found himself on the *Anthony*'s deck in a sea of blue-jacketed sailors. They were asking if he needed help. "Help the boys," he said weakly. Then he felt his legs buckle. A pair of sailors carried him to the officers' mess.

Other sailors tended to the badly weakened priest, wrapping him in blankets in the lifeboat and hoisting him over the rail. In a faint voice O'Sullivan asked for the ship's name.

"Anthony," a sailor replied.

Rory O'Sullivan nearly always saw deeper meaning, some divine hand, even in life's small and seemingly insignificant moments. Now, in this life-altering moment, O'Sullivan heard "Anthony" and determined that it must have been St. Anthony—patron saint of those looking for "lost articles"—who had saved them. It had to have been Anthony who had done the Lord's work, he thought, counting these forty-five souls among his "lost articles" on the water. St. Anthony was guiding them home, Rory O'Sullivan believed, using his namesake to finish the job.

THE PILOT DOUGHIE BAKER HAD lingered, circling the scene until he saw the destroyer reach the lifeboat. His crew snapped photographs of HMS *Anthony* and Lifeboat 12. Then Baker turned his Sunderland around. He had received orders to return to base before dusk.

"We were very glad to see those people safe," Baker told a reporter later. "All of us felt very pucked about it."

ANTHONY'S CREW COUNTED TWENTY-EIGHT "cot cases" among the forty-five *Benares* survivors. Overall the group was "in a rather bad way," as the ship's first lieutenant Ronald Brooke put it.

In the officers' mess, Bohdan Nagorski was treated to a pot of strong tea that he would never forget. "Heavenly nectar" it was, though the joy of swallowing the tea was tempered by an irrational fear that it would not last. George Purvis' fastidious rations—of water in particular—had left Nagorski and many of the others convinced they would have to ration all they were given from now on. Nagorski could not bring himself to finish the pot.

Five of the boys—all but Shearing—were delivered to the mess, too, and after tea, warm milk, porridge, and warm baths, they were outfitted in bulky sweatshirts and pants loaned them by *Anthony* sailors. They were asked what more they wanted, and when Billy Short replied, "Juice, please," he was rewarded with several jugs of orange juice to share with his friends. "Drowning in orange juice, we were," Short said later. Then they sprawled about the mess, five numb and weary boys who were able somehow to laugh and talk animatedly about the ship and about home. Nagorski watched them leaf through illustrated magazines, as though nothing had happened. *They've forgotten everything already.*

Even in these happy circumstances, after all that these people had shared and suffered together, British notions of class and social position intruded on board the destroyer. While Nagorski, Mary Cornish, and the children were billeted with the ship's officers and the British crewmen found accommodation with the *Anthony*'s sailors, the Indians from Lifeboat 12 were taken to the lower deck. So, initially, was Father Rory O'Sullivan.

It was much later that evening that a man appeared below deck and called out, "Isn't there a Catholic priest among you?"

O'Sullivan, still exhausted, held up a hand. He thought he had done something wrong, or that someone had died.

The man was the ship's doctor, and he was profoundly apologetic. "We should have cared for you better," he said.

They had taken O'Sullivan—with his sun-browned, grease-stained face, and with its week's worth of beard—for an Indian. Now that they knew he was an English priest, he would be treated differently, or at least he would be treated in a different part of the ship. A sailor brought O'Sullivan to the cabin belonging to HMS *Anthony*'s deputy commander, the first lieutenant Ronald Brooke.

MARY CORNISH WAS CARRIED TO a cabin belonging to the ship's chief engineer. He helped her into an easy chair—perfect, he told her, for "human wrecks."

It was an apt description for the music teacher from London. They had roused her with smelling salts on the deck, but Cornish still felt faint, and almost constantly on the verge of collapse. She had probably slept less than anyone during the eight days in the boat, having fretted constantly over the boys in her care. She felt too weak to utter a word. Her body was dotted with sores and scrapes and bruises; her hands and feet were swollen and jelly-like.

A ship's stoker named Potts was detailed to look after Cornish, and he soon appeared at her door with a tray of tea, honey, and bread and butter. At first she could not swallow the tea—it was too hot—and without the tea she could not manage the food, either. The room seemed to heave, much as Lifeboat 12 had rocked so often on the water. Her head swam, nausea took hold, and suddenly neither food nor drink appealed. Potts remained with her. "You'll be all right, miss."

After a time the room steadied. The tea had cooled, and now it went down smooth and soothing, warming her though the drink itself was no longer warm. Potts returned with a fresh supply, well sweetened with honey. Mary Cornish thought she had never tasted anything so good.

Strange sensations crowded her brain. How remarkable it was to stretch her limbs with no fear of striking a neighbor! The engineer's small cabin seemed the size of a gymnasium, and the door—no more than ten feet from her bed—looked to her to be a long way off. And to think—this pot of tea was hers alone! She shared Bohdan Nagorski's anxiety—her instincts telling her to guard the cup zealously and drink in small sips. Noises were odd, too. The *absence* of noise, really. She continued to listen for the wind and for the creaking of the lifeboat, for the children's voices and the relentless slap of the sea.

Before long she felt an overwhelming heat—though of course it was "hot" only to someone who had been in shirtsleeves for eight days in the North Atlantic. A fever had come over her. Mary Cornish was very sick; all her defenses were down.

Potts brought pajamas and a toothbrush, and a bucket of warm water for bathing. He helped her to a washstand in a corner of the cabin. Then he left her alone.

There was a small mirror above the washstand. Mary Cornish saw herself for the first time in eight days—and she recoiled. There were bluish bruises on one cheek and a bloodied cut on her forehead. She discovered a hideous film of salt that had crusted on her teeth. She saw and then felt her hair, matted in stiff and filthy clumps. Slowly, unsteadily, she began to wash her face.

Cornish found herself unable at first to remove her clothes; it was as if the synapses linking mind and muscle had broken down. How to lift off a shirt? How to undo a button, or unfasten a clasp? When at last she had undressed and bathed, and slipped on the pajamas, she had difficulty putting one foot in front of the other. A few feet from the bunk, she staggered, suddenly afraid. She called for Potts.

He came. Mary Cornish apologized. Potts lifted her gently to the bed, and brought her a pitcher of lime juice. She took several gulps, and then she lay down and tried to sleep.

AS DUSK APPROACHED, BOHDAN NAGORSKI found himself restless. He left the mess, found a stairwell, and climbed haltingly to deck. It was nine days since his last stroll on a ship's deck, the fateful walk he had taken aboard the *City of Benares* the night the torpedo hit. He ached terribly and he was exhausted. The logical thing would have been to lie in his bunk and sleep for however long it took to regain his strength and his senses, but Nagorski found that he craved the air. Even one hour spent indoors had left him feeling stifled, uncomfortably warm, and claustrophobic. *It makes sense,* he thought. *We've been out in the open for so long.*

From the deck he saw that the seas were crowded with ships. A sailor told him the *Anthony* was escorting an inbound convoy, HX73 from Halifax, a half dozen vessels bringing supplies and military equipment to England. It occurred to Nagorski that they were sailing in an obvious danger zone, precisely the sort of setting they had been so keen to escape nearly a fortnight before, as the *Benares'* convoy had moved west.

To Bohdan Nagorski, it did not matter. He had never felt safer.

FOR ALL OF RORY O'SULLIVAN'S suffering in Lifeboat 12, it was in the warm and welcoming confines of a well-made bunk that he began to confront a whole new set of ordeals. The pain that night was such that he cried out, feeling what seemed like a hundred knives jabbing his legs, hips to toes, while the rest of his body fought fever and nausea. *The suffering of the damned,* O'Sullivan thought, reaching as ever for a biblical phrase. A ship's doctor cut his pajama bottoms and wrapped his swollen feet, and gave the priest a morphine injection.

Like Mary Cornish, O'Sullivan was beset by what seemed a punishing heat.

In the middle of the night, *Anthony* sailors recorded his temperature at 105 degrees. They brought water and the ship's doctor, afraid they were about to lose a survivor, a man who had not seemed at risk when they first pulled him to safety. It appeared that Cornish and O'Sullivan had both seen their defenses fall away in the immediate aftermath of their rescue. Father Rory O'Sullivan was fighting for his life. Again.

STILL HOT AND DISORIENTED IN the chief engineer's cabin, Mary Cornish could not shake her anxieties. Her mind would not rest. More than anything, thoughts of the children danced in her head. *Where are they? Is Paul all right? Doesn't he need my help?* Surely the boys needed a foot rub, or a fresh installment of Bulldog Drummond? Probably they were searching for her, at that very moment . . .

Cornish lay on her back, exhausted but too tense to sleep. Her mind raced, desperate for answers. After a while she summoned the stoker again. "I need to see my boys," she told him. Her voice was shaking.

Potts smiled. He pulled up her covers. "You've handed over to the Navy now," he said. "No need to worry."

It was a simple answer, and yet with those few words an enormous burden lifted from Mary Cornish's shoulders. She smiled faintly, felt a lightness come over her; the "web of responsibility" that had kept her so anxious had come untangled, with just those few words. Her boys were "handed over to the Navy now." Potts' simple assurance had brought comfort, like a deep, plush bed. Soon she was asleep.

ALL THROUGH THE NIGHT, RORY O'Sullivan drank water. The jug at his washstand seemed to refill magically while he rested. Again and again he emptied the jug, drifted into and out of a half sleep, discovered a fresh jug, and drank once more. Delirium came, along with the dangerous fever and searing pain in his legs. Blood raced to his feet and legs; circulation was returning. All Rory O'Sullivan really understood was that it was good and necessary to drink the water.

He expected to die, in this comfortable bed. In his first night *away* from the lifeboat. A special watch was ordered, to attend to "the Catholic priest."

.   .   .

MARY CORNISH WAS STILL SLEEPING nine hours later, when someone knocked at her door. She woke gradually, no idea at first where she was.

Then came voices. And then someone was banging on the door.

"You all right?"

"Yes."

It was Thursday, September 26. In came a sailor bearing a breakfast tray, which he laid on a small table at her bedside. "How'd you sleep, miss?" Then he told Cornish that she had visitors.

The sailor laughed, and Capel, Claytor, Steels, Sparks, and Short came bounding in, with happy cries of "Morning, Auntie Mary!," "How's your cabin?" and "We're on a *destroyer*, Auntie!" They danced around her bed, told her where they had slept and what they had eaten. There was even a fresh request for another Bulldog Drummond story.

For the first time, Mary Cornish refused, politely and with an apology. "You'll excuse me, boys." Much as she had come to adore them, she also understood now that their lives no longer hung in the balance. She recalled what Potts had said: *You've handed over to the Navy now.* Her beloved boys could manage, this once, without her. And without Bulldog Drummond.

Mary Cornish laughed, and closed her eyes.

HMS *ANTHONY* SPED FOR SCOTLAND. To the people who had lived in the lifeboat for eight days, the warship's pace—roughly twenty-three knots—seemed wild. *Wonderful*, thought Ken Sparks, *to be aboard a vessel that actually moves!* Ronald Brooke radioed ahead to Gourock, just two miles from the port that had welcomed HMS *Hurricane* and the first *Benares* survivors six days before. Brooke was proud of what they had done, but still concerned that they might lose some of the group from Lifeboat 12. He asked that Gourock have ambulances and hospital beds at the ready.

From conversations with the children and the lifeboat crew, Captain Thew and Lieutenant Commander Brooke were piecing together the story of the boat's eight days on the water, and they were beginning to understand and appreciate what Mary Cornish had done for the boys in Lifeboat 12. "She was wonderful," Howard Claytor said. "She always cheered us up . . . [and] she massaged our arms and legs and made our skin quite warm again." Nagorski praised her "heroism"; Mary Cornish, he said, had "looked after the children like a mother." The steady, impeccable conduct of Cooper and Purvis was viewed as less of a surprise—they were professional seamen, after all. The children themselves had shown great character and courage. But the more they learned, the more the *Anthony*'s officers were filled with admiration for the woman who had kept the boys warm and alert, upbeat and entertained for eight days in the boat. The captain invited her to his wardroom for tea.

Cornish still felt unwell. Her throat was raw and her mind wandered, but she accepted the invitation. *How often does a ship's captain invite you to tea?* she thought. She spent a wobbly, weak time at the captain's bridge, watching the seas from there and hearing a detailed description of the *Anthony*'s workings. It was strange and frightening to gaze at the ocean and to think that this had been their home, their only company, for all those days. *I won't ever travel by sea again.* Cornish still felt faint and unsteady. Her head ached. She needed help stepping down from the bridge.

Then a cry went up behind her. They had seen land in the faraway mist.

CHAPTER 22

Home

On a still and golden evening, the sun dropping gently over the Clyde estuary, HMS *Anthony* eased herself into a berth at Gourock port. It was a few minutes after seven o'clock on Thursday, September 26.

News of the rescue had been wirelessed ahead and it had caused a sensation. The attack on the *Benares* had dominated newspaper and radio coverage for the last several days; word that some of its passengers and crew were "returned from the grave," as one reporter put it, had drawn great interest across Britain and in many other parts of the world. Forty-five people—among them a half dozen of the evacuee children—had been officially dead for one week, listed as "lost at sea through enemy action." A *Daily Mail* reporter in the crowd at Gourock wrote that "as we watched we could hardly believe our eyes. The boys were waving."

Headline writers reveled in the news of the lifeboat that had been lost, then found. The *News of the World* ran a bold banner: "Torpedoed Evacuees Back from the Dead—Thousand to One Chance Comes Off in Mid-Atlantic." They were the "Mercy Ship Survivors." "Hope Was Abandoned," read another headline, "But They Came Back." "Six Children Back from Dead," the *Daily Mail* cheered. "Plane Sees Boat After Eight Days." The *Mail* correspondent wrote that "it will take more than a Hun torpedo and [eight] days in an open boat to crush the spirits of lads like these."

The newspapers highlighted the boys' courage, and indeed the children and Mary Cornish were near-celebrities by the time the *Anthony* arrived. People on shore wept as the boys came into view, waving from the ship's deck, smiling and sporting the oversized uniforms and caps loaned them by the ship's sailors. Photographers and reporters swarmed the dock, and the boys flashed thumbs-up signs and toothy grins for the cameras. Five of the six were carried off on sailors' shoulders; Paul Shearing left the ship on a stretcher.

The story rated front-page news in other countries as well. "46 of the Benares Saved After 8 Days" ran the headline in the *New York Times*, which had the precise number wrong but provided detailed accounts from several survivors. The *Montreal Gazette* cheered the "Miracle at Sea." It was, in the *Montreal Daily Star*'s account, "An epic of courage and refusal to despair. It gives a lift to hope."

Telegrams had gone out that morning to the families of the six boys. The CORB's awful "We regret to inform you, etc. . . ." notes were now trumped by cheery messages from Gourock. "William Cunningham Short alive and well," read the missive to Sunderland, where Billy Short's family had spent a week believing the opposite to be true. Each family also received a separate, seven-word telegram from the CORB Chairman Geoffrey Shakespeare: "Rejoice at survival of your gallant son."

The "gallant sons" and thirty-nine others made for a tattered group, many among them still tired, sick, and overwhelmed. They were met on shore by more than one hundred people—a collection of local well-wishers, Scottish officials, and representatives from the CORB, in addition to the crush of reporters and photographers. Shakespeare's private secretary, N. A. Beechman, came to Gourock and gushed to a *News Chronicle* reporter, "It is a complete miracle. Their food was giving out and the [drinking] water in the boat was practically at a finish." The Duke of Kent canceled several engagements so that he could travel to Gourock; there were even three officers from the Polish government-in-exile at the port, there to greet a native son named Bohdan Nagorski. "Never at any time did the boys complain," Nagorski told a reporter at Gourock port. "They behaved magnificently." Rory O'Sullivan, speaking from a stretcher, concurred. "They were grand little fellows."

One of the *Anthony*'s sailors ran to Mary Cornish as she disembarked. He pressed his hatband into her hands. It was marked "H.M.S. Anthony."

"Like you to have it, miss," the sailor said. She would keep it as a treasured souvenir.

Doug Critchley reached his father from a Gourock post office phone. "It's me, Dad."

"Doug?" His father was stunned. "We'd given you up."

George Purvis made a similar call, and found his father at home. "Hello, Dad. This is your son Georgie-Porgie. I'm on my way home."

Fred Steels' mother had just arrived at a local bomb shelter—dressed in black—when she received the news. And Connie Peard was home in Bristol when friends called on her. She had already accepted the news of her husband Harry's death. Now she heard something very different. "Don't give up your hopes, Connie. A boat has been found."

THEY WERE TAKEN TO A Gourock hotel, given "emergency clothing" by the town authorities, and brought by train the following night to Glasgow for a more flamboyant version of the celebrations held one week before, for the first group of *Benares* survivors. Once again the lord provost of Glasgow would host. He had not imagined there would be another occasion.

Another large crowd was on hand at Glasgow Central Station. By now people there knew the faces of Mary Cornish and the boys from splashy coverage in the papers. Cornish found the adulation difficult to absorb and comprehend. Later the author Elspeth Huxley would write of Cornish that "anyone would wish to avoid disaster; she, above most, would have shunned the fame." Before leaving Gourock, Cornish had gone on a brief shopping expedition, and a Scottish policeman had helped her from a taxi. "Are ye the lady who came back wi' the wee bairns? Weel, ye didna do a bad job o' work!" Many more people seemed to recognize her at the Glasgow station, where she was mobbed by a sea of well-wishers, scores of people pressing toward her. She even heard someone cry, "Cheers to you, Auntie Mary!"

A dream...

Making her way in the crowd, she felt suddenly afraid, seized by claustrophobia and a fear that she might "drown" in the crowd. Finally a sailor took her hand and guided her to the Glasgow hotel. *Strange,* she thought. *He is rescuing me.* She thanked the sailor, who in turn asked only that Mary Cornish pose with him for a photograph.

They were brought to a Glasgow hotel that Ken Sparks pronounced "too comfortable"; accustomed to the hard boards of Lifeboat 12 and his Navy cot aboard the *Anthony,* a soft bed somehow left him restless. Sparks and the other boys were fitted with kilts, gray-green Scottish coats, and badges from the lord provost. They were given keys to the city—entitling each of them to a free meal whenever they visited Glasgow, for the rest of their lives—and before the party he gave in the survivors' honor, the lord provost awarded them all gold brooches bearing the city's coat of arms. Finally he invited Cornish and the boys to his library and told them to take any volume they liked.

The boys snapped up biographies and adventure stories. Fred Steels chose *Westward Ho!*—appropriate, he thought—and after a while Steels noticed that Mary Cornish had not chosen a book for herself.

"Ain't Auntie going to have one?" Steels asked.

Mary Cornish laughed. The lord provost smiled and scanned the shelves. He presented her with a volume of Robert Burns.

On the following day, while the boys waited for relatives to retrieve them in Scotland, they were given pens and letter paper and told they could write to their families. Ken Sparks produced a wonderful one-page letter to his parents that captured—in a single, unpunctuated run-on sentence—the essence and highlights of the ordeal.

> *Dear Mum and Daddy*
> *I hope you are well and happy as you know that I am safe we had a*
> *dreadful time on the lifeboat we had very little water and a small piece of*
> *salmon or a sardine on a ships biscuit we saw a huge whale and we were*
> *ready to drive it away in case it broke the boat one day we saw a boat*
> *which stopped for us but before we were picked up it went away and we*
> *were dissaponted [sic] three days we floated around when we saw an*
> *aeroplane which dropped us food and then went away soon after two*
> *planes came along with a destroyer which picked us up and we had good*
> *food and water.*

It was in character for Ken Sparks to say nothing of his own role in flagging the plane that had saved them.

BEFORE THE CHILDREN WENT THEIR separate ways, they received one more pleasant surprise, from a man who had been their neighbor for eight days in the lifeboat. He had been something of an enigma—the boat's elder statesman, an elegant-looking man with an accent and a homburg hat.

Bohdan Nagorski had been true to his word. After the Glasgow reception, Nagorski took the boys aside and told them he would not only return their pocket money—he would double the amounts. Together with Cornish he arrived at the appropriate sums.

The children jumped and cheered. More than one of them cried, "Hooray!" Mary Cornish, still very much their minder and "escort," had to nudge the children to "thank the gentleman."

"Thank you, sir!" they cried.

Nagorski turned to Cornish and said, "They are wonderful boys."

Two weeks earlier, six boys had left their families, heady with dreams about Canada, happy to be leaving bomb shelters and air raids behind. They had anticipated months, even years, away from home and away from war. Now, just a fortnight later, they were back in wartime Britain. They would be "evacuees" no more.

The boys understood that they might never reach Canada now. They might never really escape the war. But they had had their own adventures, as rich as any Bulldog Drummond story. They were coming home with new friends and strange memories, terrible and wondrous. They were returning with books, kilts, and brooches, and with keys to a city. And they were coming home with double their money.

ACROSS ENGLAND, COMMUNITIES AND NEIGHBORHOODS prepared for happy homecomings. The *Daily Echo* ran a fat headline: "Paul Shearing's Safe! All Bournemouth rejoiced . . ."

It was no exaggeration. Though the child lay in a Glasgow hospital bed, still dangerously ill, people Lily Shearing had never seen before were turning up at 44 King Edward Avenue in Moordown to congratulate the family. "A miracle has happened," she said. "We have not had time to realize it yet." In the previous week they had already received scores of condolence calls and telegrams.

Howard Claytor's father was roused after midnight by three air-raid wardens who banged on his door in Kenton.

"I thought they were going to tell me there was an unexploded bomb back of our house," he said, "and that my wife and I would have to leave. They greeted us with the good news. We had absolutely given up hope."

So had Fred Steel's parents. His father fetched him in Glasgow, and when they returned to Eastleigh, Peg Steels' embrace "damn near broke me ribs," as the boy remembered it.

Charles and Nora Sparks had abandoned hope, too. They quickly and happily transformed their Wembley home from a mourners' gathering place to the scene of a wild celebration.

"Now," Ken Sparks' father said, "we can look at his bike without crying."

More than one hundred people took up a collection and purchased a silver pocket watch to honor Sparks, already well known locally as "the boy who had seen the plane." The money paid for the watch and for an inscription:

Presented to Kenneth Sparks
By his neighbors in admiration
Of his dauntless courage
When torpedoed in

S.S. City of Benares

September 17, 1940

When Sparks returned to London's Euston Station, a local paper wrote that he was "still wearing the grin Hitler's terrors could not take from his face." People lined his street, Lancelot Crescent, waiting at their front gates to greet him. When Ken Sparks appeared, turning the last corner for home, he found Union Jacks hung from windows and balconies in his honor. The street erupted in applause.

Ronnie Cooper came home to a hero's reception, too, in the Scottish village of Invergowrie, where his "ain folk" had pitched in to buy him an inscribed gold wristwatch and a war bond. They then held a special reception in a crowded hall at St. Columba's Church hall, to thank the "young chap who brought back the evacuees."

Bohdan Nagorski's scattered family—wife and daughters in Montreal, siblings in London and Warsaw—had all assumed that he was dead. The *Benares*' parent company had sent a condolence telegram to his brother Zygmunt in London.

Now a new telegram went out. "Very pleased inform you further survivors landed at Northern Port Thursday night include your brother Mr B Nagorski previously reported missing." The *Montreal Gazette* picked up the story, publishing a photograph of Zosia Nagorski clutching the second telegram under a headline that read "Polish Executive Rescued."

The following day Zygmunt Nagorski received an almost amusing telegram from his brother. "Arrived here today after very interesting round trip with eight days on open lifeboat stop Am well but tired by lack of sleep and food and should like to have a short rest."

ALL THE HOMECOMINGS AND THE splashy headlines could not mask the heavy physical and emotional toll borne by the Lifeboat 12 survivors. The burdens multiplied when they learned the full scale of the *Benares* disaster. For the first time they were told of the rescues carried out by HMS

Hurricane, and the deaths of fellow passengers and sailors. And for the first time they learned about the loss of so many children.

When reporters in Scotland peppered Mary Cornish with questions, she replied with a question of her own: What had become of the other boys and girls? The answers left her shattered. Slowly Cornish absorbed the overall figures: only seven others saved, making a final roster of thirteen survivors among the child evacuees. Seventy-seven had been lost. From Cornish's initial group of fifteen girls, only Eleanor Wright was alive. Among ten escorts, only she, O'Sullivan, Marjorie Day, and Lillian Towns had made it back to Britain. She had always assumed, during those eight long days in the lifeboat, that the large majority of *Benares* passengers had been saved.

Rory O'Sullivan mourned Father William King and the divinity student Michael Rennie, men he had known only for a short time but had come to admire greatly. Nagorski heard from the Polish officers that Zygmunt Gralinski was dead. He also learned that services had been held and obituaries written in memory of Bohdan Nagorski. When Nagorski phoned his company's London office, a receptionist broke down and cried. "But sir—I've just come back from your *memorial!*"

The boys were stunned as well. Many had assumed their boat had been the unlucky one. Surely most of the others had been found? Now Derek Capel and Billy Short received the news they had long dreaded. A Red Cross worker told Capel that his brother, Alan, had not survived. Capel could not shake the memory of his mother telling him, *Look after your brother.* For decades he would strain to recall precisely what had happened to Alan, in their last minutes on board the *City of Benares.*

Nine-year-old Billy Short's parents were first among the boys' families to reach Glasgow, and after embracing his mother, Short blurted, "Mummy, I have not got Peter for you." They were his first words to her. He then discovered that a service had already been held in Sunderland for the souls of William and Peter Short.

Still, the Short and Capel families were thrilled to have one child home. When a CORB official came to the Capel home to say, "Your son's been picked up," Elizabeth Capel did not believe it. "We thought we had lost both boys," she said that afternoon. "It is a miracle that Derek has been snatched back from the grave." In a magnanimous statement to the press, Billy and Peter Short's father, John, said that "It would have been grand if I could have had both my boys saved but I thank God for sending one. The homes that have not got any back must be terrible, because I know what it is like to miss one."

John Short met Mary Cornish at Glasgow and told her, "We shall never forget your bravery." To which Cornish replied to Short and to the parents of Howard Claytor, "You have reason to be proud of such splendid sons. *They were very brave.*"

THOUGH MOST OF THE BOYS had felt well and played happily on board HMS *Anthony*, in the end every one of the six relapsed and spent time in a hospital, and they all reported experiencing effects of the trauma once they were home. For more than a month, Fred Steels woke screaming in the night. Ken Sparks dreamed a specific nightmare every few days: the *City of Benares* going down, passengers falling from wildly angled lifeboats, a sharp light blazing at the scene. Some version of this dream would stay with him for years.

They all had difficulty walking, but in this regard Paul Shearing was clearly worst off. Scottish doctors who saw him on the night of September 26 found his toes bleeding, his feet roughly double the size they should have been. And this was *after* a day and a half of care on board the *Anthony*. Ultimately both his big toes were amputated at the joint; he would suffer significant pains in his feet for decades.

BECAUSE SO MUCH ATTENTION WAS paid to the child survivors and the heroine Mary Cornish, and because only Cornish, O'Sullivan, and Nagorski wrote detailed accounts of their ordeal, considerably less is known about the condition of the British and Indian sailors who had occupied thirty-six seats in Lifeboat 12.

Witnesses at a Gourock hospital reported that when the Indians from the *City of Benares* were treated, "fingers and toes came off in their dressings." From O'Sullivan comes the only written record of the Indians in Scotland, and even this is spare: "Some of the Indians lost a leg or a foot, but considered that they had got off lightly; others lost their minds and went mad." Indeed, from hospital and infirmary records comes the disheartening news that two men whose names appear nowhere in the *Benares* and Lifeboat 12 stories—Ibrahim Balla and Abbas Bekim—died in Scotland, in the first week of October. Balla, a twenty-year-old deckhand, had suffered "gangrene of foot"; Bekim, a twenty-five-year-old seaman, was listed as "died resulting from prolonged exposure at sea." The strong suggestion from other accounts is that the Indians fared worse than the rest, either because they had been lightly dressed, inexperienced in cold climates, or because some were believed to have drunk the saltwater.

Bohdan Nagorski wrote a detailed narrative but made scant mention of his own suffering. He reached Canada in October—by plane—and his wife and daughters noticed only that a slight difficulty with his hearing had become more pronounced. Indeed, he would write years later that the torpedo's strike had sounded like the "report of a revolver near the ear."

Mary Cornish came down with a severe cold just days after landing in Scotland, and illness and insomnia stalked her for months after the attack. She was diagnosed with neuralgia, her feet "balled up and perpetually on fire." Cornish dreamed nightmares, too, violent dreams in which she found herself "back in the pitching lifeboat," the boys always huddled nearby, and always close to death.

As for Father O'Sullivan, he enjoyed reading his obituary—("If only one took the trouble," he said, "to tell people while they were alive of all the good things that are thought of them!")—but he suffered terribly in the immediate aftermath of the ordeal. His pain was constant, his nightmares vivid and powerful. O'Sullivan battled gangrene in one foot, sores in his mouth, and recurrent fever, nausea, and dizziness. These ailments would keep him hospitalized for three months after HMS *Anthony*'s arrival at Gourock.

MARY CORNISH, RONALD COOPER, AND George Purvis were each awarded the Medal of the British Empire for valor at sea. There would be no disagreement from the other passengers that all three were heroes, truly deserving of the honor.

Cooper had guided Lifeboat 12 expertly from the steeply angled *Benares* to a rough sea; he had saved at least eight lives in the tumult following the boat's launch, laboring to fish people from the water; his skill and effort during that storm and the others that followed had given Lifeboat 12 a chance. Every interview on shore made mention of the skill demonstrated by Cooper and his steward George Purvis; one of the recommendations for Cooper's award put it simply: "The seamanship and courage of the fourth officer [Cooper] were . . . outstanding."

Purvis had saved lives in different ways. Without his early judgments and careful calculations, the boat's stocks would never have lasted; certainly the drinking water would have gone too soon. Survivors also cited Purvis' ability to convince everyone on board that what he did was necessary. Mary Cornish thought Purvis had been "magnificent" in apportioning the limited food and water; Nagorski believed no one else in the boat could have managed the rations as successfully. In fact, Purvis had been stunningly prescient—and fortunate; his calculations had meant that water was available to all on board for eight and a half days, only a little while longer than was needed before the Sunderland flew into view.

As for Mary Cornish, every one of the boys said flatly that this woman had been his salvation. "Auntie Mary never slept," Derek Capel said. "It was like she was made to look after us." She had, in Capel's view, been their "Florence Nightingale." Paul Shearing wondered how Cornish herself had survived, given all the attention and energy she had lavished on them. Her near-constant massaging of their arms and legs, her insistence that the blankets be given to the children, her offer of a camisole for the boat's flag, and a jacket for Paul Shearing—the boys would never forget these details and this woman's charity. They also would never forget the "friend" she had brought along, that wartime hero named Bulldog Drummond. "Without Captain Drummond," Fred Steels observed, "we'd have died of boredom." Officials at Glasgow writing a recommendation to honor Cornish noted that "During the whole of this time Miss Cornish, though suffering, as the whole boat's company was, from the effects of exposure, directed herself to the task of saving the lives of her six young charges ... Thanks to her devotion, her cheerful resource, and her supreme endurance when herself suffering severely, the six boys survived." The September 28 edition of the *Montreal Gazette* went further, predicting that "first on the honor roll surely will stand the name of the ... London school teacher Mary Cornish. Her unbounded courage, her endurance and achievement made her one of God's heroines."

Bohdan Nagorski, who had initially considered Cornish a tiresome woman and Harry Peard an arrogant brute, ultimately credited these two for saving the lives of six English boys. Of the brash and tireless sailor, Nagorski wrote that

Gunner Peard was full of energy and good humor the whole time ... and he was always ready for any difficult job in the boat. In my opinion, he contributed more than anyone else to the fact that after eight hard days, we were found in relatively good state, without having lost the hope of rescue.

Peard had been initially disdainful of the Polish man in the homburg hat, and the others at the bow of Lifeboat 12. When their ordeal ended, however,

Peard was filled with respect and admiration for Nagorski, in particular for his ability to engage with the Indian crew. From the Royal Naval Hospital at Bristol one month later, Peard informed Nagorski that he had injured his back and suffered the effects of exposure—presumably frostbite or trench foot or something similar. But he filled most of a long letter with fond memories and warm sentiments:

> *Dear Bohdan,*
>
> *You must excuse my form of address but I would very much like to know that you suffered no ill effects from our voyage in the lifeboat together...*
>
> *I would love to meet you and talk over our trip. I feel I must take this opportunity of thanking you for your kindness during our ordeal. I also want to congratulate you on your wonderful composure during the eight days. You greatly impressed me and also impressed the others with your stolid matter-of-fact attitude, notably the [Indians] who regarded you with a little awe...*
>
> *I sincerely hope you escape danger.*
> *I am your sincere friend,*
> *Harry Peard*

The boys were also effusive in their thanks to Nagorski, not just for the pocket money he restored, but also for the constant assurances he had given that they would be saved. As Fred Steels put it, "Why should we have doubted it—when *he* was so sure?"

Ronnie Cooper filed a terse report for the Royal Navy from Scotland, taking only a page and a half of dry, matter-of-fact language to tell his version of the odyssey. Cooper praised Cornish, too, but he also credited his colleagues Doug Critchley, the signaler Johnny Mayhew, and the Indian sailor Ramjam Buxoo for their hard work, positive spirit, and for their heroism. In Cooper's opinion, Ramjam had been "most willing and helpful," a critical player as translator, diplomat, and general go-between with the thirty-one other Indians who survived.

Overall, though, Ronnie Cooper's conclusions were brief, basic, and characteristically understated: "Everyone behaved very well, and a spirit of loyalty to orders and comparative cheerfulness prevailed, through the entire seven days and 19 hours which we were in the boat."

Indeed, it was probably no exaggeration to say that "cheerfulness" and "spirit of loyalty" had saved them. Those demons mentioned in Chapter 15—"Fear," "Anxiety," "Anger," and "Loss of Faith"—had found almost no allies in Lifeboat 12. Conversely, if calm and discipline truly were lifesavers, then this little boat had been fortunate indeed.

All forty-five survivors had benefited from an uncommon calm and decorum which they maintained as a group. Given the pitiful rations, crowded conditions, and the seemingly endless crush of the sea, there had been ample motive and opportunity for selfishness, resentment, and anger. So many accounts of lifeboats stranded for long periods on the water are colored by these emotions, and the tension and violence they provoke. Reading those stories, one wonders why a battle over water or space never materialized in Lifeboat 12. It would have been perfectly understandable, and in keeping with precedent. And it never happened. Instead these eight long days and nights were marked by discipline and resilience, by selflessness and heroism.

NOT SURPRISINGLY, FATHER RORY O'SULLIVAN believed all forty-five survivors had someone else to thank. As he struggled in a Scottish hospital, long after the others had returned to their homes, O'Sullivan gave thanks for what he was convinced had been divine intervention at sea. Whether via St. Anthony, or Amadour, or the Virgin Mary herself, Rory O'Sullivan was convinced that God's hand had touched Lifeboat 12, and helped bring them home.

After five weeks O'Sullivan was permitted to walk with a pair of canes, and on a Sunday morning he ventured out for the first time. He found a taxi and asked the driver to bring him to the nearest church. They came to a chapel by the sea, where O'Sullivan discovered an inscription near the door: "To the Star of the Sea," it said. O'Sullivan limped to the nearest pew.

As the congregation began the opening hymn—"*Ave Maris Stella*"—O'Sullivan again felt the gentle hand of providence. He knew the hymn. And he knew his Latin.

"Ave maris stella, dei mater alma, atque semper virgo, felix caeli porta..."

"Hail, O star of the ocean, God's own Mother blessed, ever sinless Virgin, gate of heavenly rest..."

It was this church's traditional first hymn, but Rory O'Sullivan believed that on this particular Sunday it must have been meant for him and his fellow survivors, and as he listened he choked back tears. While the congregation sang, O'Sullivan bowed his head and said one more prayer of thanks. God's "star of the ocean," he believed, had guided them home.

"Our Lady had heard us," O'Sullivan wrote later, "[and] listened to our prayers and through so many dangers on the ocean, had guided us safely to port."

CHAPTER 23

Blame

On October 2, 1940, the British government suspended the CORB evacuation program, having determined that it could no longer assure the children's safety in the North Atlantic. The CORB chief Geoffrey Shakespeare called it a "difficult decision."

> On the one hand there is the delightful welcome and home life awaiting our children, free from the war atmosphere and particularly the nervous effects and discomforts of air raids. On the other hand the risks of achieving it seem latterly to be increasing.

That same day, the Prime Minister's Office issued a statement in which it claimed that "The recent sinking of vessels convoying children overseas has illustrated the dangers to which passenger vessels are exposed, even when in convoy . . ."

A handful of families complained that the decision would only reward the Nazis. Even some relatives of children lost on the *City of Benares* wrote to the government, urging that the evacuations be continued. Hitler's maritime terror, they argued, should not be permitted to scuttle a valuable and immensely popular program. The children's chief escort, Marjorie Day, wrote, "I hope this disaster won't put a stop to overseas evacuation—it's such a magnificent scheme." But the sorrow and anger that followed the sinking of the *Benares* were powerful emotions, and with no government promise that children sent in subsequent convoys would be safe, no real constituency existed to keep the program alive.

Anger channeled itself in another fashion. Almost immediately following the attack, there were loud calls for a government investigation. The first such demands had come on the night of September 18, before news of the attack had even been made public. That was the night that HMS *Hurricane*'s captain, Hugh Crofton Simms, telegraphed his account to the commander in chief of Western Approaches, describing what he and his men had found in the waters near the sunken liner. The commander in chief forwarded Simms' message to the Admiralty with a brief addendum: "Request Ministry of Shipping be asked to carry out necessary investigation." It seemed almost a formality, a "necessary" course of action.

By the time the first survivors landed in Scotland, several among them were already raising provocative questions about what had happened. Why had the escort destroyer HMS *Winchelsea* turned and left Convoy OB213? And why had the convoy plodded on, unguarded and slow, while U-boats prowled nearby? The cadet Doug Critchley said that the twenty hours the *Benares* had spent without a naval escort had constituted "a senseless, pointless blunder," and the purser, John Anderson, argued that this window of time had given the U-boat a chance "to pick us off." Marjorie Day gave her opinion that the *Benares* had been "an absolute sitter for any submarine crew that had the intelligence to wait." And in a long, thoughtful letter sent to the Admiralty on October 11, the BBC's Eric Davis suggested gently that the collective response to the attack could have been more efficient. A group of *Benares* passengers should have been drafted as a kind of auxiliary emergency crew, Davis wrote, and given responsibilities ranging from cabin evacuation to assistance in the launch of lifeboats. "This sink-at-sight policy is no new thing recently adopted by the enemy," Davis wrote, "and I feel certain that many passengers would have eagerly accepted even the humblest duty which would give a sense of competence and cooperation."

The most forceful of the critical voices belonged to the *Benares* survivor and retired Navy man Richard Deane. Deane was a former lieutenant commander, and he was in mourning. He had lost his wife, Dorothy, during the night of September 17–18, in the storm-tossed Lifeboat 7. Ashore in Scotland, Richard Deane let his own anger run free.

To Deane the mistakes had been many and inexcusable. In statements to reporters and letters to the Admiralty, he questioned the position of the convoy vessels, asked why the destroyer *Winchelsea* had turned, and then railed against virtually every aspect of the crew's performance immediately following the attack. Why, Deane wanted to know, had so many lifeboat falls jammed? Why had the children slept in their pajamas? Why had the crew been unable to steady the boats once they touched the water? And why had the lifeboats' Fleming handles been so stiff and so difficult to maneuver? The storm alone, Deane argued, could not be blamed for everything. "I say that in the conditions under which the ship was sunk, with a properly trained crew and efficient lifeboats, there should have been no loss of life."

This was a minority view, fueled perhaps by the bitterness that came with the loss of a loved one. Deane's report included misstatements of fact (most notably the contention that the ship was "on a perfectly even keel" as the lifeboats were lowered), and his implied criticism of the crew—that they had not been "properly trained"—was contradicted by virtually every other *Benares* survivor. Not surprisingly, Deane's remarks galled the crewmen. Anderson and the chief officer, Joe Hetherington, defended their colleagues vigorously, saying that given the heavy seas and damage done to the ship, they could imagine no sailors who could have lowered the boats cleanly and kept them all dry. Marjorie Day concurred: "The crew behaved admirably at every step."

But Deane had raised one pertinent question that was not so easily answered—the same one raised by other survivors. Why had the *Winchelsea* left when she had, and why had she not returned to the scene? "In other words," Deane wrote, "why had we to wait while HMS *Hurricane* steamed some 280 miles [301 miles, actually] in a sea in which she could not make her top speed, when it would seem that the . . . escort vessels must have been very much nearer?"

It was a good question, and the CORB executive, Geoffrey Shakespeare, had another. Why had no convoy ships been designated as rescue vessels? "This," he wrote, "had been the understanding of everyone from the start." Shakespeare cited the story of the SS *Volendam*, the CORB liner torpedoed in late August with all 321 child evacuees saved. In the *Volendam*'s case, a convoy vessel had deviated from standing rules and come to the liner's aid. Why, Shakespeare wondered, had the *Benares'* convoy partners not done the same? (It may also be asked: Why—as head of the CORB—had Shakespeare himself not been more aware of these critical rules of engagement?) The Admiralty offered a terse reply. "We do not think it would have been proper to depart from orders on account of the children," it said in a statement, "as this would possibly have endangered other ships."

Britain's Ministry of Shipping raised questions of its own, listing them alphabetically from "A" to "L" and suggesting that the "Admiralty are doubtless giving careful consideration to points 'K' and 'L.'" These were as follows:

(K) Surviving passengers and crew were in the lifeboats for at least 18 hours before being rescued. It appears that none of the vessels in the convoy had been instructed to attend to rescue, notwithstanding the large number of children among the passengers of the *City of Benares*.

(L) The escort left the convoy at 1 a.m. on September 17, 1940 and thereafter, instead of the convoy dispersing forthwith, it continued to proceed in formation at restricted convoy speed. The signal to the convoy to "scatter" was not given until after the torpedoing of the *City of Benares*.

The U-48 crewmen had remarked on this—had noted with curiosity the absence of an escort vessel. The wireless operator Rolf Hilse would argue later that the British were to blame in another way: that they had not informed Berlin, via the Red Cross, of the *City of Benares'* precious cargo. Historians I have asked say flatly that at this stage of the war the German Navy would not have been deterred by Red Cross designations. Some have even suggested it might have aroused even more attention, thereby endangering more vessels in the convoy.

While these questions, suggestions, and accusations flew about, another explanation—certainly the more politically palpable one—was put forward. Blame of any kind should rest with one party, and one party alone: the German Navy. This was certainly the prevailing opinion in the British press. "The submarine commander who loosed his torpedo in darkness and a rough sea knew how small the hope of rescue would be," argued the *Daily Telegraph*. "Brutal and barbarous slaughter . . . is the mark of German determination in war by sea, air and land." To question the crew's actions or the decisions made by the Admiralty was seen as missing the point. Worse, it was unpatriotic.

On December 20, three months after the attack, as a direct result of the sinking of the SS *City of Benares*, the Admiralty amended its rules governing maritime convoy traffic. Henceforth all maritime convoys were to be accompanied by "rescue escorts"—trawlers, tugboats, and other craft specifically designated to scoop up survivors in the event of a shipwreck or U-boat attack.

These vessels were to assist only "when a local escort is present," but they would prove their worth. Before war's end some four thousand people would be saved at sea by these newly christened "rescue vessels." The *Benares* could claim this policy, and those who were rescued, as important components of her legacy.

On that same day in December, the Admiralty concluded that the loss of the *City of Benares,* and the 256 souls who had perished in the waters around her, did not merit a formal investigation. The event, tragic though it was, was "a war casualty resulting from Germany's unrestricted warfare at sea, and the essential facts were clear." To the modern observer this may seem callous; an investigation into Richard Deane's claims might appear to have been the obvious and correct course of action. To many citizens of late-1940 England, however, there were more important matters at hand. Further horrors were already being visited on the British populace, and the European front was ever-widening. The last word would belong to the Ministry of Shipping: "The lamentable loss of life was caused primarily by the torpedoing of the *City of Benares* and proximately by swamping of lifeboats at night time and eighteen hours' exposure in the boats, in severe weather."

All of this was incontrovertible; it was also an incomplete answer. But there would be no further questions. In a memorandum that was not made public for obvious reasons, the Admiralty explained its position this way: "It appears to us that the balance of advantage would probably lie in saying nothing . . . The public disquiet at the sinking of the vessel is now dying down."

THERE WAS ANOTHER COMPLAINT FOUND in several accounts given after the survivors reached Great Britain: an alleged slow response and incompetence among some members of the Indian crew. Some of the Indians were said to have been "unhelpful" on deck; others had "lacked vitality" in the lifeboats. The implication throughout was that an English or Scottish crew would have done better, but it is a fact that just as many survivors credited Indian crew members for lifesaving bravery on the water.

More to the point, though less easy to quantify, a profound undercurrent of racism runs through the narrative of this story as told by certain participants. The CORB director, Geoffrey Shakespeare, in his final report, cites children who praised the Indians, mentions the chief officer's testimony that the Indians had "behaved very well and were good seamen," and gives a general assessment that Indian crews were traditionally brave and reliable—only to finish by recommending that the board should in the future "only send children in ships with white crews." This is all the more galling given that the Ministry of Shipping's own determination was that "it is not possible to state that the loss of life would have been less with other than an Indian crew."

The only convincing evidence against the Indians had to do with clothing: Flimsily dressed as they were, the Indians weakened or perished faster; certainly they quickly lost their ability to aid others. Of course the answer might as well have been to recommend warmer clothing, not lighter-skinned crew.

BLAME WAS ASSESSED IN A different forum after the war, when the role of the German *Unterseebootflotille* came before the War Crimes Tribunal at Nuremberg. During their deliberations regarding the indictment of Admiral Karl Doenitz, prosecutors revisited the attack on the *City of Benares*, charging that while there was no evidence the Germans knew the *Benares* had carried child evacuees, the attack was barbaric nonetheless and worthy of the tribunal's condemnation. On January 14, 1946, British colonel H. J. Phillimore recounted the story of the *Benares* as part of his case for the prosecution. "The point to be emphasized," said Phillimore, "is not the unusual brutality of the attack, but that such results are inevitable when a belligerent disregards the rules of sea warfare." Reminding the tribunal of the horrors visited on "open boats in Atlantic gales, of men in the water clinging for hours to a raft and gradually dropping off one by one," Phillimore argued that "The enemy must know that such things are the inevitable result of the warfare he has chosen to employ."

Heinrich Bleichrodt was held on war crimes charges for having knowingly attacked a vessel—the *Benares*—that carried a large complement of children. Bleichrodt refused to testify or even speak with investigators, who eventually dropped their case for lack of evidence.

Ultimately, only one U-boat commander was prosecuted at Nuremberg. Heinz Eck and two of his officers were executed for the indisputably heinous crime of firing on survivors of the torpedoed Greek merchant steamer *Peleos* as they languished in the water. There had of course been nothing comparable in the behavior of Heinrich Bleichrodt and his crew on board U-48. They were seen to have been doing their job—namely, hunting for and destroying large liners. Despite all the fulminations of the British press in late September 1940

Peter Collinson
Chief Surgeon and Code Officer,
HMS *Hurricane*

Albert Gorman
Leading Seaman, HMS *Hurricane*

Moment of rescue—a *Hurricane* sailor
hauls in a raft from the *City of Benares*.

HMS *Hurricane*

Hugh Crofton Simms
Commander, HMS *Hurricane*

Rex Thorne, Louis Walder, and Colin Richardson
on board HMS *Hurricane*

Colin Richardson reads accounts of his own rescue
Abergavenny, Wales
October 1940

Beth Cummings in hospital
Scotland, September 1940

Lifeboat 12
September 25, 1940

Ken Sparks, Derek Capel, and Fred Steels
on board HMS *Anthony*

Ken Sparks returns home
October 1, 1940

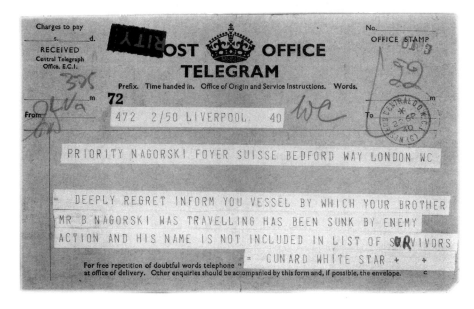

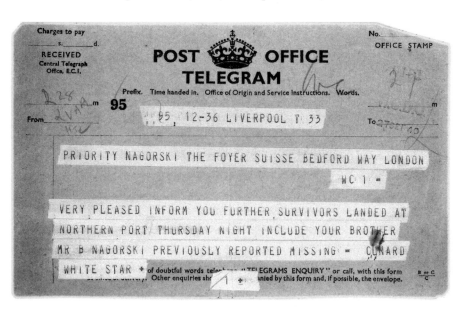

Telegrams from Cunard/White Star Lines to Bohdan Nagorski's brother
September 22 (*above*) and September 27, 1940

Reunion: (*back*) Anthony Quinton, John Baker, Beth Williams (nee Cummings), Colin Richardson, Jack Keeley; (*seated*) Bess Cummings (nee Walder), Derek Bech, Sonia Williams (nee Bech), Barbara Partridge (nee Bech)—September 1989

Five Lifeboat 12 "boys" reunited
September 1990
(*left to right*: Ken Sparks, Fred Steels, Derek Capel, Billy Short, Paul Shearing)

Bohdan Nagorski and George Nagorski (the author's father)
Hampton Bays, New York, 1979

("Nazis Torpedo Mercy Ship, Kill Children," etc.) no evidence ever surfaced that the U-48 men knew that children were aboard the ship they struck on the night of September 17.

There has never been a formal investigation into the sinking of the SS *City of Benares.*

CHAPTER 24

Reunions

On a chilly morning in September 2000, a group of elderly men and women gathered in the Church of the Annunciation at Wembley, England. They waited in a rear alcove as the church filled, talking softly and pausing occasionally to embrace one another. At a signal from the rector, the organist and the Preston Park Junior Choir struck the opening phrases of "O God Our Help in Ages Past." The guests of honor filed in.

Children were paired with the older men and women, and they walked arm in arm down the aisle, reaching their pews as the hymn neared its final stanza, ". . . and our eternal home."

There was a time for silent prayer, and then Kenneth Sparks was called forward to read from the Book of Proverbs. Sparks—who as a child had famously flagged down a Sunderland plane from his perch in Lifeboat 12—was a slightly stooped but otherwise hearty seventy-three-year-old. "When your panic comes as a storm and desolation," Sparks read, "and calamity comes on like a whirlwind, when distress and anguish come upon you, then will you call upon me." When he had finished, the priest began reading names, a long, alphabetical procession, the names of boys and girls lost in a disaster at sea precisely sixty years before.

"Allen, Patricia. Baker, Robert. Barrett, Kathleen. Beesley, Edna."

The morning's program was called "Memorial: Service for the Lost Children, and Reunion of the Survivors of the *City of Benares*." The Preston Park Junior School had lost five of its own in the tragedy; their names were carved into the church's baptismal font.

"Came, Lewis. Capel, Alan. Carr, Beryl." The reading carried on, slow and deliberate.

The men and women in the front pews—the honored guests—were in their late sixties and early seventies. One of them, a stocky, silver-haired woman, cried hard as the names were read. "Willis, Peter. Wood, Dorothy." When the list was finished, the woman stood with some effort, daubing her eyes as she gathered herself and walked the few steps to the lectern. She had written a prayer for the occasion:

Lord God and tender Father of us all, we are still your children just as we were when we set out on our dangerous journeys over the sea so long ago. At this very special time of many remembrances, we ask that you accept silent prayers for the children and their escorts of the *City of Benares*, who were lost at sea, but were taken up into your divine care. We, who have survived our journeyings through life, pray for them and remember them now. Amen.

The woman returned to her seat. The congregation stood for another hymn. From the row behind, a stocky man in a dark blue suit extended an arm, touching the woman's shoulder. She smiled back, a look of warmth and recognition shining through her tears. He was Albert Gorman, Royal Navy veteran, looking fit and strong for his eighty-eight years. The woman, now seventy-five, was the person he had known as Bess Walder, an immensely brave fifteen-year-old with a lovely smile. Albert Gorman remembered that smile well. And for as long as Bess lived she would know that face, wind-weathered and wrinkled as it was, as the face of her salvation, the face she associated with a sixty-year-old miracle at sea.

"It's good to see you, Bess," Gorman said with a smile.

AMONG THE SURVIVORS OF THE *City of Benares*, one became a lord, another won an Oscar, one credited his ordeal on the water for his successful battle against cancer, and at least two became casualties of war on a different front. All six of the Lifeboat 12 boys served in the Navy, inspired at least in part by their brief time aboard HMS *Anthony*. Beyond a boyish excitement and admiration for the *Anthony*'s crew, they had also returned home with a fresh and profound sense of patriotism. All told, the 148 people who were brought "back from the dead" had resolved, in their own ways, to make the most of it.

Many of the *Benares* survivors have lived long lives, long enough so that I was able to find them when I began my own investigations, more than sixty years later.

As for Bess and Beth—the girls on the overturned lifeboat—they became sisters-in-law. In 1946 Beth's brother, Geoff Cummings, returned from his military service—he had been an artilleryman guarding British oilfields in Iraq—and came home to the Woolwich Barracks in southeast London. By this time Bess Walder and Beth Cummings were speaking almost every week by telephone, and it was Beth's suggestion that Bess get together with her brother. "It's been forever since he's been in London," Beth Cummings told her friend. "Will you show him around?" Bess agreed, and today a twinkle comes to her eye as she tells the story. "I've been showing that man around ever since." On August 16, 1947, Bess Walder and Geoff Cummings were married in London. Bound by fate, and their remarkable and harrowing time in the cold North Atlantic, Bess and Beth would now share a family tie as well.

"Must've been meant to be," Beth told me when we first spoke. "P'raps we hung on to that boat long as we did, so Bess could meet me brother."

TEN OF THE THIRTEEN CHILD evacuee survivors were in the Wembley church that morning on September 17, 2000. Howard Claytor had been killed in a car accident in 1969; Louis Walder died of a massive heart attack in 1986, when he was only fifty-six. The only surviving evacuee not at the reunion was Eleanor Wright, who had retreated from public view and from the rest of the group after her rescue. Presumably Wright had chosen to do everything possible to forget what had happened.

It was an emotion the other survivors could well understand. "I spent all those years forgetting," John Baker told the others at their reunion, and when I spoke with Rex Thorne his first reply to my questions was "I've been able to blot the memory." Bill Short found that the memories had come rushing back as he made his way to Wembley. "We'll shed a tear here," Short said, in his heavy Scottish brogue. " 'Bout time we did." Of his own memory of the event, Short said, "It's a ghost, is what it is. Come out of the cupboard."

Baker, Thorne, and Short had all lost siblings in the attack; they were bound to feel a particular pang when the memories resurfaced. Derek Capel had come enthusiastically to the Wembley church and to earlier reunions, but the gatherings sent Capel on a fresh and obviously difficult journey through the morass of memory, searching for any strands that might help him to better understand what had become of his little brother, Alan, and what more might have been done to save him. Derek Capel had been unable to walk properly for six months after the ordeal and he had suffered headaches and nightmares for twenty-odd years after, but the pain that endured was mental, and it involved the loss of his brother.

"All my life I've been haunted by the thought that I could have been there for him," Capel told me when we met in the spring of 2004. "That I should have saved him. Logic tells me there was nothing a young boy could do, but I feel it deeply just the same. Alan was a lovely little lad."

It had not helped that the details of Alan Capel's death and the way in which they were communicated to the family had been shrouded in confusion. Two months after the attack, Derek Capel's parents received an official letter stating that Alan had been "buried at sea." The family assumed this meant that he had been lost during that terrible night like all the others—never realizing that "buried at sea" referred to the poignant memorial held aboard HMS *Hurricane* on September 19, 1940. A small matter, perhaps, but it was 1990 before Derek Capel learned, from other survivors, that his little brother had in fact been brought alive on board the *Hurricane*.

Derek Capel continues at this writing to speak to children about his experiences—about what he calls "the positive lessons of optimism and survival." Indeed many of the *Benares* "children" have carried such "positive" associations into their later years, believing that their rescue at sea not only offered a second chance at life, but also bestowed upon them an inner strength that bordered on invincibility.

In Scotland in 1940, Colin Richardson's mother had instructed her son to banish the ordeal from his mind. "He must forget as soon as he can," she told a friend, "and I do not want him questioned about it." But Colin Richardson has not heeded this advice. In 1979 Richardson was diagnosed with stomach cancer and given a 10 percent chance of survival. He is still alive today, more than a quarter century later, and with great conviction he tells a visitor that he has eluded death precisely because of his brief but traumatizing time in the North Atlantic. "I am a survivor," he said when we first met. "I beat the ice water, and I've beaten cancer." Richardson founded the Association for New Approaches to Cancer, wrote a book called *I Beat My Cancer*, and the positive outlook and spirit exhibited in a *Benares* lifeboat are quite apparent in the way he speaks about his life. "The only way to face such matters," he told me— "matters" in this case meaning a torpedo attack and stomach cancer—"is to face them head-on."

Paul Shearing had lost two toes and suffered chronic pain in his feet and legs for much of his adult life, but he never felt anything but great gratitude for his lot, and in particular for those in Lifeboat 12 who had kept him alive. "We all know, every one of us, that we've no business being on this earth," Shearing told me. "Likewise we all know that every day has been a gift. We must make the days count." At the Wembley reunion Bess Walder (now Bess Cummings) fell into conversation with Shearing, and at one point she remarked that from what she had learned about the experience of Lifeboat 12 he had suffered mightily. "You *really* had a rough time," she observed.

Paul Shearing shrugged. "All I did," he replied, "was step into a lifeboat one awful night, and get lifted from it eight days later."

As for Bess herself, she had become a doyenne of sorts for the survivors, organizing these occasional get-togethers and helping people like me to find the survivors. Every September 17 since 1940 has stirred her deeply, and not just because the memory brings tears to her eyes. "I don't want this to sound arrogant," she said at Wembley, "but it made us feel almost invincible, and that we could do anything." Later she told me that the clear lesson of the *Benares* story was that "one can always cope. No matter what comes, one can always look trouble in the eye."

Other survivors came to the reunion. Here were all three Bech "children"—Derek, Sonia, and Barbara. They were the ones who first put the word "miracle" in my mind, reflecting on the rescue of their entire family from the torpedoed liner. They also believed that they had benefited in the aftermath from one another's comfort and confidence. "Perhaps it's been easier for us," Derek Bech said. "We've had each other to deal with the memories." Also present, sixty years on, was Anthony Quinton, a bookish teenager in 1940 and now a highly regarded author and professor of philosophy, a former president of Trinity College, and member of the British House of Lords. Colin Richardson was there, too, still flashing the infectious smile that had captured so many hearts sixty years before. And here was Jack Keeley, still voluble and effervescent and—all these years later—still awed by his experience on the water. "Hard to imagine," he said, "how exactly we managed."

Certainly the survivors of the *Benares* were a hardy group. Only a few had died young. A second act of war felled the BBC correspondent Eric Davis, who reached the Far East but was killed when the plane carrying him from Singapore to Java was shot down by a Japanese fighter. (His kindness and generosity toward raft mate Jack Keeley had continued after their rescue; in October 1940 Davis twice visited the child and his family, bearing food and gifts from

Harrods on both occasions. Keeley never forgot the gesture.) The *Benares'* carpenter Angus MacDonald—the man who had skippered Lifeboat 2—was killed in the 1943 attack on the *California*, which was ferrying British troops to North Africa. MacDonald was said to have returned below deck to search for survivors—never to be seen again.

Cancer claimed Mary Cornish in 1964, and Ronnie Cooper was only sixty-one when he died in 1979, still remembered as "the young chap who brought back the evacuees." Among the child evacuees who survived, all but two would reach their seventies. The children of the paying passengers lived long lives as well, and two of the adult Lifeboat 12 survivors—Rory O'Sullivan and my great-uncle Bohdan Nagorski—lived into their late nineties.

During a conversation with Jack Keeley, I reviewed these facts and remarked upon the apparent longevity of the *Benares* survivors. It was strange, I suggested, that so many in the group had lasted so long, considering all they had suffered. Keeley, himself seventy-three at the time, reflected for a moment. And then he laughed. "Well," he said, "it's probably the saltwater."

IN FACT IT WAS REMARKABLE that all these people ever found one another, six decades later. While Bess and Beth had become family, and some of the Lifeboat 12 "boys" had stayed in touch in the years immediately following the attack (including a joint appearance they made with Father Rory O'Sullivan on a 1956 television program called *The Wilfred Pickles Show*), most of the *City of Benares* survivors had been out of touch for decades. They went their own ways and would probably never have met again had it not been for a man who had never even been on board the *Benares*.

Blake Simms was only one year old when the *Benares* was sunk. His father was Hugh Crofton Simms, commander of HMS *Hurricane*, the destroyer that had raced for the scene and brought more than one hundred of the ship's survivors aboard. Simms had gone on to lead several more rescue missions with *Hurricane*, most notably spearheading the rescue of more than four hundred passengers and crew from the torpedoed *City of Nagpur* in April 1941. Hugh Crofton Simms was awarded the Distinguished Service Order for sinking three German U-boats, and in 1942 he was given command of the junior class destroyer *Snapdragon* as she was deployed in support of General Montgomery's Eighth Army in the bombardment of Benghazi, Libya. On December 21, an Italian fighter plane bombed the *Snapdragon*, scoring a direct hit to the captain's bridge. Hugh Crofton Simms was mortally wounded, at the age of thirty-five.

A proud son who had scarcely known his father, Blake Simms began in the 1970s to research his father's naval career and then to locate those who had benefited from Hugh Crofton Simms' heroism at sea. Blake Simms found hundreds of grateful souls, the *Benares* veterans among them, and organized their first formal reunion in the late 1980s.

Simms had done more than find the surviving children. Working like a historian or documentary filmmaker, he had also located a few surviving members of U-48's crew, men in their eighties who all said they had been stunned and saddened upon learning that the liner they struck that September night had carried so many children. U-48's two wireless operators, Wilhelm Kruse and Rolf Hilse, both said they had never known the *Benares* was on a mercy mission, and they described their commander, Heinrich Bleichrodt, as having fallen silent when he heard about the *Benares'* special mission. "None of us knew," said Kruse. "We had no way to know." It was, he said, "a dark day for all of us." This may have been self-serving talk, and in the case of Hilse his remarks about the attack sounded more defensive than remorseful. In a long interview conducted sixty years later for the Imperial War Museum, Hilse appeared to want desperately to convince survivors and the public that any submariner would have done what he and his crewmates had done. Hilse never apologized and expressed no regret during the interview.

As for the claim that U-48's crew never knew about the children aboard the *Benares,* I can say only that Simms and all the *Benares* survivors—even the bitter ones—believed it. Kruse and U-48's engineer Edouard Hansen came to the reunion, smiling and posing for photographs with several of the survivors. They laid a wreath of white flowers at the Royal Naval War Memorial at Portsmouth, and a larger group of U-48's crew sent a bouquet of flowers to the church and single carnations for the *Benares* survivors.

Billy Short refused to pose for the pictures—and he tossed his carnation. "Didn't like it," Short told me later. "Not one bit."

Short, the youngest of the "Lifeboat boys," is today a modest, unassuming man of few words. He described himself as a forgiving person, and insisted that he held no personal animus for the Germans he met at the *Benares* reunion. But Short believed that to the extent the event was to be remembered at all, it ought to be remembered in the company of men and women who had survived the attack and the sailors who had rescued them. "Not," Billy Short said bluntly, "with the fellows who fired the bloody torpedoes."

The survivors had mixed feelings about this. Bess and Beth sat with Kruse and Hansen and traded stories. Jack Keeley said he had carried a virulent hatred for years after the attack, and then felt it dissolve, slowly but unmistakably, to the point at which he could now lunch without misgiving with a U-48 veteran. "I've got no hate left in me now," he said. Ken Sparks believed that the Germans "were just out there doing their job." Perhaps the most intriguing reunion story involved Hilse, the U-48 wireless operator. He had read about an earlier *Benares* get-together and called Beth Williams (nee Cummings). Hilse had been held prisoner by the British after the war, and he had later married an Englishwoman and settled outside London. His wife had discouraged him from calling any of the *Benares* survivors—"Let it die" were her words—but in the late 1990s Hilse called anyway.

Hilse met and made a peace of sorts with Beth and several other survivors, and then he found a *Sunday Express* article about the reunion that referred to him as "the Nazi Rolf Hilse." Hilse called the paper's editors, and they retracted the adjective "Nazi."

Bess Cummings wrestled with these questions of memory and forgiveness as part of her remarks from the Wembley church lectern:

> We who were saved have had to come to terms with a problem of forgiveness. To forgive those who did so much harm to so many people and who have a left a trail of misery and horror in their wake is not easy, and to obey Christ's teachings on forgiveness when we say the Lord's Prayer is still, for some, greatly difficult in this context . . . Forgiveness can be very beneficial to the soul, reciprocal and helpful in healing deep wounds of the mind. It sometimes has to be a long process, one that may never quite be completed.

THERE REMAIN A FEW REMARKABLE footnotes to this story.

The freighter *Marina*'s second lifeboat—piloted by Captain R. T. Paine, who had sailed briefly alongside the *Benares'* Lifeboat 12—had made an extraordinary journey back to Great Britain. Paine had sailed for Ireland early on the morning of September 18, having set rations at three biscuits and a dipper and a half of water per day, per man. Paine kept a journal of the event, finishing with an entry on Wednesday, September 25:

> Strong NW wind and high sea. 4 a.m. arrived off Tory Island Light, and whilst waiting for daylight to look for a landing place the SS *Carlingford*, a coaster bound from the west of Ireland to Glasgow, came along

and offered to take boat's crew on board and tow lifeboat to Londonderry, and as by this time all hands were in a pretty weak state, I accepted the master's offer, and at 4 p.m. the *Carlingford* berthed at
Londonderry.

Another footnote involves the man who carried out the attack, and who
may have become a casualty of his own action. In September 1942 Heinrich
Bleichrodt was awarded the Knight's Cross with Oak Leaves, one of the highest honors ever bestowed on a U-boat commander. That same month found
Bleichrodt in command of U-109, and it found him in trouble.

The accounts are sketchy, but it appeared to his U-109 crewmate Wolfgang
Hirschfeld that Bleichrodt had come to a point in his career at which he
"could no longer take the heat." In November 1942 U-109 was engaged in a
particularly dangerous fight with a destroyer in the Bay of Biscay. One of his
torpedoes jammed, the destroyer dropped a depth charge, and Bleichrodt and
his submarine narrowly escaped. In December Bleichrodt launched an attack
on a merchant vessel off French Guyana, and after his torpedoes missed their
mark the following dispatch was sent from U-109: "For ten days the commander has been suffering from nervous debility with loss of energy, together
with a serious depression. Request return." The response from headquarters
was a firm warning that the mission had to be completed "under all circumstances," but then Bleichrodt himself sent a message, on December 31: "At the
moment I am not fully fit. Request medical advice."

Hirschfeld believed Bleichrodt had suffered a nervous breakdown, the result of a long, intense, and sometimes harrowing career of undersea warfare.
There is no way to know whether the attack on the *Benares* and the children
she carried had anything to do with the mental state of this illustrious commander. In one of the many remarkable twists to the story, Heinrich Bleichrodt
was assigned to watch over the repair and upkeep of old submarines at the
German-occupied Baltic port of Gdynia. This was the Polish city Bohdan
Nagorski called home—the place from which his wartime odyssey had begun,
three years before.

Finally there was the story of the Oscar winner. On March 4, 1943, at the
Ambassador Hotel in Los Angeles, Arthur Wimperis won the Academy Award
for Best Screenplay for *Mrs. Miniver*, an account of upper-middle-class life in
wartime England. Wimperis' survival at sea was remarkable not only for the
efforts he had expended to save several children, but also for the fact that
he was sixty-three years old at the time, one of the eldest passengers to have

escaped with his life from the *City of Benares*. Wimperis made something of a heroic return to Hollywood; *Mrs. Miniver* starred Greer Garson and Walter Pidgeon, and in addition to its critical acclaim, the film was heralded by Winston Churchill for its depiction of the struggles facing Great Britain. Its "propaganda value," Churchill said, "was worth a dozen battleships."

I BEGAN MY OWN INVESTIGATIONS of these events assuming I would primarily be scouring obituaries, visiting nursing homes, and interviewing sons and daughters of those *Benares* children who had survived. But other than Howard Claytor, all the Lifeboat 12 boys were still alive, and all were vigorous, warm, and welcoming. Bess and Beth were not only alive— they were funny, kind, and insistent that I get to all the survivors and also to some of the men who had been responsible for their rescue. "You'll need to see Albert Gorman," Bess said matter-of-factly, one among a long list of ideas she offered over a three-year period. I did—or tried to do—just about everything Bess suggested. And I was rarely disappointed.

As I wrote at the opening of this book, the story of the *City of Benares* lifts the spirit as much as it drags it down. The people I encountered have had everything to do with that. Albert Gorman, ninety-one at the time of our meeting, invited me to his home and almost immediately directed me to a table upon which notebooks and loose-leaf binders had been laid out in orderly piles. Gorman asked me to burrow through these—most were journals he had kept at the time—and then come to him afterward with whatever questions remained. "You go in there and *read*," he said gruffly. His wife made tea, and Gorman himself shuffled out, retreating to their garden. If I still had questions when I was finished, he said, I could ask them. "I'll be in the garden, whenever you're through." I asked how much time I could spend with the stacks on their dining table. "Take your time," he said, with a chuckle. "I'm not going anywhere."

Everyone seemed to have maintained some sort of personal archive. Fred Steels kept a small suitcase under his television; Colin Richardson lugged a fat file to his terrace; Derek Capel and Ken Sparks not only laid out papers and photographs, they also allowed me to borrow many of these and carry them back to New York. Derek Bech made copies for me of every document in his possession, brought his sisters together for a *Benares* family reunion—and then peppered me with helpful e-mails once I had returned home. Lord Anthony Quinton and I spoke by phone—and then he turned up in New York, where he invited me to lunch and regaled me with stories about the *Benares* and about his mother, Letitia; about the philosopher Immanuel Kant; and about the relative merits of the cities of London and New York. Listening to this brilliant and deeply engaging man, it was hard to imagine that his life had very nearly been snuffed out on a night when he was only fifteen years old.

Other mementos of the story have been more broadly and publicly shared. Blake Simms has donated the bell from HMS *Hurricane* to the Imperial War Museum in London, together with a pair of binoculars Hugh Crofton Simms used to scan the sea on the afternoon of September 18, 1940. It was through these binoculars that Simms had seen the first of the *Benares'* lifeboats. Colin Richardson's scarlet-colored life vest hangs currently in a glass cabinet, not far from Simms' binoculars, at the Imperial War Museum. And in an alcove of St. Jude on the Hill Church in London's Hampstead Garden, where Michael Rennie's father was the vicar, an arc-shaped painting honors Rennie, showing him struggling valiantly to pull small children aboard a wave-wracked lifeboat.

As I said at the outset, I owe a profound debt to all the survivors. For one thing, each of them has answered my questions—even the reticent Rex Thorne, who kept saying, "I still find it so hard to describe," and Billy Short, who apologized profusely for his scattered memories. "I was only nine, y'see ..." More than this, the survivors have inspired me, each in his or her own way. I first met Bess Cummings (nee Walder) after an overnight flight to London and subsequent two-and-a-half-hour drive from Heathrow Airport to her home in Bishop's Cleve. A nap was in order, but Bess had a pot of tea waiting; she had a warm and engaging manner, a gentle wit, and of course she had her remarkable story. A nap was out of the question.

When I called on Paul Shearing, he had already shared much of his story over the phone and in letters, so he began by telling me about his wife, who had died recently after a long struggle with Alzheimer's disease. Shearing spoke sweetly about her, and said he had been surprised at how hard it had been to manage after her death. "I thought I was prepared for it," he said. He still had difficulty walking, but he had tea waiting, too, and he had his own stack of clippings and photographs. And then Paul Shearing brought out something else. A cardboard box, perhaps a foot square, with my name on it.

"For you," he said.

I looked at the box. I was the one who should have been bearing gifts, I protested, and while I had brought him some chocolates and a coffee table book about New York, Shearing's box made me a little uncomfortable. And as it happened, his was the far more thoughtful gift.

Paul Shearing had been an amateur wood-carver since his late teenage years, and inside the box I found a lovely oval-shaped wooden frame, with curved holes cut into either end. Under the glass Shearing had nestled a photograph I knew well: a view of Lifeboat 12, taken from the deck of the *Anthony* at the moment of rescue.

"There's your great-uncle," said Shearing, indicating the hunched figure under a homburg hat.

"Yes," I said. "That's him."

BOHDAN NAGORSKI WAS NO LONGER living when I began my research, but his daughters shared old clippings and letters and memories of their own. It helped that I had a clear memory of their father, and this inspired me, too. Bohdan Nagorski was a lovely man. While I was writing one night, I remembered Colin Richardson's words—*I am a survivor*—and it brought back a story about Bohdan. Surely, I thought, my great-uncle was a survivor, too.

In the summer of 1979 my father and I were spending a week in Hampton Bays, New York, just a few hundred yards from the house where Bohdan and his wife, Zosia, were living. One night a fireman banged on our door and asked if we knew the elderly couple who lived down the street. Yes, my father said. We expected the worst.

The man told us that Bohdan and Zosia had been watching television when a fuse blew, igniting a small blaze in the wiring behind the set. Soon the flames were leaping high, and while Zosia did the smart thing—she called 911 and implored her husband to come with her to the front door—Bohdan Nagorski attempted to smother the flames with an old oriental rug. The fire department later told us that Bohdan had probably saved the house—and that he could easily have been killed. He was eighty-eight years old at the time.

We found Bohdan at the local hospital. He waved weakly at us, smiling and pointing to his face. The nurses had smeared a white ointment across his forehead.

"Don't touch!" he said through a weary smile. "Wet paint!"

After a while a nurse appeared, with a clipboard and forms that needed to be completed. Bohdan was almost completely deaf at this late stage of life, and we helped communicate the nurse's questions.

"Date of birth?" the nurse asked, and my father repeated the words, enunciating clearly for Bohdan's sake. "Date—of—birth?"

"Eighteen twelve," Bohdan replied without hesitation, grinning broadly. The nurse had begun writing this down when she caught herself.

"You're something else, Mr. Nagorski," she said.

It is a cliché, but I can well imagine, given the terrible circumstance of a shipwreck and a protracted time spent in a cramped lifeboat, that you would be happy for the company of such a man in your boat. As I worked on the book in the late and lonely hours, when my wife and children slept, it helped immensely to summon Bohdan's voice, his gentle face and manner, and above all his wonderful sense of humor.

Bohdan Nagorski was not an overtly spiritual man, but just as God had played a role in Rory O'Sullivan's reflections, so too did Bohdan see some divine hand in what he called the "miracle of his rescue." In 1941 he wrote an eighteen-page account of his time on board the *City of Benares* and one of her lifeboats. This is how he finished:

In my innermost heart I never lost hope during those long bleak days and still longer nights. Sometimes, when overcome with fatigue, I lost all sense of reality, and in my semi-conscious state I imagined myself to be sailing in an open boat on my native Baltic—sailing back to Gdynia harbour. There, on the hill overlooking the city and the port, an illuminated cross proudly marked the site selected for the Cathedral of the Redeemer, to be erected by my people as a thank-offering for liberty and independence. And on the high altar of that cathedral I shall place my own votive offering in thanksgiving for the miracle of my rescue, when after the horrors of this war have been overcome I return to my native land.

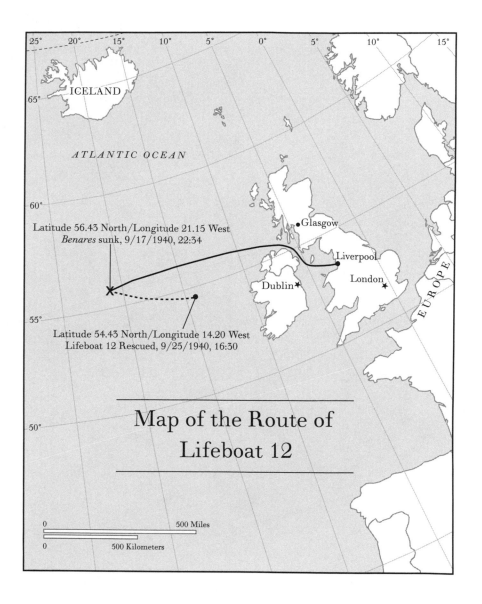

25° 20° 15° 10° 5° 0° 5° 10° 15°

ICELAND

65°

ATLANTIC OCEAN

60°

Latitude 56.43 North/Longitude 21.15 West
Benares sunk, 9/17/1940, 22:34

• Glasgow

Liverpool
London

Dublin ✶

55°

Latitude 54.43 North/Longitude 14.20 West
Lifeboat 12 Rescued, 9/25/1940, 16:30

EUROPE

50°

Map of the Route of
Lifeboat 12

0   500 Miles

0   500 Kilometers

Of the 406 passengers and crew aboard the SS *City of Benares*, 258 perished as a result of the attack. This figure includes the three children who died on board the HMS *Hurricane* and two Indian crewmen who died soon after their return, in Scottish hospitals. There were 148 survivors of the attack on the *Benares*.

The breakdown was as follows:

	SURVIVED	DIED
Child Evacuees	13	77
Child Escorts	4	6
Paying Passengers	40	51
Crew (includes Royal Navy sailors)	91	124

Below, what I have been able to learn about some of the survivors:

JOHN ANDERSON served as purser on two more ships, the *City of Exeter* and the *City of York*, before retiring in the early 1960s.

JOHN BAKER says it took years before he really understood that his brother was gone. "I kept thinking Bobby would be there again, someday." He spent most of his professional career with Rolls-Royce Engines, as a project controller. Today Baker claims to still love the sea. "They couldn't take that from me." John Baker is an avid golfer and lives in Derby.

BARBARA BECH and her family returned to their home in Bognor Regis in southern England after the attack on the *Benares*. Barbara (now Barbara

Partridge) worked as a secretary for a legal and medical publishing firm in London. Today she lives in Sussex.

DEREK BECH joined the Royal Air Force to fulfill his military service and later worked for a British import-export firm in South India. He returned to England as an accountant for a building company. Today he lives in Bognor Regis, within a mile of the home where he grew up.

MARGUERITE BECH took her children by train from Scotland to Bognor Regis, and then by taxi to their home. The driver—well aware of the story of the *Benares* and her survivors—looked at her when they arrived and said, "Madam, I do not want a fare. This has been an honor." Marguerite Bech never recovered her full strength after the attack—though she lived to the age of seventy-eight. She died in 1962.

SONIA BECH trained as a kindergarten teacher and taught at schools in Bognor Regis and then for three years in Canada—making it at last to the country she was to have visited in 1940. Sonia (today Sonia Williams) returned to England and took up drama and stage acting, which she pursued until retirement. She lives in Sussex.

HEINRICH BLEICHRODT commanded two other U-boats—U-67 and U-109—to round out one of the most illustrious careers of any German submariner. U-boats under Bleichrodt's command sank twenty-four ships for a total of 158,402 tons destroyed. He was heavily decorated and in September 1942 became one of only twenty-eight men to receive the coveted Knight's Cross with Oak Leaves. His difficulties in 1943 led to the job at the port of Gdynia before war's end, and in May 1945, Heinrich Bleichrodt surrendered to British forces at Wilhelmshaven. Bleichrodt was held on war crimes charges for having knowingly attacked a vessel—the *City of Benares*—that was carrying child evacuees; he refused to testify or even to speak with investigators, who ultimately dropped their case for lack of evidence. After the war Bleichrodt worked at an ironware factory, rising ultimately to the post of director. Heinrich Bleichrodt died at Munich in 1977. He was sixty-six years old.

RONALD BROOKE enjoyed a distinguished career at sea. Still at the helm of HMS *Anthony*, Brooke held leading roles in the evacuation of Spitsbergen, Norway, and a successful allied raid on the German-occupied Lofoten Islands. Brooke was heavily decorated for his heroism, and in 1944 he was appointed to Lord Mountbatten's Supreme Allied Headquarters in India. Later he served in Korea and the Suez, in times of crisis for both those parts of the world. Ronald Brooke died at age ninety-two in November 2004.

DEREK CAPEL spent seven years in the Royal Navy, beginning as an aircraft fitter at Somerset. He later transitioned to a career as an inspector for Westland Helicopters. Capel says the *Benares* ordeal left him with, among other things, "far more feeling for my fellow man." In retirement he has spoken to church groups, scout troops, and schools about the experience and its power to teach, as

Capel puts it, "the lesson that one must always have faith." A pious man, Derek Capel is also quite superstitious. When we fixed a date to meet at his home, he laughed and said, "That's the thirteenth!" He reminded me that the *City of Benares* had sailed on the thirteenth; that he and the others in Lifeboat 12 had spent thirteen days at sea, between Liverpool and Gourock; that thirteen of the evacuee children had been saved; and that—when one added the lone *Marina* lifeboat—a total of thirteen boats had been found on the water. Today Derek Capel lives in Hanworth, not far from where he grew up.

REG CHARLTON spent a long career in the Royal Navy before pursuing work in education, rising eventually to the position of schoolmaster. Charlton retired to Newcastle upon Tyne, where he died in 2005.

HOWARD CLAYTOR died in a car accident in 1969. He was only forty years old.

PETER COLLINSON finished his service in the Royal Navy and returned to lead the third generation of the family's medical practice; his son is now taking on the fourth generation. Collinson says he will never forget the night he tended to two girls named Bess and Beth, and the bravery they and so many others exhibited on board HMS *Hurricane*. Dr. Peter Collinson lives in Rotherham.

RONNIE COOPER was awarded the Order of the British Empire in 1941, for his courage on board the *Benares* and his stewardship of Lifeboat 12. In his village of Invergowrie, residents gathered in St. Columba's Church to present him with a gold watch and a war bond on his return. Cooper died in Invergowrie in 1979, still remembered and revered as the "young chap who brought back the evacuees."

MARY CORNISH corresponded with the Lifeboat 12 boys for a few years following the attack, but none of them saw her again. Like Cooper, she was awarded the Order of the British Empire in 1941, and like Cooper, Cornish tended to deflect compliments and say that others in Lifeboat 12 deserved the bulk of the credit for their survival. She died of cancer in 1964.

DOUG CRITCHLEY, the young yachtsman who had longed for a career as a sailor, suffered severe frostbite after his eight days in Lifeboat 12. He never returned to the sea.

BETH CUMMINGS required another three weeks in the hospital after her return to Liverpool, suffering as she was from badly frostbitten and infected feet. It was her mother, Anne Cummings, who suggested to Beth that she make something of the time in the hospital. "Busy yourself!" she said. "Write everything down!" Her daughter did precisely that, and consequently Beth's recollections are particularly sharp, and close in their detail to accounts given by survivors immediately after their landing in Scotland. At seventeen, Beth took a secretarial course and went to work for the Marconi International Marine Communication Company in Liverpool. She worked there until 1956, when she began a three-decade career with a pair of insurance firms, finishing as a welfare officer for the Royal Insurance Group. Beth Cummings is today Beth Williams; she lives in High Bentham.

ERIC DAVIS recorded a strident, angry essay for the BBC after the attack, a statement that would literally represent his final words on the subject. Davis was killed when the plane he was on was shot down by a Japanese fighter over Java in 1942.

HENRY DIGBY-MORTON founded his own design house and became a member of the Incorporated Society of London Fashion Designers. Among his creations were uniforms for the Women's Voluntary Service in Britain. He later designed several collections for American manufacturers. Today two photographs of Henry Digby-Morton hang in Britain's National Portrait Gallery. He closed his design house in 1957 and died in 1983, at the age of seventy-seven.

PHYLLIS DIGBY-MORTON helped support her husband's design house and edited a collection called *The Christmas Book*—described as an "anthology of poems, stories, recipes, quizzes, and cartoons all on a Christmas theme."

ALBERT GORMAN was injured during the D-day landings on Omaha Beach. After the war he worked as a builder and then ran a general contracting business. Later he became a security officer for the Shell Oil Corporation, and he worked for that company for more than twenty years. Albert Gorman lives in Hampshire.

EDDIE AND HANNAH GRIMMOND did not see their suffering end after the tragedy of their five children's deaths at sea. On September 17, 1943—exactly three years after the sinking of the *City of Benares*—their son Sergeant Joseph Ronald Grimmond was killed in action while serving with the Royal Air Force Volunteer Rescue Service. He was nineteen years old; he had been one of the Grimmond siblings too old to qualify for the CORB evacuation program. As for the other Grimmond children, the three others who had been too old for the CORB program—Frederick, Gladys, and Lesley Grimmond—died in 2004, 1997, and 1995, respectively. The two who were mercifully too *young* to have traveled on the evacuee ships—Ralph and Gerald Grimmond—are still alive at this writing. As for their parents, Eddie was refused his request to join his World War I regiment and signed on instead with the photography department of the Royal Air Force. Later he worked at an antiques shop in Southeast London. Eddie Grimmond died of lung cancer in 1948. He was only fifty-one. His wife lived another four decades, reaching the age of eighty-nine. Hannah Grimmond went to her grave having scarcely discussed the tragedies of war that had claimed her children—six in all.

ROLF HILSE'S U-boat surrendered to U.S. forces off New Orleans, and from June 1945 to February 1946 he was a prisoner of war at the U.S. air base at El Paso, Texas. Hilse was later transferred to British custody, where as described earlier he spent two years as a prisoner and later married an Englishwoman. Rolf Hilse found work as a truck driver and farm laborer and still lives in England.

HMS *HURRICANE* returned immediately to sea (indeed, she was almost never in harbor in the years that followed the attack on the *Benares*). This busy destroyer became known as the "Atlantic Lifeboat" or "HMS *Rescue*" for her exploits. *Hurricane* saved more than one thousand more people—including one Jimmy Proudfoot, the *Benares'* barman, rescued a second time less than one year after the *Benares* was sunk. It was Proudfoot's first trip to sea after a period of "shock leave" back home. HMS *Hurricane* was attacked and sunk by U-415 northeast of the Azores, on Christmas Eve 1943.

JACK KEELEY returned home in late September, and before long his family had received a half dozen offers to pay airfare for the boy to the United States or Canada. His parents refused. Keeley wound up working for twenty-seven years with the postal service and another twenty-one with the national railway. Jack Keeley's father, a stoic man with what Keeley called "a Victorian sensibility," never spoke of the *Benares* sinking again. "He didn't want it on my mind." Keeley retired to East Sussex, where he died in 2005.

MONIKA LANYI was one of 717 passengers to reach New York aboard the *Cameronia*, in late 1940. Her husband, Jeno Lanyi, had not survived. Her mother, Mrs. Thomas Mann, met her at the pier and brought her to the family residence in Princeton, New Jersey. Monika Lanyi had never been to the United States before. She took her maiden name and published novels as Monika Mann. She died in Leverkusen, Germany, in 1992.

LESLIE LEWIS believed he had witnessed and participated in a "miracle" in the rescue of Marguerite Bech and her three children. Nothing less, he believed, could have accounted for their survival on a small raft, and then the serendipitous meeting of that raft with his own lifeboat. Lewis ran a successful hairdressing business in Wiltshire for many years after the war.

ANGUS MACDONALD was killed on July 11, 1943, when the troop ship SS *California* was bombed three hundred miles off the coast of Portugal. He was only twenty-nine years old.

JOHNNIE MAYHEW returned to Britain badly frostbitten, but he was able ultimately to resume a prewar career working for Siemens as an electrician and then as projects foreman. Later he accepted an offer from Friedland Wagner, granddaughter of the composer Richard Wagner, to be "chief handyman" on her estate outside Stockton, England. Today Mayhew lives in Hartlepool, in northeast England.

TOMMY MILLIGAN worked in Scotland as a design engineer for Massey Ferguson, a manufacturer of heavy equipment. He died in 1993, at the age of seventy-two.

BOHDAN NAGORSKI was made director of the New York office of the Gdynia-America Line in 1941, a job he held for a few years, until he came to believe the company had adopted a too-conciliatory line toward the Soviet Union. He worked after that for the British Ministry of Transport's New York office and in 1952 took a position with the United Nations Technical Assistance Organization as a port and shipping expert. Nagorski's first mission took him to Jordan, where he led a feasibility study to build a deep-water port at Aqaba. His success there won him that country's Order of Independence, and he later advised the governments of Greece, Egypt, Congo, and Saudi Arabia, among others, on matters of port design and engineering. His *Port Problems in Developing Countries* is a highly regarded work in the field. Bohdan Nagorski died in New York in 1987. He was ninety-six.

RORY O'SULLIVAN received his Navy chaplaincy in late 1940, while he was still convalescing, and he served as chaplain until the end of the war. In 1956 O'Sullivan was reunited with the Lifeboat 12 boys, who reported that they had kept their promise and gone to church to say prayers of thanks for their rescue. By then O'Sullivan had returned to Annecy in southern France, where he became a teacher of English and geography and other subjects at St. Michael's College. One good source—Paul Shearing—reported that O'Sullivan was a revered figure there. Shearing visited Annecy several times, and on each occasion he received a similar greeting: "Ahh—you are a friend of *Père Rory!*" Everyone seemed to know the man. Shearing found it hard to reconcile his old image of O'Sullivan—frail and prostrate on the lifeboat floor—with this vigorous and outgoing priest. The two men developed a powerful bond—perhaps not surprising, given that they were the two Lifeboat 12 survivors who had suffered most on the water. O'Sullivan made an effort to reach Bohdan Nagorski in the 1960s, but in what today seems an example of a Dark Age of communications, O'Sullivan's written query to Nagorski's publisher yielded no contact information, and the effort went nowhere. Rory O'Sullivan still lives in Annecy. At this writing he is ninety-seven years old.

HARRY PEARD suffered significantly after the ordeal in Lifeboat 12, despite the stamina and bravado he had shown during those difficult eight days. Peard's feet were badly damaged, his back gave him near-constant pain, and he was forced to take menial work—including a long tenure for a uniform manufacturer, where Peard helped maintain steam presses and sewing machines. He suffered from peritonitis as well—though Peter Peard stresses that his father was "always a very happy person and did not allow these shortcomings to affect his life." Harry Peard died in 1985.

GEORGE PURVIS, like Cooper and Cornish before him, was ultimately awarded the Order of the British Empire, in 1941.

ANTHONY QUINTON says he shouted in his sleep for a long time after the attack on the *Benares,* invariably rousing his fellow boarders at school. Quinton has since then enjoyed a distinguished academic career. He is author of several books about philosophy, including *The Nature of Things, The Politics of Imperfection,* and *Thoughts and Thinkers.* Anthony Quinton has also hosted popular radio programs about philosophy, and he is past president of Trinity College at Oxford, Chairman of the British Library, President of the Aristotelian Society, and a member of the British Arts Council. Quinton is a lord and baron and lives today in London.

LETITIA QUINTON settled in England after the war and returned later to her native Victoria, in British Columbia. She died there in 1980.

COLIN RICHARDSON won a King's Commendation in January 1941 "for brave conduct in the Merchant Navy." There may have been some confusion behind the awarding of that prize (Richardson was almost certainly the youngest recipient, before or since, of such an honor for "conduct in the Merchant Navy"), but there was no doubt that Richardson was deserving of honor. Nearly everyone who had been near him after the torpedo's strike testified later to the child's courage and stoicism in the face of danger and death. As has been said, Colin Richardson has waged a long, public, and courageous battle against cancer for more than a quarter century. He lives in Surrey.

ANNIE RYAN won the King's Commendation for Good Services for her courage in Lifeboat 10; Chief Officer Joe Hetherington had offered public recommendations for Ryan, who he felt had shown "outstanding coolness and resource and did much to maintain the morale of the children whilst they were waiting to get away in the lifeboat."

PAUL SHEARING'S suffering persisted after he returned home. His convalescence was long, his mother died in 1943, and Shearing left school soon after that, at age fourteen. One year later he joined the Army. "You could say I never was a teenager, really." Shearing had a two-decade career as a pipefitter and welder, and later became a lecturer in pipefitting and welding at Southampton College. "Why were we saved?" Shearing asked rhetorically, during one of our conversations. "No one was looking for us!" Over the years, when people noticed his limp and asked, "What've you done to your foot, then?" Shearing developed a standard response: "Oh, it's a long story." He shared his long story with me at his home in Bournemouth, in June 2004, and it was only two months later that he died peacefully there. Paul Shearing was seventy-six.

BILLY SHORT suffered nightmares for roughly six months after the ordeal, and recalls that when he returned to school, "the other lads kept their distance." Short had always been shy, but now the other children knew something profound had happened to him. Adults in Sunderland who knew Billy Short showered him with generosity. " 'Give a little extra for the boy,' " he remembers a shopkeeper saying. "They all knew what had happened. They knew I'd lost me brother." The manager at the paper mill where Short's father worked took up a collection. "Take yer son a little vacation." Like the other boys, Short served in the Navy, and later he became a shipyard carpenter and then a site manager for the Tarmac Company. More than sixty years later he confesses a peculiar fondness for condensed milk and sardines—two of the staples of Lifeboat 12. Billy Short still lives in Sunderland.

HUGH CROFTON SIMMS had a storied, if brief, career with the Royal Navy. As described earlier, he won the Distinguished Service Order for sinking three submarines, led the rescue of thousands of shipwrecked civilians, and was greatly admired by the men who served under his command. The *Benares* rescue and recovery mission had made him, in the words of his son, "one of the most determined and vengeful destroyer Captains." Simms was killed off the coast of Libya on December 21, 1942.

KEN SPARKS still has the occasional nightmare, a dream in which a harsh light burns over a wild sea, and a liner slips away. In the dream's most violent form, people tumble from lifeboats. Sparks joined the Navy in 1944 as a "boy bugler," and later spent a long career with the postal service. He says he takes enormous pleasure in life's "small events"—pottering in the garden, taking a walk with his wife—and that he thinks of the *Benares* and Lifeboat 12 every day, amazed each time at how the story unfolded. "I'm a survivor," Sparks said emphatically when we first met. "That's it. Definitely a survivor." Ken Sparks lives in Sprowston.

FRED STEELS narrowly escaped death one week after his rescue, when the train he and his father were taking back to England was bombed. Steels was confined to a wheelchair for eight months after he returned home, and wore special slippers to ease the pain frostbite had brought to his feet. Later he spent eight years in the Navy, before launching a career at the Saunders Row Aircraft Factory, where he painted aircraft interiors and maintained planes in other ways. Steels still suffers in winter from the lingering effects of the frostbite. He lives in Eastleigh.

REX THORNE had a long career in banking before retiring in the 1980s. He lives in Malmesbury.

U-48 became the most prolific U-boat of the Second World War. The submarine sank fifty-three ships for a total of 308,000 tons destroyed before being retired to Kiel in June 1941 and used as a model for training missions. U-48 was decommissioned in October 1943 and scuttled at Neustadt, just one week before V-E Day.

BESS WALDER married Geoff Cummings in 1947. She became a teacher, and later head teacher at Bishop Cleve Primary School, which with six hundred children was the largest such school in Gloucestershire. She is among other things a superb organizer of information and people, and while she insists each *Benares* reunion is to be "the last," she arranged yet another gathering in September 2005, to mark the sixty-fifth anniversary. I suspect she will continue to find a way to bring these remarkable men and women together as long as their strength allows. "I love and admire these people," Bess is fond of saying. She also professes an unbroken passion for the sea. "May seem strange, but I've never stopped loving the sea."

LOUIS WALDER died in 1986, at the age of fifty-six.

ARTHUR WIMPERIS resumed his career as a screenwriter and—as mentioned above—won an Academy Award for *Mrs. Miniver* in 1943. He wrote the screenplays for two other films—*Random Harvest* and *Young Bess*—to round out a career in which he had authored the scripts for fifteen motion pictures. Arthur Wimperis died in 1953. He was seventy-eight.

ELEANOR WRIGHT spoke to reporters in Scotland, volunteered to care for the younger survivors, and returned to Sunderland. She vanished from public view after that.

On September 17, 2005, thanks to another successful organizational effort by Bess Cummings and Blake Simms, a group of twenty-five people gathered to commemorate the sixty-fifth anniversary of the attack on the *City of Benares*. Nine survivors were there—Bess, Derek Capel, Ken Sparks, John Baker, Colin Richardson, the three Bech siblings, and a woman who was something of a surprise guest.

Dorothy Perkins Silver had been a passenger in Lifeboat 2, with Richardson and the *Benares'* carpenter Angus MacDonald. She was twenty years old then, traveling to Canada with her father, and she had lived since the war in Rochester, New York. For some reason Dorothy Perkins' name never appeared on the *Benares'* manifest, and consequently she had been a kind of invisible fellow survivor. Decades later, she had found Colin Richardson's name on the Internet—and so it was that two lifeboat passengers embraced in the Cotswolds after sixty-five years, filled with stories and memories that produced laughter and tears. Dr. Peter Collinson—now ninety-two years old—was there, too; when he saw an old photograph, he recalled treating young Dorothy Perkins in one of his triage wards on board the *Hurricane*. "She was beautiful," Collinson said with a smile.

Bess Cummings watched this small group in wonder. So did I. So did John MacDonald, Angus' son. And so did Barbara and Christine Nagorski, whom I had brought with me to England, to meet some people who had known their father—albeit briefly—six and a half decades later.

"Maybe," said Bess, "we'll do this again in five years' time."

SOURCES

My research for this book drew first on interviews with the surviving passengers and crew of the SS *City of Benares*, HMS *Hurricane*, and HMS *Anthony*. I have also interviewed relatives of survivors and victims, and relied on newspaper accounts and records kept at the Imperial War Museum and the Public Records Office at Kew, for information about the CORB program, the Admiralty, and the war years generally. Finally, it was an enormous help to find that so many people who survived the attack on the *Benares* had given interviews at the time, and that many more had written detailed accounts of the journey, the attack, and of their subsequent rescues.

INTERVIEWS

John Baker, Derek Bech, Derek Capel, Reg Charlton, Margaret Claytor, Peter Collinson, Bess Cummings (nee Walder), Geoff Cummings, Albert Gorman, Gerald Grimmond, Jimmy Grimmond, Jack Keeley, John MacDonald, John Mayhew, Christine Nagorski, Zygmunt Nagorski, Jr., Rory O'Sullivan, Patricia Parker (nee Milligan), Barbara Partridge (nee Bech), Peter Peard, Dorothy Perkins Silver, Anthony Quinton, Colin Richardson, Charles Salisbury, Paul Shearing, Bill Short, Blake Simms, Edward Smith, Ken Sparks, Fred Steels, Rex Thorne, Barbara Wierzbianski (nee Nagorski), Beth Williams (nee Cummings), and Sonia Williams (nee Bech).

RECORDINGS

Derek Bech. 9/5/2002. Imperial War Museum.
Patricia Bulmer. 9/27/1940. Imperial War Museum.

Mary Cornish. 9/27/1940. BBC.

Bess Cummings. 3/31/2000. Imperial War Museum.

Eric Davis. 9/23/1940. BBC.

Rolf Hilse. April 2004. Imperial War Museum.

Jack Keeley. November 1992. BBC; also 6/28/2000. Imperial War Museum.

Memorial Service and interviews with John Baker, Derek Capel, Beth Cummings, Jack Keeley, Paul Shearing, Billy Short, Ken Sparks, Fred Steels, Bess Walder, Church of the Annunciation, Wembley, England. 9/17/1990.

Barbara Partridge (nee Bech). 7/28/2000. Imperial War Museum.

Colin Richardson. 10/1/2000. Imperial War Museum.

Blake Simms' Address, Church of the Annunciation, Wembley. 9/17/1995.

Ken Sparks. 9/27/2001. Imperial War Museum.

Fred Steels. 8/6/2002. Imperial War Museum.

Sonia Williams (nee Bech). 5/8/2002. Imperial War Museum.

WRITTEN ACCOUNTS

Martin Bum, Ronald Cooper, Mary Cornish, J. R. Creswell, Doug Critchley, Beth Cummings, Eric Davis, John Percival Day, Marjorie Day, Richard Deane, Albert Gorman, Joseph Hetherington, Leslie Lewis, Bohdan Nagorski, Rory O'Sullivan, R. T. Paine, John Rennie, Dorothy Perkins Silver, Hugh Crofton Simms, Louis Walder.

BIBLIOGRAPHY

Ralph Barker. *Children of the Benares.* London: Methuen, 1987.

Kapitanlieutenant Heinrich Bleichrodt. *Kriegstagebuch U-48.* Ministry of Defence Collections, Naval Historical Branch, 1940.

Tony Bridgland. *Waves of Hate: Naval Atrocities of the Second World War.* Annapolis: Naval Institute Press, 2002.

Winston Churchill. *The Second World War: Their Finest Hour.* Boston: Houghton Mifflin, 1949.

Joseph Conrad. *Lord Jim.* Cambridge (Massachusetts): Riverside Press, 1958.

Phil Craig and Tim Clayton. *Finest Hour: The Battle of Britain.* New York: Simon & Schuster, 2002.

Karl Doenitz, translated by R. H. Stevens and David Woodward. *Admiral Karl Doenitz: Memoirs—Ten Years and Twenty Days.* Cleveland and New York: The Wall Publishing Company, 1958.

Michael Fethney. *The Absurd and the Brave: The True Account of the British Government's World War II Evacuation of Children Overseas.* Sussex: The Book Guild, 2003.

Martin Gilbert. *Second World War.* London: Heinemann, 1989.

Derek Haffner. *The Papers of Derek Haffner.* Imperial War Museum. London.

Arnold Hague. *The Allied Convoy System, 1939–45: Its Organization, Defence & Operation.* Annapolis: Naval Institute Press, 2000.

Wolfgang Hirschfeld as told to Geoffrey Brooks. *Hirschfeld: The Secret Diary of a U-Boat.* London: Cassell Military Paperbacks, 1996.

Elspeth Huxley. *Atlantic Ordeal: The Story of Mary Cornish.* London: Chatto and Windus, 1941.

Derek E. Johnson. *Exodus of Children.* Essex: Pennyfarthing Publications, 1985.

Tony Lane. *The Merchant Seaman's War.* New York: Manchester University Press, 1990.

W. W. Lowther. *Wish You Were Here: An Account of Sunderland's Wartime Evacuation.* Wallsend-On-Tyne: Walton Publications, 1989.

Herman McNeile. *Bulldog Drummond.* London: Hodder & Stoughton, 1920.

Janet Menzies. *Children of the Doomed Voyage.* Chichester: John Wiley & Sons, 2005.

Jean Merrien, translated by J. H. Watkins, *Lonely Voyagers.* New York: Putnam's, 1954.

David Miller. *U-Boats: The Illustrated History of the Raiders of the Deep.* Dulles, Virginia: Brassey's, 2000.

Frank Mulville. *Schooner Integrity.* New York: Sheridan House, 1979.

Emmie and Tom Myatt. *The Papers of Emmie and Tom Myatt.* Imperial War Museum. London. 1940.

Bohdan Nagorski. "Eight Days in a Lifeboat." Chapter in *They Fight for Poland: The War in the First Person.* Edited by F. B. Czarnomski. London: George Allen and Unwin Ltd, 1941.

Nuremberg War Crimes Tribunal. Transcripts for January 14, 1946.

Official Report on the Sinking of the S.S. City of Benares. *10/1940.* Imperial War Museum. London.

Father Rory O'Sullivan. *Join the Navy? Get Torpedoed First!* Annecy, 2001.

Thomas Parrish. *The Submarine: A History.* New York: Viking, 2004.

Nathaniel Philbrick. *In the Heart of the Sea: The Tragedy of the Whaleship Essex.* New York: Penguin, 2000.

Phil Richards and John J. Banigan. *How to Abandon Ship.* New York: Cornell Maritime Press, 1942.

Dougal Robertson. *Sea Survival: A Manual.* New York: Praeger, 1975.

Jurgen Rohwer. *Axis Submarine Successes: 1939–45.* Annapolis: Naval Institute Press, 1998.

Geoffrey Shakespeare. *Let the Candles Be Brought In.* London: MacDonald, 1949.

John R. Stilgoe, *Lifeboat: A History of Courage, Cravenness and Survival at Sea.* Charlottesville: University of Virginia, 2003.

John Terraine. *The Right of the Line: The Royal Air Force in the European War, 1939–1945.* London: Hodder and Stoughton, 1985.

Bess Walder. *Letter to Headmistress of School.* October 1940. Imperial War Museum. London.

John Winton. *Convoy: The Defence of Sea Trade 1890–1990.* London: M. Joseph, 1983.

PHOTO CREDITS

p. 2. Peter Collinson: Courtesy of Peter Collinson
Albert Gorman: Courtesy of Albert Gorman
Raft rescue: Courtesy of Peter Collinson
p. 3. Rex Thorne, Louis Walder, and Colin Richardson: Courtesy of Peter
Collinson
Colin Richardson: Courtesy of Colin Richardson
p. 4. Beth Cummings: Courtesy of Beth Williams
Lifeboat 12: Copyright Associated Press
p. 5. Ken Sparks: Courtesy of Ken Sparks
p. 6. Telegrams: Courtesy of Christine Nagorski
p. 7. *Benares* reunion: Courtesy of Bess Cummings
Lifeboat 12 reunited: Courtesy of Blake Simms
p. 8. Bohdan and George Nagorski: Courtesy of Christine Nagorski

The author has made every effort to locate the owners of copyrighted material
and to secure permission to reprint. Permission to reprint copyrighted material is
gratefully acknowledged. All other material is believed to be in the public domain.

INDEX